MASTERING THE ART OF
FRENCH PASTRY

AN ILLUSTRATED COURSE
BY BRUCE HEALY & PAUL BUGAT

WITH DRAWINGS BY PAUL BUGAT
PHOTOGRAPHS BY PIERRE GINET

BARRON'S
New York • London • Toronto • Sydney

For Alice and Danielle

All inquiries should be addressed to:
Barron's Educational Series, Inc.
250 Wireless Boulevard
Hauppauge, New York 11788

Library of Congress Catalog Card No. 82-13874
International Standard Book No. 0-8120-5456-3

Library of Congress Cataloging in Publication Data

Healy, Bruce. Mastering the Art of French Pastry.

Includes indexes.
1. Pastry. 2. Cookery, French. I. Bugat, Paul.
II. Title.
TX719.H33   1983   641.8'65   82-13874
ISBN 0-8120-5456-3

PRINTED IN THE UNITED STATES OF AMERICA
890   790   987654
CREDITS:
Photography by Pierre Ginet
Drawings by Paul Bugat
Jacket and cover design by Milton Glaser, Inc.
Book design by Milton Glaser, Inc.

TABLE OF CONTENTS

Foreword

*D*uring my professional life, especially as president of the Confederation Nationale, I have had several opportunities to introduce books about gastronomy and French pastry. This honor has always been one which I have undertaken with great pleasure, because of the respect I have for these arts of the table, as well as for the art of good eating. It is with double pleasure that I preface this great book on traditional French pastry.

My first pleasure comes from the recognition that this book was written for the enjoyment of an English-speaking audience. In so doing, the authors provide a complementary understanding of French pastry, which is a world-renowned jewel of our country.

The second pleasure is in the knowledge that this book is the result of close collaboration by two men of quality. One is Bruce Healy, doctor of physics, grand gourmet, and leading American teacher of cooking. The other, Paul Bugat, is a *pâtissier, confiseur,* and *chocolatier* born of one of the greatest families to contribute to the art of making desserts. Indeed, when you pronounce the name Bugat, with which must be associated that of Gavillon, how can you not envisage the nobility, the respect for tradition, and the considerable contributions which this family has brought to our profession?

Today the most noted of our Parisian pastry shops are directed and vitalized by members of the Bugat and Gavillon family. Paul Bugat is the worthy successor and professional heir of the pastry pioneers. He has brought to this book his precision, artistic sense, and devotion, in order that the reader may here discover and learn to enjoy the art of French pastry.

This book has required three years of long and hard work, multiple meetings, recipe testing and revising, and some 400 illustrations for these two people to complete this project. In the name of our entire profession, I offer them my congratulations and thanks for their dedication in making us more familiar with and appreciative of this fine craft, which so many men and women are proud to practice.

Jean Millet, President
Confederation Nationale de la
Pâtisserie-Confiserie-Glacerie

PREFACE AND ACKNOWLEDGMENTS

*T*his book is grounded in a body of knowledge which has been evolved over generations and handed down from one pastry chef to another in the professional pastry kitchen. We wish to express our sincere gratitude to those who have had the patience, love, and devotion to their craft to teach and encourage us. Paul would like to thank Marcel Bugat in particular for guiding him to his career as pastry chef and artist.

In the course of preparing this book we have been fortunate to receive the generous help and cooperation of many friends, relatives, colleagues, and students. It is a pleasure for us to convey our special appreciation to the following people:

Alice Healy for making it possible for Bruce to devote the enormous amount of time required to complete this book; for reading the manuscript and giving many valuable comments and suggestions; for her critical assessment of every pastry; and, by maintaining her weight at 96 pounds, for proving that French pastries need not be fattening.

Danielle Bugat for taking on added responsibilities in directing the operation of Pâtisserie Clichy while Paul was working on the manuscript and preparing the illustrations, and for her patience during the months when he spent every night at the drawing table.

André Neveu for introducing us nearly seven years ago and thereby making our collaboration possible.

Peggy Peabody for her capable assistance in the kitchen, for reading the manuscript and contributing helpful criticisms, and for testing many of the recipes in her own kitchen.

Isabelle Bugat for her help in shading some of the drawings.

Dr. Gabor Huszar for a critical reading of the chapter on ingredients.

Carole Berglie, our editor, for her fine job coordinating the many tasks required to transform our original manuscript into this book.

Alan Chodos, Leonard and Ann Drabkin, Ruth Goldfarb, James and Margaret Healy, Harvey Koizim, Peter and Nancy Kranz, and Paula Wolfert for their suggestions, advice, and support.

Finally we wish to thank the following manufacturers and suppliers for giving us the opportunity to test and evaluate samples of their products:

B.I.A. Cordon Bleu, Inc.
Bon Jour Imports Corporation
Chambers Corporation
Chicago Metallic
Ranier Devido Stone & Marble Company
F. Dick
R. H. Forschner Company, Inc.
General Electric Company
Kitchen Glamor, Inc.
Charles F. Lamalle
Leyse Aluminum Company
Lincoln Manufacturing Company, Inc.
Market Forge
Moulinex Products, Inc.

Penn Scale Manufacturing Company
Rival Manufacturing Company
Robot Coupe International Corporation
Robot Coupe U.S.A., Inc.
Taylor Instrument
Terraillon Corporation
Thermador
Thorn Kenwood, Inc.
Thorpe Rolling Pin Company
Waring Products Division, Dynamics Corporation of America
Wear-Ever Aluminum Inc.
The West Bend Company
Wüsthof-Trident, Inc.

HOW TO USE THIS BOOK

*T*his book is a thorough introduction to the art and science of French pastry for American home cooks. Our recipes are based on the elegant and delicious desserts which are the repertoire of Paul Bugat's Pâtisserie Clichy in Paris. We use these recipes as examples to teach you the professional techniques of pastry making, just as you would learn them in Bruce Healy's cooking classes in Boulder. With Paul's drawings to complement the text, we explain in detail the methods that will transform the mysterious domain of the pastry chef into an easily comprehensible and practicable skill for the amateur cook. Pierre Ginet's exquisite color photos illustrate some of the mouth-watering desserts you will be learning to create.

To make the best use of this book we encourage you to learn and take advantage of the intrinsic structure of French pastry. All pastries are prepared by combining components of four basic types—pastry doughs, cake and pastry batters, fillings, and toppings. Whether these components are assembled before or after baking, they retain their distinct identities. In addition to its conceptual simplicity, this division has very practical implications. The components of a dessert can be prepared one at a time and stored for later use. Also, each component can be used in many different pastries. With the bulk of the work done in advance, you will be amazed at the efficiency and speed with which you can assemble even the most complex desserts.

We have divided this book into three parts. The heart of the book is in Part 1. In the four chapters here we teach you how to prepare the basic components. We discuss the properties of each component so you will learn to use it to fullest advantage. Since so many home kitchens are equipped with electric mixers and food processors, we give directions for preparation by machine as well as by hand whenever appropriate. And with every recipe we provide complete storage instructions, including directions for freezing when it can be done without loss of quality.

Ultimately you are reading this book because you want to enjoy the finished pastries, and in Part 2 we explain how to assemble the components from Part 1. Here you will find recipes for some of the most sought-after and imitated creations in Paris. Our structural approach will not only enable you to reproduce the superb pastries for which Pâtisserie Clichy is famous, but will also provide a framework within which you can improvise new variations according to your own taste.

Much of the beauty and richness of French pastry derives from the fact that a few themes generate an infinite range of sensual combinations and juxtapositions. *Tartes* contrast the crisp and flaky textures of pastry doughs with the tender textures and delicate flavors of fresh fruits. *Feuilletés,* such as napoleons, emphasize buttery flakiness. Brioches are breads rich in butter and eggs, and *babas* are drenched in rum syrup. In *gâteaux* layers of cake alternate with luxurious butter creams, while meringues bring sweet crispness to the fore and *choux* (such as éclairs) enclose soft pastry creams in gentle, puff-like shells. *Bavarois* and charlottes highlight light, creamy mousses flavored with fresh fruits and liqueurs.

Most of our pastries are desserts—some as simple as apple *tarte,* and others (like our sumptuous mango charlotte) appropriate to your most sophisticated dinner party. Brioches and croissants are destined to grace your breakfast table, and *chaussons aux pommes* and *brioche bordelaise* might accompany mid-morning coffee or afternoon tea.

Part 3 of the book is devoted to reference material. Here we describe the tools that are important for pastry making and tell you how to use them. We discuss many of the general techniques for handling important ingredients, such as milk, cream, butter, eggs, flour, sugar, nuts, and chocolate, and we explain in nontechnical language how the scientific properties of these ingredients come into play in French pastry. We also include sources for baking equipment and specialty ingredients and an American-Metric-British conversion table.

To help you coordinate the preparation of components in Part 1 with the pastries in Part 2, we have included in the reference section a cross-index of components, listing the pastries in which each is used, as well as a complete general index. You can, of course, start by choosing a dessert, go back to prepare the necessary components, and then assemble them to produce the finished pastry. Or, having some components prepared in advance, you can check the cross-index to find which pastries can be made by assembling them. For example, if you have in your refrigerator some *crème pâtissière* (French pastry cream) and a pad of the flaky pastry dough *rognures,* you could combine them in a round fruit tart, *tarte alsacienne, mille-feuilles, pont neuf, puit d'amour,* or *St.-Honoré.*

You can already see that the systematic nature of French pastry simplifies it enormously and makes it easy to adapt to the needs and limitations of the home cook. Another advantage is that a small group of fundamental methods is the basis for a wide range of components and pastries. For example, there are three types of pastry doughs, and all the doughs of each type are produced by a single general method or set of techniques. So, in the process of mastering just three recipes, you can acquire the skills needed to prepare all French pastry doughs.

In each of our recipes we give a concise, self-contained set of instructions. We also provide a thorough lesson on general techniques in a *tours de main* section at the beginning of each chapter or subchapter. You can prepare any of our recipes without consulting the *tours de main* sections or reference chapters, but whenever you would like a more detailed explanation of a technique or want to learn more about the reasons behind what you are doing, they are there to help.

We would be unfair if we did not admit that some of the techniques we describe will require a certain amount of practice before you can use them with confidence and expertise. On the first attempt, no one can smooth the topping of a cake into a perfect cylindrical drum with a few sweeps of the palette knife or deftly roll a lump of brioche dough into shape with a flick of the wrist. Don't let that deter you. Everything you need to know is here, and after a couple of tries you will be turning out pastries of professional polish and style.

PART

COMPONENTS

Chapter One

PASTRY DOUGHS

*A*ll pastry doughs are composed primarily of flour, butter, and some liquid—most typically water, eggs, or milk. The doughs are rolled and molded to give them shape and then baked.

The characteristics that differentiate the three basic classes of pastry doughs—*pâtes à foncer, pâtes feuilletées,* and *pâtes levées*—derive from the manner in which the flour, butter, and liquid are combined and the additional ingredients that appear in the recipe. The key factor in all of this is the gluten in the flour, which gives pastry doughs varying degrees of elasticity and strength.

For the *pâtes à foncer* (sweet and short pastry doughs), which are used primarily for lining flan rings for *tartes,* it is essential to minimize the elasticity of the dough so it will be easy to roll out, won't shrink in the oven, and will produce a tender crust after baking. Consequently, these doughs are mixed quickly and worked as little as possible.

In the *pâtes feuilletées* (flaky pastry doughs) the butter is not actually mixed with the other ingredients at all. Rather, a pad of butter is wrapped in an envelope of a flour-and-water dough called the *détrempe,* and a sequence of rolling and folding operations (called turns) transforms the initial butter-filled envelope into a pastry dough consisting of many alternating layers of butter and *détrempe.* The turns partially activate the gluten, giving the *détrempe* the strength required to maintain the separation of the butter layers.

The *pâtes levées* (leavened pastry doughs) are distinguished by the presence of yeast. These doughs must be kneaded vigorously to activate the gluten in the flour to the fullest extent. The fibers of gluten become extremely elastic and are inflated like tiny balloons by carbon dioxide, which is a by-product of fermentation of the yeast. After baking, the result is the light, airy texture characteristic of yeast breads.

Les Pâtes à Foncer

These are the most simple and basic pastry doughs. They are used to line (*foncer*) flan rings and molds for *tartes* and for cookies. We include three doughs of this type: *pâte à foncer spéciale, pâte sablée,* and *pâte sucrée.*

Spéciale is a *pâte brisée,* or short pastry dough. It is the best dough to use for *tartes* that are not served soon after baking or that have juicy fillings, since it is more resistant to soaking than *pâte sablée* and *pâte sucrée.*

Pâte sablée and *pâte sucrée* are the sweet pastry doughs. *Sablée* is even better than *spéciale* for dessert pastry crusts, but it is also more perishable than *spéciale* and should be used only for *tartes* that will be consumed relatively quickly and that don't contain juicy fillings. *Sucrée* contains ground almonds, which give it a special flavor and make it ideal for almond cream *tartes* and cookies. However, *sucrée* is very dry and gets soggy much more quickly than *sablée,* so it should be used for fruit *tartes* only if the filling is not at all juicy and the *tarte* will be served immediately after baking and cooling. Because of their high sugar content, both *sablée* and *sucrée* are quite fragile, and they require more care to roll out and mold than does *spéciale.*

TOURS DE MAIN

It is ironic that so many people are intimidated by these pastry doughs because, of all the fundamental components of French pastry, they are among the easiest to prepare. In fact, there is only one real technique to learn, a kneading motion called *fraisage.*

Fraisage

In making all of the *pâtes à foncer,* you quickly mix the ingredients to form a loose, crumbly dough. The trick is to finish the mixing in such a way that you produce a smooth dough without warming it (which would melt the butter) or working it too much (which would activate the gluten in the flour and make the dough elastic). The technique that accomplishes this is *fraisage.*

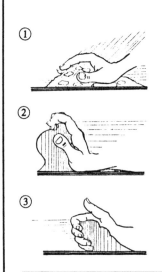

To *fraiser* the dough you simply smear it, a little at a time, across the counter with the heel of your hand ①-②. Press firmly so that each push breaks off a piece of dough from the remaining mass. When all of the dough has been pushed across the counter, gather it together in a mound ③ and repeat the *fraisage* procedure until the dough is smooth. Be careful, however, not to overwork the dough. We have called *fraisage* a kneading motion, but, for the *pâtes à foncer,* it is really only a mixing technique.

About "Softened" Butter

We want to expand upon one other general point about the preparation of the *pâtes à foncer*. All of our recipes here call for "softened" butter, which means that the butter should be removed from the refrigerator far enough in advance to become malleable. However, it is important that the butter not warm enough to melt before or during the preparation. Actually, as long as the butter is malleable, the colder it is the better. If you forget to remove it from the refrigerator far enough in advance, you can soften it by working it on the counter with the heel of your hand or with the leaf beater in your electric mixer.

Pâte à Foncer Spéciale

For about 2 pounds 14 ounces (1,300 g) of *spéciale*, *or* enough for three or four 9½-inch (24 cm) *tarte* shells

INGREDIENTS

1 pound 7 ounces (650 g), or about 4¾ cups, flour

1 pound (450 g) butter, softened

1 tablespoon (13 g) salt

4 teaspoons (20 g) sugar

7 tablespoons (1 dL) cold water

1 large egg, lightly beaten

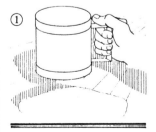

By hand:

1 Sift the flour onto your countertop ①. Cut the butter into pieces about 1 tablespoon (15 g) in size and add it to the flour. Roughly mix the butter and flour, pinching the pieces of butter with the flour between your fingertips and working quickly so you don't warm the butter ②.

2 Gather the flour and butter into a mound and make a well in the center. Dissolve the salt and sugar in the cold water and pour it and the beaten egg into the well ③. Stir the butter and flour mixture into the liquid in the well with your fingertips ④. Then gather this very crumbly dough into a mound and *fraiser* the dough, repeatedly smearing it across the counter a little at a time with the heel of your hand and then gathering it back into a mound ⑤. Stop as soon as the dough is smooth and no longer crumbly, and proceed to step 3.

In an electric mixer equipped with dough hook:

1 Sift the flour into the bowl of the electric mixer. Cut the butter into pieces about 2 tablespoons (30 g)

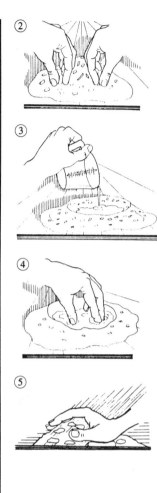

in size and add it and the remaining ingredients to the flour. Dissolve the salt and sugar in the cold water.

2 Mix the flour and butter at low speed with the dough hook. Gradually pour in the dissolved salt and sugar and the beaten egg. If some of the flour cakes around the bottom and sides of the bowl, stop the machine and push the flour into the center with a rubber spatula, then start the machine again. Stop mixing as soon as the dough is smooth, and proceed to step 3.

In a food processor:
Many home food processors do not have a capacity large enough to handle the quantities of ingredients listed above. For all but the largest machines, cut our recipe in half or process the dough in two batches.

1 Sift the flour into the bowl of your food processor. Cut the butter into pieces about 2 tablespoons (30 g) in size, and add it and the salt and sugar to the flour. Using the steel blade of the food processor, cut the butter into the flour until the mixture resembles coarse meal.

2 With the machine on, pour in the cold water and beaten egg through the feed tube, and continue processing until the dough is smooth and gathers itself into a ball on top of the blade. Stop!

By whichever method you have chosen to use:

3 The dough should now be smooth and homogenous and should hold together in a cohesive mass without being sticky. If the dough seems too dry and crumbly, sprinkle it with a little more cold water; on the other hand, if it seems too moist or sticky, dust it with a little flour. Then mix (by hand, electric mixer with dough hook, or food processor) for a few seconds longer to get a smooth dough of the proper consistency.

4 Gather the dough into a ball. Depending on how you plan to use the dough, leave it in one piece or divide it into several pieces of appropriate size. If you plan to use the dough for large *tartes,* you will minimize the waste when you roll it out if you divide the dough now into several pieces, one for each *tarte*—for example, about 11½ to 15 ounces (325 to 425 g) for a 9½-inch (24 cm) *tarte* shell. For small pastries, it is best to roll out one sheet of dough and cut from it the circles for each pastry.

5 To facilitate the eventual rolling out of the dough, flatten each piece with the palm of your hand and form it into a round pad about 1 to 1½ inches (2½ to 4 cm) thick. Wrap each pad of dough in waxed paper and refrigerate for at least 2 hours before rolling out or freezing.

Storage: Wrapped in waxed paper, for up to 3 days in the refrigerator. Or cover tightly with freezer wrap and freeze for up to 3 months. If frozen, defrost in the refrigerator for 24 hours before using.

Pâte Sablée and Pâte Sucrée

For about 3 pounds (1,350 g) of *sablée* or *sucrée, or* enough of either dough for three or four 9½-inch (24 cm) *tarte* shells

SABLÉE:

14 ounces (400 g) butter, softened

7 ounces (200 g), or about 1½ cups, confectioners sugar

9 tablespoons (1.3 dL) cold milk

2 teaspoons (9 g) salt

1 pound 7½ ounces (670 g), or about 5 cups, flour

By hand:

1 On your countertop, cream the butter with the confectioners sugar and (for *sucrée*) *TPT blanc* or (for *sablée*) ¾ cup (100 g) of the flour ①.

2 A little at a time, add (for *sablée*) the milk and salt or (for *sucrée*) the eggs and work it into the creamed butter with your fingertips ②. Work quickly so the warmth of your hands doesn't melt the butter.

3 Sift the flour over the butter mixture ③ and mix it in with your fingertips to form a loose, crumbly dough ④. Gather the dough into a mound and *fraiser* the dough, repeatedly smearing it across the counter a little at a time with the heel of your hand and then gathering it back into a mound ⑤. Stop as soon as the dough is smooth and no longer crumbly, and proceed to step 4.

SUCRÉE:

10½ ounces (300 g) butter, softened

5⅓ ounces (150 g), or about 1 cup plus 2 tablespoons, confectioners sugar

5⅓ ounces (150 g), or about 1 cup, *TPT blanc* (see page 413)

3 large eggs

1 pound 5⅓ ounces (600 g), or about 4½ cups, flour

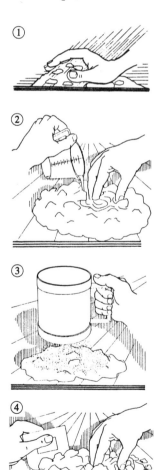

In an electric mixer equipped with leaf beater and dough hook:

1 Cream the butter with the confectioners sugar and (for *sucrée*) *TPT blanc* or (for *sablée*) ¾ cup (100 g) of the flour, using the leaf beater of your mixer.

2 Add (for *sablée*) the milk and salt or (for *sucrée*) the eggs and mix, still using the leaf beater.

3 Remove the leaf beater and sift the flour over the butter mixture. Attach the dough hook and mix in the flour at low speed. If some of the flour cakes around the bottom and sides of the bowl, stop the machine and push the flour into the center with a rubber spatula, then start the machine again. Stop mixing as soon as the dough is smooth, and proceed to step 4.

In a food processor:

Many home food processors do not have a capacity large enough to handle the quantities of ingredients listed above. For all but the largest machines, cut our recipes in half or process the dough in two batches.

1 Cream the butter with the confectioners sugar and (for *sucrée*) *TPT blanc* or (for *sablée*) ⅒ of the flour, using the steel blade of your food processor.

2 Add (for *sablée*) the milk and salt or (for *sucrée*) eggs and continue processing until blended.

3 Take the cover off the processor bowl and sift the flour over the butter mixture. Then continue processing just long enough to make the dough smooth. Stop!

By whichever method you have chosen to use:

4 The dough should now be smooth and homogenous, and it should hold together in a cohesive mass without being sticky. If the dough seems too dry and crumbly, sprinkle it with a little cold water; on the other hand, if it seems too moist or sticky, dust it with a little flour. Then mix (by hand, electric mixer with dough hook, or food processor) for a few seconds longer to get a smooth dough of the proper consistency.

5 Gather the dough into a ball. Depending on how you plan to use the dough, leave it in one piece or divide it into several pieces of appropriate size. If you plan to use the dough for large *tartes*, you will minimize the waste when you roll it out if you divide the dough now into several pieces, one for each *tarte*—for example, about 12 to 16 ounces (335 to 450 g) for a 9½-inch (24 cm) *tarte* shell. For small pastries, it is best to roll out one sheet of dough and cut from it the circles for each pastry.

6 To facilitate the eventual rolling out of the dough, flatten each piece with the palm of your hand and form it into a round pad about 1 to 1½ inches (2½ to 4 cm) thick. Wrap each pad of dough in waxed paper and refrigerate for at least 2 hours before rolling out or freezing.

Storage: Wrapped in waxed paper, fo up to 3 days in the refrigerator. Or cover tightly with freezer wrap and freeze for up to 3 months. If frozen, defrost in the refrigerator for 24 hours before using.

Les Pâtes Feuilletées
Flaky Pastry Doughs

Pâtes feuilletées are composed of hundreds of layers of butter alternating with layers of a flour and water dough called the *détrempe*. The principle of their preparation is based on simple multiplication. Start with a single layer of butter wrapped between two layers of *détrempe*. Roll out this sandwich and fold it in three, like a letter. You now have three layers of butter. Roll it and fold it again, and you get nine layers of butter—and so on. After six turns you have 729 layers.

The elasticity of the gluten in the flour keeps the layers of butter separated. And when the *pâte feuilletée* is baked, water in the butter forms steam, pushing the layers of *détrempe* apart, at the same time as the butter fat melts into the layers of *détrempe*. The result is a pastry dough that is miraculously flaky and inundated with the flavor of sweet butter.

Flaky pastry doughs originated with the ancient Romans. They were reintroduced and popularized in the seventeenth century by the great French painter and pastry chef Claude Gelée, le Lorrain. Then, in the nineteenth century,

Carème established the modern method of developing the layered structure by six "turns."

Actually there are two types of *pâtes feuilletées—feuilletage* and *pâte à croissant*—which are somewhat different in character and use. *Feuilletage*, the classic flaky pastry dough which is frequently referred to as "puff pastry" in the United States, is the more basic and versatile.

Pâte à croissant is prepared in essentially the same way as *feuilletage*, but includes yeast in the *détrempe* and requires a total of only four turns. It is used exclusively for *croissants* and *pains au chocolat*.

When you use *feuilletage*, you will inevitably end up with trimmings from the dough. *Rognures* is a by-product of *feuilletage* made simply by collecting the *feuilletage* trimmings into a pad of dough. it is similar to *feuilletage* but less flaky. In its character and uses, it stands between the *pâtes à foncer* and *feuilletage*.

The *pâtes feuilletées* are more complicated to make than the *pâtes à foncer* because they involve more steps. However, there is nothing particularly difficult about their preparation. Still, we realize that many of you are intimidated by the prospect of making *feuilletage* and are anxious to learn a "simpler" method for making "puff pastry." To help you take the step from the *pâtes à foncer* to the *pâtes feuilletées*, we have included a discussion of such methods at the end of the *Tours de Main* section, and a recipe for one of them called *feuilletage rapide*.

TOURS DE MAIN

The preparation of *feuilletage* and *pâte à croissant* is carried out in three stages: (1) making the *détrempe;* (2) the *beurrage,* or wrapping a block of butter (*beurre,* in French) in the *détrempe;* and (3) the *tourage,* the repeated rolling and folding of the dough that develops its multilayered structure.

Both *feuilletage* and *pâte à croissant* are always made in a *paton,* or pad, of fixed size. This optimal size is large enough to minimize edge effects in the layering due to the folds in the *tourage* process, yet small enough to be manageable. The *pâtes feuilletées* freeze very well, so, if you are preparing the *détrempe* by hand or in a heavy duty electric mixer, then for efficiency we recommend that you make two *patons* at once. On the other hand, if you make the *détrempe* in a food processor, the capacity of your machine will limit you to making one *paton* at a time.

La Détrempe

The ingredients for the *détrempe* will be flour and a liquid. For *feuilletage* the liquid is water and melted butter; for *pâte à croissant* it is water and the *pouliche,* a yeast-leavened "sponge" that is prepared in a preliminary step and contains milk.

What is important in preparing the *détrempe* is to mix the liquid into the flour without working the dough too much. You don't want to activate the gluten in the flour any more than necessary, since that would make the dough elastic (hence difficult to use) and the finished pastry tough. Of course, the *détrempe* must have a little elasticity to keep the layers of butter separated, but the repeated rolling of the *pâte feuilletée* in the *tourage* will activate the gluten sufficiently.

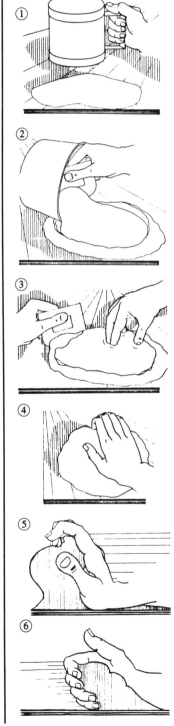

To begin, sift the flour onto the counter ① and make a large well in the center. Pour most of the liquid into the center of the well ②, reserving some of the water to add later. Gradually stir the flour into the liquid in the well. At first you will form a smooth paste, but then, as you add more flour, the dough will become very dry and will not absorb more flour. Continue pulling in more flour and stirring and tossing the dough with one hand. With your other hand, push in flour from the outside of the well, using your dough scraper ③. As you work, gradually sprinkle more water over the dough, adding it alternately with the flour. When you have added all of the flour and water to the well, continue tossing the dough with both hands until it is well mixed. By tossing this very loose dough to mix it, you minimize the stretching that would activate the gluten in the flour and make the dough elastic.

Now gather the dough into a ball. It will be very loose and crumbly. Gather together any flour and dough that is too dry to hold together, sprinkle with a little more water, and toss it until mixed. Then gather it together and add it to the ball of dough.

To make the dough smooth, you must finish mixing it by the *fraisage* technique: With the heel of your hand, break off a piece of the dough ④ and smear it across the counter ⑤. Repeat until all the dough has been pushed across the counter. Then gather the dough together again ⑥. Repeat this *fraisage* technique until the dough is fairly smooth and homogeneous, and dry to the touch.

If, during the mixing of the *détrempe,* any of the dough is too dry to hold together, sprinkle it with a few more drops of water; or, if any of the dough becomes sticky from adding too much water, lightly dust it with flour. Then mix in the added flour or water by the *fraisage* technique.

When you are finished, the *détrempe* should hold together in a single coherent mass. But don't worry if there are a few tiny cracks in the ball of *détrempe.* It will be smoothed still more in the successive rollings of the *tourage.*

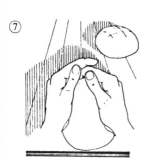

Divide the *détrempe* into pieces of equal size, one for each *paton* of the *pâte feuilletée* you are making. Form each piece of *détrempe* into a ball ⑦.

If you are making *feuilletage,* lightly dust the balls of *détrempe* with flour, wrap them in waxed paper, and let them rest in the refrigerator for 30 minutes to relax the gluten. (Or, if your kitchen is cool, you can omit the flour and waxed paper and let the *détrempe* rest on your countertop.)

If you are making *pâte à croissant,* place the balls of *détrempe* on your countertop and let them rest (and begin to rise) for 15 minutes. Then deflate the *détrempe* by striking each ball two or three times with the heel of your hand.

Beurrage

The *beurrage* is the incorporation of the butter in the *détrempe.* The most commonly used method of *beurrage,* and the one we recommend, is to enclose a single pad or block of butter in an envelope of *détrempe.* This makes it possible to obtain layers of butter and *détrempe* of approximately equal thickness. The uniform development of the *feuilletage* in the oven and its beautiful appearance after baking depend on this regularity of layering.

In order for the *tourage* (see page 15) to produce this regular layering, the butter and *détrempe* must have the same softness so the rolling process will flatten and thin the layers of butter and *détrempe* equally. To give the butter the required consistency, it must be removed from the refrigerator and softened. At the cool (57° F, or 14° C) basement pastry-dough station in the kitchen at Pâtisserie Clichy, the butter is simply left on the counter overnight, and then cut into rectangular blocks of the appropriate size in the morning.

Most home kitchens are too warm for that, and most American butter contains more water than the best French butter. So we recommend that you work the cold butter by hand until it reaches the right consistency; and then work in a little flour to absorb the extra moisture in the butter. In our recipes, we have subtracted this flour from the amount that would normally be used in the *détrempe*. If you were to put all of the flour in the *détrempe*, then you would also have to add a little more water to the *détrempe*, and the moisture in the butter would make the *pâte feuilletée* a little too soft.

To soften the cold butter and make it malleable, first place the butter on your countertop and cut it into 1- to 2-ounce (25 to 50 g) pieces with your dough scraper. Work the butter by smearing it across the counter a little at a time with the heel of your hand ⑧—just like the *fraisage* mixing technique. Gather the butter together with your dough scraper and repeat until the butter is malleable. Then add the reserved flour and continue smearing the butter across the counter with the heel of your hand and gathering it together with your pastry scraper until the butter-flour mixture is smooth and about as soft as the *détrempe*. Gather the butter together and form it into a rectangular pad. Lightly dust the pad with flour on all sides so it will be easy to handle. If it has softened too much, wrap it in waxed paper and let it rest in the refrigerator until it is as firm as the *détrempe*.

When you have gotten the pad of butter to the required consistency, lightly dust your countertop with flour and place a ball of *détrempe* on it. Place the heel of your hand on the top of the *détrempe* just to the far side of the top center of the ball, and press down on it to push the dough out and away from you into a flattened corner ⑨. Rotate the dough 90° and repeat, then two more times, until you have four corners extending from a thick central mound of dough.

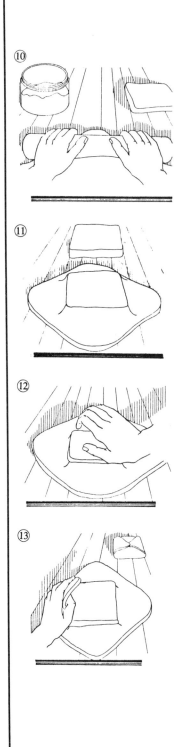

If the top of the *détrempe* seems at all sticky, lightly dust it with flour.

Firmly roll your rolling pin out from the central mound over each corner of the *détrempe* to flatten and enlarge it, making a square of *détrempe* with the mound in the center ⑩. Roll your rolling pin over the central mound to flatten it into a thick, roughly square central cushion oriented at 45° with respect to the square of *détrempe* and a little larger than the square pad of butter. The butter will go on this central cushion of *détrempe,* and the corners of the *détrempe* must be large enough to completely envelop the butter. If they are too small, roll out a little more *détrempe* from the central pad into the corners to enlarge them.

Place the square pad of butter on the square central cushion of *détrempe* ⑪ and pound it once or twice with the heel of your hand to flatten it ⑫. The pad of butter should not extend beyond the thick central cushion of *détrempe*.

Fold one of the corners of the square of *détrempe* over the butter ⑬. Fold the opposite corner over the butter so it overlaps the first corner and press firmly with the heel of your hand to seal the corners together. Fold a third corner of the square over the butter, being careful to seal the edges of the *détrempe* tightly around the butter, and press the corner down where it overlaps the first two corners. Finally, fold the fourth corner of the square over the butter, sealing the edges around the butter, and give this top corner a couple of firm blows with the heel of your hand. You now have a *paton* of *pâte feuilletée* consisting of a pad of butter enclosed in an envelope of *détrempe*. Be sure that all of the corners of the square of *détrempe* overlap sufficiently so the envelope will not open during the *tourage*.

For *feuilletage* give the *paton* a few blows with your rolling pin to flatten it slightly and make it into a more even rectangle. First strike the *paton* one or two times parallel to the last envelope fold so that it won't open up, then strike it in the other direction as well. Lightly dust the *paton* with flour, wrap it in waxed paper, and let it rest in the refrigerator for 30 minutes so the gluten will relax and the *feuilletage* will be easier to roll.

For *pâte à croissant,* you should not strike the *paton* with your rolling pin, because the *détrempe à croissant* is much softer than the *détrempe à feuilletage.* And because the *détrempe à croissant* contains yeast, the *paton* should not be allowed to rest at this stage. Rather proceed directly to the *tourage.*

At this point, the bottom layer of *détrempe* in your *paton* should be about the same thickness as the butter and about twice as thick as the top layer of *détrempe,* so the rolling and folding in the subsequent *tourage* will produce layers of butter and *détrempe* of approximately equal thickness, and the exterior layer of *détrempe* (which at this stage is the bottom of the *paton*) is thick enough to hold the butter inside. If the *beurrage* has been well executed, then the *tourage* should proceed with no difficulties.

Tourage

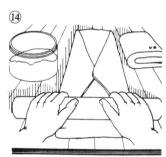

Lightly dust your countertop and the *paton* of *pâte feuilletée* with flour and roll out the *paton* in the direction perpendicular to the last envelope fold . Start with your rolling pin on the near edge of the *paton* and roll it firmly and evenly to, but not over, the far end of the *paton.* Then reverse direction and roll the rolling pin to the near end of the *paton.* Continue rolling forward and backward over the *paton,* always rolling firmly and evenly so that the butter and *détrempe* are flattened and extended in uniform layers, until the *paton* has reached three times its initial length. Dust the counter and the dough with flour as needed to prevent it from sticking to counter or rolling pin.

Never roll your rolling pin out over the end of the *paton* of *pâte feuilletée,* since this can force the butter to escape out the end of its envelope of *détrempe.* Always flatten the ends of the paton by rolling the rolling pin from the edge in toward the center of the *paton,* so you push the butter in toward the center.

Don't be afraid to turn the dough over and roll it on the back side, if this helps to roll it more evenly. But always be sure that the last previous fold is on top when you make the next fold.

If the *paton* starts to lose its rectangular shape while you are rolling it, you can roll your rolling pin in the perpendicular direction over part of the *paton* to even out the width. Ideally, you should roll the *paton* into a perfect rectangle with squared-off ends, but even professionals aren't always that proficient. Just do the best you can, and, if the ends aren't square, stretch the corners a little to make them more square just before folding the *paton*.

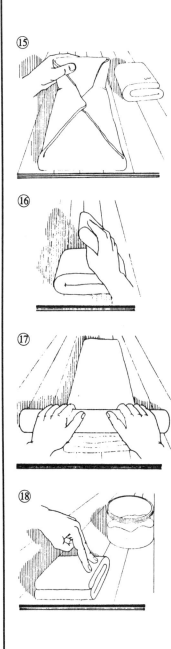

If there is excess flour on the dough, brush it off so it won't be incorporated into the *paton*. Then fold the dough in thirds like a letter ⑮. This makes one turn, or one rolling and folding step ⑯.

Rotate the *paton* 90° and repeat the operation, this time rolling and folding the *paton* in the direction perpendicular to the first turn ⑰. This makes two turns.

Lightly dust the *paton* with flour. Mark the *paton* by pressing the tips of two fingers on the surface of the dough to indicate the number of turns ⑱. Wrap the *paton* in waxed paper and place it in the refrigerator.

For feuilletage: let the dough rest in the refrigerator for at least 30 minutes, and preferably 2 hours. Then give the *feuilletage* two more turns, always rotating the *paton* 90° between each successive turn. Lightly dust the *paton* with flour and mark it with the imprint of four fingertips to indicate four turns. Then wrap the dough in waxed paper and let it rest in the refrigerator for at least 2 hours and preferably overnight.

For pâte à croissant: let the dough rest in the refrigerator for a least 1 hour and preferably overnight. Notice that *pâte à croissant* gets two fewer turns than *feuilletage*.

This finishes the initial preparation of the *pâte feuilletée*. When you are ready to use the dough, you will give it additional turns (following the same procedure described here) as the first step in the recipe you are making. *Pâte à croissant* will get two more turns, making four turns altogether. *Feuilletage* will get one and a half or two more turns, for five and a half or six turns altogether.

The time-consuming aspect of making *pâtes feuilletées* is the rest periods between turns. These rest periods are necessary to prevent the gluten in flour from building up too much strength and making the dough elastic. The turns are always done in pairs so the *paton* of *pâte feuilletée* is rolled equally in both directions. If the *pâte feuilletée* were rolled much more in one direction than the other, the gluten would be activated more in that direction, and as a result the dough could shrink unevenly during baking.

About Quick Pâtes Feuilletées

There are two standard short-cut methods for making *feuilletage*, called *feuilletage rapide* and *feuilletage inversé*. These both differ from true *feuilletage* primarily in the method of *beurrage*. They produce pastry doughs that do not rise as high or as evenly as true *feuilletage*, so they are never used in a first-class professional pastry kitchen. Their practical advantage is not so much that they are easier to make than true *feuilletage*, but that they require shorter rest periods between turns and so can be produced more quickly. We will sketch both methods here and then later give a recipe for *feuilletage rapide*, which we feel has greater practical and pedagogical value.

For *feuilletage inversé* the *détrempe* is rolled out in a rectangle and softened butter is spread over half of its surface. Then the *détrempe* is folded in half to enclose the butter and the *tourage* proceeds as usual. In our opinion, this is no simpler than making true *feuilletage*, and we will not give a recipe for it.

Feuilletage rapide accomplishes the *beurrage* by incorporating the butter as dice in the *détrempe*. The *tourage* then smears out the dice horizontally and develops the layered structure characteristic of flaky pastry doughs. Thus, from a pedagogical point of view, *feuilletage rapide* forms a natural bridge between the *pâtes à foncer* and true *feuilletage*. So if you are hesitant about trying to make *feuilletage*, you might try *feuilletage rapide* first. Also, since *feuilletage rapide* does not rise as high as true *feuilletage*, it can be used in recipes that call for *rognures*.

Feuilletage

Incredibly rich in butter, and light and flaky when baked, this is the most refined and elegant of all pastry doughs. You can make the *détrempe* for *feuilletage* by hand, in a heavy duty electric mixer, or in a large-capacity food processor. After the *détrempe* has been made, the remainder of the preparation is always done by hand. We have included a tiny amount of vinegar in the *détrempe* to help prevent it from developing too much strength.

For 2 *patons* of *feuilletage*, each weighing about 3¼ pounds (1,475 g), or 1 *paton* if made with food processor

---

INGREDIENTS

2 pounds 15 ounces (1,330 g), or about 10 cups, flour

2 tablespoons (28 g) salt

4 teaspoons (2 cL) vinegar

2¼ cups (5.3 dL) cold water

4⅔ ounces (133 g) barely melted butter

2 pounds (900 g) cold butter

By hand:

1 Set aside ½ cup (65 g) of the flour. Sift the remaining flour onto your countertop. Gather it into a wide mound and make a large well in the center.

2 Dissolve the salt and vinegar in 1¼ cups (3 dL) of the cold water, and pour this mixture and the melted butter into the well.

3 With the fingertips of one hand, gradually stir flour into the liquid in the well. At first you will form a smooth paste. Then, as you pull more flour into the well, it will become very dry and crumbly. Using your dough scraper in the other hand, continue adding flour to the well, and alternately add the remaining water, a little at a time, as you stir and toss the dough to mix it. When you have finished adding the flour and water, continue tossing the dough with both hands until it is well mixed, then gather the dough together into a ball. If there is any flour or dough that is too dry to hold together, sprinkle it with a little more cold water and toss it to mix. Then gather it together and add it to the ball of dough.

4 Finish mixing the dough by the *fraisage* technique: that is, with the heel of your hand, break off a little of the dough at a time and smear it across the countertop. Then gather the dough together into a ball again and repeat until the dough is fairly smooth and homogeneous and holds together in a coherent mass. If the dough is too dry or too damp, sprinkle it with a little cold water on the one hand or flour on the other, and continue mixing by this *fraisage* method until smooth.

5 Gather the dough together. This is the *détrempe*. Divide the *détrempe* into two equal pieces of about 2 pounds 3 ounces (990 g) each, and form each piece into a ball. Lightly dust each ball of *détrempe* with flour, wrap in waxed paper, and let rest in the refrigerator for 30 minutes. Proceed to step 6.

In an electric mixer equipped with leaf beater:
That's right, the leaf beater, not the dough hook!

1 Set aside ½ cup (65 g) of the flour. Sift the remaining flour into the bowl of your electric mixer and attach the leaf beater.

2 Dissolve the salt and vinegar in the cold water. Mix with the melted butter.

3 Turn on the mixer at low speed and pour in the liquid in a slow, steady stream. The dough will be very crumbly and resemble coarse meal at first, then quickly start to come together in small lumps. Stop the machine! Do not let the mixer work the dough or it will activate the gluten in the flour and make the *détrempe* elastic.

4 Turn the dough out onto the countertop and gather it together. If there is any loose flour or dough that is too dry to hold together, sprinkle it with a little more cold water, toss to moisten it, and then gather it together and add it to the bulk of the dough. If necessary, *fraiser* the dough—repeatedly smearing it across the counter, a little at a time, with the heel of your hand—to make it fairly smooth and homogeneous. This dough is the *détrempe*.

5 Divide the *détrempe* into two equal pieces of about 2 pounds 3 ounces (990 g) each, and form each piece into a ball. Lightly dust each ball of *détrempe* with flour, wrap them in waxed paper, and let them rest in the refrigerator for 30 minutes. Proceed to step 6.

In a food processor:
To make the *détrempe* for one *paton* of *feuilletage* in a food processor, you need a workbowl capacity of

INGREDIENTS

1 pound 7½ ounces (665 g), or about 5 cups, flour

1 tablespoon (14 g) salt

1 cup plus 2 tablespoons (2.7 dL) cold water

2 teaspoons (1 cL) vinegar

2⅓ ounces (67 g) barely melted butter

1 pound (450 g) cold butter

at least 9 cups (2.1 L), or a 7-cup (1.7 L) workbowl with a "Dough Dome." These ingredients are for one *paton* of *feuilletage,* weighing about 3¼ pounds (1,475 g).

1 Set aside ¼ cup (35 g) of the flour. Sift the remaining flour into the workbowl of your food processor (fitted with the steel blade).

2 Dissolve the salt and vinegar in the cold water. Mix with the melted butter.

3 With the feed tube open, pour a little of the liquid into the workbowl of the food processor and pulse the machine on and off once or twice. Repeat, alternately adding the liquid and pulsing the machine on and off, until all the water and melted butter have been added. Pulse the food processor on and off a few more times to be sure the liquid is uniformly incorporated with the flour. The dough should be very loose and resemble coarse meal.

4 Turn the dough out onto the counter and gather it together. If there is any loose flour or dough that is too dry to hold together, sprinkle it with a little more cold water, toss to moisten it, and then gather it together and add it to the bulk of the dough. If necessary *fraiser* the dough—repeatedly smearing it across the counter, a little at a time, with the heel of your hand—to make it fairly smooth and homogeneous. This dough is the *détrempe.*

5 Form the *détrempe* into a ball and lightly dust it with flour. Wrap the ball in waxed paper and let it rest in the refrigerator for 30 minutes.

By whichever method you have chosen to use:

6 Meanwhile, take 1 pound (450 g) of cold butter and soften it by repeatedly pushing it across the countertop, a little at a time, with the heel of your hand. Use your dough scraper in your other hand to gather the butter together after each time you finish pushing it across the counter. When the butter is malleable, add ¼ cup (35 g) of reserved flour and work it into the butter by the same technique. When the butter-flour mixture is smooth, form it into a pad

4½ inches (11½ cm) square and about 1⅝ inch (4 cm) thick. Lightly dust the pad of butter with flour. If you are making more than 1 *paton* of *feuilletage,* repeat with the remaining cold butter and reserved flour. The butter should have the same softness as the détrempe. If it has softened too much, wrap each pad in waxed paper and refrigerate until the butter is as firm as the *détrempe.*

7 Lightly dust your countertop with flour and place a ball of *détrempe* on it. With the heel of your hand, press out four corners from the ball of dough to make a square with a mound in the center. Then roll your rolling pin out over the corners to thin them and enlarge the square to about 12 inches (30 cm). Roll your rolling pin over the central mound to make a cushion 5 inches (12½ cm) square and about 1¼ inch (3 cm) thick and oriented on the diagonal with respect to the square of *détrempe.*

8 Place a pad of butter on the thick, square cushion in the center of the square of *détrempe.* Flatten the butter by striking it once or twice with the heel of your hand. Fold two opposite corners of the *détrempe* over the butter pad, overlapping the corners. Then fold the remaining two corners over the butter pad, overlapping them as well. The *détrempe* should now enclose the butter like an envelope. Seal the envelope by pressing it on top with the heel of your hand, then strike it a few times with your rolling pin to flatten it into a square about 2 inches (5 cm) thick and 6½ inches (16½ cm) on a side. (If you are making more than one *paton* of *feuilletage,* repeat steps 7 and 8 with the remaining balls of *détrempe* and pads of butter.)

9 Lightly dust each *paton* of *feuilletage* with flour, wrap it in waxed paper, and let it rest in the refrigerator for 30 minutes.

10 Lightly dust your counter with flour, place a *paton* on it, and dust the *paton* with flour. Roll out the *paton,* in the direction perpendicular to the last envelope fold of the *détrempe,* into a rectangle three times the original length of the *paton.* Fold it in three like a letter. This is the first turn. Rotate the *paton* 90°—so that the folds are at the sides—and repeat this rolling and folding operation. Mark the *paton* by pressing the tips of two fingers into the surface of the dough to indicate two turns. (Repeat with the remaining *paton,* if any.) Dust the *paton* with flour, wrap it in waxed paper, and let it rest in the refrigerator for at least 30 minutes, and preferably for 2 hours.

⁄⁄ Give the *paton* (or *patons*) two more turns, rotating the *paton* 90° after each successive turn. Mark the *paton* with the imprint of four fingertips to indicate four turns. Dust the *paton* with flour, wrap it in waxed paper again, and return it to the refrigerator for at least 2 hours, and preferably overnight. This completes the initial preparation of the *feuilletage.*

Storage: Wrapped in waxed paper, in the refrigerator for up to 3 days. For longer storage, the *feuilletage* can be covered with freezer wrap and frozen for up to 2 months. If you want to cut the *paton* in half before freezing, first roll it out to about one and a half times its length in the direction perpendicular to the last turn, then cut it in half, wrap it, and freeze it as for a whole *paton.* If the *feuilletage* is frozen, let it defrost overnight in the refrigerator before using.

Feuilletage Rapide

The proportions of flour, butter, water, and salt in this recipe for *feuilletage rapide* are identical to those in our recipe for *feuilletage.* Unlike *feuilletage,* there is no optimum size for a *paton* of *feuilletage rapide.* Since cooks who are unfamiliar with the *tourage* process may find it easier to deal with a smaller amount of dough, we have chosen the quantities to give a *paton* of 1 pound 10 ounces (735 g), or the equivalent of half a *paton* of *feuilletage.*

Feuilletage rapide works well in *bandes de tarte* and in most of our recipes for *feuilletage* desserts and cookies. It is also a good substitute for *rognures* if you are very thorough in pricking the dough, whenever this is called for in the recipe, to prevent it from rising too high or unevenly. We do not recommend *feuilletage rapide* for *pithiviers, galette des rois,* or *vols-au-vent* shells where even rising is essential.

For 1 *paton* weighing 1 pound 10 ounces (735 g)

INGREDIENTS

½ pound (225 g) well-chilled butter

¾ pound (340 g), or about 2½ cups, flour

5 teaspoons (24 g) butter, barely melted

1½ teaspoons (7 g) salt

10 tablespoons (1½ dL) cold water

1 Cut the butter into ½-inch (1 cm) dice. This is easiest if the butter is very cold, almost frozen, so the dice won't stick together. After cutting the dice, put the butter in a bowl and let it rest in the refrigerator to soften a little. For the next step, the butter dice should be at, not below, refrigerator temperature.

2 Dissolve the salt in the cold water and mix in the melted butter.

3 Sift the flour onto the countertop. Add the butter dice and toss to mix without breaking down the dice.

4 Slowly pour and sprinkle the liquid over the flour using one hand, while with the other hand you toss the flour and butter to mix in the liquid. After you have added all of the liquid, continue tossing with both hands to be sure it is thoroughly blended, but leaving the butter dice intact. Then gather the dough together into a ball. The dough should be very loose and crumbly and barely hold together. If there is any loose flour or dough that is too dry to hold together, sprinkle it with a little more cold water, toss to moisten it, and then gather it together and add it to the ball of dough.

5 Form the ball of dough into a rough rectangular pad, about 1½ inches (4 cm) thick. Dust the countertop and the pad of dough with a little flour and roll out the dough into a rectangular sheet about 6 inches (15 cm) wide and 16 inches (40 cm) long. In the process of rolling out the dough, the butter in it will stick to the counter and rolling pin. Each time it does, stop rolling, lift the dough from the counter with your dough scraper, and dust the counter and dough with a little more flour. Use as little flour for dusting as you can. Then continue rolling. When you have rolled the dough out to a rectangle of the required size, fold it in thirds like a letter. This completes the first turn. Lightly dust the *paton* of dough with flour, wrap it in waxed paper, and refrigerate for 30 minutes to 1 hour to keep the butter cold.

6 Give the *paton* two more turns: Lightly dust your counter and the *paton* with flour, and roll out the *paton,* in the direction perpendicular to the first turn, into a rectangle about three times its original length. Fold it in three like a letter. This is the second turn. Rotate the paton 90°—so the folds are on the sides—and repeat this rolling and folding operation. This makes three turns. While you are doing the turns, lightly dust the counter and the dough with flour as needed to prevent the dough from sticking to counter or rolling pin. Then, at the end of the third turn, dust the *paton* with flour, wrap it in waxed paper, and refrigerate again for 30 minutes to 1 hour. The dough is now ready to use.

Storage: Wrapped in waxed paper, in the refrigerator for up to two days. Or cover the dough with freezer wrap and freeze for up to 2 months. If frozen, defrost overnight in the refrigerator before using.

Note: *Feuilletage rapide* gets only three turns as part of its initial preparation, but it can be used in most of our recipes that call for four turns *feuilletage*.

Rognures

The word *rognures* in French means "trimmings." In pastry making, *rognures* is the dough formed from trimmings of *feuilletage*. *Rognures* is used when you want a flaky pastry dough that won't rise too high, for example in *tarte* shells, bases for *bandes de tarte*, and *mille-feuilles*.

For any quantity of dough

INGREDIENTS

Trimmings from
  rolling out and
  cutting *feuilletage*

1 Gather the trimmings together and form them into a tight ball. Flatten this ball into a round pad by pressing it with the heel of your hand.

Alternatively, to get a slightly better-quality (i.e., more flaky) *rognures,* lay out some flat pieces of *feuilletage* tight against each other in one layer with all the long pieces running roughly parallel to each other in one direction. Then arrange a second layer of trimmings on top, placing the long pieces perpendicular to the long pieces in the first layer. Continue with 1 or 2 more layers, depending on the quantity of trimmings you have. The idea is to keep as much of the layered structure of the *feuilletage* as possible. Press the trimmings tightly together and form them into a round or rectangular pad.

2 Lightly dust the pad of *rognures* with flour and wrap it in waxed paper. Refrigerate the *rognures* for at least 2 hours, and preferably overnight, to be sure it is well chilled and the gluten in the dough has completely relaxed.

Storage: If the *feuilletage* from which the trimmings came was freshly made, the *rognures* can be kept in the refrigerator for 2 or 3 days, or wrapped in freezer wrap and frozen for up to 2 or 3 months. If frozen, defrost the *rognures* overnight in the refrigerator before using.

If the *feuilletage* from which the trimmings came was not freshly made, reduce the storage times accordingly.

Pâte à Croissant

This is just a leavened version of *feuilletage*. If you have already mastered *feuilletage* and any one of the *pâtes levées—pâte à brioche*, for example—you will have no difficulty turning out a perfect *pâte à croissant*.

There are several distinct methods for incorporating the yeast in the *détrempe* for *pâte à croissant*. We prefer the method of preparation *"sur pouliche"* in which a yeast sponge is made as an initial step in the preparation. As for *feuilletage*, the *détrempe à croissant* can be prepared by hand, in a heavy duty electric mixer, or in a large-capacity food processor. After the *détrempe* has been made, the remainder of the preparation is always done by hand.

For 2 *patons* of *pâte à croissant*, each weighing about 3 pounds (1,350 g), or 1 *paton* if made with food processor

INGREDIENTS

2⅔ pounds (1,200 g), or about 9 cups, flour

1.8 ounces (34 g), or

By hand:

1 Sift 3 cups (400 g) of the flour into a bowl. Crumble the yeast into a small bowl and dissolve it and the sugar and molasses in the warm milk. Add this to the flour and stir with your fingertips to form a

3 cakes, fresh yeast

5 tablespoons (60 g)
sugar

2 teaspoons (20 g)
light molasses

1¾ cups (4 dL)
warm milk

1½ pounds (700 g)
cold butter

2 tablespoons (25 g)
salt

1 cup (2.4 dL) warm
water

smooth, soft paste. This is the *pouliche*. Put the bowl in a warm place (75° to 85° F or 25° to 30° C) and let the *pouliche* rise until tripled in volume, about 1 hour.

2 Meanwhile, take ¾ pound (350 g) of the butter and soften it by repeatedly pushing it across the countertop, a little at a time, with the heel of your hand. Use your dough scraper in your other hand to gather the butter together after each time you finish pushing it across the counter. When the butter is malleable, add 3 tablespoons (25 g) of the remaining flour and work it into the butter by the same technique. When the butter-flour mixture is smooth, form it into a pad 4 inches (10 cm) square and about 1½ inches (4 cm) thick. Lightly dust the pad of butter with flour. Repeat with the remaining ¾ pound (350 g) of butter and another 3 tablespoons (25 g) of the flour. If the butter pads are too soft, wrap them in waxed paper and refrigerate until after you have made the *détrempe*.

3 Sift the remaining flour onto your countertop. Gather it into a wide mound and make a large well in the center.

4 When the *pouliche* has risen, turn it out into the center of the well. Dissolve the salt in half of the warm water, and stir it into the *pouliche*.

5 With the fingertips of one hand, gradually stir flour into the *pouliche* in the well. At first you will have a smooth paste. Then, as you pull more flour into the well, it will become very dry and crumbly. Using your dough scraper in the other hand, continue adding flour to the well, and alternately add the remaining water a little at a time, as you stir and toss the dough to mix it. When you have finished adding the flour and water, continue tossing the dough with both hands until it is well mixed, then gather the dough together into a ball. If there is any loose flour or dough that is too dry to hold together, sprinkle it with a little more warm water and toss to moisten it. Then gather it together and add it to the bulk of the dough.

6 Finish mixing the dough by the *fraisage* technique: that is, with the heel of your hand, break off a little of the dough at a time and smear it across the countertop. Then gather the dough together into a ball again and repeat until the dough is fairly smooth and homogeneous and holds together in a coherent mass. If you feel that the dough is too dry or too damp during the mixing process, sprinkle it with a little warm water on the one hand or flour on the other, and continue mixing by this *fraisage* method until smooth. The finished dough should be softer than *feuilletage,* and not quite as dry.

7 Gather the dough together. This is the *détrempe à croissant.* Divide the *détrempe* into two equal pieces, of about 2 pounds 2 ounces (975 g) each, and form each piece into a ball. Let the *détrempe* rest— and begin to rise—on your countertop for 15 minutes. Proceed to step 8.

In an electric mixer equipped with leaf beater:
As for *feuilletage,* our method is unconventional in that we use the leaf beater rather than a dough hook.

1 Sift 2 cups (267 g) of the flour into a bowl. Crumble the yeast into a small bowl and dissolve it and the sugar and molasses in 1¼ cup (3 dL) of the warm milk. Add this to the flour in the bowl, and stir with your fingertips to form a smooth, soft paste. This is the *pouliche.* Put the bowl in a warm place (75° to 85° F, or 25° to 30° C) and let the *pouliche* rise until tripled in volume, about 1 hour.

2 Meanwhile, take ¾ pound (350 g) of the butter and soften it by repeatedly pushing it across the countertop, a little at a time, with the heel of your hand. Use your dough scraper in your other hand to gather the butter together after each time you finish pushing it across the counter. When the butter is malleable, add 3 tablespoons (25 g) of the remaining flour and work it into the butter by the same technique. Do not work the butter too much or it will become too soft. When the butter-flour mixture is smooth, form it into a pad 4 inches (10 cm) square and about 1½ inches (4 cm) thick. Lightly dust the pad of butter with flour. Repeat with the remaining ¾ pound (350 g) of butter and another 3 tablespoons (25 g) of flour. If the butter pads are too soft, wrap them in waxed paper and refrigerate until after you have made the *détrempe*.

3 Sift the remaining flour into the bowl of your electric mixer and attach the leaf beater.

4 Dissolve the salt in the warm water and the remaining warm milk. When the *pouliche* has risen, stir in the milk-salt mixture with your fingertips to get a smooth, heavy liquid.

5 Turn on the mixer at low speed and slowly pour in the liquid in a slow, steady stream. Stop the machine as soon as the dough starts to hold together.

6 Turn the dough out onto the counter and gather it together. If there is any loose flour or dough that is too dry to hold together, sprinkle it with a little more warm water and toss to moisten it. Then gather it together and add it to the bulk of the dough. If necessary, *fraiser* the dough—repeatedly smearing it across the counter, a little at a time, with the heel of your hand—to make it fairly smooth and homogeneous. This dough is the *détrempe à croissant*.

7 Divide the *détrempe* into two equal pieces of about 2 pounds 2 ounces (975 g) each, and form each piece into a ball. Let the *détrempe* rest—and begin to rise—on your countertop for 15 minutes. Proceed to step 8.

INGREDIENTS

1⅓ pounds (600 g), or about 4½ cups, flour

0.9 ounces (25 g), or 1½ cakes, fresh yeast

2½ tablespoons (30 g) sugar

1 teaspoon (10 g) light molasses

In a food processor:
As for *feuilletage,* you need a food processor with a workbowl capacity of at least 9 cups (2.1 L), or a 7-cup (1.7 L) workbowl with a "Dough Dome." These ingredients are for 1 *paton* of *pâte à croissant,* weighing about 3 pounds (1,350 g).

1 Sift 1½ cups (200 g) of the flour into a bowl. Crumble the yeast into a small bowl and dissolve it and the sugar and molasses in the warm milk. Add this to the flour in the bowl, and stir with your fingertips to form a smooth, soft paste. This is the *pouliche*. Put the bowl in a warm place (75° to 85° F or

¾ cup plus 2
  tablespoons (2 dL)
  warm milk
¾ pound (350 g)
  cold butter
1 tablespoon (13 g)
  salt
½ cup (1.2 dL)

25° to 30° C) and let the *pouliche* rise until tripled in volume, about 1 hour.

2 Meanwhile, soften the butter by repeatedly pushing it across the countertop, a little at a time, with the heel of your hand. Use your dough scraper in your other hand to gather the butter together after each time you finish pushing it across the counter. When the butter is malleable, add 3 tablespoons (25 g) of the remaining flour and work it into the butter by the same technique. Do not work the butter too much or it will become too soft. When the butter-flour mixture is smooth, form it into a pad 4 inches (10 cm) square and about 1½ inches (4 cm) thick. Lightly dust the pad of butter with flour. If it is too soft, wrap it in waxed paper and refrigerate until after you have made the *détrempe*.

3 Sift the remaining flour into the workbowl of your food processor (fitted with the steel blade).

4 When the *pouliche* has risen, add it to the flour in the food processor and turn on the machine just long enough to cut the *pouliche* into the flour.

5 Dissolve the salt in the warm water. With the feed tube open, pour a little of the water into the workbowl of the food processor and pulse the machine on and off once or twice. Repeat, alternately adding the water and pulsing the machine on and off, until all the water and salt have been added. Pulse the machine on and off a few more times to be sure the water is uniformly incorporated in the flour. The dough should be fairly loose and just beginning to come together.

6 Turn the dough out onto the countertop and gather it into a ball. If there is any loose flour or dough that is too dry to hold together, sprinkle it with a little warm water and toss to moisten it. Then gather it together and add it to the bulk of the dough. If necessary, *fraiser* the dough—repeatedly smearing it across the counter, a little at a time, with the heel of your hand—until fairly smooth and homogeneous. This dough is the *détrempe à croissant*.

7 Form the *détrempe* into a ball, and let it rest—and begin to rise—on your countertop for 15 minutes.

29

By whichever method you have chosen to use:

8 Lightly dust your countertop with flour and place a ball of *détrempe* on it. With the heel of your hand, deflate the *détrempe* and press out four corners from the ball of dough to make a square with a mound in the center. Then roll your rolling pin out over the corners to thin them and enlarge the square to about 11 inches (28 cm). Roll your rolling pin over the central mound to make a cushion 4½ inches (11½ cm) square and about 1½ inches (3.8 cm) thick and oriented on the diagonal with respect to the square of *détrempe*.

9 The butter should have about the same softness as the *détrempe*. If it is too hard, work it a little more with the heel of your hand, then form it back into a square pad. Place the pad of butter on the thick square cushion in the center of the square of *détrempe*. Flatten the butter by striking it once or twice with the heel of your hand. Fold two opposite corners of the *détrempe* over the butter pad, overlapping the corners. Then fold the remaining two corners over the butter pad, overlapping them as well. The *détrempe* should now enclose the butter like an envelope. Seal the envelope by pressing it on top with the heel of your hand. You should have a *paton* 6 to 6½ inches (15 to 16 cm) square and 2 inches (5 cm) thick. (If you are making more than one *paton* of *pâte à croissant,* repeat steps 8 and 9 with the remaining ball of *détrempe* and pad of butter.)

10 Lightly dust your countertop and the *paton* with flour. Roll out the *paton,* in the direction perpendicular to the last envelope fold of the *détrempe,* into a rectangle about three times the original length of the *paton.* Fold it in three like a letter. This is the first turn. Rotate the *paton* 90°—so that the folds are at the sides—and repeat this rolling and folding operation. Mark the *paton* by pressing the tips of two fingers into the surface of the dough to indicate two turns. (Repeat with the remaining *paton,* if any.) Dust the *paton* with flour, wrap it in waxed paper, and let it rest in the refrigerator for at least 1 hour and preferably overnight.

Storage: Wrapped in waxed paper, in the refrigerator for no longer than 24 hours. For longer storage,

cover with freezer wrap and freeze for up to 1
month. If frozen, then let the *pâte à croissant* defrost
overnight in the refrigerator before using.

Les Pâtes Levées
Leavened Pastry Doughs

The essential ingredients of the pastry chef's oeuvre are butter, eggs, flour, and
sugar. Those of the baker's are yeast, flour, salt, and water. In *les pâtes levées,*
the two domains intersect. From the baker's point of view, the subject of this
section is butter- and egg-rich breads; but for us it is leavened pastry doughs.
The four we have chosen to share with you are *pâte à brioche, pâte à kugelhopf,
brioche aux fruits,* and *pâte à baba.*

TOURS DE MAIN

All of the *pâtes levées* are prepared by variations of one general method. First,
yeast (dissolved in water), eggs, and sugar and salt (also dissolved in water) are
mixed with flour. The resulting dough is kneaded to give it body and strength,
and then butter is mixed into the dough. The dough is allowed to rise, and
finally the risen dough is deflated and refrigerated to allow the yeast to mature
and give body to the dough.

In contrast to the *pâtes à foncer* and *pâtes feuilletées,* here it is essential to
activate the gluten in the flour maximally so that the gas produced by the yeast
will inflate the dough, making it rise when baked. The kneading process that
accomplishes this can be carried out with equal success by hand, in an electric
mixer, or in a food processor.

Mixing the Dough
(Pétrissage, Première Étape)

At the outset of this step, you will have flour, dissolved yeast, eggs, dissolved sugar and salt, and
possibly some additional liquid (depending on the
recipe). The mixing of these ingredients is a delicate
process, and it is important that you maintain the
proper consistency from start to finish. The dough
will be "burned" (that is, the eggs will be dehy-
drated by the flour, making lumps in the dough) if it

gets too dry, but it will not develop enough strength if it is too loose at the beginning of the kneading process that follows.

Sift the flour onto the counter and gather it into a mound ①. Make a large well in the center of the mound. To the side of the main well, make a second, smaller well. Pour the dissolved yeast into the small well and pour some of the eggs into the main well ②. Using the fingertips of one hand, break the yolks of the eggs and gradually stir in some of the surrounding flour until you get a smooth, soft paste. With your index finger, stir some flour into the dissolved yeast to get a smooth paste of similar consistency to the egg-flour mixture in the main well ③. Then push into the main well and thoroughly mix the yeast-flour paste with the egg-flour paste by stirring with your fingertips ④.

Continue mixing in a circular motion with the fingertips of one hand, dragging the flour into the center of the well a little at a time. With your other hand, use a dough scraper to prevent the well from spreading out too much on the countertop and to push flour into the well as needed. Do not let the dough become too dry. When it begins to lose its sheen and softness, add another egg, break the yolk with your fingertips, and stir the egg into the paste until it is soft, smooth, and glistening again. Continue mixing in the flour and adding the remaining eggs, one at a time, as you need them to keep the dough from becoming too dry. Try to keep approximately the same consistency throughout the mixing process.

When you have used all of the eggs, stir in the dissolved sugar and salt and any additional liquids. If these liquids amount to more than about ¼ cup (6 cL), then add them a little at a time, alternately with the flour, in the same way you added the eggs. Finally, stir in the remaining flour and mix until the dough is smooth, then gather the dough into a mound in the center of the counter.

The dough should now be soft, sticky, and slightly elastic, forming a limp, amorphous mass on your countertop. The kneading process that follows will activate the gluten in the flour by repeatedly stretching the dough. If the dough is too firm and dry, holding together in a well defined form and not sticking to the countertop and your fingers, then it will not stretch easily and will be difficult to knead, but if the dough is too moist, it will not hold together when it is stretched in the kneading procedure, and consequently the strength of the gluten will not be activated sufficiently. If you decide that the dough is either too dry or too moist, then mix in a little more liquid (beaten egg for *pâte à brioche,* water for *pâte à kugelhopf* and *pâte à baba*) on the one hand or flour on the other to reach the required consistency. The first time you make one of the *pâtes levées,* you may think this discussion is a little abstract, but when you begin the kneading you will quickly learn to assess the consistency by the feel of the dough. If necessary, you can always adjust the consistency after you start the kneading and see how it goes.

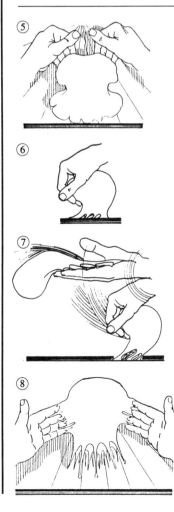

Kneading the Dough
(Pétrissage, Deuxième Étape)

The dough must now be kneaded to increase its strength and give it body.

With your palms facing up and your fingertips overlapping slightly, lift the mass of dough (or as much of it as pulls free of the counter) up and toward your body ⑤ - ⑥. Moving your hands in a roughly circular path, continue lifting the dough up, then away from you ⑦, and finally throw it vigorously down onto the counter ⑧.

You must repeat this motion until the dough develops sufficient strength, and it will probably take 15 to 20 minutes. In the beginning, lift the dough about 4 to 6 inches (10 to 15 cm) off the countertop. As it becomes more elastic and holds itself together more strongly, you can lift it higher and throw it down more forcefully. Continue kneading until the dough is very smooth and rubbery, with sufficient strength and elasticity to pull cleanly off the countertop when you lift it. If the dough becomes too dry before acquiring the requisite strength, add a little extra liquid (beaten egg for *pâte à brioche,* water for *pâte à kugelhopf* and *pâte à baba*) by dipping your fingers in the liquid and then continuing to knead the dough ⑨.

When the dough is ready, gather it into a thick pad. Whereas at the beginning of this step the dough was a limp, amorphous mass, now its strength and elasticity hold it together in a resilient and well defined form. This is the property that is referred to as ''body.''

Incorporating the Butter (*Beurrage*)

To mix butter into this very elastic dough without melting the butter requires another special technique.

First, take the butter out of the refrigerator and let it barely begin to soften before using; but do not allow it to warm above 59° F (15° C) or it will get too soft. Work the butter with the heel of your hand, repeatedly smearing it across the countertop and gathering it back together with your dough scraper, until it has the same softness as the dough.

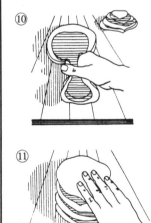

With your dough scraper, cut off one third of the pad of dough and spread the butter on top of it. Lift one end of the butter-dough pad off the counter with the fingertips of one hand. Wrap the thumb and index finger of your other hand around the pad and cut off about one quarter of it by constricting it between thumb and index finger ⑩. Lay this piece out flat next to the rest of the pad. Repeat this process, cutting the butter-dough pad into four approximately equal pieces and piling one on top of the other as you proceed ⑪. As you place each piece on top of the preceeding one, pat it down gently so you end up with a butter-dough pad of about the same dimensions as the original one. Repeat the cutting and piling procedure until the butter and dough are well mixed and smooth, with no lumps of butter. Then combine with the remaining two thirds of the dough by the same method.

Dust the countertop and your hands with flour. Gather the dough into a ball by rolling it in a circular motion under your palms.

On Rising and Deflating (*La Première Pousse et Rabattage*)

The dough is now ready to rise. Transfer it to a bowl with a capacity about triple the volume of the dough. To prevent a crust from forming on top of the dough, dust it very lightly with flour and cover the bowl with a damp kitchen towel. Put the bowl in a warm place (75° to 85° F, or 25° to 30° C) and let the dough rise until doubled in volume, about 2 to 3 hours. This rise serves three purposes: the yeast cells process the starch and sugar in the dough, developing its flavor; the yeast cells reproduce, multiplying their numbers so that the final dough will have plenty of rising power; and the expansion of the dough works the gluten in the flour, giving the dough added strength, which is necessary for it to rise properly in the oven. Do not, however, allow the dough to rise to more than triple its original volume. If it rises too much or at too high a temperature, the yeast can overferment, producing an unpleasant sour taste.

When the dough has risen to double its original volume, turn it out onto a lightly floured countertop, using a rubber spatula or pastry corne. Dust your hands lightly with flour and pat down the dough with your palms to deflate it. Fold the dough in half three or four times, flattening it each time by patting it down with the palms of your hands, to redistribute the yeast cells evenly in the dough. Lightly dust the counter and your palms with flour as needed to prevent the dough from sticking, but try to use as little flour as possible so you don't alter the proportions of ingredients in the dough.

Gather the dough into a ball and return it to the bowl. Dust the top of the ball very lightly with flour and cover the bowl with a damp towel again. Place the dough in the refrigerator and let it rest overnight. During this time, the dough will begin to rise again and develop more flavor. The next day it will be cold and ready to shape and mold.

La Pouliche—a Method for Kneading and Baking the Same Day

In the general method we have described (and its electric-mixer and food-processor equivalents), you prepare the *pâte levée* one day and mold and bake it the next. Because of the rising times required by leavened pastry doughs, this is especially convenient for pastries that will be served early in the day, at breakfast or for midday snacks, for example. Sometimes, however, it is desirable to be able to knead and bake the dough on the same day, and there is a slight modification of our general method that makes this possible.

The modified method is called preparation *"sur pouliche,"* a name that derives from the fact that, in the eighteenth century, brewers' yeast was introduced into France from Poland, replacing the leaven that had been used to make these pastry doughs up to that time.

To make the dough by this method, first mix 15 to 20 percent of the flour called for in the recipe with the dissolved yeast and some additional liquid (if needed) to form a very soft, sticky dough. This dough is the *pouliche*. Transfer the *pouliche* to a bowl and let it rest in a warm place (the usual 75° to 85° F, or 25° to 30° C) until doubled in volume, 1 to 2 hours.

Sift the remaining flour onto the countertop, gather it into a mound, and make a single, large well in the center. The *pouliche* has replaced the second well and its contents. Pour some of the eggs into the well, and start mixing flour into the eggs by the method described in Mixing the Dough, above. Then add the *pouliche* and mix it into the egg-flour paste. (If you are making the dough by machine, add the *pouliche* as though it were just the dissolved yeast.) The remaining steps in mixing the dough, kneading it, and incorporating the butter are the same as those of the standard method.

For *pâte à brioche* and *brioche aux fruits,* the dough is allowed to rise and deflated just as in the standard method, and then it is refrigerated for an hour or two until it is firm enough to shape and mold.

Because of the way they are molded, *pâte à kugelhopf* and *pâte à baba* need less strength that the other *pâte levées*. Consequently, the second rise is superfluous for these two, and the dough is molded immediately after the butter has been incorporated.

In the recipes that follow, we use the standard method for *pâte à brioche* and *brioche aux fruits*. For *pâte à kugelhopf*, we prefer the same-day baking feature of the *pouliche* modification, and we give our recipe using this method. For *pâte à baba*, we also like to knead and bake the dough the same day, and our recipe follows a method that includes all of the flour in the *pouliche* and that is traditionally used to make this extremely soft and sticky dough.

Pâte à Brioche

Brioche is the bread of kings, the mistranslated "cake" that Marie Antoinette thought the peasants should eat if they had no ordinary French bread. Of all the *pâtes levées*, brioche dough is the richest in eggs and butter. Unlike most recipes for *pâte à brioche*, ours contains a little molasses, which gives the baked brioche added softness.

For 2 pounds 10 ounces (1,200 g) of dough, or 1 pound 2 ounces (510 g) if made in food processor

INGREDIENTS

1 pound 1½ ounces (500 g), or about 3⅔ cups, flour

1.2 ounces (34 g), or 2 cakes, fresh yeast

1 tablespoon (25 g) light molasses or malt extract

1 tablespoon (1½ cL) warm water

3 tablespoons (40 g) sugar

By hand:

1 Sift the flour onto the counter and gather it into a mound. Make a large well in the center of the mound and a second, smaller well to the side.

2 Combine the yeast and molasses with 1 teaspoon (½ cL) of the warm water and stir until the yeast dissolves. Mix the sugar and salt with the remaining 2 teaspoons (1 cL) of warm water.

3 Pour the dissolved yeast into the small well and 3 of the eggs into the main well. Using the fingertips of one hand, break the yolks of the eggs and gradually stir in some of the surrounding flour to get a smooth, soft paste. With your index finger, stir some

2½ teaspoons (10 g)
  salt

7 large eggs, at room
  temperature

¾ pound (340 g)
  butter, softened

flour into the dissolved yeast to get a smooth paste of similar consistency to the one in the main well. Then push into the main well and thoroughly mix the two pastes. Continue mixing with your fingertips, gradually dragging in the surrounding flour and alternately adding the remaining eggs, one at a time, to keep a smooth, soft consistency. Mix in the moistened sugar and salt and finally the remaining flour.

4 Knead the dough by repeatedly lifting it and throwing it down on the counter until it is very smooth and rubbery, with sufficient strength and elasticity to pull itself cleanly off the counter when you lift it. Then gather the dough into a thick pad.

5 Work the butter with the heel of your hand, repeatedly smearing it across the countertop to give it the same softness as the dough. With your dough scraper, cut off one third of the pad of dough and spread the butter on top of it. Cut the butter-dough pad into 4 pieces by wrapping your thumb and index finger around the pad and constricting, and pile the pieces on top of each other, pressing them down gently, to form a new pad. Repeat until the butter-dough mixture is smooth. Then mix with the remaining two thirds of the dough by the same method.

6 Dust your hands lightly with flour and gather the brioche dough into a ball by rolling it in a circular motion under your palms. Transfer the dough to a large bowl, with a capacity about triple the volume of the dough, and proceed to step 7.

In an electric mixer equipped with dough hook:

1 Sift the flour into the bowl of the mixer and make a small well in the center.

2 Combine the yeast and molasses with 1 teaspoon (½ cL) of the warm water and stir until the yeast dissolves. Mix the sugar and salt with the remaining 2 teaspoons (1 cL) of warm water.

3 Pour the dissolved yeast into the well on top of the flour. With the tip of your index finger, stir in a little flour to form a soft, smooth paste. Add 3 of the eggs and start the mixer at medium-low speed, using the dough hook. When the eggs are mixed well with the yeast-flour paste, start pushing the flour, a little at a time, into the center of the bowl with a rubber spatula. Add the remaining eggs, one at a time, alternately with the flour, to keep the dough soft, moist, and smooth. Then pour in the moistened sugar and salt and gradually push the remaining flour into the center of the bowl as you continue mixing the dough. When all of the flour has been mixed in, the dough should be soft, sticky, and slightly elastic, clinging to the bottom and sides of the bowl and to the dough hook in a limp, amorphous mass. If the dough seems too dry and holds together in a lump around the dough hook without adhering strongly to the bottom and sides of the bowl, then mix in a little beaten egg to moisten it.

4 Turn up the mixer to medium-high speed and knead the dough to give it body and strength. This will take 15 to 20 minutes. Toward the end the dough will repeatedly gather around the dough hook, get thrown off the hook and slap against the side of the bowl, then gather around the hook again. If the dough becomes too dry before acquiring the requisite strength, moisten it with a little beaten egg. The dough is ready when it is very smooth and rubbery, with sufficient elasticity and strength to pull cleanly off the sides of the bowl and hold itself together in a resilient and well-defined form.

5 Work the butter with the heel of your hand, repeatedly smearing it across the countertop to give it the same softness as the dough. Take one third of the dough out of the mixer and mix it with the butter, following the method described in step 5 of the ''by hand'' instructions (see page 38). When smooth and homogeneous, return this butter-dough mixture to the mixer bowl with the remaining dough and mix at medium-high speed with the dough hook until the dough is completely smooth and homogeneous.

6 Turn the dough out onto a lightly floured countertop. Dust your hands lightly with flour and gather the brioche dough into a ball by rolling it in a circular motion under your palms. Transfer the dough to a large bowl, with a capacity about triple the volume of the dough, and proceed to step 7.

INGREDIENTS

7½ ounces (215 g),
  or about 1½ cups,
  flour

0.6 ounce (17 g), or
  1 cake, fresh yeast

1¼ teaspoon (10 g)
  light molasses or
  malt extract

1¼ teaspoons (0.7
  cL) warm water

4 teaspoons (17 g)
  sugar

1 teaspoon (4 g) salt

3 large eggs, at room
  temperature

5⅓ ounces (150 g)
  butter, softened

In a food processor:

For 1 pound 2 ounces (510 g) of dough.

1 Sift the flour into the workbowl of the food processor (fitted with the steel blade).

2 Combine the yeast and molasses with ½ teaspoon (0.3 cL) of the warm water and stir until the yeast dissolves. Mix the sugar and salt with the remaining ¾ teaspoon (0.4 cL) of warm water.

3 Cut the butter into pieces about 2 tablespoons (30 g) in size and add it to the flour in the bowl of the food processor. Process until the mixture resembles coarse meal.

4 Add the dissolved yeast and 2 of the eggs to the butter-flour mixture in the food processor bowl. Turn on the machine, open the feed tube, and pour in the remaining egg and the moistened sugar and salt with the machine running. Do not turn off the machine.

5 Continue processing until the brioche dough gathers around the center of the blade, about 2 to 3 minutes. Do not stop the machine until the dough is ready. If the food processor stalls, let it rest for 5 minutes and then start it again. The finished dough will be very soft and elastic.

6 Pour and scrape the dough into a bowl with a capacity about triple the volume of the dough. Then proceed to the rising instructions below.

By whichever method you have chosen to use:

7 To prevent a crust from forming on top of the dough, dust it very lightly with flour and cover the bowl with a damp kitchen towel. Put the bowl in a warm place (75° to 85° F, or 25° to 30° C) and let the dough rise until doubled in volume, 2 to 3 hours.

8 Turn the dough out onto a lightly floured countertop. Dust your hands lightly with flour and pat down the dough with your palms to deflate it. Fold the dough in half three or four times, patting it down with your palms each time to flatten it. Lightly dust the counter and your hands with flour as needed to prevent the dough from sticking, but use as little flour as possible.

9 Gather the dough into a ball and return it to the bowl. Dust the top of the ball very lightly with flour and cover the bowl with a damp towel again.

10 Place the dough in the refrigerator and let it rest overnight.

Storage: Covered with a damp cloth, for no more than 24 hours in the refrigerator. The brioche dough can be frozen after molding and before baking, or after baking (see page 200 for details).

Brioche aux Fruits

This unusual brioche dough, flavored with citrus zests, orange flower water, and rum, is used to make the *gâteau des rois,* or Twelfth-Night cake, of the south of France. In contrast to the other *pâtes levées,* for this recipe the butter is melted with the sugar, salt, zests, and some of the liquids to form a syrup that is mixed into the flour before the dough is kneaded.

For 1 pound 14 ounces (850 g) of dough, or 1¼ pounds (565 g) if made with a food processor

INGREDIENTS

6 tablespoons (75 g) sugar

1½ teaspoons (6 g) salt

Grated zest of ½ orange

Grated zest of ½ lemon

3½ tablespoons (½ dL) dark rum

6 ounces (170 g) butter

3½ tablespoons (½ dL) orange flower water

By hand:

1 Combine the sugar, salt, grated orange and lemon zests, rum, and butter in a saucepan and bring to a simmer, stirring to dissolve the sugar and melt the butter. Remove the saucepan from the heat, add the orange flour water, and allow the syrup to cool to about 90° F (32° C).

2 Sift the flour onto the countertop and gather it into a mound. Make a large well in the center of the mound, and a second, smaller well to the side of the main well.

3 Combine the yeast and warm water and stir until the yeast dissolves.

4 Pour the dissolved yeast into the small well and the eggs into the main well. Using the fingertips of

14 ounces (400 g), or about 3 cups, flour

0.9 ounce (25 g), or 1½ cakes, fresh yeast

3½ tablespoons (½ dL) warm water

3 large eggs, at room temperature

one hand, break the yolks of the eggs and gradually stir in some of the surrounding flour to get a smooth, soft paste. With your index finger, stir some flour into the dissolved yeast to get a smooth paste of similar consistency to the one in the main well. Then push into the main well and thoroughly mix the two pastes. Continue mixing with your fingertips, gradually dragging in the surrounding flour and alternately pouring in the warm syrup, a little at a time, to keep a smooth, soft, and very sticking consistency. When all of the flour and syrup have been added, the dough will be very soft and sticky. Do not add more flour. This is the correct consistency for this dough.

5 Knead the dough by repeatedly lifting it and throwing it down on the counter until it is very smooth and rubbery, with sufficient strength and elasticity to pull itself cleanly off the counter when you lift it. At the beginning of the kneading, you must be especially careful with this dough, in order not to splatter it all over the room: As you lift the dough off the counter, gather any loose strands hanging from the dough in your hands, and as you move your hands up, press the sides of your hands together before throwing the dough down onto the counter. As the dough develops body, it will become easier to handle, and, when you have finished kneading it, the dough will feel similar to finished *pâte à brioche* (after adding the butter), but a little softer because the dough will be warmer.

6 Dust your hands lightly with flour and gather the dough into a ball by rolling it in a circular motion under your palms. Transfer the dough to a large bowl, with a capacity about triple the volume of the dough, and proceed with step 7.

In an electric mixer equipped with dough hook:

1 Combine the sugar, salt, grated orange, and lemon zests, rum, and butter in a saucepan and bring to a simmer, stirring to dissolve the sugar and melt the butter. Remove the saucepan from the heat, add the orange flower water, and allow the syrup to cool to about 90° F (32° C).

2 Sift the flour into the bowl of the mixer and make a small well in the center.

3 Combine the yeast and warm water and stir until the yeast dissolves.

4 Pour the dissolved yeast into the well on top of the flour. With the tip of your index finger, stir in a little flour to form a soft, smooth paste. Add the eggs, and start the mixer at medium-low speed, using the dough hook. When the eggs are mixed well with the yeast-flour paste, start pushing the flour, a little at a time, into the center of the bowl with a rubber spatula. Pour in the warm syrup, a little at a time, alternately with the flour to keep the dough smooth, soft, and rather sticky. When all of the flour and syrup have been added, the dough will be very soft and sticky.

5 Turn the mixer up to medium-high speed and knead the dough to give it body and strength. This will take 15 to 20 minutes. Toward the end, the dough will repeatedly gather around the dough hook, get thrown off the dough hook and slap against the side of the bowl, then gather around the dough hook again. The dough is ready when it develops body and sufficient strength and elasticity to pull cleanly off the side of the bowl.

6 Turn the dough out onto a lightly floured countertop. Dust your hands lightly with flour and gather the dough into a ball by rolling it in a circular motion under your palms. Transfer the dough to a large bowl, with a capacity about triple the volume of the dough, and proceed with step 7.

INGREDIENTS

¼ cup (50 g) sugar

1 teaspoon (4 g) salt

Grated zest of ½
  small orange

Grated zest of ½
  small lemon

2 tablespoons plus 1
  teaspoon (3½ cL)
  dark rum

In a food processor:
For 1¼ pounds (565 g) of dough.

1 Combine the sugar, salt, grated orange and lemon zests, rum, and butter in a saucepan and bring to a simmer, stirring to dissolve the sugar and melt the butter. Remove the saucepan from the heat, add the orange flower water, and allow the syrup to cool to about 80° F (27° C).

2 Sift the flour into the workbowl of the food processor (fitted with the steel blade).

4 ounces (115 g) butter

2 tablespoons plus 1 teaspoon (3½ cL) orange flower water

9½ ounces (270 g), or about 2 cups, flour

0.6 ounces (17 g), or 1 cake, fresh yeast

2 tablespoons plus 1 teaspoon (3½ cL) warm water

2 large eggs, at room temperature

3 Combine the yeast and warm water and stir until the yeast dissolves.

4 Add the dissolved yeast and the eggs to the flour in the processor bowl. Turn on the machine, open the feed tube, and gradually pour in the syrup. Do not turn off the machine.

5 Continue processing until the dough gathers around the center of the blade, about 2 to 3 minutes. Do not stop the machine until the dough is ready. If the food processor stalls, let it rest for 5 minutes and then start it again. The finished dough will be very soft and elastic.

6 Pour and scrape the dough into a bowl with a capacity about triple the volume of the dough. Then proceed to the rising instructions below.

By whichever method you have chosen to use:

7 To prevent a crust from forming on top of the dough, dust it very lightly with flour and cover the bowl with a damp kitchen towel. Put the bowl in a warm place (75° to 85° F, or 25° to 30° C) and let the dough rise until doubled in volume, 2 to 3 hours.

8 Turn the dough out onto a lightly floured countertop. Dust your hands lightly with flour and pat down the dough with your palms to deflate it. Fold the dough in half three or four times, patting it down with your palms each time to flatten it. Lightly dust the counter and your hands with flour as needed to prevent the dough from sticking, but use as little flour as possible.

9 Gather the dough into a ball and return it to the bowl. Dust the top of the ball very lightly with flour and cover the bowl with a damp towel again.

10 Place the dough in the refrigerator and let it rest overnight.

Storage: Covered with a damp cloth, for no more than 24 hours in the refrigerator. *Brioche aux fruits* can be frozen after it is formed into rings and before baking, or after baking—see page 200 for details).

Pâte à Kugelhopf

Kugelhopf probably orginated in Austria (where it is called *gugelhupf*), but in France it has been considered an Alsatian specialty for nearly two centuries. It is thought to have been a favorite of Marie Antoinette. Some people make kugelhopf from *pâte à brioche,* but we feel brioche dough is too rich for it. Our recipe uses the *pouliche* variation of the standard method, so you can bake the kugelhopf on the same day as you prepare the dough.

For 2 pounds 14 ounces (1,300 g) of dough, or 1 pound 15 ounces (875 g) if made with a food processor

INGREDIENTS

3½ tablespoons (½ dL) dark rum

7 ounces (200 g), or about 1½ cups, seedless raisins

1.2 ounces (34 g), or 2 cakes, fresh yeast

½ cup plus 2 tablespoons (1½ dL) warm water

1 pound 1½ ounces (500 g), or about 3⅔ cups, flour

¼ cup (50 g) sugar

2½ teaspoons (10 g) salt

1 tablespoon (25 g) light molasses or malt extract

3 large eggs, at room temperature

9 ounces (250 g) butter, softened

By hand:

1 Bring the rum to a simmer and pour it over the raisins. Cover and let the raisins soak until the rum is cool, an hour or longer.

2 Dissolve the yeast in 3½ tablespoons (½ dL) of the warm water. Mix the dissolved yeast with about ½ cup (70 g) of the flour to form a smooth, very soft dough, which is the *pouliche.* Put the *pouliche* in a bowl, cover it, and let it rise in a warm place until doubled in volume, 1 to 2 hours.

3 Sift the remaining flour onto the countertop and gather it into a mound. Make a large well in the center of the mound.

4 Dissolve the sugar and salt in the remaining 6½ tablespoons (1 dL) of warm water. Drain the raisins, reserving any rum that has not been absorbed.

5 Place the *pouliche* in the center of the well with the molasses and eggs, and, using your fingertips, thoroughly mix the molasses and eggs into the *pouliche* to form a smooth paste. Gradually stir in the surrounding flour, adding the dissolved sugar and salt and the excess rum from the raisins, a little at a time, to maintain a soft smooth consistency and prevent the dough from becoming too dry.

6 Knead the dough by repeatedly lifting it and throwing it down on the counter until it is very smooth and rubbery, with sufficient strength and elasticity to pull itself cleanly off the counter when you lift it. Then gather the dough into a thick pad.

7 Work the butter with the heel of your hand, repeatedly smearing it across the countertop to give it the same softness as the dough. With your dough scraper, cut off one third of the pad of dough and spread the butter on top of it. Cut the butter-dough pad into four pieces by wrapping your thumb and index finger around the pad and constricting, and pile the pieces on top of each other, pressing them down gently, to form a new pad. Repeat until the butter-dough mixture is smooth and homogeneous. Then mix with the remaining two thirds of the dough by the same method.

8 Spread the dough out on the countertop and sprinkle the raisins over it. Fold the dough in half to enclose the raisins, and mix the raisins with the dough by the same cutting procedure as you used to mix in the butter. The dough is now ready to mold. For storage instructions see page 48.

In an electric mixer equipped with dough hook:

1 Bring the rum to a simmer and pour it over the raisins. Cover and let the raisins soak until the rum is cool, 1 hour or longer.

2 Sift the flour into the bowl of the electric mixer. Make a small well in the center of the flour.

3 Dissolve the yeast in 3½ tablespoons (½ dL) of the warm water. Pour the dissolved yeast into the well on top of the flour. Using the tip of your index finger, stir in about ½ cup (70 g) of the flour to form a smooth, very soft dough, which is the *pouliche*. Put the bowl in a warm place and let the *pouliche* rise until it has doubled in volume, 1 to 2 hours.

4 Dissolve the sugar and salt in the remaining 6½ tablespoons (1 dL) warm water. Drain the raisins, reserving any rum that has not been absorbed.

5 Add the eggs and molasses to the *pouliche* on top of the flour in the bowl. Return the bowl to the mixer, and start mixing with the dough hook at medium-low speed. When the eggs and molasses are well mixed with the *pouliche,* start pushing the flour, a little at a time, into the center of the bowl with a rubber spatula. Gradually add the dissolved sugar and salt and the excess rum from the raisins, alternately with the flour, to keep the dough soft, moist, and smooth. Then gradually push the remaining flour into the center of the bowl as you continue mixing the dough. When all of the flour has been mixed in, the dough should be soft, sticky, and slightly elastic, clinging to the bottom and sides of the bowl and to the dough hook in a limp, amorphous mass. If the dough seems too dry and holds together in a lump around the dough hook without adhering strongly to the bottom and sides of the bowl, then mix in a little more warm water to moisten it.

6 Turn up the mixer to medium-high speed and knead the dough to give it body and strength. This will take 15 to 20 minutes. Toward the end, the dough will repeatedly gather around the dough hook, get thrown off the hook and slap against the side of the bowl, then gather around the hook again. The dough is ready when it is very smooth and rubbery, with sufficient elasticity and strength to pull cleanly off the bottom and sides of the bowl.

7 Work the butter with the heel of your hand, repeatedly smearing it across the countertop to give it the same softness as the dough. Take one third of the dough out of the mixer and mix it with the butter following the method described in step 7 of the "by hand" instructions (see page 46). When smooth and homogeneous, return this butter-dough mixture to the mixer bowl with the remaining dough and mix at medium-high speed with the dough hook until the dough is completely smooth and homogeneous.

8 Add the raisins and mix at medium-high speed just long enough to distribute them uniformly throughout the dough. The dough is now ready to mold. For storage instructions see page 48.

INGREDIENTS

2 tablespoons plus 1 teaspoon (3½ cL) dark rum

In a food processor:
For 1 pound 15 ounces (875 g) of dough.

1 Bring the rum to a simmer and pour it over the raisins. Cover and let the raisins soak until the rum is cool, 1 hour or longer.

5 ounces (135 g), or about 1 cup, seedless raisins

0.9 ounce (25 g), or 1½ cakes, fresh yeast

7 tablespoons (1 dL) warm water

¾ pound (340 g), or about 2½ cups, flour

2 tablespoons plus 2 teaspoons (35 g) sugar

1¾ teaspoons (7 g) salt

2 teaspoons (17 g) light molasses or malt extract

2 large eggs, at room temperature

6 ounces (170 g) butter, softened

2 Dissolve the yeast in 2⅓ tablespoons (3½ cL) of the warm water. Mix the dissolved yeast with about ⅓ cup (45 g) of the flour to form a smooth, very soft dough—the *pouliche*. Put the *pouliche* in a bowl and let it rise in a warm place until doubled in volume, 1 to 2 hours.

3 Sift the remaining flour into the workbowl of the food processor (fitted with the steel blade).

4 Dissolve the sugar and salt in the remaining 4⅔ tablespoons (6½ cL) of warm water. Drain the raisins, reserving any rum that has not been absorbed.

5 Cut the butter into pieces about 2 tablespoons (30 g) in size and add it to the processor bowl. Process until the mixture resembles coarse meal.

6 Add the *pouliche*, molasses, and eggs to the butter-flour mixture in the processor bowl. Turn on the machine, open the feed tube, and pour in the dissolved sugar and salt and the excess rum from the raisins. Do not turn off the machine.

7 Continue processing until the kugelhopf dough gathers around the center of the blade, about 2 to 3 minutes. Do not stop the machine until the dough is ready. If the food processor stalls, let it rest for 5 minutes and then start it again. The finished dough will be very soft and elastic.

8 Pour and scrape the dough into a bowl. Add the raisins and mix them thoroughly into the dough. The dough is now ready to mold.

Storage: Mold the dough right away. If desired it can be frozen after molding and before baking, or after baking. See page 200 for details).

Pâte à Baba

Pâte à baba is the dough used for a group of pastries, the *babas*, which are soaked in rum syrup. The dough is very soft and sticky, but after baking it becomes quite dry. Soaking the pastries in syrup supplies both moisture and flavor.

For about 2 pounds 10 ounces (1,200 g) of dough, or 1 pound 1 ounce (480 g) if made with food processor

---

INGREDIENTS

1 pound 1½ ounces (500 g), or about 3⅔ cups, flour

1.2 ounces (34 g), or 2 cakes, fresh yeast

1 cup (2.4 dL) warm water

5 large eggs, at room temperature

3 tablespoons (40 g) sugar

2½ teaspoons (10 g) salt

½ cup plus 2 tablespoons (150 g) butter, softened

By hand:

1 Sift the flour onto the countertop and gather it into a mound. Make a large well in the center of the mound, and a second, smaller well to the side of the main well.

2 Dissolve the yeast in 2 tablespoons (3 cL) of warm water.

3 Pour the dissolved yeast into the small well and 3 of the eggs into the main well. Using the fingertips of one hand, break the yolks of the eggs and gradually stir in some of the surrounding flour to get a smooth, soft paste. With your index finger, stir some flour into the dissolved yeast to get a smooth paste of similar consistency to the one in the main well. Then push into the main well and thoroughly mix the two pastes. Continue mixing with your fingertips, gradually dragging in the surrounding flour and alternately adding the remaining eggs, one at a time, to keep a smooth consistency. Gradually mix in ¼ cup (6 cL) of warm water and the remaining flour. At the end of this step, the dough should be smooth and as firm as possible—too firm to knead. If necessary, you can add a little more of the warm water while mixing to keep the dough smooth and prevent it from becoming too dry.

4 Gather the dough into a ball, transfer it to a bowl, and dust the top of the ball very lightly with flour. Cover the bowl with a damp towel and let it rest in a warm place until the dough rises to double its original volume, about 1½ to 2 hours.

5 Mix the sugar and salt with 2 tablespoons (3 cL) of the warm water. Turn out the dough onto your countertop and gradually work in the moistened sugar and salt with your fingertips.

6 Knead the dough by repeatedly lifting it and throwing it down on the counter until it is very smooth and rubbery, with sufficient strength and elasticity to pull itself cleanly off the counter when you lift it.

7 Put the dough in a bowl and gradually work in the remaining ½ cup (1.2 dL) of warm water with your fingertips to get a very soft, sticky, almost liquid dough.

8 Work the butter with the heel of your hand, repeatedly smearing it across the countertop until it is almost as soft as the dough. Take about one third of the dough from the bowl, place it on the countertop, and spread the butter on it. Cut the butter-dough pad into four pieces by wrapping your thumb and index finger around the pad and constricting, and pile the pieces on top of each other, pressing them down gently to form a new pad. Repeat until the butter-dough mixture is smooth and homogenous. Then mix with the remaining two thirds of the dough by the same method. The dough is now ready to mold. For storage instructions see page 53.

In an electric mixer equipped with dough hook:

1 Sift the flour into the bowl of the mixer and make a small well in the center.

2 Dissolve the yeast in 2 tablespoons (3 cL) of warm water.

3 Pour the dissolved yeast into the well on top of the flour. With the tip of your index finger, stir in a little flour to form a soft, smooth paste. Add 3 of the eggs and start the mixer at medium-low speed, using the dough hook. When the eggs are mixed well with the yeast-flour paste, start pushing the flour, a little at a time, into the center of the bowl with a rubber spatula. Add the remaining eggs, one at a time, alternately with the flour, to keep the dough smooth. Then gradually add ¼ cup (6 cL) of warm water and push the remaining flour into the center of the bowl as you continue mixing the dough. When all of the flour has been mixed in, the dough should be smooth and as firm as possible—too firm to knead. If the dough is not quite smooth, gradually add a little more warm water with the machine on.

4 Stop mixing, remove the bowl from the mixer, and dust the top of the dough with a little flour. Cover the bowl with a damp kitchen towel and let it rest in a warm place until the dough rises to double its original volume, about 1½ to 2 hours. At this point, the dough should already have developed some strength by rising.

5 Mix the sugar and salt with 2 tablespoons (3 cL) of the warm water. Return the bowl to the mixer, and gradually mix the moistened sugar and salt into the dough at medium-low speed using the dough hook.

6 Turn up the mixer to medium to medium-high speed and knead the dough to give it body and strength. This will take 15 to 20 minutes. Toward the end, the dough will repeatedly gather around the dough hook, get thrown off the hook and slap against the side of the bowl, and then gather around the hook again. If the dough becomes too dry before acquiring the requisite strength, moisten it with a little warm water. The dough is ready when it is very smooth and rubbery, with sufficient elasticity and strength to pull cleanly off the sides of the bowl and hold itself together in a resilient and well-defined form.

7 Turn down the mixer to medium-low speed and gradually add the remaining ½ cup (1.2 dL) of warm water to get a very soft, sticky, almost liquid dough.

8 Work the butter with the heel of your hand, repeatedly smearing it across the countertop until it is almost as soft as the dough. Take about one third of the dough from the bowl, place it on the counter-top, and spread the butter on it. Cut the butter-dough pad into four pieces by wrapping your thumb and index finger around the pad and constricting, and pile the pieces on top of each other, pressing them down gently to form a new pad. Repeat until the butter-dough mixture is smooth. Return this butter-dough mixture to the mixer bowl with the remaining dough and mix at medium-high speed with the dough hook until the dough is completely smooth and homogenous. The dough is now ready to mold. For storage instructions see page 53.

INGREDIENTS

7 ounces (200 g), or
about 1½ cups,
flour

0.6 ounces (17 g), or
1 cake, fresh yeast

6½ tablespoons
(1 dL) warm water

4 teaspoons (16 g)
sugar

1 teaspoon (4 g) salt

¼ cup (60 g) butter,
softened

2 large eggs, at room
temperature

In a food processor:

Here we recommend making the *pâte à baba "sur pouliche,"* because once the dough begins to develop elasticity it is much more difficult for the food processor to get started. These ingredients are for about 1 pound 1 ounce (480 g) of dough.

1 Dissolve the yeast in 2 tablespoons (3 cL) of warm water. In a small bowl, mix the dissolved yeast with about 3½ tablespoons (30 g) of the flour to form a smooth, very soft dough—the *pouliche.* Cover the bowl with a damp cloth, put it in a warm place, and let the *pouliche* rise until doubled in volume, 1 to 1½ hours.

2 Sift the remaining flour into the workbowl of the food processor (fitted with the steel blade).

3 Dissolve the sugar and salt in 1½ tablespoons (2 cL) of warm water.

4 Cut the butter into pieces about 2 tablespoons (30 g) in size and add it to the flour in the processor bowl. Process until the mixture resembles coarse meal.

5 Add the *pouliche* and one of the eggs to the butter-flour mixture in the processor bowl. Turn on the machine, open the feed tube, and pour in the second egg and the dissolved sugar and salt. Do not turn off the machine.

6 Continue processing until the *pâte à baba* begins to gather around the center of the blade, about 2 or 3 minutes. Do not stop the machine. If the food processor stalls, let it rest for 5 minutes and then start it again.

7 As soon as the dough begins to gather around the blade, open the feed tube and immediately pour in the remaining 3 tablespoons (5 cL) of warm water. When the water has been thoroughly mixed with the dough, turn off the machine.

8 The dough is now ready to mold. Because the high-speed cutting action of the food processor warms the dough, it will be too liquid to mold by the same methods as will be used for *pâte à baba* made by hand or in an electric mixer. Instead, it must be piped from a pastry bag and tube.

Storage: Mold the *pâte à baba* right away. If desired it can be frozen after baking. See page 222 for details.

Chapter Two

CAKE AND PASTRY BATTERS

*E*ggs and sugar are the two invariable ingredients for cake and pastry batters. Baking powder is rarely used in French cakes, so the eggs are the only leavening agent.

There are four distinct types of cake batters, corresponding to the ways in which the eggs are used:

For *génoises* the whole eggs are beaten with sugar over hot water until they warm and begin to froth. Then the water is removed and the eggs are whipped until they are very light and cool. Finally, flour and melted butter are folded into the beaten eggs.

Pound cakes contain much more butter than do *génoises,* and it would be pointless to whip the eggs and then deflate them by adding the butter at the end. Instead, the butter is first creamed with sugar and then the eggs are beaten into it, one at a time. As for *génoises,* the flour is folded in at the end.

Biscuits (spongecakes) are similar to *génoises* in composition, but the method for preparing them is altogether different. Here the eggs are separated and the yolks beaten with sugar. The whites are beaten until very light and stiff, and *meringuéed* by whipping in sugar. Then flour and the meringue are folded into the beaten yolks.

Meringues contain no yolks at all and little or no flour. For these the egg whites are also whipped until very light and stiff, then *meringuéed* by whipping in sugar. If ground nuts are folded into the batter, the meringue becomes an *appareil meringuée.*

The *pâtes à choux* are the pastry batters used for cream puffs and eclairs. For these a thick, heavy batter (called a *panade*) is prepared by cooking flour, water or milk, butter, salt, and sugar over direct heat. Then whole eggs are beaten into the hot *panade* to get a soft, sticky batter.

All cake and pastry batters must be baked immediately after they are prepared. They can be stored before (and sometimes after) assembling the finished dessert

TOURS DE MAIN

Cake and pastry batters can be baked in many forms, in molds or on baking sheets. Prepare the mold or baking sheet before you start making the batter so you won't have to delay baking the cake after the batter is ready.

Preparing and Filling Molds

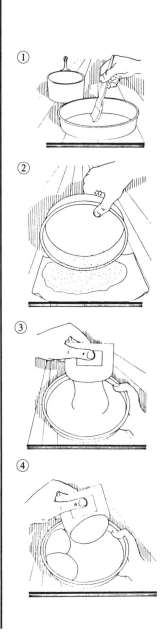

The molds we use most often for cake batters are round molds (layer-cake pans, tarte molds, and *brioche parisienne* molds) and rectangular loaf pans. The inside of the mold must be brushed with melted butter ①, and the butter shouldn't be hot or it won't coat the surface of the mold heavily enough. For some batters with low butter content, the mold must be dusted with flour. To do that, spoon flour into the mold, and gradually tilt, rotate, and shake the mold to distribute an even coating of flour over the butter on the bottom and sides of the mold. Then invert the mold and tap it to dislodge the excess flour ②.

Transfer the batter to the mold by pouring and scraping it from the mixing bowl into the mold or by scooping up the batter with a pastry corne and depositing it in the mold, a little at a time. Smooth the top surface of the batter with your pastry corne or rubber spatula. If the mold is round, make a depression in the center, using the curved edge of your pastry corne ③ or a rubber spatula. This prevents the top of the cake from forming a dome when baked.

If you have a pastry corne, there is also a more sophisticated way to fill a round mold. Hold the mold in one hand and tilt it. Scoop up some batter on your pastry corne and transfer it to the lowest side of the tilted mold. Rotate the mold and repeat ④. It will take about a half-dozen scoops to work your way around the mold. Then deposit a small scoop of batter in the center of the mold. By controlling the amount of batter you take with each scoop, you can get the correct distribution of batter in the mold without smoothing the surface afterward, thus lessening the chances of deflating the batter.

Usually the mold should be filled to only about three quarters of its height so the batter has room to expand in the oven. However, if the mold you are using is deeper than the one we suggest, naturally you should fill it to a lower proportion of its height.

Preparing Baking Sheets

If you are baking the batter directly on a baking sheet, the baking sheet can be prepared in several ways. For some cakes (*russe, biscuits à la cuillère, meringue ordinaire, succès,* and *progrès*) it is simply brushed with melted butter ⑤ and dusted with flour. The flour prevents the batter from slipping on the baking sheet as your spread it. To dust the sheet with flour, sprinkle over it more flour than you need. Tilt, shake, and tap the sheet to distribute the flour and coat the sheet evenly. Then invert the baking sheet and tap it to dislodge the excess flour ⑥.

For other cakes (*génoise, joconde,* and *dijonnaise*) the baking sheet is lined with newsprint or kitchen parchment. To accomplish this, first brush a band 1½ to 2 inches (3 to 5 cm) wide around the edge and down the diagonals of the baking sheet with melted butter ⑦ so that the paper will stick to the baking sheet. Then line the baking sheet with the specified paper. If you have a French baking sheet with a low, turned up lip around the edge you can cut off the excess paper by running the back edge of a chef's knife over the paper around the edge of the baking sheet ⑧. Otherwise cut off the excess paper with a scissors. The paper should then be brushed with melted butter for *joconde* or *génoise*, but not for *dijonnaise*.

For *pâte à choux*, use a seasoned, heavy baking sheet, but do not butter or flour it because that would make the batter lift off the sheet as you terminate each piped shape. However, if the baking sheet is not seasoned and doesn't have a nonstick surface, coat it with a thin film of butter to prevent the batter from sticking after baking.

Spreading Batter on Baking Sheets

To make thin, rectangular sheets of cake (for *génoise, russe,* or *joconde*), scoop the batter from the mixing bowl and transfer it to the prepared bak-

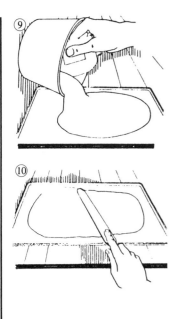

ing sheet ⑨. Deposit the batter uniformly over the baking sheet so you can spread it more quickly and deflate it as little as possible. Spread the batter with the face of your palette knife and smooth the surface with the edge of your palette knife ⑩. On a French baking sheet use the lip around the edge to guide the palette knife as you sweep it across the surface of the batter to get a uniform thickness which will bake evenly; and occasionally draw the face of the palette knife over the edge of the baking sheet as you work to get batter that sticks to the palette knife back onto the baking sheet. If you have an American jelly-roll pan, or you don't have a palette knife, you can smooth the batter with the flat edge of a pastry corne or with the edge of a ruler, holding it with two hands as you drag it over the surface of the batter. In any case, work quickly so you don't deflate the batter too much.

Piping Batter on Baking Sheets (*Dressage à la Poche*)

Biscuit à la cuillère, meringue ordinaire, dijon-naise, succès, and *progrès* are piped onto baking sheets in circular discs, using a pastry bag fitted with a large plain pastry tube. *Biscuit à la cuillère, meringue ordinaire,* and *pâte à choux* are piped in fingers, domes, ovals, teardrops, and rings. There are also many more specialized ways of piping *meringue ordinaire* and *pâte à choux* which are explained in the relevant recipes.

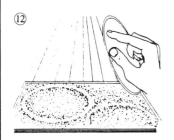

CIRCULAR DISCS AND RINGS: First mark circles of the size you want to make on the baking sheet using a *vol-au-vent* disc, flan ring, or round mold as a guide. On a paper-lined baking sheet, mark the circles with a pencil ⑪. On a buttered and floured baking sheet, just placing or tapping the disc or ring on the sheet will mark the circles in the flour ⑫. And on an uncoated, seasoned sheet you can mark the circles by dipping the edge of the disc or ring in flour and then tapping it on the baking sheet ⑬. After you have marked the circles, fill your pastry bag with batter.

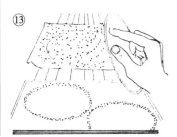

To pipe a circular disc, hold the pastry bag almost vertical, with the tip of the pastry tube about 1 to 1½

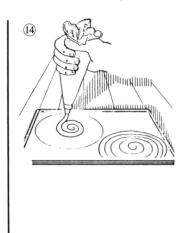

inches (2½ to 3½ cm) above the baking sheet. Pressing steadily on the pastry bag, and starting from the center of the circle, pipe the batter in a continuous spiral that completely fills the circle. ⑭. Move the tip of the pastry tube in a smooth and continuous motion and let the batter drop over the outside third of the previous arc of the spiral. The batter will fall down onto the baking sheet, leaving no gaps in the final disc of batter. If there are gaps, fill them later by piping in a little more batter. When you have filled the circle, release the pressure on the pastry bag and quickly flick the tip of the pastry tube horizontally along the outside of the disc to terminate the spiral.

To pipe a ring, hold the pastry bag almost vertical with the tip of the pastry tube ½ to 1 inch (12 mm to 2½ cm) above the baking sheet. Pressing steadily on the pastry bag, move the tip of the tube in a smooth continuous motion and let the batter drop just inside the circle marked on the baking sheet. When you have piped a complete circle, release the pressure on the pastry bag and quickly flick the tip of the pastry tube horizontally along the batter piped at the beginning of the circumference to terminate the circle with no gaps or excess thickness of batter.

DOMES: Hold the pastry bag at an angle of 60° with respect to the baking sheet, with the tip of the pastry tube about ⅛ inch (3 mm) above the baking sheet. Press the pastry bag and hold the tube fixed until the batter starts to spread evenly around the tip of the tube. Continue pressing on the pastry bag and slowly raise the tip of the tube until the batter spreads to a symmetrical dome of the required size. Then release the pressure on the pastry bag and cut the batter by flicking the tip of the tube in a quick clockwise semi-circle and then across the baking sheet to the place where you will pipe the next dome ⑮. Separate the domes by at least 1 to 1½ inches (3 to 4 cm) so that they will remain separated when they expand in the oven.

FINGERS: Hold the pastry bag at an angle of 60° with respect to the baking sheet, with the tip of the pastry tube about ¼ inch (6 mm) above the baking sheet. Press on the pastry bag and hold the tube fixed until the batter spreads evenly around the tip of the

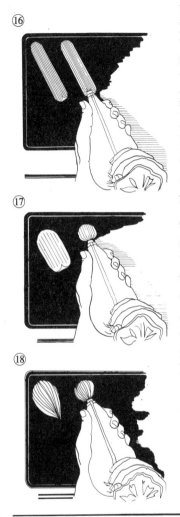

tube to the required width. Maintain the pressure on the pastry bag and move the tip of the tube toward you in a straight line to make a finger of the size you want. Adjust the pressure on the pastry bag and the speed at which you move the pastry tube to get a uniform width. At the end of the finger, release the pressure on the bag, reverse direction, and cut the batter with a quick, nearly horizontal flick of the pastry tube ⑯. Separate the fingers by 1 to 1½ inches (3 to 4 cm) so that they stay separated when they expand in the oven, and pipe them on the diagonal to make piping easier and get more fingers on the baking sheet.

OVALS: The method is the same as for fingers, but adjust the pressure on the pastry bag and the speed at which you move the pastry tube to get an elongated oval ⑰ rather than a finger of uniform width.

TEARDROPS: Hold the pastry bag at an angle of 60° with respect to the baking sheet, with the tip of the pastry tube about ¼ inch (6 mm) above the surface of the baking sheet. Press on the pastry bag and hold the tube fixed until the batter spreads evenly around the tip of the tube to the required width. Then gradually reduce the pressure on the pastry bag and move the tip of the tube toward you in a straight line to make a teardrop. At the tip of the teardrop release the pressure on the pastry bag, reverse direction, and cut the batter with a quick, nearly horizontal flick of the pastry tube ⑱.

Les Génoises

The most versatile and widely used of all French cakes are *les génoises*. Firm and fine textured, they are made from eggs, sugar, and flour. Enriching them with melted butter gives them a better flavor, but makes the batter more delicate to mix and the finished cakes a bit heavier.

Génoises can also be flavored with vanilla, liquors, coffee, chocolate, or almonds. We almost invariably brush our *génoises* with syrups flavored according to the *gâteaux* in which they will be used, and we prefer the flexibility of leaving our basic *génoise* unflavored. However, chocolate and almond *génoises* are special, since for them the flavoring elements are integral to the cakes and cannot be replaced by a brushing of syrup.

We most often bake *génoises* in layer-cake pans or in thin layers on baking sheets. They can also be baked in many other forms, such as *bûche de Noël* molds.

For: Two 9-inch (23 cm) layer-cake pans *or* one 8-inch (20 cm) and one 10-inch (25 cm) layer-cake pan *or* two 12 × 16-inch (30 × 40 cm) baking sheets *or* one 13 × 20-inch (33 × 50 cm) baking sheet *and* one 8-inch (20 cm) layer-cake pan

---

INGREDIENTS

Melted butter for molds or sheets

Either flour for dusting *or* newsprint or parchment for lining baking sheets

GÉNOISE

8 large eggs, at room temperature

1¼ cups (250 g) sugar

9 ounces (250 g), or about 1¾ cups, flour

Optional: 2 tablespoons (30 g) melted butter

GÉNOISE CHOCOLAT

8 large eggs, at room temperature

1¼ cups (250 g) sugar

8 ounces (225 g), or about 1⅔ cups, flour

2 ounces (50 g), or about ⅓ cup, cocoa powder

Optional: 2 tablespoons (30 g) melted butter

1 If the *génoise* will be baked in molds, brush them with melted butter and dust them with flour. If it will be baked in a thin layer on a baking sheet, brush the edges and diagonals of the baking sheet with melted butter, line it with newsprint or kitchen parchment, and brush the paper with melted butter.

2 Preheat the oven to 375° F (190° C).

3 Combine the eggs and sugar in a large bowl (minimum 4 quarts, or 4 L) and break up the yolks with a fork or whisk. Set the bowl in a larger bowl containing hot (but not boiling) water and stir the eggs and sugar with a wire whisk or at low speed in an electric mixer until warm (100° F, or 40° C), frothy, and pale yellow.

4 Remove the bowl from the hot water and continue beating, preferably at high speed in an electric mixer, until the batter is risen and cool. It should coat your finger very thickly ① and form ribbons when dropped from a spoon.

5 Sift the flour, with the cocoa powder for *génoise chocolat*. For *génoise aux amandes*, mix the *TPT blanc* with the sifted flour.

6 A little at a time, dust the flour over the batter and fold it in very gently. If you are including the butter, add it just before the flour is completely incorporated and continue folding until mixed.

7 *Molds:* Transfer the batter to the prepared molds, filling them to three fourths of their height. Smooth the surface of the batter and make a slight depression in the center. Place the molds on a baking sheet.

Baking Sheets: Scoop the batter from the mixing bowl onto the prepared baking sheet. Spread and

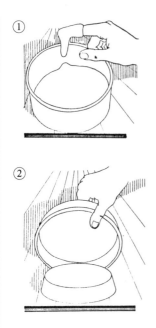

GÉNOISE AUX AMANDES

8 large eggs, at room
  temperature

¾ cup (150 g) sugar

7 ounces (200 g), or
  about 1½ cups,
  flour

7 ounces (200 g), or
  about 1⅓ cups, *TPT
  blanc* (see page
  413)

Optional: 2
  tablespoons (30 g)
  melted butter

smooth the batter with your palette knife to completely cover the baking sheet in an even layer about ⅜ inch (1 cm) thick.

8 Bake until the top of the *génoise* is lightly browned and firm to the touch, but not crusty. This should take 15 to 25 minutes for an 8- to 10-inch (20 to 25 cm) layer-cake pan. A skewer inserted in the center of the cake should come out clean. For thin sheets of *génoise* the baking time will be 5 to 10 minutes. If you are baking on 2 oven racks simultaneously, switch the baking sheets 2 or 3 times during the baking period.

9 If the *génoise* was molded, unmold it onto a cooling rack ②. Invert the *génoise* and let it cool right side up on the rack. If the *génoise* was baked as a thin sheet, slide it off the baking sheet onto a cooling rack. When it is no longer hot (but still warm enough that the butter between paper and *génoise* hasn't solidified), place a second cooling rack upside down on top of the sheet of *génoise* and invert the *génoise* onto the second rack. Carefully peel the paper away from the back of the *génoise,* but leave the paper against the *génoise* until ready to use in order to prevent the *génoise* from drying. Turn the sheet of *génoise* right side up again and allow it to finish cooling on the rack.

Storage: If the *génoise* was baked in a mold, cover it airtight with plastic wrap and keep for up to 2 days in the refrigerator. Or freeze the *génoise* for as long as 2 months, then defrost overnight in the refrigerator before using. If the *génoise* was baked in a thin sheet it will dry very quickly and is best used the same day as it is prepared.

Pound Cakes

As for *les génoises,* the primary ingredients in pound cakes are eggs, sugar, flour, and butter. However, pound cakes contain relatively fewer eggs and much more butter, so they are much richer.

In contrast to the other cakes in this chapter, pound cakes are not components for more elaborate *gâteaux.* They are finished desserts in themselves. In France, where the tradition of home baking is not so strong as it is here in the United States and fancy desserts are usually purchased at the family's favorite *pâtisserie*, pound cakes are regarded as *gâteaux de ménagère* (''home-style'' cakes).

Quatre Quarts

CLASSIC POUND CAKE

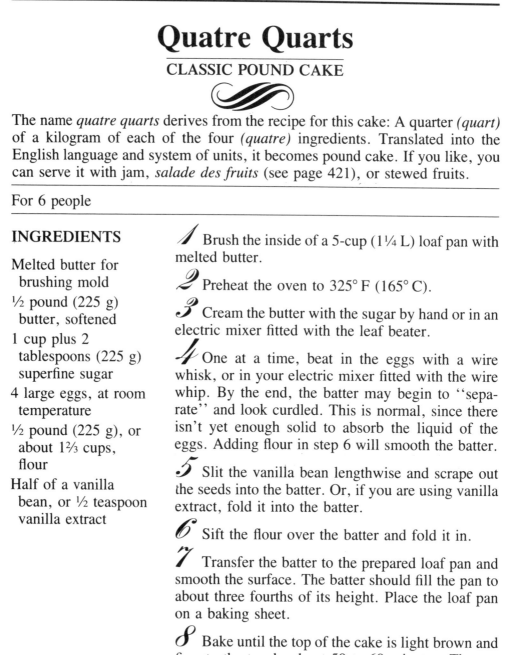

The name *quatre quarts* derives from the recipe for this cake: A quarter *(quart)* of a kilogram of each of the four *(quatre)* ingredients. Translated into the English language and system of units, it becomes pound cake. If you like, you can serve it with jam, *salade des fruits* (see page 421), or stewed fruits.

For 6 people

INGREDIENTS

Melted butter for brushing mold

½ pound (225 g) butter, softened

1 cup plus 2 tablespoons (225 g) superfine sugar

4 large eggs, at room temperature

½ pound (225 g), or about 1⅔ cups, flour

Half of a vanilla bean, or ½ teaspoon vanilla extract

1 Brush the inside of a 5-cup (1¼ L) loaf pan with melted butter.

2 Preheat the oven to 325° F (165° C).

3 Cream the butter with the sugar by hand or in an electric mixer fitted with the leaf beater.

4 One at a time, beat in the eggs with a wire whisk, or in your electric mixer fitted with the wire whip. By the end, the batter may begin to ''separate'' and look curdled. This is normal, since there isn't yet enough solid to absorb the liquid of the eggs. Adding flour in step 6 will smooth the batter.

5 Slit the vanilla bean lengthwise and scrape out the seeds into the batter. Or, if you are using vanilla extract, fold it into the batter.

6 Sift the flour over the batter and fold it in.

7 Transfer the batter to the prepared loaf pan and smooth the surface. The batter should fill the pan to about three fourths of its height. Place the loaf pan on a baking sheet.

8 Bake until the top of the cake is light brown and firm to the touch, about 50 to 60 minutes. The top surface of the cake will have split open down the center, revealing the yellow interior. When the cake is done, a skewer into the center will come out clean.

9 Unmold the *quatre quarts* onto a cooling rack. Turn right side up; let cool to room temperature.

Storage: Cover the *quatre quarts* airtight with plastic wrap and keep for up to 2 days at room temperature (or refrigerated in hot weather). Or freeze the *quatre quarts* for as long as 3 months. If frozen, defrost overnight in the refrigerator, and unwrap the cake at least 2 hours before serving to allow condensation produced by defrosting to evaporate. Serve the *quatre quarts* at room temperature.

Pain de Gênes

ALMOND POUND CAKE

This is the most luxurious of all pound cakes.

For 8 people

INGREDIENTS

Melted butter for brushing mold

1 tablespoon (10 g) sliced almonds for mold

6 ounces (170 g) butter, softened

1 pound (450 g), or about 3 cups, *TPT blanc* (see page 413)

4 large eggs, at room temperature

2 ounces (60 g), or about 7 tablespoons, flour

2 ounces (60 g), or about 7 tablespoons, cornstarch

3 tablespoons (4½ cL) maraschino liqueur or dark rum

1 Brush the inside of a deep 9-inch (23 cm) fluted *tarte* mold with melted butter, and sprinkle the sliced almonds over the bottom of the mold. If you don't have a deep, fluted *tarte* mold, you can use a plain layer-cake pan instead.

2 Preheat the oven to 325° F (165° C).

3 Cream the butter with the *TPT blanc* by hand or in an electric mixer fitted with the leaf beater.

4 One at a time, beat in the eggs with a wire whisk, or in your electric mixer fitted with the wire whip. By the end, the batter may begin to "separate" and look curdled. This is normal, since there isn't yet enough solid to absorb the liquid of the eggs. Adding the flour in the next step will smooth the batter.

5 Sift the flour and cornstarch over the batter, and fold them in. Sprinkle the maraschino liqueur or dark rum over the batter and fold it in.

6 Transfer the batter to the prepared mold, filling it almost to the rim. Smooth the top of the batter with a pastry corne or rubber spatula, and make a depression in the center. Place on a heavy baking sheet.

7 Bake until the top of the cake is light brown and firm to the touch, about 40 to 50 minutes. A skewer inserted in the center of the cake should come out clean.

8 Unmold the *pain de Gênes* onto a cooling rack. Turn right side up, and let cool to room temperature.

Storage: Cover the *pain de Gênes* airtight with plastic wrap and keep for up to 2 days at room temperature (or refrigerated in hot weather). Or freeze the *pain de Gênes* for as long as 3 months. If frozen, defrost overnight in the refrigerator, and unwrap the cake at least 2 hours before serving to allow condensation produced by defrosting to evaporate. Serve the *pain de Gênes* at room temperature.

Le Cake

FRENCH FRUITCAKE

Adding raisins and candied fruit to pound cake produces the dessert that the French call *le cake*. It is traditionally flavored with rum and served during the Christmas holiday season.

For 6 people

INGREDIENTS

Melted butter for
  brushing mold
Brown wrapping
  paper for lining
  mold
5⅓ ounces (150 g)
  butter, softened
¾ cup (150 g)
  superfine sugar
3 large eggs, at room
  temperature
6½ ounces (180 g),
  or about 1⅓ cups,
  flour

1 Brush the inside of a 5-cup (1¼ L) loaf pan with melted butter. Cut an 8 × 12-inch (20 × 30 cm) rectangle of brown wrapping paper. Cut out the corners to make a pattern that will fit the mold and fold the paper along the lines that will be along the edges of the mold. Line the mold with the cut and folded paper and brush it with melted butter.

2 Preheat the oven to 325° F (165° F).

3 Cream the butter with the sugar by hand or in an electric mixer fitted with the leaf beater.

4 One at a time, beat in the eggs with a wire whisk, or in your electric mixer fitted with the wire whip. By the end, the batter may begin to "separate" and look curdled. This is normal, since there

1 teaspoon (3 g) baking powder

5⅓ ounces (150 g) candied fruits, cut into ¼-inch (6 mm) dice

5⅓ ounces (150 g), or about 1 cup, golden raisins

3 to 4 tablespoons (4½ to 6 cL) plus ½ teaspoon (¼ cL) dark rum

1 tablespoon (10 g) sliced almonds

About 1 tablespoon (20 to 25 g) strained apricot jam

2 tablespoons (15 g) confectioners sugar

Candied cherries or other candied fruits for decorating top of cake

isn't yet enough solid to absorb the liquid of the eggs. Adding the flour in step 6 will smooth the batter.

5 Sift the flour with the baking powder onto a sheet of waxed paper. Toss the candied fruits and the raisins with the sifted flour.

6 Add the flour, raisins, and candied fruits to the batter and fold them in. Then fold in 2 tablespoons (3 cL) of the rum.

7 Transfer the batter to the prepared loaf pan and smooth the surface. The batter should fill the pan to about three fourths of its height. Sprinkle the sliced almonds over the top of the batter. Place the loaf pan on a baking sheet.

8 Bake until the top of the cake is a rich, deep brown and firm to the touch, 1 hour to 1 hour 15 minutes. When done, a skewer inserted in the center of the cake will come out clean.

9 Unmold the cake onto a rack. Turn it right side up and sprinkle the top with 1 to 2 tablespoons (1.5 to 3 cL) of dark rum while the cake is hot. Let cool to room temperature. Do not remove the paper from the cake until you are ready to serve it.

10 Warm the apricot jam over low heat, stirring occasionally, until melted. Brush the top of the cake with jam until lightly coated and glistening.

11 Preheat the oven to 450° F (230° C).

12 Prepare a *glace à l'eau*. Add the ½ teaspoon (¼ cL) of rum to the confectioners sugar and stir in enough cold water to make it smooth, creamy, and just liquid enough to spread easily with a pastry brush. Brush this *glace à l'eau* over the jam on top of the cake. Place the cake on a baking sheet and finish glazing in the preheated oven to melt the sugar and turn the glaze from opaque white to almost transparent, about 1 or 2 minutes. If the *glace à l'eau* starts to bubble, remove it from the oven immediately.

13 Decorate the top of the cake with a few candied cherries or other candied fruits.

14 When ready to serve, remove the paper from the outside of the cake.

Storage: Uncovered (the glaze on top and paper around the sides and bottom prevent the *cake* from drying out), for up to 3 days at room temperature (or refrigerated in hot weather). Or, before glazing and decorating the cake, cover it airtight with plastic wrap and freeze for as long as 3 months. If frozen, defrost overnight in the refrigerator; then proceed to glaze and decorate following steps 10 through 13 above. Serve *le cake* at room temperature.

Les Biscuits (Spongecakes)

The name "spongecake" obviously derives from the texture of these cakes, but why they are called *biscuits* (meaning "twice-baked") in French is a mystery.

Biscuit de Savoie
SAVOY SPONGECAKE

This cake is a specialty of the Savoy region in the French Alps. Like the pound cakes, it is a simple, family-style dessert, complete in itself, and not a component for more elaborate desserts. While *biscuit de Savoie* can be baked in anything from a deep, decorative tube pan to an ordinary layer-cake pan, we think it is especially handsome when baked in a *brioche parisienne* mold. If you like, you can serve it with jam, *salade des fruits* (see page 421), or stewed fruits.

For 6 people

INGREDIENTS

Melted butter for
  brushing mold
1 tablespoon (10 g)
  sliced almonds
3 large eggs,
  separated, at room
  temperature

1 Thoroughly brush the inside of an 8-inch (20 cm) *brioche parisienne* mold with melted butter. Scatter the sliced almonds over the bottom and sides of the mold.

2 Preheat the oven to 325° F (165° C).

3 Combine the egg yolks and 6 tablespoons (75 g) of the superfine sugar and beat with a wire whisk or

½ cup (100 g) superfine sugar

½ teaspoon (¼ cL) orange flower water or ¼ teaspoon (1 mL) vanilla extract

1¾ ounces (50 g), or about 6 tablespoons, flour

1¾ ounces (50 g), or about 6 tablespoons, cornstarch

Optional: ⅛ teaspoon (a pinch) cream of tartar

About 2 teaspoons (5 g) confectioners sugar

at medium speed in an electric mixer until cream-colored and light. Then stir in the orange flower water or vanilla extract.

4 Sift the flour and cornstarch over the beaten egg yolks.

5 Whip the egg whites with a clean wire whisk or at medium-high speed in an electric mixer. If you are not whipping the whites in a copper bowl, then when they start to froth add the cream of tartar. Continue whipping until the whites form very stiff peaks and just begin to streak and slip around the side of the bowl. Add the remaining superfine sugar and continue beating just long enough to make the meringue smooth and shiny, 10 to 20 seconds.

6 Scoop about ⅓ of the meringue into the bowl with the beaten egg yolks, flour, and cornstarch, and quickly and thoroughly fold it in. Then add the remaining meringue and gently fold it into the batter.

7 Transfer the batter to the prepared mold. Smooth the surface of the batter and make a depression in the center.

8 Place the mold on a baking sheet and bake until the top is a rich, uniform beige and firm to the touch and a skewer inserted in the center of the cake comes out clean, 35 to 45 minutes.

9 Carefully unmold the cake onto a cooling rack and allow to cool to room temperature.

10 When ready to serve, dust the top of the cake with the confectioners sugar.

Storage: Covered airtight with plastic wrap, for up to 3 days in the refrigerator.

Biscuit à la Cuillère

~~~~~

Biscuits à la cuillère are so called because up until the 17th century this batter was formed into the now classic "ladyfinger" shapes by dropping it from a spoon (*cuillère* in French). Today a pastry bag makes the process quick and easy. *Biscuits à la cuillère* have two primary uses, namely as tea cookies and for lining charlottes. The name can be slightly confusing, since we often pipe the same batter into circular discs to make bases for charlottes. When *biscuit* is singular we mean the batter, and when it is plural *(biscuits)* we mean ladyfingers.

For about 75 ladyfingers *or* three 8- to 9-inch (20 to 23 cm) circular discs *or* twenty-five ladyfingers and two 8- to 9-inch (20 to 23 cm) circular discs

INGREDIENTS

Melted butter for
  brushing baking
  sheet
Flour for dusting
  baking sheet
6 large eggs,
  separated, at room
  temperature
¾ cup (150 g)
  superfine sugar
Orange flower water
5⅓ ounces (150 g),
  or about 1 cup plus
  2 tablespoons, flour
Optional: ¼ teaspoon
  (a pinch) cream of
  tartar
Confectioners sugar
  for dusting

1 Brush 2 large heavy baking sheets with melted butter and dust them with flour.

2 Preheat the oven to 400° F (200° C).

3 Combine the egg yolks with ½ cup (100 g) of the superfine sugar and beat with a wire whisk or at medium speed in an electric mixer until cream-colored and light. Stir in a drop or two of orange flower water.

4 Sift the flour over the beaten egg yolks.

5 Whip the egg whites with a clean wire whisk or at medium-high speed in an electric mixer. If you are not whipping the whites in a copper bowl, then when they start to froth add the cream of tartar. Continue whipping until the whites form very stiff peaks and just begin to streak and slip around the side of the bowl. Add the remaining superfine sugar and continue beating just long enough to make the meringue smooth and shiny, 10 to 20 seconds.

6 Scoop about one third of the meringue into the bowl with the beaten egg yolks and flour, and quickly and thoroughly fold it in. Then add the remaining meringue and gently fold it into the batter.

7 Transfer the batter to a large pastry bag fitted with an ¹¹⁄₁₆-inch (18 mm) plain pastry tube (Ateco 9) for fingers or with a ⁹⁄₁₆-inch (14 mm) plain pastry tube (Ateco 7) for circles or decorative discs.

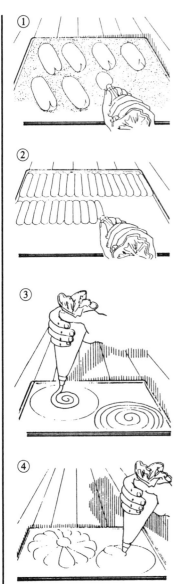

Fingers: Pipe the batter in fingers about 1 inch (2½ cm) wide, 3 inches (8 cm) long, and ½ inch (1 cm) thick. If the ladyfingers will be used as tea biscuits, pipe them 1 to 1½ inches (2½ to 3½ cm) apart so they will stay separated when baked ①. If they will be used to line *charlottes,* pipe them adjacent to each other so they will hold together in long strips when baked ②.

Circular discs: Tap an 8- to 9-inch (20 to 23 cm) flan ring, *vol-au-vent* disc, or round mold on your baking sheet to mark the circles in the flour. Starting from the center of each circle, pipe the batter in a continuous spiral that completely fills the circle ③.

Decorative discs: Tap a 7-inch (18 cm) flan ring, *vol-au-vent* disc, or round mold on your baking sheet to mark a circle. Starting inside the perimeter of the far side of the circle, pipe a teardrop ending with the tip at the center of the circle ④. Rotate the baking sheet and pipe another teardrop adjacent to the first one. Repeat until you have piped 6 to 8 adjacent teardrops that fill the circle, with their tips meeting at the center. Finally pipe a 1-inch (2½ cm) dome of batter on the center.

8 Sift the confectioners sugar over the *biscuits à la cuillère* until the surface of the batter is white. Wait until the sugar dissolves, about 2 minutes, then dust with confectioners sugar a second time. Quickly turn the baking sheet upside down, tap it firmly with a wooden spoon to remove the excess sugar, and turn the baking sheet right side up again before the batter has a chance to move.

9 Place the baking sheet in the preheated oven and splash some water on the bottom of the oven (the water produces steam, which dissolves the sugar on top of the *biscuits à la cuillère* and gives the finished cakes a pearly look). Bake until the *biscuits à la cuillère* are lightly colored and crusty outside, but still soft inside and not dry, 10 to 15 minutes. Since the cooking time is very short, if the *biscuits à la cuillère* are on 2 baking sheets and you can't bake them simultaneously, there is no harm in baking one sheet first and then the other.

10 Place the baking sheet on a cooling rack and allow the *biscuits à la cuillère* to cool on the baking sheet.

Storage: Piled in an airtight cookie tin, with as little air space between them as possible, for up to 2 or 3 days. Or place them in a plastic bag, seal airtight, and freeze for up to 1 month. If frozen, defrost overnight in the refrigerator before using.

Joconde

ALMOND SPONGECAKE

This *biscuit* is named for the Mona Lisa (La Joconda in French). In addition to containing almonds, it differs from other spongecakes by having whole eggs (rather than just yolks) beaten with the sugar and ground almonds before the meringue is folded in. *Joconde* is baked in thin layers on baking sheets. It is used in such sumptuous, multilayered *gâteaux* as the *clichy;* and it is rolled or layered with jams, then sliced to make linings for the outsides of *charlottes royales*.

For one 13 × 20-inch (33 × 50 cm) sheet or one 12 × 16-inch (30 × 40 cm) sheet

INGREDIENTS

Melted butter for brushing baking sheet

Newsprint (preferably) or kitchen parchment for lining baking sheet

13 × 20-INCH SHEET

3 large eggs, at room temperature

½ pound (225 g), or about 1½ cups, *TPT blanc* (see page 413)

1 Brush the edges and diagonals of the baking sheet with melted butter, and line the baking sheet with the newsprint or kitchen parchment. Brush the paper with melted butter.

2 Preheat the oven to 425° F (220° C).

3 Combine the whole eggs with the *TPT blanc* and beat with a heavy wire whisk or at medium speed in an electric mixer until cream colored and light.

4 Sift the flour over the beaten eggs.

5 Whip the egg whites with a clean wire whisk or at medium-high speed in an electric mixer. If you are not whipping the whites in a copper bowl, then when they start to froth add the cream of tartar. Continue whipping until the whites form very stiff peaks and just begin to streak and slip around the side of the

1 ounce (30 g), or about 3½ tablespoons, flour

3 large egg whites, at room temperature

Optional: ⅛ teaspoon (a pinch) cream of tartar

2½ tablespoons (30 g) superfine sugar

1½ tablespoons (22 g) butter, melted

12 × 16-INCH SHEET

2 large eggs, at room temperature

5⅓ ounces (150 g), or about 1 cup, *TPT blanc* (see page 413)

⅔ ounce (20 g), or about 7 teaspoons, flour

2 large egg whites, at room temperature

Optional: ⅛ teaspoon (a pinch) cream of tartar

5 teaspoons (20 g) superfine sugar

1 tablespoon (14 g) butter, melted

bowl. Add the superfine sugar and continue beating just long enough to make the meringue smooth and shiny, 10 to 20 seconds.

6 Scoop about one third of the meringue into the bowl with the beaten eggs and flour, and quickly and thoroughly fold it in. Then add the remaining meringue and gently fold it into the batter until almost mixed. Finally add the melted butter and continue folding gently until the batter is evenly mixed.

7 Scoop the batter from the mixing bowl onto the prepared baking sheet, and spread and smooth it with your palette knife to completely cover the baking sheet in an even layer about ⅜ inch (1 cm) thick.

8 Bake until the cake is lightly browned and firm to the touch, but not dry, 5 to 10 minutes.

9 Slide the *joconde* off the baking sheet onto a cooling rack. When it is no longer hot (but still warm enough that the butter between the paper and *joconde* hasn't solidified), place a second cooling rack upside down on top of the *joconde* and invert the *joconde* onto the second rack. Carefully peel the paper away from the back of the *joconde,* but leave the paper against the *joconde* until ready to use in order to prevent the *joconde* from drying. Turn the sheet of *joconde* right side up again and allow to finish cooling on the rack.

Storage: Covered airtight with plastic wrap, for up to 3 days in the refrigerator. Or freeze for as long as 3 months. If frozen, defrost overnight in the refrigerator before using. If the *joconde* will be rolled or layered with jam for lining the outside of a *charlotte royale,* it can also be frozen after rolling (see pages 328 and 330).

Meringue and Les Appareils Meringuées Plain and Nut Meringues

Meringues are based on egg whites and sugar, and they never contain egg yolks. There are three basic types of plain meringue. *Meringue ordinaire* is made by beating the egg whites until stiff and then whipping in sugar. It is always baked for use in cake layers and for meringue desserts and decorations. For *meringue italienne*, the egg whites are also beaten until stiff, but then a hot sugar syrup is whipped into the whites. Italian meringue is used primarily as a topping and to lighten butter creams and pastry creams, and the recipe for it appears in Chapter Four (page 101). It may or may not be baked. Finally, to make *meringue suisse*, the egg whites and sugar are beaten together over low heat. Swiss meringue is heavy and old-fashioned, and we rarely use it except for cookies.

Appareils meringuées are just ordinary meringue with ground almonds or filberts (always in the form of *TPT*) folded in before baking. Their textures depend on the proportions in the recipe: *dijonnaise* is dry and crisp like *meringue ordinaire; succès, progrès*, and *russe* are softer and more cakelike. *Succès, progrès*, and *russe* are especially delicate because the whites are whipped with a very small amount of sugar and they contain large quantities of almonds, so, for these batters, the sugar is added gradually to the whites before they become stiff rather than by ''meringuing'' the whites at the very end.

Meringue Ordinaire

This basic meringue is very light, dry, and crisp when baked. Piped and baked in circular discs, it makes an excellent foil for the richness of butter creams in some *gâteaux*. It can also be piped in many special shapes for meringue desserts and decorations.

For about 4 cups (440 g) of meringue batter *or* two 8½- to 9½-inch (22 to 24 cm) circular discs *or* twenty 2½-inch (6 cm) domes *or* twenty 3½-inch (9 cm) fingers

INGREDIENTS

Melted butter for brushing baking sheet

Flour for dusting baking sheet

1 Brush one or two heavy baking sheets with melted butter and dust with flour. If you are piping circular discs of meringue, tap a flan ring, *vol-au-vent* disc, or round mold on the surface of the baking sheet to mark two circles 8½ to 9½ inches (22 to 24 cm) in diameter in the flour. Fit the 2 circles on one baking sheet, if possible.

4 large egg whites, at room temperature

Optional: ⅛ teaspoon (a pinch) cream of tartar

¾ cup (150 g) superfine sugar

5⅓ ounces (150 g), or about 1 cup plus 2 tablespoons, confectioners sugar

1 tablespoon (10 g) flour

2 Preheat the oven to 275° F (135° C).

3 Whip the egg whites with a wire whisk or at medium-high speed in an electric mixer. If you are not whipping the whites in a copper bowl, then when they start to froth add the cream of tartar. Continue whipping until the whites form very stiff peaks and just begin to streak and slip around the side of the bowl. Add the superfine sugar and continue beating at high speed just long enough to make the meringue smooth and shiny, 10 to 20 seconds.

4 Sift together the confectioners sugar and flour. A little at a time, dust them over the meringue and fold them in very gently.

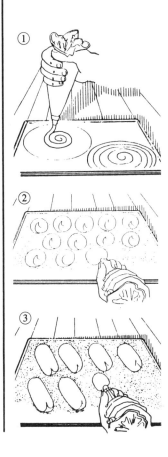

5 Transfer the batter to a large pastry bag fitted with a plain pastry tube, and pipe it onto the prepared baking sheets.

Circular Discs: Use a ½-inch (12 mm) plain pastry tube (Ateco 6). Starting from the center of each circle marked on the baking sheet, pipe the batter in a continuous spiral that completely fills the circle ①.

Domes: Use a ⅝-inch (16 mm) plain pastry tube (Ateco 8). Pipe the batter onto the prepared baking sheet in twenty domes 2½ inches (6 cm) in diameter and ¾ to 1 inch (2 to 2½ cm) high ②. Pipe the domes in staggered rows and separate them by 1 to 1½ inches (2½ to 4 cm).

Fingers: Use a ⅝-inch (16 mm) plain pastry tube (Ateco 8). Pipe the batter onto the prepared baking sheet in twenty fingers, each 3½ inches (9 cm) long and 2 inches (5 cm) wide ③. Pipe the fingers on the diagonal in staggered rows, separating them by 1 to 1½ inches (2½ to 4 cm).

Meringue Mushrooms and Vacherins: Proceed to the recipes in Chapter Ten.

6 Bake until set, dry, and firm to the touch, 40 to 60 minutes. (If you are baking on 2 oven racks simultaneously, switch the baking sheets every 15 minutes during the baking period.)

7 Place the baking sheet on a cooling rack and allow the meringues to cool on the baking sheet.

Storage: Up to 2 weeks in a very dry place, preferably in a tin cookie box, or covered airtight in a plastic bag.

Dijonnaise

This light, crisp almond meringue is named for Dijon, the capital of the province of Burgundy.

For two 8½- to 9½-inch (22 to 24 cm) circular discs

INGREDIENTS

6½ ounces (185 g), or about 1¼ cup, *TPT blanc* (see page 413)

3½ ounces (100 g), or about ¾ cup, confectioners sugar

3½ tablespoons (½ dL) milk

Melted butter for sticking parchment to baking sheet

Kitchen parchment for lining baking sheet

6 large egg whites, at room temperature

Optional: ¼ teaspoon (a pinch) cream of tartar

½ cup plus 2 tablespoons (125 g) superfine sugar

1 Mix the *TPT blanc,* confectioners sugar, and milk in a large bowl.

2 Brush the edges and diagonals of one or two heavy baking sheets with a little melted butter. Line the baking sheet (or sheets) with kitchen parchment. Draw two circles 8½ to 9½ inches (22 to 24 cm) in diameter on the parchment. Fit the two circles on one baking sheet if possible.

3 Preheat the oven to 300° F (150° C).

4 Whip the egg whites with a wire whisk or at medium-high speed in an electric mixer. If you are not whipping the whites in a copper bowl, then when they start to froth add the cream of tartar. Continue whipping until the whites form very stiff peaks and just begin to streak and slip around the side of the bowl. Add the superfine sugar and continue beating just long enough to make the meringue smooth and shiny, 10 to 20 seconds.

5 Scoop about one third of the meringue into the bowl with the *TPT blanc* mixture and quickly mix it. Add the remaining meringue and fold it in gently.

6 Transfer the *dijonnaise* batter to a large pastry bag fitted with a ⅝-inch (16 mm) plain pastry tube (Ateco 8). Starting from the center of each circle,

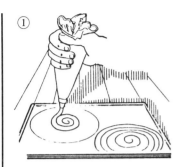

pipe the batter in a continuous spiral that completely fills the circle ①. All of the batter must be piped out and baked right away or it will deflate.

7 Bake until the *dijonnaise* puffs up and the top turns a very pale brown, 25 to 35 minutes. Then reduce the oven temperature to 275° F (135° C) and continue baking until the *dijonnaise* is dry, firm to the touch, and a uniform light brown, about 25 to 45 minutes longer. Carefully lift the edge of the parchment and feel the undersides of the *dijonnaise* rounds to be sure that they are dry. (If you are baking on 2 oven racks simultaneously, switch the baking sheets every 15 minutes during the baking period.)

8 Place the baking sheet on a cooling rack and allow the *dijonnaise* to cool on the baking sheet. Then carefully remove the rounds of *dijonnaise* from the parchment.

Storage: Up to 2 weeks in a very dry place, preferably in a tin cookie box, or covered airtight in plastic wrap.

Succès and Progrès

These are made exactly like *meringue ordinaire*. But they contain a high percentage of ground nuts, which makes them more cakelike in texture. If you have trimmings of *succès* or *progrès* left over from the results of a previous baking, you can powder them in your food processor or electric blender and substitute this powder for the *TPT blanc* called for in these recipes.

For two 8½- to 9½-inch (22 to 24 cm) circular discs

INGREDIENTS

Melted butter for brushing baking sheet

Flour for dusting baking sheet

1 Brush one or two heavy baking sheets with melted butter and dust with flour. Tap a flan ring, *vol-au-vent* disc, or round mold on the surface of the baking sheet to mark two circles 8½ to 9½ inches (22 to 24 cm) in diameter in the flour. Fit the two circles on one baking sheet if possible.

SUCCÈS:

6 large egg whites, at room temperature

Optional: ¼ teaspoon (a pinch) cream of tartar

3½ tablespoons (45 g) superfine sugar

9½ ounces (270 g), or about 1¾ cups, *TPT brut* (see page 413) made with almonds or half almonds and half filberts

½ cup (75 g) *TPT blanc* (page 413)

PROGRÈS:

6 large egg whites, at room temperature

Optional: ¼ teaspoon (a pinch) cream of tartar

3½ tablespoons (45 g) superfine sugar

9½ ounces (270 g), or about 1¾ cups, *TPT brut* (see page 413) made with filberts

½ cup (75 g) *TPT blanc* (page 413)

2 Preheat the oven to 300° F (150° C).

3 Whip the egg whites with a wire whisk or at medium-high speed in an electric mixer. If you are not whipping the whites in a copper bowl, then when they start to froth add the cream of tartar. Whip the whites until they form soft peaks. Gradually whip in the superfine sugar and continue whipping until the meringue is very stiff, smooth, and shiny. It should not slip or streak around the side of the bowl.

4 Mix the *TPT brut* and *TPT blanc*. A little at a time, dust it over the meringue and fold it in very gently.

5 Transfer the *succès* or *progrès* batter to a large pastry bag fitted with a ⁹⁄₁₆-inch (14 mm) plain pastry tube (Ateco 7). Starting from the center of each circle, pipe the batter in a continuous spiral that completely fills the circle ①. All of the batter must be piped out and baked right away or it will deflate.

6 Bake until the *succès* or *progrès* puffs up and the top turns a light brown, 20 to 30 minutes. Then reduce the temperature to 275° F (135° C) and continue baking until the *succès* or *progrès* is dry, firm to the touch, and a uniform medium brown, about 20 to 30 minutes longer. (If you are baking on 2 oven racks simultaneously, switch the baking sheets every 15 minutes during the baking period.)

7 Place the baking sheet on a cooling rack and allow the *succès* or *progrès* to cool on the baking sheet.

Storage: Up to 2 weeks in a very dry place, preferably in a tin cookie box, or covered airtight in plastic wrap.

Russe

Russe means "Russian." Unlike the other *appareils meringuées* and *meringue ordinaire*, which are piped from a pastry bag, this almond meringue is always spread in a thin layer on a baking sheet.

For one 13 × 20-inch (33 × 50 cm) sheet or one 12 × 16-inch (30 × 40 cm) sheet

INGREDIENTS

Melted butter for
brushing baking
sheet
Flour for dusting
baking sheet

13 × 20-INCH SHEET

7 ounces (200 g), or
about 1⅓ cup, *TPT
blanc* (page 413)
4 teaspoons (10 g)
cornstarch
8 large egg whites, at
room temperature
Optional: ¼ teaspoon
(a pinch) cream of
tartar
6½ tablespoons (80
g) superfine sugar
Optional: ¼ cup (40
g) chopped blanched
almonds; and 2
tablespoons plus 2
teaspoons (34 g)
granulated sugar

12 × 16-INCH SHEET

5⅓ ounces (150 g),
or about 1 cup, *TPT
blanc* (page 413)

1 Brush the baking sheet with melted butter and dust it with flour.

2 Preheat the oven to 350° F (175° C).

3 Mix the *TPT blanc* and cornstarch.

4 Whip the egg whites with a wire whisk or at medium-high speed in an electric mixer. If you are not whipping the whites in a copper bowl, then when they start to froth add the cream of tartar. Whip the whites until they form soft peaks. Gradually whip in the superfine sugar and continue whipping until the meringue is very stiff, smooth, and shiny. It should not slip or streak around the side of the bowl.

5 A little at a time, dust the *TPT blanc* and cornstarch over the meringue and fold it in very gently.

6 Scoop the batter from the mixing bowl onto the prepared baking sheet, and spread and smooth it with your palette knife to completely cover the baking sheet in an even layer about ⅜ inch (1 cm) thick.

7 If the *russe* is to be used for a *russe praliné*, sprinkle the optional chopped almonds and sugar over the sheet of batter.

8 Bake until the top of the *russe* is dry, firm to the touch, and a uniform light brown, 20 to 30 minutes.

9 Remove from the oven and loosen the edges of the *russe* with your palette knife. Place the baking sheet on a cooling rack, and, when the *russe* is no

1 tablespoon (8 g)
cornstarch

6 large egg whites, at
room temperature

Optional: ¼ teaspoon
(a pinch) cream of
tartar

5 tablespoons (60 g)
superfine sugar

Optional: 3
tablespoons (30 g)
chopped blanched
almonds; **and** 2
tablespoons (25 g)
granulated sugar

longer hot (but still warm), slide it off the baking sheet onto the rack. If the *russe* sticks to the baking sheet, loosen it by sliding your palette knife or a pancake turner under it. Allow the *russe* to finish cooling on the rack.

Storage: *Russe* dries out quickly, so if possible use it the day it is made. Otherwise, cover it airtight with plastic wrap and keep for up to 2 days in the refrigerator.

Les Pâtes à Choux
Cream Puff Pastry Batters

These pastry batters are always piped from a pastry bag. The most familiar shapes are domes (cream puffs) and fingers (eclairs), but they can also be transformed into swans, rims on pastry dough bases for elaborate desserts such as *St. Honoré* and *tartes alsaciennes,* and numerous other forms. Whatever the shape, *pâte à choux* puffs up to form a hollow shell when baked.

The texture of the baked *pâte à choux* depends on the amount of butter and the choice of water or milk as the liquid in the recipe. *Pâte à choux ordinaire* is light and crisp and is good for all pastries that call for *pâte à choux.* The softer and richer *pâte à choux spéciale* should be used only for small pastries.

For about 2½ cups (600 g) of batter, *or* twenty 2½-inch (6 cm) domes, *or* twenty 4½-inch (12 cm) fingers, *or* twenty 3½-inch (9 cm) ovals, *or* eighty 1¼-inch (3 cm) domes

**PÂTE À CHOUX
ORDINAIRE**

4 large eggs

1 cup (2.4 dL) water

1 Preheat the oven to 400° F (200° C).

2 Lightly beat one of the eggs, but leave the remaining three eggs unbeaten.

7 tablespoons (100 g)
  butter

2 teaspoons (8 g)
  sugar

¾ teaspoon (3 g) salt

5⅓ ounces (150 g),
  or about 1 cup plus
  2 tablespoons, flour

PÂTE À CHOUX SPÉCIALE

4 large eggs

1 cup (2.4 dL) milk

9 tablespoons (125 g)
  butter

2 teaspoons (8 g)
  sugar

¾ teaspoon (3 g) salt

4½ ounces (125 g),
  or about 1 cup,
  flour

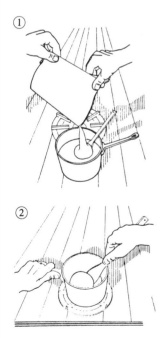

3 Combine the water or milk, butter, salt, and sugar in a 1½- to 2-quart (1½ to 2 L) saucepan. Bring to a boil over high heat, stirring occasionally with a wooden spoon until all the butter melts.

4 Remove the saucepan from the heat and add the flour all at once ①. Stir with the wooden spoon until thoroughly mixed.

5 Return the saucepan to the stove and cook over medium-high heat, beating constantly and vigorously with the wooden spoon, until a thin film forms on the bottom of the saucepan and the batter no longer sticks to the sides of the saucepan or to the wooden spoon but holds together in a mass in the center of the pan (about 1 or 2 minutes for this quantity of batter) ②. The batter should have a matte surface and feel dry, but slightly buttery.

6 Remove the saucepan from the heat and transfer the batter to a medium-sized bowl. (Or, if you want to make a larger quantity, doubling our recipe, you may find it easier to use an electric mixer fitted with the leaf beater.) Add the 3 unbeaten eggs and mix them into the batter using a wooden spoon (or at low speed in your electric mixer). When the batter is smooth, add lightly beaten egg, a little at a time, stirring to mix after each addition, until the batter is smooth, soft, and shiny and sticks to your fingers, pulling up in strings from the bulk of the dough in the bowl ③. Add only as much of the beaten egg as needed to achieve this consistency and do not over-work the batter. If there is any beaten egg left, it can be used to brush the batter after it is piped.

7 *Large domes, fingers, and ovals:* Transfer the batter to a large pastry bag fitted with a large fluted pastry tube (Ateco 9B or 8B). Pipe the batter onto a heavy, seasoned baking sheet in dome shaped mounds 2½ inches (6 cm) in diameter and 1 inch (2½ cm) high ④, or fingers 4½ inches (12 cm) long and 1 inch (2½ cm) wide ⑤, or oval mounds 3½ inches (9 cm) long and 1½ inch (4 cm) wide ⑥. Pipe them in staggered rows and separate them by at least 1½ inches (4 cm).
Small domes: Transfer the batter to a pastry bag fitted with a ⅜-inch (1 cm) plain pastry tube (Ateco 5).

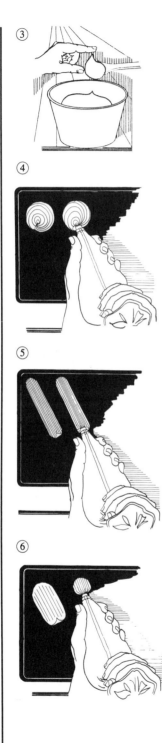

③

④

⑤

⑥

Pipe the batter onto a heavy, seasoned baking sheet in dome shaped mounds 1¼ inches (3 cm) in diameter. Separate the domes by at least 1 inch (2½ cm) and pipe them in staggered rows.

For cygnes, ponts neufs, puits d'amour, St. Honoré, paris-brest, and négus: See recipes in Chapter 11.

8 Dip a soft pastry brush in the beaten egg and gently pat the egg wash on the mounds to lightly moisten the surface of the batter. Use the egg wash sparingly, and if the batter was piped from a star tube try not to destroy the grooves in the mounds. If there are tails sticking up, pat down with the brush. If you have piped domes for *choux praliné,* scatter sliced almonds on top of each.

9 Bake in the preheated oven, using a wooden spoon to hold the oven door ajar, until the batter puffs up and turns a medium golden brown with any cracks or scars a pale to medium golden brown. The cooking time should be 15 to 25 minutes for small domes and 25 to 35 minutes for large shapes.

10 Place the baking sheet on a cooling rack and allow the pastries to cool on the baking sheet. After cooling, slide a pancake turner or palette knife under the pastries to remove them without tearing bottoms.

Storage: After piping and brushing with egg wash, the unbaked *pâte à choux* can be frozen for up to 1 month. Remove the frozen mounds of batter from the baking sheet and seal airtight in a plastic bag. When ready to bake, arrange the frozen mounds on a heavy, seasoned baking sheet and, without defrosting them first, bake following the instructions above. After baking the pastries can be kept in the refrigerator, covered airtight in a plastic bag, for up to 3 days. If the pastries become soft, dry them briefly in a 200° F (90° C) oven before filling.

Note on Pastry Tubes: *Pâte à choux* is most often piped from a fluted pastry tube. If necessary you can use a plain pastry tube instead, and then after brushing with egg wash draw the tines of a fork across the batter in the direction in which it was piped. The grooves produced by a fluted pastry tube or by the tines of the fork make the batter rise more evenly.

Chapter Three

FILLINGS

*S*oft, flavorful fillings nestle between the pastry and cake layers of desserts. Some, for example *crème chantilly* and *crème au beurre*, can also be used as toppings; and toppings, such as *meringue italienne* and jams, occasionally serve as fillings. But the distinction between the two is usually obvious.

Of the fillings for which we give recipes, only three (*crème d'amandes*, *compote de pommes*, and *pommes sautées au beurre*) must be baked, and 2 others (*crème pâtissière* and lemon curd) may be baked or not, depending on the dessert. Our other fillings must not be baked.

The Fundamental Creams

More than half of all French pastries contain *crème chantilly* (whipped cream), *crème pâtissière* (French pastry cream), or *crème au beurre* (butter cream). These three are very different in character, yet they share a certain neutrality which allows them to serve as carriers for other more assertive flavors or as foils for the flavors in other layers of desserts.

To be more specific, *crème pâtissière* is by far the most common filling for *tartes*, and *crème au beurre* is nearly ubiquitous in *gâteaux*. *Crème chantilly* and *crème pâtissière* share honors in *babas* and *choux*.

Crème Chantilly

WHIPPED CREAM

Crème chantilly is just sweetened whipped cream, and the only "secret" to making it is that the cream and the utensils you use to whip it should be cold. *Crème fraîche* is more delicate to whip than ordinary heavy cream, but produces a more flavorful *crème chantilly*.

For 4 cups (500 g)

INGREDIENTS

Either 2 cups (½ L) heavy cream *or* 1¾ cups (4½ dL) *crème fraîche* (see page 387) and ¼ cup (6 cL) crushed ice (preferably) or cold water or milk

¼ cup plus 2 tablespoons (50 g) confectioners sugar

Optional: One quarter vanilla bean or 2 tablespoons (3 cL) dark rum, kirsch, Grand Marnier, or other liqueur

1 Mix the heavy cream or *crème fraîche* with the sugar, and, if possible, chill the cream for an hour or so while the sugar dissolves. This makes for a lighter *crème chantilly*. Chill the bowl and the whisk or beater you will be using to whip the cream.

2 If you are whipping *crème fraîche*, thin it with the crushed ice, water, or milk to reduce the risk of overbeating the cream.

3 If you want a vanilla-flavored *crème chantilly*, slit open the vanilla bean lengthwise and scrape out the seeds into the cream.

4 Whip the cream at medium speed with a wire whisk or in an electric mixer. Slow down when the cream forms soft peaks to avoid overbeating. Continue whipping until the cream is light, thick, and stiff. Do not overbeat or the cream will curdle.

5 If you want to flavor the *crème chantilly* with dark rum or another liqueur, gently fold it in with a rubber spatula.

Storage: *Crème chantilly* is best used right away, but you can keep it in the refrigerator for a short time if necessary. If you don't use it within 2 hours, it will begin to separate. When that happens you can beat the cream with a wire whisk for a few seconds to pull it back together, but it will no longer be as firm and light as when it was first made.

Crème Pâtissière

FRENCH PASTRY CREAM

Crème pâtissière is a stovetop custard thickened with eggs, flour, and cornstarch. Using both flour and cornstarch gives it both stability and a smooth, refined texture.

For about 2⅔ cups (720 g)

INGREDIENTS

One quarter vanilla
  bean
2 large eggs
2 large egg yolks
2 cups (½ L) milk
¾ cup (150 g) sugar
1¼ ounces (35 g),
  or about ¼ cup,
  flour
1¼ ounces (35 g), or
  about ¼ cup,
  cornstarch
Optional: Up to 5
  tablespoons (70 g)
  butter, softened

1 Cut open the vanilla bean lengthwise and scrape out the seeds.

2 Combine the vanilla seeds and pod with the milk in a heavy 2-quart (2 L) saucepan and bring to a simmer. Be careful not to let the milk boil over.

3 Meanwhile, beat together the eggs, egg yolks, sugar, flour, and cornstarch with a wire whisk until lemon-colored and smooth. Slowly pour in half of the simmering milk, stirring constantly with a wire whisk. Pour this mixture back into the saucepan with the remaining milk and stir until thoroughly blended and smooth.

4 Place the saucepan over medium heat and bring the *crème pâtissière* to a boil, stirring constantly with a wire whisk. The *crème pâtissière* should already be quite thick. Reduce the heat and continue boiling, stirring constantly and vigorously with a wire whisk, until the *crème pâtissière* no longer tastes of raw flour, 2 to 3 minutes. It should now be very thick and smooth.

5 Remove the saucepan from the heat and strain the *crème pâtissière* through a sieve into a bowl.

6 If you want a softer *crème pâtissière,* enrich it by stirring in up to ¼ cup (55 g) of the softened butter. This also helps cool the *crème pâtissière.*

7 If the *crème pâtissière* continues to cool undisturbed, a skin will form on the top. You can avoid this either by coating the surface of the *crème pâtissière* with about 1 tablespoon (15 g) of the optional butter while the *creme pâtissière* is still hot, or by stirring the *crème pâtissière* occasionally with a wire whisk as it cools. Alternatively, you can let the skin form, then puree the *crème pâtissière* in a food processor to make it smooth before using it.

8 In any case, let the *crème pâtissière* cool to room temperature.

Opposite: Conversation (page 173). Following page: Breakfast pastries: Croissants, page 189; Pains au chocolat, page 192; Pains aux raisins, page 207.

Storage: Covered airtight, for up to 1 week in the refrigerator. If the surface of the *crème pâtissière* is coated with butter, remove it from the refrigerator and let it warm to room temperature, then beat in the butter with a wire whisk before using.

Crème au Beurre

BUTTER CREAM

Crème au beurre is the richest of our fundamental creams. Making *crème au beurre* by hand is hard work, and we strongly advise preparing it in a heavy-duty electric mixer. If you must make it by hand, cut this recipe in half.

For about 7 cups (1,260 g)

INGREDIENTS

1⅔ cups (335 g) sugar

½ cup (1.2 dL) water

8 large egg yolks

1½ pounds (680 g) butter, softened

Optional: 2 cups (120 g) *meringue italienne* (see page 101)

1 Combine the sugar and water in a saucepan or caramel pot and stir to thoroughly moisten the sugar. Bring to a boil. Continue boiling over medium heat, washing down the walls of the pot with a moistened pastry brush as needed to dissolve any sugar crystals that form there. Cook until the sugar reaches the low end of the firm ball stage or about 242° F (117° C).

2 Start beating the egg yolks at low speed in an electric mixer fitted with the wire whisk, or beat it by hand if you don't have an electric mixer. Very slowly, pour the syrup into the yolks in a thin steady stream while you beat the yolks, gradually increasing the speed at which you beat them. Do not pour syrup on the whisk or it will splatter around the sides of the bowl. Try to pour the syrup directly into the yolks, but in a mixer with a steep sided bowl you may have to pour the syrup down the side of the bowl in order to avoid pouring it onto the whisk. When all of the syrup has been added, continue beating at medium-high speed until the mixture is white, stiff, and cool.

3 Gradually add the softened butter, beating vigorously with the leaf beater of your electric mixer or a wooden spoon.

Opposite: Assorted meringues, pages 294–296. Preceding page: Charlotte poire with sauce au chocolat (pear Charlotte with chocolate sauce), pages 336 and 128.

4 If you want a lighter *crème au beurre* (for most purposes we prefer it lighter) stir in the *meringue italienne* with the leaf beater or wooden spoon.

5 Use the *crème au beurre* right away, or refrigerate it for later use. If refrigerated, remove it from the refrigerator and let it soften at room temperature before using. When the *crème au beurre* has softened, beat it vigorously with a wooden spoon or the leaf beater of your electric mixer to make it smooth and spreadable.

Storage: Covered airtight, for up to 1 week in the refrigerator. Or divide the *crème au beurre* into quantities suitable for the desserts you expect to make (say 1½ to 2½ cups, or 270 to 450 g) and freeze it for up to 3 months. If frozen, allow the *crème au beurre* to defrost overnight in the refrigerator before softening at room temperature in step 5.

Note A: If you forget to remove the *crème au beurre* from the refrigerator in advance, you can warm and soften it quickly in a stainless-steel bowl. Briefly warm it over direct heat, stirring constantly and cutting the butter cream into pieces with a wooden spoon. Remove it from the heat and beat it vigorously with the wooden spoon. Return it to the heat and repeat as often as necessary to make the *crème au beurre* smooth and spreadable. If you do not warm the *crème au beurre* enough while softening, it may become grainy and deflate. This can also result from adding too much liquid flavoring or the right amount of flavoring in too soft a butter cream. When this happens, continue warming the *crème au beurre* and beating it vigorously with a wooden spoon until it is soft. Then beat it with a heavy wire whisk or in your electric mixer with the leaf beater to make it light again. If the *crème au beurre* still doesn't look right, melt about one tenth as much butter as you have *crème au beurre*; and beat the melted butter into the *crème au beurre* with the heavy wire whisk or the leaf beater of your electric mixer to make it light and smooth again.

Note B: You can make a softer, less rich butter cream by mixing 2 parts (by weight) *crème au beurre* with 1 part *crème pâtissière*. The result is called *crème au beurre au lait* and can be used interchangeably *with crème au beurre.* Occasionally the proportions are varied to get a texture ideally suited to a particular dessert.

Intrinsically Flavored Fillings

For these the flavoring elements are intrinsic to the preparation of the fillings. You simply can't have *compote de pommes* without apples or *ganache* without chocolate, for example. The distinctive flavors and textures of these fillings give them a special appeal.

Crème d'Amandes

ALMOND PASTRY CREAM

Crème d'amandes is a luxurious, almond- and butter-enriched pastry cream that, unlike most fillings, is always baked in the desserts in which it is used.

For about 5 cups (1,350 g)

INGREDIENTS

½ pound (225 g) butter

1 pound 1½ ounces (500 g), or about 3⅓ cups, *TPT blanc* (see page 413)

3 tablespoons (40 g) superfine sugar

3 large eggs

1¼ cups (340 g) *crème pâtissière* (see page 83)

2½ ounces (70 g), or about ½ cup, cornstarch

3 tablespoons (4½ cL) dark rum

1 Cream the butter with the *TPT blanc* and superfine sugar by hand, in an electric mixer with leaf beater, or in a food processor.

2 One at a time, beat the eggs into the creamed butter using a wooden spoon, the leaf beater of your electric mixer, or your food processor. Then beat in the *crème pâtissière* and finally the cornstarch.

3 Mix in the dark rum to flavor the *crème d'amandes*.

Storage: Covered airtight, for up to 1 week in the refrigerator. Or freeze the *crème d'amandes* for up to 3 months. If frozen, defrost overnight in the refrigerator before using.

Compote de Pommes

APPLE COMPOTE

Compote de pommes is used in apple tartes and turnovers, and it is always baked in the pastry.

For about 2 cups (600 g)

INGREDIENTS

1½ pounds (675 g) tart cooking apples

One half vanilla bean

3 tablespoons (4½ cL) strained fresh lemon juice

¾ cup (150 g) superfine sugar

7 tablespoons (1 dL) water

1 Peel, core, and coarsely chop the apples.

2 Split the vanilla bean lengthwise and scrape out the seeds. Combine both the pod and seeds with the chopped apples and the remaining ingredients in a 2-quart (2 L) saucepan.

3 Bring the apple mixture to a simmer. Then reduce the heat to low and continue cooking, stirring occasionally, until the apples become almost a purée and the excess liquid has evaporated, about 20 minutes. Stir the compote occasionally to avoid scorching the apples at the bottom of the saucepan.

4 Remove from the heat and cool to room temperature.

Storage: Covered airtight, for up to 1 week in the refrigerator. When ready to use, remove the vanilla bean.

Pommes Sautées au Beurre

Here is a second apple filling, made by gently cooking diced apples in butter, which has more texture than *compote de pommes*. You can substitute *pommes sautées au beurre* for *compote de pommes* in most recipes, or use a mixture of the two, depending on the texture you like best.

For about 1½ cups (450 g)

INGREDIENTS

1½ pounds (675 g)
 tart cooking apples
3 tablespoons (45 g)
 butter
¼ cup (50 g) sugar

1 Peel and core the apples, and cut them into ½-inch (1 cm) dice.

2 Melt the butter in a sauté pan or saucepan. Add the apple dice and turn them with a wooden spoon until they are coated with the butter.

3 Add the sugar and mix with the apple dice. Cook gently, turning the apple dice frequently with a wooden spoon, until they are no longer crisp but not yet soft, about 5 minutes.

4 Remove from the heat and cool to room temperature.

5 Drain the apples before using.

Storage: Covered airtight, for up to 1 week in the refrigerator.

Les Ganaches

Ganaches are rich chocolate fillings made from semi-sweet chocolate and cream and used in *gâteaux* and chocolate candies.

For about 2 cups (500 g)

GANACHE CLICHY

10½ ounces (300 g)
 semisweet chocolate
1 cup (2.4 dL) heavy
 cream

GANACHE AU RHUM

10½ ounces (300 g)
 semisweet chocolate

1 Coarsely chop the chocolate with your chef's knife and put it in a bowl.

2 Bring the cream just to a boil, then reduce the heat and sterilize the cream by simmering it for at least 2 minutes, stirring constantly with a wire whisk to prevent the cream from boiling over.

3 Gradually pour the hot cream into the chocolate, stirring constantly with the wire whisk. Continue stirring until the chocolate is completely melted and the *ganache* is smooth. (If all of the chocolate does not melt, dip the bottom of the bowl of *ganache* in a bowl of hot water and stir over the hot water until

¾ cup plus 2
  tablespoons (1.8 dL)
  heavy cream
3 tablespoons plus 1
  teaspoon (5 cL)
  dark rum

**GANACHE AU
GRAND MARNIER**

10½ ounces (300 g)
  semisweet chocolate
¾ cup (1.8 dL)
  heavy cream
3 tablespoons plus 1
  teaspoon (5 cL)
  Grand Marnier

smooth.) Then stir in the rum or Grand Marnier if required.

4 Allow the *ganache* to cool to room temperature.

5 Use the *ganache* before it sets. Or refrigerate the *ganache,* then remove it from the refrigerator 1 hour before using; and when it has warmed to room temperature, place it in a stainless-steel bowl over hot water and beat it vigorously with a wooden spoon until it is smooth and spreadable.

Storage: Covered airtight, for up to 1 week in the refrigerator.

Mousse à Paris

CHOCOLATE MOUSSE

This chocolate mousse is designed for a sumptuous *gâteau* called *Paris*.

For about 4 cups (500 g)

INGREDIENTS

7 ounces (200 g)
  semisweet chocolate
7 tablespoons (100 g)
  butter, melted
2 large egg yolks
4 large egg whites
Optional: ⅛ teaspoon
  (a pinch) cream of
  tartar
¼ cup (50 g)
  superfine sugar

1 Temper the chocolate as follows: Melt the chocolate. Dip the bottom of the pot of chocolate in cold water. Stir until it starts to thicken. Immediately return it to the heat and gently warm the chocolate a second time, stirring constantly until just melted again.

2 Remove the chocolate from the heat and stir in the melted butter with a wire whisk. When smooth, beat in the egg yolks.

3 Whip the egg whites with a wire whisk or in an electric mixer. If you are not whipping the whites in a copper bowl, then, when they begin to froth, add the cream of tartar. Continue whipping until the whites form very stiff peaks and just begin to slip and streak around the side of the bowl.

4 Dust the sugar over the egg whites and continue whipping for a few seconds longer, until the meringue is smooth and shiny.

5 Transfer the chocolate mixture to a medium size bowl and thorougly mix in about one third of the meringue with a rubber spatula. Then gently fold in the rest of the meringue.

Storage: None. Use the mousse before it sets.

Lemon Curd

There is no French name for *lemon curd*. This is an English lemon custard that Paul adapted for use in lemon tartes and charlottes.

For about 2⅔ cups (700 g)

INGREDIENTS

4 small or 3 medium
  fresh lemons
4 large eggs
1¼ cups (250 g)
  sugar
6 ounces (170 g)
  butter, softened

1 Finely grate the aromatic yellow zest from the outsides of the lemons. Juice the lemons, and strain the juice. You should have about ½ cup (1.2 dL) of strained lemon juice.

2 Combine the grated lemon zest and lemon juice with the eggs and sugar in a 1-quart (1 L) saucepan. Mix well by beating with a wire whisk.

3 Place the saucepan over medium heat and, stirring constantly with a wooden spoon, bring the mixture to a simmer. Reduce the heat to very low and continue cooking, stirring constantly, until the mixture coats the spoon heavily. Do not boil or the custard will curdle.

4 Immediately transfer the mixture to a bowl and stir in the softened butter, one tablespoon (15 g) at a time.

5 Let the lemon curd cool to room temperature.

Storage: Covered airtight, for up to 1 week in the refrigerator. Or freeze for up to 1 month. If frozen, defrost overnight in the refrigerator before using.

Crème de Marrons

CHESTNUT CREAM

This is an extremely luxurious filling based on puréed chestnuts and butter.

For 5 cups (900 g)

INGREDIENTS

2 cups (400 g) sugar

½ cup (1.2 dL) water

One 15½-ounce
(439 g) can of *purée
de marrons*

9 ounces (250 g)
butter, softened

3 tablespoons (4½
cL) dark rum or
bourbon

1 Combine the sugar and water in a saucepan or caramel pot and stir to thoroughly moisten the sugar. Bring to a boil. Continue boiling over moderate heat, washing down the walls of the pot with a moistened pastry brush as needed to dissolve any sugar crystals that form there. Cook until the sugar reaches the hard ball stage, or about 255° F (125° C).

2 While the syrup is cooking, drain off any excess water from the *purée de marrons* and place the purée in the workbowl of your food processor.

3 When the syrup is ready, immediately remove the pot from the heat and plunge the bottom of the pot in cold water to cool the pot and stop the cooking. Then quickly remove the pot from the water so you don't cool the syrup.

4 Turn on the food processor, open the feed tube, and pour in the hot syrup in a thin stream. Continue processing until the chestnut and sugar mixture is completely smooth.

5 Transfer the sweetened chestnut purée to a 2- to 3-quart (2 to 3 L) saucepan and simmer it gently, stirring occasionally with a wooden spoon, to evaporate excess moisture and reduce the mixture to about 2 cups (600 g) of very thick *pâte de marrons*. The *pâte de marrons* should be so thick that when you draw the wooden spoon across the bottom of the saucepan, it takes a few seconds to flow back together and cover the bottom of the saucepan.

6 Remove from the heat and cool to room temperature.

7 Mix the *pâte de marrons* with the softened butter, using a wooden spoon or the leaf beater of your electric mixer. Beat in the dark rum or bourbon. Switch to a wire whisk or, preferably, the wire whip of your electric mixer, and whip this *crème de marrons* until it is smooth and light like *crème au beurre*.

Storage: Covered airtight, in the refrigerator for up to 1 week. Remove from the refrigerator 1 hour before using and let soften at room temperature, then beat vigorously with a wooden spoon or the leaf beater of your electric mixer to make it smooth.

You can also freeze the *crème de marrons* for up to 1 month. If frozen, defrost overnight in the refrigerator before softening at room temperature.

Composite Creams

Some of the lightest, most ethereal fillings are made by combining our fundamental creams with various toppings.

Crème Chiboust

LIGHT PASTRY CREAM

Named after a nineteenth-century Parisian pastry chef, *crème chiboust* is a very light, sweet pastry cream. Some people call it *crème légère*. It is made by folding *meringue italienne* into an ordinary pastry cream, with a little gelatin added to stabilize the meringue. *Crème chiboust* is excellent in tarts as a foil for very sour fruits, such as red currants, and it can be used in desserts like *St.-Honoré*, which require the pastry cream to be piped in a decorative way.

For about 4 cups (500 g)

INGREDIENTS

1 teaspoon (4 g)
 unflavored gelatin
¾ cup (1.8 dL) milk

1 Soften the gelatin in 1 tablespoon (1½ cL) of cold water.

2 Prepare an ordinary pastry cream as follows: Cut open the vanilla bean lengthwise and scrape out

One quarter vanilla bean

3 large egg yolks

3 tablespoons (40 g) sugar

2 tablespoons (17 g) cornstarch

Optional: 1 tablespoon plus 2 teaspoons (2½ cL) very strong black coffee (see page 416), dark rum, or kirsch

MERINGUE ITALIENNE

¾ cup (150 g) sugar

3 tablespoons (4½ cL) water

3 large egg whites

Optional: ⅛ teaspoon (a pinch) cream of tartar

the seeds. Combine the seeds and bean with the milk in a heavy 1-quart (1 L) saucepan and bring to a simmer. Meanwhile, beat together the egg yolks, sugar, and cornstarch until smooth. Pour in half the simmering milk, stirring constantly with a wire whisk, then pour this mixture back into the saucepan with the remaining milk and stir until thoroughly blended. Place the saucepan over medium heat and, stirring constantly with a wire whisk, bring the pastry cream to a boil. Reduce the heat and continue cooking, stirring constantly, until the pastry cream is very thick and smooth, 1 to 2 minutes. Remove from the heat and stir in the softened gelatin to dissolve it. Then strain the pastry cream through a sieve into a bowl.

3 Allow the pastry cream to cool, stirring occasionally, but do not let it set.

4 Meanwhile, prepare a *meringue italienne* with the egg whites and sugar. Combine the sugar and water in a small saucepan and cook to the high end of the firm ball stage, or about 248° F (120° C). Whip the egg whites with a wire whisk or, preferably, in an electric mixer. If you are not whipping the whites in a copper bowl, then when they start to froth add the cream of tartar. Continue whipping until the whites form very stiff peaks and just begin to slip and streak around the side of the bowl. Pour in the syrup in a thin, steady stream while you continue whiping at maximum speed. After all the syrup has been added, continue whipping briefly until the meringue is smooth and shiny. Then let the meringue cool to room temperature, stirring at low speed in the electric mixer or stirring occasionally with a wire whisk to prevent it from forming a skin on top.

5 If you want to flavor the *crème chiboust* for use in a *St.-Honoré,* stir the optional coffee, dark rum, or kirsch into the pastry cream.

6 Quickly and thoroughly mix about one third of the *meringue italienne* into the pastry cream with a rubber spatula. Then gently fold in the remaining meringue.

Storage: None. Use the *crème chiboust* immediately, before it sets.

Crème Bavaroise

The classical pastry cream for molding is *crème bavaroise*. It combines the velvety egginess of *crème anglaise* with the lightness of *crème chantilly,* stabilized with gelatin. *Crème bavaroise* is usually flavored with liqueur.

For about 4 cups (1 L)

INGREDIENTS

2¼ teaspoon (8 g) unflavored gelatin

1 cup (2.4 dL) milk

¼ cup plus 2 tablespoons (75 g) sugar

4 large egg yolks

Optional: 3 tablespoons (4½ cL) dark rum, kirsch, Curaçao, or other liqueur

1¼ cups (3 dL) heavy cream

1 Chill the bowl and the whisk or beater you will be using to whip the cream.

2 Soften the gelatin in 1 tablespoon (1½ cL) of cold water.

3 Prepare the *crème anglaise*. Bring the milk to a simmer in a 1-quart (1 L) saucepan. Beat together the egg yolks and sugar until smooth and lemon-colored, then slowly pour in the simmering milk, stirring constantly with a wire whisk. Pour back into the saucepan. Cook over low heat, stirring constantly with a wooden spoon, until the *crème anglaise* coats the back of the wooden spoon and the bubbles formed when you stirred the milk into the yolks have disappeared. Do not boil.

4 Remove the *crème anglaise* from the heat immediately and stir in the softened gelatin to dissolve it. Strain the *crème anglaise* into a stainless-steel bowl. Set the bowl in another bowl of crushed ice or ice water, and cool the *crème anglaise,* stirring constantly. When it has cooled to room temperature, remove the bowl of *crème anglaise* from the ice so it doesn't start to set. Stir in the optional alcohol to flavor the *crème anglaise.*

5 Whip the cream in the chilled bowl, using a wire whisk or electric mixer. Stop whipping when the cream is light, thick, and holding medium-firm peaks.

6 Place the bowl of *crème anglaise* over the ice again and stir constantly with a rubber spatula until it just begins to thicken. Immediately remove the bowl from the ice and stir about one third of the whipped cream into the *crème anglaise* with the rubber spatula. Then gently fold in the remaining whipped cream.

Storage: None. Use the *crème bavaroise* immediately, before it sets.

Fruit Mousses

The fruit mousses we use for filling *charlottes* are simply whipped cream mixed with sweetened fruit purées and stablized with gelatin. They are light and creamy and have the intense and compelling flavors of the fresh fruits themselves.

For about 6 cups (1½ L)

INGREDIENTS

3½ teaspoons (12 g) unflavored gelatin

1 pound 5⅓ ounces (600 g), or 2¼ to 2½ cups (5.3 to 6 dL), fruit purée or *coulis de fruit* (for details on each fruit, see below)

2 cups (4.7 dL) heavy cream

1 Chill the bowl and the whisk or beater you will be using to whip the cream.

2 Combine the gelatin with about one third of the fruit purée or *coulis* in a small saucepan and, stirring constantly, warm it over low heat until the gelatin dissolves. Remove from the heat and pour into a large bowl.

3 Stir the remaining fruit purée or *coulis* into the gelatin-purée mixture. Allow the purée to cool, stirring occasionally, but do not let it set.

4 Meanwhile, whip the cream with the chilled wire whisk or in an electric mixer. Stop whipping when the cream is light and thick, and holds medium-firm peaks.

5 Dip the bottom of the bowl of fruit purée or *coulis* in a larger bowl of crushed ice or ice water, and stir with a rubber spatula until it just begins to thicken. Immediately remove the bowl from the ice and quickly and thoroughly stir about one third of the whipped cream into the fruit purée or *coulis* with the rubber spatula. Then gently fold in the remaining whipped cream.

Storage: None. Use the mousse immediately, before it sets.

Mousse aux Fraises (Strawberry Mousse): Use a *coulis de fraise* (see page 127).

Mousse aux Cerises (Cherry Mousse): Use a *coulis de cerise* (see page 127).

Mousse aux Framboises (Raspberry Mousse): Since raspberries have a stronger taste than the other fruits, use only 2 to 2¼ cups (½ L), of *coulis de framboise* (see page 127) and increase the amount of heavy cream to 2¼ cups (5.3 dL).

Mousse aux Mangues

MANGO MOUSSE

Prepare a fresh mango purée as follows:

INGREDIENTS

Two 1 pound (450 g) ripe fresh mangoes

¼ cup plus 2 tablespoons (75 g) sugar

2 tablespoons (3 cL) strained fresh lemon juice

1 Slit the skin all the way around each mango and peel off the skins. With a spoon, scrape off any of the flesh that clings to the skins. Slice the flesh off the pit of each mango. You should have about 1¼ pounds (570 g) of flesh. If you don't have enough, then cut open another mango and add as much of its flesh as necessary.

2 Purée the mango flesh with the sugar and lemon juice in an electric blender or food processor. Then strain it through a fine sieve to remove any bits of fiber from the mango.

Storage: Tightly cover and refrigerate for up to 3 or 4 days. Or freeze for as long as 1 or 2 months. If frozen, defrost overnight in the refrigerator before using.

Mousse aux Poires

PEAR MOUSSE

Since pears have a relatively weak flavor, reduce the amount of heavy cream to 1¾ cups plus 2 tablespoons (4.4 dL), and use 2½ cups (650 g) of a purée of fresh pears, prepared as follows:

INGREDIENTS

1 pound 5⅓ ounces (600 g) poached fresh pears (4 or 5 pears, see page 422)

2 tablespoons (25 g) sugar

2 teaspoons (1 cL) strained fresh lemon juice

2 tablespoons (3 cL) *eau de vie de poire*

1 Purée the poached pears with the sugar and lemon juice in a blender or food processor. Strain the purée through a fine sieve.

2 Stir the *eau de vie de poire* into the purée.

Storage: Tightly cover and refrigerate for up to 3 or 4 days. Or freeze for as long as 1 or 2 months. If frozen, defrost overnight in the refrigerator before using.

Mousse aux Myrtilles

BLUEBERRY MOUSSE

Prepare a fresh blueberry purée as follows:

INGREDIENTS

1½ pints (700 g) fresh blueberries

½ cup (100 g) sugar

1 tablespoon plus 2 teaspoons (2½ cL) strained fresh lemon juice

1 Combine the blueberries with the sugar and lemon juice and coarsely purée them in the blender or food processor. The pieces of blueberry skin should be fairly large, so they can be easily strained out later.

2 Pour the puréed blueberries into a 2-quart (2 L) saucepan. Bring to a simmer over moderate heat, stirring constantly with a wooden spoon. Then remove from the heat.

3 Strain the hot blueberry purée through a fine sieve to remove the skins. Cool to room temperature.

Storage: Tightly cover and refrigerate for up to 3 or 4 days. Or freeze for as long as 1 or 2 months. If frozen, defrost overnight in the refrigerator before using.

Mousse aux Airelles

CRANBERRY MOUSSE

Prepare a fresh cranberry purée as follows:

INGREDIENTS

1½ pounds (680 g)
  fresh cranberries
2 cups (400 g) sugar
¼ cup (6 cL) water

1 Combine the cranberries with the sugar and water and coarsely purée them in the food processor or blender. The pieces of cranberry skin should be fairly large, and can be easily strained out later.

2 Pour the puréed cranberries into a 2-quart (2 L) saucepan. Bring to a simmer over moderate heat, stirring constantly with a wooden spoon. Continue cooking over low heat, stirring occasionally, until the cranberry purée is very soft and a uniform red color, 5 to 7 minutes. Then remove from the heat.

3 Strain the hot cranberry purée through a fine sieve to remove the skins. Cool to room temperature.

Storage: Tightly cover and refrigerate for up to 3 or 4 days. Or freeze for as long as 1 or 2 months. If frozen, defrost overnight in the refrigerator before using.

Mousse aux Citron

LEMON MOUSSE

Because the taste of lemon juice is so intense, the method for preparing this mousse is different from the others.

For about 6 cups (1½ L)

INGREDIENTS

3 tablespoons (4½
  cL) strained fresh
  lemon juice
3 tablespoons (4½
  cL) *sirop à trente*
  (see page 398)
1½ teaspoons (5 g)
  unflavored gelatin
2¼ cups (5.3 dL)
  heavy cream

1 Chill the bowl and the whisk or beater you will be using to whip the cream.

2 Combine the gelatin with the lemon juice and *sirop à trente* in a small saucepan and, stirring constantly, warm it over low heat until the gelatin dissolves. Remove from the heat and pour into a large bowl.

3 Whip the cream with the chilled wire whisk or in an electric mixer. Stop mixing when the cream is light and thick and holds medium-firm peaks.

1 cup (260 g) lemon curd (see page 91)

4 Add the lemon curd to the dissolved gelatin and stir to mix thoroughly. Quickly and thoroughly fold in about one third of the whipped cream. Then gently fold in the remaining whipped cream.

Storage: None. Use the *mousse au citron* immediately, before it sets.

Chapter Four

TOPPINGS

*T*oppings are the components used on the outsides of desserts. Very few of them are baked, but their textures vary from hard and crisp to soft and smooth. Many toppings are also fillings, and vice versa.

Frostings

Frostings are toppings that are spread over the outsides of *gâteaux* with a palette knife. These include *crème au beurre*, *crème chantilly*, *ganache*, *mousse à paris*, and *meringue italienne*, but not glazes such as fondant or *pâte à glacé*, which are poured over *gâteaux*. Most of our frostings are also used as fillings, and the recipes for all but *meringue italienne* appear in the previous chapter.

Meringue Italienne
ITALIAN MERINGUE

Meringue italienne is an incredibly versatile meringue made by whipping hot sugar syrup into stiffly beaten egg whites. Not only is it used by itself as a frosting, but it can be piped from a pastry bag and tube and baked like ordinary meringue, or mixed with other ingredients to make a filling, or folded into pastry creams and butter creams to lighten them.

For 9½ ounces (270 g), or about 4½ cups

INGREDIENTS

1 cup (200 g) sugar
¼ cup (6 cL) water
3 large egg whites

1 Combine the sugar and water in a small saucepan or caramel pot and stir to thoroughly moisten the sugar. Bring to a boil over medium heat. Continue boiling, washing down the walls of the pot with a moistened pastry brush as needed to dissolve any

Optional: ⅛ teaspoon (a pinch) cream of tartar

sugar crystals that form there. Cook until the sugar reaches the high end of the firm ball stage, or about 248° F (120° C).

2 Meanwhile, whip the egg whites in an electric mixer fitted with the wire whisk; or whip them by hand if you don't have an electric mixer. If you are not whipping the whites in a copper bowl, then, when they begin to froth, add the cream of tartar. Continue whipping until the whites form very stiff peaks and just begin to slip and streak around the side of the bowl. Adjust the speed at which you whip the whites and the rate at which you cook the sugar so they are ready simultaneously.

3 Pour the syrup into the egg whites in a thin, steady stream while you continue to whip the whites at maximum speed. The meringue will rise and become very light. Do not pour the syrup on the whisk or it will splatter around the sides of the bowl. Try to pour the syrup directly into the whites, but, in an electric mixer with a steep-sided bowl, you may have to pour the syrup down the side of the bowl in order to avoid pouring it onto the beater.

4 After all of the syrup has been added, continue whipping briefly until the meringue is smooth and shiny.

5 If you are making the meringue as a topping or to be piped and baked, then use it while it is still hot. Otherwise, let the meringue cool to room temperature, stirring at very low speed in the electric mixer or gently stirring occasionally with a wire whisk to prevent it from forming a skin on top.

Storage: For frosting or for piping from a pastry bag and then baking, the meringue should be used within an hour after it is prepared. It will always have the best consistency and lightness when freshly made, but for other purposes it can be kept in the refrigerator, covered airtight, for up to 2 days, if necessary.

Glazes

Many pastries are glazed to give them a shiny surface. The glazes are applied in a variety of ways. Jams and jellies and *glace à l'eau* are painted on with a pastry brush. Small pastries can be dipped in fondant, *caramel blond,* or *pâte à glacé;* and fondant and *pâte à glacé* are poured over *gâteaux. Glace royale* is spread with a palette knife and baked on some *feuilletés.*

Jams and Jellies

Apricot jam and red currant jelly are by far the most common ones used for glazing in French pastry. Others that occasionally take their places are peach jam and cherry jelly. Strongly flavored jams and jellies should not be used as glazes, because they would distract from the pastry itself.

STRAINED APRICOT JAM: Apricot jam must be melted and forced through a sieve before using as a glaze. Work the jam through the sieve with a wooden pestle or a rubber spatula. Don't try to purée the jam with a food processor or blender, since that would trap air bubbles in the jam and make it opaque. After you have forced as much of the solid pieces of fruit through the strainer as you can, stir the strained jam to make it homogeneous.

If you frequently make pastries that are glazed with apricot jam, strain one or two jars at a time and store the strained jam in the refrigerator.

Always melt jams over low heat, stirring occasionally with a wooden spoon. Do not stir constantly or use a whisk because you don't want to introduce air bubbles into the jam. If the jam is too thin and watery, simmer it over low heat, stirring occasionally, to reduce it to a better consistency.

RED CURRANT JELLY: Unlike jams, red currant jelly should not be melted. Instead work the jelly through a fine sieve with a wooden pestle or a rubber spatula. It will then have the right consistency for brushing.

Glace à l'Eau

This is a water and confectioners sugar glaze that is often brushed over apricot jam. The glaze can be made more transparent by briefly placing the pastry in a hot oven. Usually *glace à l'eau* is flavored with an alcohol, such as rum.

For about ½ cup (1.2 dL) of *glace à l'eau*

INGREDIENTS

¾ cup (100 g) confectioners sugar

Optional: 2 teaspoons (1 cL) dark rum, or other liqueur

Cold water

1 Sift the confectioners sugar.

2 Stir the optional rum into the confectioners sugar. Slowly stir in cold water until the mixture becomes smooth and creamy. The *glace à l'eau* should be just liquid enough to spread easily with a pastry brush. If you add too much water and the *glace à l'eau* becomes runny, stir in more confectioners sugar.

Storage: Covered airtight, in the refrigerator for up to 3 or 4 days. If a crust forms on top, pour a little water over it and stir to dissolve the crust. In any case, before using, stir the *glace à l'eau* until it is smooth and add more water if necessary.

Glace Royale

Glace royale is used as a glaze on cakes and pastries in England, where it is called "royal icing." In France, a few pastries—including Conversation and *alumettes*—are glazed with *glace royale* before baking, and it is also used for writing and decorating (see Piped Decoration, page 117) on *gâteaux*.

For about 6 tablespoons (175 g)

INGREDIENTS

¾ cup (100 g) confectioners sugar

2 tablespoons (3 cL) of egg white

A few drops of lemon juice

1 Sift the confectioners sugar.

2 Using a wooden spoon, stir the confectioners sugar into the egg white to make a smooth paste. Beat the paste vigorously with the wooden spoon until it whitens and stiffens.

3 Beat in the lemon juice to whiten the *glace royale* still more. It should be just soft enough to spread easily with a palette knife.

Storage: Cover the surface of the *glace royale* with a damp cloth to keep it from drying and forming a skin on top. Cover airtight with plastic wrap and keep for up to 3 days in the refrigerator. Beat vigorously with a wooden spoon before using.

Fondant

To make fondant by hand, you need a marble or Formica work surface. Marble is better because it cools the fondant more quickly, giving a smoother texture and requiring less time and effort. Also, unless your work suface is very large, you will need fondant rails. These are just four steel rods that you arrange on your work surface to make a rectangle of variable size to contain the fondant and prevent it from flowing off the work surface. We use 18 × 1-inch (45 × 2½ cm) steel angle rods, seasoned with oil to prevent rust.

We have also discovered that you can work the fondant in a Kitchen-Aid K5, using the leaf beater and the ice jacket. The ice jacket is essential for quickly cooling the fondant.

For 2 pounds 7 ounces (1,100 g) or about 3¼ cups

INGREDIENTS

5 cups (1 kg) sugar

1¾ cups (4 dL) water

⅓ cup (100 g) glucose, or ¼ cup plus 3 tablespoons (133 g) light corn syrup

1 Combine the sugar and water in a saucepan or caramel pot and stir to thoroughly moisten the sugar. Bring to a boil over medium heat.

2 Add the glucose or corn syrup.

3 Continue boiling over medium heat without stirring, washing down the walls of the pot with a moistened pastry brush as needed to dissolve any sugar crystals that form there. Cook until the syrup reaches 239° F (115° C) on a candy thermometer, or the high end of the soft ball stage.

4 While the sugar is cooking, wipe your marble slab or Formica countertop with a cold wet cloth to moisten it, and arrange your fondant rails on the work surface to contain a rectangle about 12 × 16 inches (30 × 40 cm). Or rinse out the bowl of your Kitchen-Aid K5 with cold water, attach the bowl, the ice jacket, and the leaf beater to the machine, and fill the ice jacket with crushed ice (preferably) or ice water.

5 As soon as the syrup reaches 239° F (115° C), remove it from the heat.

By hand: Pour the hot syrup onto the prepared work surface ① and sprinkle it lightly with cold water. Allow the syrup to cool to about 150° F (65° C). Then begin stirring it constantly with a wooden spoon in one hand, and use a dough scraper in the other hand to scrape it from the work surface and gather it to the center of the work surface ② . Gradually the fondant will become very thick, white, and opaque. When it solidifies into a dull white, dry mass and is barely warm, stop working it.

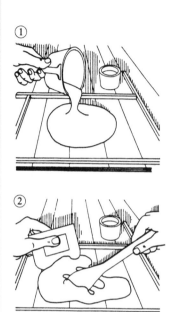

In your Kitchen-Aid K5: Pour the syrup into the prepared bowl of the K5 and turn on the machine. Stir at very low speed with the leaf beater until the syrup begins to thicken. Turn up the speed to medium-low and continue stirring over the crushed ice. Gradually the fondant will become very thick, white, and opaque. Add more crushed ice to the ice jacket as needed. When the fondant solidifies into a dull white, dry mass around the leaf beater, turn off the machine.

6 Gather the fondant together, cover it with a damp cloth, and let cool to room temperature.

7 Scrape the fondant from the work surface or bowl. Take a small amount at a time and work it on the counter by repeatedly flattening it with the heel of your hand and folding it onto itself until it becomes a smooth, coherent mass.

8 Gather the fondant into a ball and place it in a bowl. Cover the surface of the fondant with a damp cloth and cover the bowl with plastic wrap so that the fondant won't dry and form a crust on top. Allow the fondant to rest for at least 24 hours.

Storage: Covered airtight at room temperature for up to 2 weeks or in the refrigerator for up to 2 months.

About using fondant
When you are ready to use the fondant, warm it in a saucepan over very low heat, stirring constantly with a wooden spoon until melted. The correct temperature for glazing with fondant is about 100° to 105° F

(38° to 40° C); when you touch it to the back of your index finger it should feel warm but not hot. At this temperature the fondant should be fluid and have just enough body that it pours easily without being runny. If the fondant is too hot it can melt a frosting such as *crème au beurre* over which it is poured, and it will become dull when it sets. On the other hand, if the fondant is too fluid (or fluid at a lower temperature), it can drip before setting.

The precise consistency of the fondant depends on the pastries you are glazing. To glaze a *gâteau* the fondant is poured on top of the dessert and must be fluid enough to flow easily over the surface of the *gâteau* and coat it quickly before the fondant starts to set. To accomplish this the fondant should have about the same body as heavy cream or a light *crème anglaise*.

Les choux are glazed by dipping the pastries in the fondant. For them the consistency should be slightly thicker and the fondant should coat a wooden spoon heavily, like a thick *crème anglaise*.

In either case, you will almost certainly have to adjust the consistency of the fondant, probably by thinning it. If the fondant is too thick and viscous, gradually stir in some *sirop à trente* (see page 398) to thin it. (It is not unusual to use up to 1 part syrup for 3 parts fondant when the fondant will be used for glazing a *gâteau*.) On the other hand, if it is too fluid, stir in some confectioners sugar to thicken it.

If you accidentally overheat the fondant, dip the bottom of the saucepan in cold water and stir until the fondant has returned to the proper temperature.

Flavored Fondants

Fondant is frequently flavored and tinted with food coloring. For *gâteaux*, where you use a large amount of fondant, this is part of the recipe of the dessert. But, for *les choux*, it is more convenient to have the fondant flavored in advance. The ones we use most often are chocolate, coffee, kirsch, and Grand Marnier, and they are tinted according to the flavor. For each version, use 1 cup (340 g) of plain fondant.

CHOCOLATE FONDANT

2 ounces (55 g)
  unsweetened
  chocolate
Red food coloring

COFFEE FONDANT

1 tablespoon (1½ cL)
  very strong black
  coffee (see page
  416)
Caramel food
  coloring (see page
  431)

KIRSCH FONDANT

1 tablespoon (1½ cL)
  kirsch
Green food coloring

GRAND MARNIER FONDANT

1 tablespoon (1½ cL)
  Grand Marnier
Red food coloring

Warm the plain fondant over low heat, stirring constantly with a wooden spoon until melted. If you are making chocolate fondant, gently melt the chocolate. Stir the melted chocolate, coffee, kirsch, or Grand Marnier into the fondant. Add a drop or so of food coloring to tint the fondant pale green for kirsch, pink for Grand Marnier, or tan for coffee, or to enrich the brown color for chocolate.

Note: If you want a very dark chocolate fondant, you must use more chocolate. However, that will thicken the fondant and you will have to compensate by adding *sirop à trente* (see page 398) to thin the fondant back to the proper consistency.

Caramel Blond

This is not a true caramel, but rather sugar cooked to a very hard crack stage. Several types of *choux* are glazed with it. This is done by dipping, so you will always need much more *caramel blond* than actually ends up coating the pastries. And, since you will rarely be glazing a large number of *choux* at once (an exception is *croquembouche*), the amount you must have in the caramel pot will depend more on the size of the pot than on the pastries themselves. The recipe below is as small as is practical to make and will be sufficient for several batches of *salambos* or *St.-Honoré*.

For 9 ounces (250 g)

INGREDIENTS

1¼ cups (250 g)
  sugar

¼ cup plus 1
  tablespoon (7½ cl)
  water

1 tablespoon plus 1
  teaspoon (25 g)
  glucose, or
  substitute 1
  tablespoon plus 2
  teaspoons (30 g)
  light corn syrup

¼ teaspoon (1 mL)
  lemon juice

1 Combine the sugar and water in a small sauce-pan or caramel pot and stir to thoroughly moisten the sugar. Bring to a boil over medium heat, then skim off any foam and scum that come to the surface of the syrup.

2 Add the glucose or corn syrup.

3 Continue cooking over medium heat, washing down the walls of the pot with a moistened pastry brush as needed to dissolve any sugar crystals that form there.

4 When the syrup reaches the soft crack stage, or about 270° F (135° C), add the lemon juice and reduce the heat to low.

5 Continue cooking until syrup passes through the hard crack stage and reaches 317° to 320° F (158° to 160° C). Depending on how evenly the sugar was cooked, it may turn a very pale golden color.

6 Immediately remove the pot from the heat and plunge the bottom of the pot in a bowl of cold water to stop the cooking. Quickly remove the pot from the water so you don't cool the syrup, and swirl the syrup in the pot for a few seconds until most of the air bubbles formed in the syrup during the cooking have disappeared.

7 The *caramel blond* is now ready to use. Or you can let it cool and reheat it later. Reheat the *caramel blond* over low direct heat, and, when it begins to melt, swirl it around in the pot so it melts evenly. Be careful not to overheat it or it will color more and cook past the correct stage.

Note: When dipping pastries in *caramel blond,* keep it on the side of the stove and warm it occasionally, swirling it in the pot, to maintain a fluid consistency.

Storage: Covered airtight, at room temperature for up to 1 month.

Pâte à Glacé

Chocolate that will be used for glazing must be thinned so it will have a more fluid consistency when melted and will spread easily, yet set quickly. This could be done by adding cocoa butter or using *couverture*, but the high cocoa-butter content would make a brittle coating that would shatter easily when cut. The chocolate glaze *pâte à glacé* that is sold for professional use in France contains vegetable oil, so it doesn't shatter so easily and still stores well. However, for home use we recommend thinning the chocolate with dairy butter, which gives a superior flavor and texture. Note that *couverture* should not be used in this recipe.

For 8 ounces (225 g)

INGREDIENTS

6 ounces (170 g) semisweet chocolate

¼ cup (55 g) butter, barely melted

1 tablespoon (1½ cL) water

1 Melt the chocolate.

2 Remove the chocolate from the heat and stir in the butter. When smooth, stir in the water.

3 Dip the bottom of the pot of chocolate in cold water and stir until it begins to thicken. Immediately return it to the heat.

4 Gently warm the chocolate a second time, stirring constantly until just melted again. The temperature of the chocolate should be between 85° and 88° F (29° to 31° C), and the *pâte à glacé* is now finished and ready to use.

Note: What you have done in making the *pâte à glacé* is to temper the chocolate with the butter. The temperature of the tempered *pâte à glacé* is lower than that of chocolate alone because dairy butter has a lower melting point than does cocoa butter.

Storage: Covered airtight, in the refrigerator for up to 1 week. If the *pâte à glacé* is prepared in advance, temper it again before using.

Rolled and Shaped Toppings

Pâte d'amandes, chocolat plastique, and *nougatine* can be rolled into sheets with a rolling pin or formed into decorative shapes by hand or in molds.

110

Pâte d'Amandes

ALMOND PASTE

There are many types of *pâte d'amandes*. Those used for filling chocolates contain a relatively high proportion of almonds and are soft. The *pâte d'amandes* we give here contains more sugar than almonds, making a much firmer almond paste for rolling into sheets and for modeling to decorate the tops of *gâteaux*. Because of its high sugar content, it stores extremely well.

Pâte d'amandes is easy to make in a food processor, and it can also be made in an electric blender if you reduce the quantity to about one quarter of the amount in our recipe.

Because *pâte d'amandes* is very firm, it is easier to roll out into sheets if you use a very heavy rolling pin. Marble is best of all, then steel, but you can also use a wood rolling pin.

For about 2¼ pounds (1 kg)

INGREDIENTS

2¼ cups (450 g) sugar

½ cup plus 1 tablespoon (1.4 dL) water

¼ cup (75 g) glucose, or substitute ⅓ cup (100 g) unflavored light corn syrup

10 ounces (285 g) blanched almonds

1½ cups (200 g) confectioners sugar

Additional confectioners sugar for dusting

1 Combine the sugar and water in a saucepan or caramel pot and stir to thoroughly moisten the sugar. Bring to a boil over medium heat.

2 Add the glucose or corn syrup.

3 Continue boiling over medium heat without stirring, washing down the walls of the pot with a moistened pastry brush as needed to dissolve any sugar crystals that form there. Cook until the syrup reaches the high end of firm ball stage, or 248° F (120° C).

4 While the sugar is cooking, put the almonds and confectioners sugar in the workbowl of your food processor or an electric blender.

5 When the syrup is ready, turn on the food processor and pour in the syrup. Continue processing until the *pâte d'amandes* is completely smooth.

6 Remove the *pâte d'amandes* from the food processor, gather it together, and put it in a bowl. It will be hot. Cover the *pâte d'amandes* with a damp kitchen towel to prevent it from drying out. When cooled to room temperature, remove the damp cloth. The *pâte d'amandes* is ready to use.

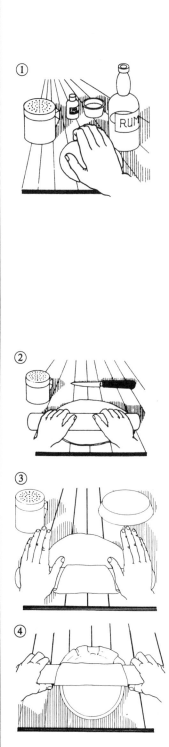

7 When you want to use some of the *pâte d'amandes*, dust a marble slab or your countertop with confectioners sugar. Work the *pâte d'amandes* on the counter with your hands, repeatedly flattening it with the heel of your hand and then folding it back onto itself to make it smooth and soften any crust that has formed during cooling or storing. The *pâte d'amandes* must be firm, but smooth and malleable. If it is too firm or dry, soften it by working in a little *sirop à trente* (see page 398) or an alcohol such as rum or Grand Marnier ①. On the other hand, if the *pâte d'amandes* is too soft, dust it with confectioners sugar and work in the confectioners sugar to make it more firm. If the recipe for the dessert you are making calls for it, add a drop or so of food coloring and work it in with the heel of your hand to tint the *pâte d'amandes* uniformly.

8 *To roll out a sheet of pâte d'amandes:* Form the *pâte d'amandes* into a round pad, and lightly dust the countertop and the pad with confectioners sugar. Roll out the pad with your rolling pin, lifting and rotating the pad after each forward and backward motion to get a round sheet of *pâte d'amandes* ②. The *pâte d'amandes* will be very firm, so press down firmly and evenly as you roll it. Lightly dust the counter and the *pâte d'amandes* with confectioners sugar as needed to prevent sticking, and wipe the sheet with your palm to spread the confectioners sugar evenly and eliminate any white blotches of sugar. Use the sugar sparingly. When the sheet of *pâte d'amandes* becomes thinner, stop lifting and rotating it, but continue rolling it in both directions, pressing down very firmly and evenly with the rolling pin, to get a rough circle of *pâte d'amandes* about $\frac{1}{16}$ inch (1½ mm) thick. To lift the sheet without tearing, first roll or drape it over your rolling pin so that the rolling pin supports its weight evenly ③. (Alternatively you can lift the sheet with your hands, folding it in half if necessary so that you can support its weight and move it without tearing.) Then transfer the sheet to the dessert you are making and unroll (or unfold) it ④.

To make pâte d'amandes leaves: Tint the *pâte d'amandes* a pale green and roll it out into a sheet ³/₃₂

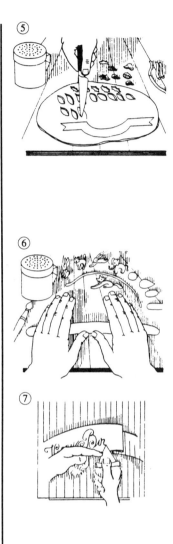

inch (2 mm) thick. Cut the leaves from the sheet with the tip of your paring knife ⑤. Draw veins on top of each leaf with the tip of your paring knife, then press each leaf into a gentle arch to make it look more realistic.

To make pâte d'amandes ropes, vines, and twigs: Press the *pâte d'amandes* into a thick pad or ball. Roll the pad back and forth on the counter under the palm of one hand to thin and elongate it into an even cylinder. As the cylinder gets longer, use both hands. Dust the *pâte d'amandes* very lightly with confectioners sugar if necessary to prevent it from sticking to your hands. By continuing to roll the *pâte d'amandes* under your palms, you can get a rope or string of whatever thickness you want ⑥. Cut it to the required length or lengths for ropes, vines, or twigs to decorate the top of a *gâteau*. Use it right away so it doesn't dry and loose its flexibility.

Writing cards: Roll out a small piece of *pâte d'amandes* about ³⁄₃₂ inch (2 mm) thick, and cut from it a rectangle or parallelogram (or a more fanciful shape with curved sides). Then place this card on top of a *gâteau* and write the name of the *gâteau* or a message on it in *pâte à écrire* or *glace royale* ⑦.

Other decorations in pâte d'amandes: You can model all sorts of decorations in *pâte d'amandes*—flowers, fruits, animals, the list is endless ⑥.

Storage: Covered airtight, at room temperature for up to 1 month. Or divide the *pâte d'amandes* into quantities suitable for finishing individual desserts (say 7 to 10 ounces, or 200 to 300 g, for a typical *gâteau*), wrap it airtight in small plastic bags, and freeze for up to 6 months. If frozen, defrost overnight in refrigerator and use within a few days.

Chocolat Plastique

This technique for making a chocolate with enough tensile strength to roll into sheets or model in decorative shapes is a relatively modern development. The trick is to temper the chocolate with corn syrup or glucose.

If you have a marble slab and a marble or steel rolling pin, this is a good place to use them, but a Formica countertop and conventional wood rolling pin will do fine.

For ⅓ pound (150 g) or one 12-inch (30 cm) circular sheet

INGREDIENTS

4 ounces (114 g) semisweet chocolate

2 tablespoons (38 g) unflavored light corn syrup, or substitute 1 tablespoon plus 2 teaspoons (32 g) glucose thinned with 1 teaspoon (½ cL) water

Confectioners sugar for dusting

①

②

③

1 Temper the chocolate as follows: Melt the chocolate. Dip the bottom of the pot of chocolate in cold water and stir until it begins to thicken. Immediately return it to the heat and gently warm the chocolate a second time, stirring constantly until just melted again.

2 Remove the chocolate from the heat and stir in the corn syrup or glucose.

3 Dust your countertop with confectioners sugar and turn out the *chocolat plastique* onto it. Use your palette knife or dough scraper to spread it on the counter and then gather it together by lifting the edges and folding them onto the center. Repeat until the *chocolat plastique* is no longer liquid but is still pliant and malleable. Then gather it into a ball and work it on the countertop, repeatedly flattening it with the heel of your hand and folding it back onto itself, to make it smooth ①.

4 *To roll out a sheet of chocolat plastique:* Form it into a round pad and lightly dust the counter and the pad with confectioners sugar. Roll out the pad with your rolling pin, lifting and rotating the pad after each forward and backward motion to get a round sheet ②. The *chocolat plastique* will be very firm, so press down firmly and evenly as you roll it. Lightly dust the counter and the *chocolat plastique* with confectioners sugar as needed to prevent sticking, and wipe the sheet with your palm to spread the sugar evenly and eliminate any blotches. Use the confectioners sugar sparingly. When the sheet becomes thinner, stop lifting and rotating it, but continue rolling it in both directions to get a rough circle about ¹⁄₁₆ inch (1½ mm) thick. To lift the sheet, roll or drape it over your rolling pin so that the rolling pin supports its weight evenly and the sheet doesn't tear ③. (Alternatively you can lift the sheet with your hands, folding it in half if necessary to support its weight.) Use the sheet of *chocolat plastique* right away so it doesn't dry and lose its flexibility.

Other decorations in chocolat plastique: You can model many decorative shapes in *chocolat plastique*. For example, you could make a single chocolate rose and a couple of leaves to decorate the top of a *gâteau*. Form the petals one at a time by pressing a small piece of *chocolat plastique* between your thumb and index and middle fingers, then gradually build up the rose by pressing the petals together at the base of the rose. Make leaves by first rolling out a small sheet of *chocolat plastique* and then cutting out the leaves with the tip of your paring knife.

Storage: Gather the *chocolat plastique* into a ball or pad and cover it airtight in plastic wrap. Keep at 60° to 75° F (15° to 24° C) for up to 1 or 2 months. When ready to use, place it on your countertop and work it with the heel of your hand to make it smooth and malleable again.

Nougatine

Nougatine, which is also referred to as *nougat brun,* is a mixture of caramel and sliced or chopped almonds. While hot, it can be rolled into thin sheets and cut into circles or other shapes to make bases or decorations for desserts. A hot sheet of *nougatine* can also be molded to make more elaborate pedestal bases or bowls that can serve as containers for ice creams or chocolates. The best rolling pin to use for *nougatine* is a steel one, but an old wood rolling pin will suffice if you oil it to prevent the *nougatine* from sticking to it.

For about 1 pound (450 g)

INGREDIENTS

1½ cups (300 g) sugar

1 tablespoon (20 g) glucose, or 4 teaspoons (25 g) unflavored light corn syrup

1 Oil a baking sheet or jelly-roll pan.

2 Warm the almonds in a very low (200° F, or 95° C) oven.

3 Put the sugar in a 1½- to 2-quart (1½ to 2 L) caramel pot or heavy saucepan and stir in the glucose. Cook over medium to high heat without stirring. As soon as the sugar begins to melt around the sides of the pot, begin stirring with a wooden spoon.

6 ounces (170 g) sliced almonds, coarsely chopped; or use finely chopped almonds and sift them to remove the almond powder

2 teaspoons (1 cL) lemon juice

When the sugar becomes fluid, with small lumps of unmelted sugar floating in the syrup, reduce the heat to low and continue cooking, stirring constantly and crushing the solid lumps of sugar with a wooden spoon, until the sugar is completely melted and turns a pale to medium amber.

4 Stir in the warmed almonds and the lemon juice. Continue heating, stirring with a wooden spoon, until the nuts and caramel are well mixed and hot, with the caramel syrupy.

5 Pour the *nougatine* onto the oiled baking sheet and spread it with your wooden spoon so it will cool quickly.

6 If you are preparing the *nougatine* in advance, let it cool to room temperature. If you will use the *nougatine* right away, put the baking sheet in a warm place and allow the *nougatine* to cool until it is no longer fluid but still very soft. It will be quite hot, and the hotter the *nougatine* is when you roll it the easier the rolling will be.

7 Oil your countertop. Take as much of the *nougatine* as you need for the shape you are making, lifting it with your dough scraper so you don't burn your fingers. Place the *nougatine* on the oiled countertop, and roll it into a sheet ⅛ inch (3 mm) thick with your rolling pin ①. Cut the sheet into shapes while it is still hot. To make a circle, use a flan ring, a *vol-au-vent* disk, or a round mold as a guide and cut the *nougatine* with your chef's knife. To cut triangles, first trim the sheet into a neat rectangle with your chef's knife, then cut the triangles from the rectangle with your chef's knife.

To mold pedestals and bowls in nougatine: Layer-cake pans and American pie pans are two convenient shapes, and you can use a plate to mold the lid for a bowl. Oil the mold. Carefully lift the rolled-out sheet of *nougatine* from your counter by draping it over your rolling pin. Drape the sheet over the mold, and gently press it down into the mold to shape it ②. If necessary, use a small lemon to press it into the mold. Trim the excess *nougatine* around the top of the mold with your paring knife while the *nougatine* is still hot ③.

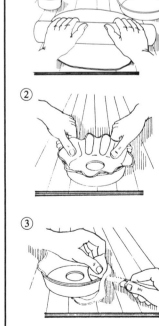

Opposite: Tarte aux cerises (cherry tarte), page 145. Following page: Tarte aux pommes (apple tarte), page 146.

8 Allow the *nougatine* to cool to room temperature before using.

Storage: After shaping, store the *nougatine* in a dry place, preferably in a tin cookie box, for up to 1 month. If it is kept too long it will tarnish.

Before shaping, cover the *nougatine* airtight in a plastic bag. It can be kept at room temperature for up to 2 or 3 months, depending on the freshness of the almonds. To use the *nougatine*, place it on an oiled baking sheet and warm it in a 250° F (120° C) oven until it is very soft. Then proceed with step 7 above.

Piped Decoration

Many pastries are embellished by piping toppings on them in decorative shapes and patterns. *Crème au beurre* and *Crème chantilly* are piped from a pastry bag, usually with a fluted pastry tube. Occasionally *meringue italienne* and *ganache* are piped in the same way. *Glace royale, pâte à écrire,* and sometimes *pâte à glacé* are used for writing on *gâteaux* with a parchment cornet or decorating tube.

TOURS DE MAIN

Rosettes and Rosaces

These are small, stylized flowerlike shapes piped from a fluted decorating tube or a small to medium-size fluted pastry tube. At a nontechnical level, the two words *rosace* and *rosette* share a common meaning in both French and English. But, to the professional pastry chef, *rosaces* is the correct term for all such piped decorations. The round, swirled pipings we refer to as "rosettes" are merely a particular type of *rosaces*.

When you are piping with a pastry tube, the topping must have the proper consistency. *Crème chantilly* and *meringue italienne* must be very stiff in order to hold a precise shape, but they must not be at all grainy. *Crème au beurre* and *ganache* must be soft-

Opposite: Tarte catalane, page 159. Preceding page: Tarte alsacienne, page 149.

ened so they can be piped, but they must still have enough consistency to hold their shape.

To pipe a rosette, hold the pastry bag nearly vertical, with the tip of the pastry tube just above the surface of the pastry you are decorating. Press on the pastry bag, and when the *crème au beurre* or *crème chantilly* spreads around the tip of the tube, slowly lift the tube at the same time as you move it in a tight circle to make an upward spiral. Finish the rosette by releasing the pressure on the pastry bag and sweeping the tip of the tube to the center of the rosette and up ①. Adjust the pressure on the pastry bag, the rate at which you move the pastry tube, and the size of the circle you move it in to get a round swirl of topping with a well-defined fluting.

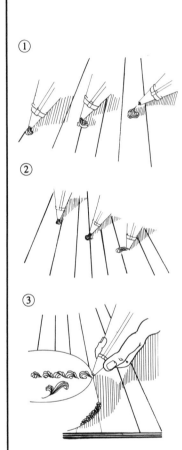

There is one other form of *rosace* we use frequently, namely the teardrop. To pipe a teardrop-shaped *rosace,* hold the pastry bag at an angle of about 60° with respect to the surface of the pastry, with the tip of the pastry tube touching the surface. Press gently on the pastry bag, start moving the tip of the pastry tube up and away from you, and then quickly move the tip in a small loop—up, back toward you, and down onto the pastry again ②. Finish by releasing the pressure on the pastry bag and drawing the tip of the pastry tube toward you to make the point of the teardrop. Adjust the pressure on the pastry bag (greatest at the beginning and middle of the motion, then decreasing quickly through the second half of the loop) and the rate at which you move the pastry tube (slow at first, more quickly as you loop up and back down, then slow again at the end) to get a teardrop with well-defined fluting ③.

How to Make and Use a Parchment Cornet

For writing and very fine decorative work, even a small pastry bag with a decorating tube is too large. You can easily make a decorating tube called a *cornet* from a piece of kitchen parchment. (You can also use waxed paper but it is more difficult to work with.) While you are at it, make at least four of them so you can master the technique more quickly and

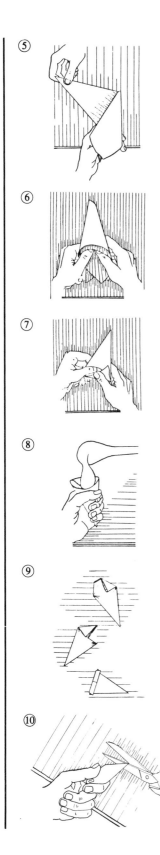

won't have to fumble with the parchment each time you need a cornet.

TO MAKE FOUR CORNETS: Cut a sheet 10 inches (25 cm) long from a 15-inch (38 cm) wide roll of kitchen parchment. Cut each sheet in half to make two 10 × 7½-inch (25×19 cm) rectangles. Cut each rectangle in half along the diagonal to make four right triangles. Place one triangle on the countertop in front of you with the 10-inch (25 cm) side on the bottom and the 7½-inch (19 cm) side on the right. Place your right hand, palm up, over the upper right corner of the triangle and grasp the corner between thumb and index finger ④. Turn your right hand over, palm down, to roll up half of the triangle into a tight cone, with the point of the cone near the center of the hypoteneuse of the triangle ⑤. With your left hand, wrap the lower left corner of the triangle around the outside of the cone. Grasp the edges of the paper between your thumbs inside the cone and your index and middle fingers outside the cone, and slide them in opposite directions to tighten the cone and give it a sharp point ⑥. The corners of the parchment will extend beyond the base of the cone. Fold the corners over and down against the inside of the cone to hold the finished cornet tightly in place ⑦. Repeat with the remaining triangles of parchment.

TO USE THE CORNET: Fill the cornet with about 1 tablespoon (1½ cL) of the topping you want to pipe ⑧. The topping must be liquid enough to pipe easily from the cornet, but just viscous enough to hold its shape and set quickly after piping.

Press the top of the cornet flat above the topping inside, and fold over the 2 top corners of the cornet to close it ⑨. Then fold over the top center in the opposite direction as the first folds to hold the cornet tightly closed. Cut the tip of the cornet to make a tiny hole ⑩.

Grasp the folded end of the cornet between the thumb and index finger of one hand, and use it to pipe writing, scrolls, or other decorations on the pastry ⑪. The topping should flow easily from the tip of the cornet with minimal pressure from your

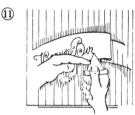

⑪ fingers. To stop the flow, turn the cornet so the tip is up.

When you are finished, empty and discard the cornet.

Pâte à Écrire

This chocolate topping is used exclusively for writing. The quantity in our recipe is quite small, but it should be enough for several *gâteaux*.

For about 3½ tablespoons (70 g)

INGREDIENTS

1 ounce (30 g) unsweetened chocolate

About 2 tablespoons (3 cL) *sirop à trente* (see page 398)

1 Gently warm the chocolate until melted. Warm the *sirop à trente*.

2 A little at a time, stir the *sirop à trente* into the melted chocolate. The chocolate will thicken and will probably seize, becoming thick and granular. Keep adding the *sirop à trente* until the chocolate becomes smooth and fluid again. Add only as much syrup as necessary to make the chocolate smooth and soft enough to pipe from a parchment cornet.

3 Transfer 2 to 3 teaspoons (1 to 1½ cL) of the *pâte à écrire* to a parchment cornet and use it right away. Let the excess *pâte à écrire* cool to room temperature and save it for later use. It is melted like ordinary chocolate.

Storage: Covered airtight, in a small container, for up to 1 week at room temperature.

Garnishes

Many ingredients are used to garnish pastries. The list includes a variety of nuts, candied fruits, confectioners sugar, cocoa powder, and chocolate sprinkles. These are all discussed in Chapter Fourteen.

Here we will explain the garnishes that require special preparation.

Sucre Filé

Sucre filé is spun sugar. The preparation is a little messy, so make it out on the back porch or on a kitchen floor covered with newspaper. You need two pieces of equipment: a wire cooling rack and an old (or inexpensive) flexible wire whisk with the wires cut off at about two thirds of their length.

Sucre filé is most often formed into a garland or pompon to veil the top of a *St.-Honoré* or *croquembouche*.

For one garland or pompon

INGREDIENTS

2½ cups (500 g) sugar

⅔ cup (1½ dL) water

⅓ cup (100 g) glucose, or 6½ tablespoons (133 g) unflavored light corn syrup

½ teaspoon (¼ cL) lemon juice

1 Wipe a large wire cooling rack with vegetable oil so the *sucre filé* won't stick to it.

2 Combine the sugar and water in a small saucepan or caramel pot and stir to thoroughly moisten the sugar. Bring to a boil over medium heat, then skim off any foam and scum that come to the surface of the syrup.

3 Add the glucose or corn syrup.

4 Continue cooking over medium heat, washing down the walls of the pot with a moistened pastry brush as needed to dissolve any sugar crystals that form there.

5 When the syrup reaches the soft crack stage, or about 270° F (135° C), add the lemon juice and reduce the heat to low.

6 Continue cooking until the syrup reaches the hard crack stage, or 300° to 305° F (150° to 152° C). It should be colorless, and, cooked to this temperature, it will give a very dry spun sugar.

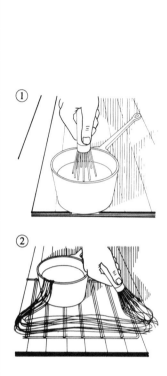

7 Immediately remove the pot from the heat and plunge the bottom of the pot in a bowl of cold water to stop the cooking. Quickly remove the pot from the water so you don't cool the syrup, and swirl the syrup in the pot for a few seconds until most of the air bubbles formed during cooking have disappeared.

8 Dip the end of your cut-off whisk in the syrup ①. Then hold the whisk vertically over the wire rack and flick the whisk back and forth across the wires of the rack. The syrup will fall through the rack in droplets. Try again every 15 to 30 seconds. As the syrup cools, it will begin to form threads across the rack when you flick it back and forth with your whisk ②. When this happens, repeatedly dip the end of the whisk in the syrup and flick it back and forth over the rack to build up a wide, feathery mesh of spun-sugar threads. If the syrup cools and thickens too much, warm it gently over low heat until it is fluid again and continue spinning the sugar.

9 Wipe a scissors with vegetable oil and use it to cut the ends of the sugar threads at the sides of the rack. Starting from one end of the rack, carefully lift the spun sugar mesh from the rack and gather it into a very loose roll of *sucre filé*. Bend the ends around in a circle to overlap each other, and shape the *sucre filé* into a garland or pompon. Work quickly before the threads harden and become brittle.

Storage: Keep the *sucre filé* dry at room temperature until ready to serve the pastry it will decorate. The *sucre filé* should easily last 6 to 12 hours if it doesn't come into contact with moisture or humidity. When ready to serve the pastry, place *sucre filé* on top.

Copeaux en Chocolat and Cigarettes en Chocolat

CHOCOLATE SHAVINGS AND CHOCOLATE CIGARETTES

These are easiest to make on a marble slab, but if necessary you can work on a Formica countertop or a black steel baking sheet. You will need a very flexible putty knife with a blade 3½ to 5 inches (9 to 13 cm) wide. You can also shave chocolate directly from a solid block using a paring knife or a swivel bladed vegetable peeler; this is easier for a small quantity of shavings, but the shavings won't look as good as the *copeaux en chocolat* made by the method described below.

For forty to fifty cigarettes or 3 ounces (85 g) of shavings

INGREDIENTS

3 ounces (85 g)
  semisweet chocolate

Optional: Up to ⅓
  ounce (10 g) cocoa
  butter

1 Temper the chocolate as follows: Melt the chocolate. Dip the bottom of the pot of chocolate in cold water, and stir until it begins to thicken. Immediately return it to the heat and gently warm the chocolate a second time, stirring constantly until just melted again.

2 Optional: If you are using a chocolate that is low in cocoa butter, dip the bottom of the pot of chocolate in warm water and shave the cocoa butter into the tempered chocolate with your paring knife. Stir until the cocoa butter melts and is thoroughly mixed with the chocolate.

3 Pour the chocolate onto a marble slab. Spread and smooth the chocolate into a thin layer with your palette knife. Press firmly on the face of the blade and sweep the blade back and forth until the chocolate covers a rough rectangle about 18 × 12 inches (45 × 30 cm) and the surface of the chocolate is smooth ①. Allow the chocolate to cool until it is no longer liquid and is beginning to set.

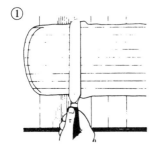

4 You will form the shavings or cigarettes by scraping the chocolate off the marble slab with your putty knife, holding the blade at a 30° angle with respect to the slab and pushing it away from you— like shoveling snow. The chocolate must be at just the right consistency in order to produce the desired result. When the chocolate is too warm and soft it will gather into a mass and stick to the putty knife. As it cools to the right temperature, the chocolate will come off the slab in a thin, pleated sheet that holds its shape and doesn't stick to the putty knife. Whenever any chocolate sticks to the blade of the putty knife, scrap it off with your palette knife or a dough scraper.

5 Cigarettes en chocolat: To make cigarettes, the chocolate must cool a little more, until when you scrape it off the marble slab it rolls up into a cylinder rather than forming a pleated sheet. As soon as this begins to happen, place the edge of your putty knife on the layer of chocolate about ¾ to 1 inch (2 to 2½ cm) in from the far side. Hold the handle of the putty knife in one hand and press down on the center of the blade with the other. Push the putty knife forward to roll the chocolate into a cigarette as long as your putty knife is wide ②. Lift the putty knife, place the blade ¾ to 1 inch (2 to 2½ cm) in from the new far edge of the chocolate, and repeat. Continue, working quickly and rythmically, until all of the chocolate has been rolled into cigarettes.

②

Copeaux en chocolat: For chocolate shavings, the consistency of the chocolate isn't quite so crucial as for cigarettes. The best is to let the chocolate cool on the marble a little more than for cigarettes. Then shave the chocolate off the marble like planing wood. It will shatter and flake into small to medium-size shavings. If the chocolate is too warm and soft when you shave it and forms sheets or rolls into cigarettes, allow them to cool completely and then coarsely chop them with your dough scraper to shatter the chocolate into shavings.

Storage: After cooling, cover airtight and keep at 60°-75° F (15°-24° C) for 1 or 2 months.

Feuilles à Noëlla

These small chocolate petals are designed to decorate a *gâteau* called *noëlla*, but they can be used on other *gâteaux* as well. To make them you will need a small, very flexible 4-inch (10 cm) palette knife. You can also decorate the bases of *gâteaux* with larger petals using an 8-inch (20 cm) palette knife.

For about 100 petals

INGREDIENTS

2 ounces (55 g)
  semisweet chocolate

1 Temper the chocolate as follows: Melt the chocolate. Dip the bottom of the pot of chocolate in cold water, and stir until it begins to thicken. Immediate-

Optional: Up to ¼ ounce (7 g) cocoa butter

ly return it to the heat and gently warm the chocolate a second time, stirring constantly until just melted again.

2 Optional: Ideally, you should add some cocoa butter to the chocolate to make it set more quickly and give it more sheen and bite. Dip the bottom of the pot of chocolate in warm water to keep it from cooling, and shave some cocoa butter into the tempered chocolate with your paring knife. Stir until the cocoa butter melts and is thoroughly mixed with the chocolate.

3 Have ready several sheets of waxed paper on your countertop. Place the pot of chocolate on your counter and tilt it by placing a small mold under one side so you can easily dip the tip of your palette knife in the chocolate. Lightly touch the face of the blade on the chocolate in the pot and clean any excess chocolate off the edges of the blade by wiping them on the edge of the pot. Make a petal on a sheet of waxed paper by pressing the chocolate coated face of the blade on it, bending the blade slightly and dragging it toward you ①. The petal should be about ¾ to 1 inch (2 to 2½ cm) wide, 1 to 1¼ inches (2½ to 3 cm) long, and less than ¹⁄₁₆ inch (1½ mm) thick, with the center thinner than the edges. Continue making petals in this fashion until there is no longer enough chocolate in the pot to dip your palette knife in. If the chocolate begins to thicken, gently warm it to keep it fluid so that the petals will be thin and have a smooth surface. Don't worry if the petals vary in size, since you can take advantage of this variation when you decorate with them. When you have finished, any chocolate remaining in the pot can be used for chocolate shavings or cigarettes.

4 Allow the petals to cool and set.

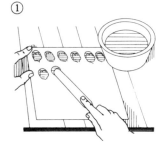

Storage: Cut the sheets of waxed paper to the size of a tin cookie box or plastic freezer storage container, and store the *feuilles à noëlla* on the paper sheets in the box, covered airtight, so they don't get damaged. Keep at 60° to 75° F (15° to 24° C) for up to 1 or 2 months. When ready to use, carefully peel them off the paper.

Sauces

Sauces are rather different from our other toppings, since they aren't actually part of the construction of pastries. Instead, they are served separately in a sauceboat to accompany such desserts as charlottes, *bavarois,* kugelhopf, *diplomate, savarins,* and *biscuit de Savoie.*

Crème Anglaise

This delicate, egg-thickened custard sauce also serves as a base for some fillings, such as *crème bavaroise.* Unlike *crème pâtissière,* it contains no starch and must not be boiled or it will curdle. The more egg yolks you put in the *crème anglaise,* the thicker it will be. However a *crème anglaise* made with a larger number of yolks will curdle more easily. When making *crème anglaise* as a sauce, use the minimum number of egg yolks in our recipe.

For 3½ to 4 cups (8 to 10 dL)

INGREDIENTS

2 cups (½ L) milk
One quarter to one
 half vanilla bean
¾ cup (150 g) sugar
6 to 8 large egg
 yolks

1 Pour the milk into a 1½- to 2-quart (1½ to 2 L) saucepan. Slit the vanilla bean lengthwise and scrape out the seeds into the milk. Add the pod to the milk and bring it to a simmer.

2 Meanwhile, beat together the egg yolks and sugar with a wire whisk until smooth and lemon colored. Slowly pour in about half the simmering milk, stirring constantly with the wire whisk. Pour this mixture back into the saucepan and stir until thoroughly blended.

3 Place the saucepan over low heat and, stirring constantly with a wooden spoon, bring the *crème anglaise* almost to a simmer. Turn down the heat to very low and continue cooking, stirring constantly with the wooden spoon, until the custard coats the back of the wooden spoon and the bubbles formed when you stirred the milk and yolks together have disappeared. The custard has thickened sufficiently when, if you draw a line across the back of the custard coated spoon with your fingertip, the custard won't flow back over the line ①.

4 Remove the saucepan from the heat immediately and strain the *crème anglaise* through a sieve into a stainless-steel bowl. Set the bowl of *crème anglaise* in crushed ice or ice water, and cool the *crème anglaise,* stirring occasionally. Cooling the *crème anglaise* quickly prevents bacteria from developing.

5 Chill the *crème anglaise* either by continuing to stir it over the ice or by placing in the refrigerator.

Note: If the egg yolks just began to curdle in step 3, and the *crème anglaise* is grainy, you may be able to salvage it by puréeing in an electric blender after cooling. If that doesn't produce a smooth, velvety sauce that holds itself together, then you have overcooked the sauce and must discard it.

Storage: The *crème anglaise* is best served as soon as it has been chilled. However, you can keep it in the refrigerator, covered airtight for up to 2 or 3 days, if necessary.

Coulis des Fruits

These are just sweetened fruit purées. They are usually made from strawberries or raspberries, and sometimes sour cherries. Fresh fruits are best, but you can also use frozen ones if you reduce the amount of sugar in the recipe to compensate for the sugar used in freezing.

In addition to their primary function as sauces, *coulis des fruits* serve as bases for some *fruit mousses* (see pages 96–97).

For about 2¼ to 2½ cups (5.4 to 6 dL)

COULIS DE FRAISE

1¼ pints (560 g) fresh strawberries

½ cup (100 g) superfine sugar

3 tablespoons (4½ cL) fresh orange juice

1 Hull the strawberries or stone the cherries.

2 Purée the fruit with the sugar in an electric blender or food processor, adding the orange juice or kirsch to enhance the fruit flavor.

3 Strain the puréed fruit through a fine sieve to eliminate the raspberry seeds, cherry skins, or any

127

COULIS DE FRAMBOISE

1 pint (500 g) fresh
  raspberries
½ cup plus 2
  tablespoons (125 g)
  superfine sugar
3 tablespoons (4½
  cL) fresh orange
  juice

COULIS DE CERISE

1½ pounds (675 g)
  fresh sour cherries
½ cup plus 2
  tablespoons (125 g)
  superfine sugar
Optional: 1
  tablespoon (1½ cL)
  kirsch

hard unripe pieces of strawberry.

Storage: Covered airtight, in the refrigerator for up to 2 or 3 days. Or freeze for as long as 2 or 3 months. If frozen, defrost overnight in the refrigerator before using.

Sauce au Chocolat

This is the classic sauce to serve with *poires Belle Hélène* or *profiteroles*. It also goes well with *charlotte poire*.

For about 1½ cups (3½ dL)

INGREDIENTS

½ pound (225 g)
  semisweet chocolate
½ cup (1.2 dL)
  boiling water
2 tablespoons (30 g)
  butter, softened

1 Finely chop the chocolate with your chef's knife, and put it in a small bowl.

2 A tablespoon (1½ cL) at a time, add the boiling water to the chocolate, stirring constantly with a wire whisk. When you have added all of the water, continue stirring until the chocolate is completely melted and smooth. If necessary, gently warm the sauce while stirring to finish melting the chocolate.

3 Add the softened butter and stir until it is melted and the sauce is smooth.

4 Serve the *sauce au chocolat* while it is warm.

Storage: Covered airtight, in the refrigerator for up to 3 days. When ready to serve, melt the sauce over hot water.

PART

PASTRIES

Chapter Five

TARTES

*T*artes are the French equivalents of pies and tarts. They have a pastry shell with some filling and, most commonly, fruit on top. The fruit can be coated with jam, jelly, confectioners sugar, or caramel. Occasionally, the fruit goes under the filling, or there is no filling at all. And there are even almond cream *tartes* with no fruit at all.

Whatever the fruit and filling, the techniques for preparing the *tarte* shell are always the same. This first step has an undeserved reputation for being difficult.

In this chapter, pastry doughs refer to *pâtes à foncer* and *rognures,* unless otherwise stated. *Feuilletage* and *pâte à brioche* are rolled and shaped in the same way, subject to the precautions mentioned on pages 161–162 and 195–197 of the chapters on *feuilletés* and *brioches,* respectively.

For most dessert *tartes,* you should use *pâte à foncer spéciale, rognures,* or *pâte sablée,* depending on how sweet you want the shell to be and whether you want it to be flaky or crisp like a sweet cookie. *Pâte sucrée* is used primarily for almond cream *tartes.*

TOURS DE MAIN

Rolling out Pastry Doughs *(Abaissage)*

The pastry dough should be firm but not too hard when you roll it out. Unless your kitchen is warm (in which case it is essential that the dough be rolled out as quickly as possible to prevent it from warming and softening too much), remove the dough from the refrigerator about 30 minutes before you intend to roll it. The best work surface is a cool marble slab, but an ordinary Formica countertop is more than adequate.

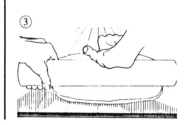

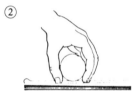

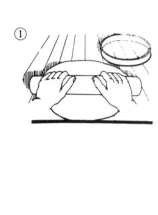

Lightly dust your countertop and the pad of dough with flour. Place the center of your rolling pin on the end of the pad nearest you, and, pressing down firmly and evenly, roll it in a smooth forward motion to (but not over) the far end of the dough ①. Then reverse direction and roll the rolling pin in a smooth backward motion to the end of the pad nearest you. Rotate the pad and roll it forward and backward again. Continue rolling the dough, rotating it after each forward and backward motion, into a rough circular or rectangular sheet about ½ inch (12 mm) thick. Dust the counter and the dough with flour as needed to prevent the dough from sticking to countertop or rolling pin.

Next you should alter the backward part of the rolling motion so it levels out irregularities in the thickness of the dough, while the forward motion continues to flatten the dough into a progressively larger and thinner sheet. Arch your hands over the rolling pin, with your fingertips touching the far side of the counter and the tips of your thumbs touching the near side ②. Keeping the tips of your fingers and thumbs on the counter and letting the rolling pin slip in your palms, roll the rolling pin back over the dough to the end nearest you to flatten any bumps in the dough and even its thickness. You must have just the right amount of flour between the dough and countertop. Too little flour and the dough will stick to the counter and stretch or tear; but too much flour will make the dough slide across the counter as you try to level it. This backward motion should not be used on *feuilletage, rognures,* or *pâte à brioche* because the strength and elasticity of these doughs require more downward pressure than you can apply with this motion.

Continue rolling the sheet of dough and rotating it after each forward and backward motion, occasionally lifting the dough from the counter and dusting both counter and dough with flour to prevent the dough from sticking to counter or rolling pin, until the dough is about ⅛ inch (3 mm) thick. Always roll with a firm, even motion so you don't stretch or tear the dough ③. If the dough becomes too warm and soft before you reach this thickness, place it on a baking sheet and refrigerate for 10 to 15 minutes before proceeding. If you find it too difficult to roll the dough to a thickness of ⅛ inch (3 mm), then try a thickness of 3/16 inch (5 mm), using a larger quantity of dough. As you become more experienced, you can gradually decrease the thickness to ⅛ inch (3 mm). Be especially careful with *pâte sablée* and *pâte sucrée*, which are more fragile than the other pastry doughs and therefore more difficult to handle when they are rolled this thin.

Cut the dough to the required size and shape with the tip of a paring knife, using a flan ring, a *vol-au-vent* disc, or a straightedge as a guide. Or make straight-line cuts with your chef's knife: place the tip of the blade on the countertop and cut through the dough by pressing down on the handle, pivoting the blade from the tip ④. If you have a pastry cutter of the required size and shape, place it on the dough and press down firmly to cut the dough.

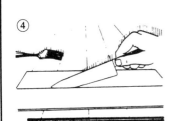

Form the cut dough immediately; or, if it is too soft to handle, slide it onto a baking sheet and refrigerate for about 20 minutes before molding.

Gather the excess dough together into a ball and flatten the ball into a thick pad. Add more trimmings to the pad each time you make a *tarte* until you accumulate enough to make a *tarte* shell; or combine the trimmings with another pad of the pastry dough.

Forming Tarte Shells
(*Fonçage des Tartes*)

TARTES RONDES (ROUND TARTES): Brush the inside of a flan ring with melted butter; or take a small piece of butter on the middle of your index and middle fingers and rub the inside of the flan ring with it. This helps the pastry stick to the ring while you are lining it and prevents the pastry from sticking.

Depending on your skill, you will need 11½ to 16 ounces (325 to 450 g) of *pâte à foncer* (see pages 5–7) or *rognures* (see page 24) to line a 9½-inch (24 cm) flan ring. An 8-inch (20 cm) flan ring will require 9 to 12 ounces (250 to 340 g) of dough, and an 11-inch (28 cm) ring 14 to 19 ounces (400 to 550 g) of dough.

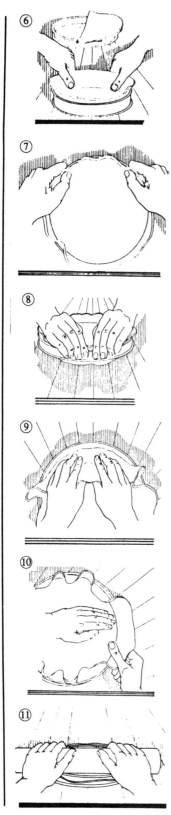

Roll out the dough into a rough circle about 4 inches (10 cm) larger in diameter than the ring. From this rough circle, cut a true circle 3 to 3½ inches (8 to 9 cm) larger in diameter than the ring, using a larger ring as a guide ⑤.

Place the buttered flan ring on the floured counter-top. Fold the circle of pastry in half, lift it from the counter, and center it on the ring. Unfold the dough and ease it down into the ring, rotating the ring as you proceed ⑥.

To help prevent the side of the *tarte* shell from slipping down as it bakes, you must make the side form a right angle with the base of the *tarte* shell, eliminating any air space between the pastry and the flan ring. Lift the far side of the ring off the counter a little and place the fingertips of both hands under that side of the ring ⑦. Use your thumbs to slide the pastry (don't stretch it) down the inside of the ring to your fingertips so the pastry reaches just past the bottom of the ring ⑧. As you work, alternately rotate the ring and press the ring down on the counter to finish the bottom edge of the pastry flush against the counter.

Alternatively, instead of lifting the edge of the ring off the counter, you can fold the far side of the pastry back away from the ring and press down on the fold with your fingertips to pinch it and press it into the corner where the ring meets the counter ⑨. Then press the pastry back against the inside of the ring ⑩. Work around the circumference, rotating the ring as you go.

By either method, the dough should now be flush against the countertop and ring should extend ½ to ¾ inch (12 to 20 mm) above the upper edge of the ring. For *tartes* that will be filled flush with the top of the ring (primarily almond cream *tartes*), drape the excess dough over the top of the ring and trim it off by rolling your rolling pin over the top of the ring ⑪. For other *tartes*, the extra pastry will become a rim.

To form the rim, bend and fold the pastry extending above the ring to form a double thickness of pastry about ¼ inch (6 mm) wide extending over the inside

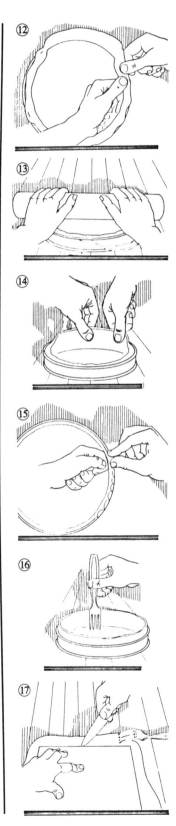

edge of the *tarte* shell. Pinch this lip between the fingertips of one hand (inside the ring, under the lip) and the thumb of the other (on top of the lip), rotating the ring as you work around the circumference of the *tarte* shell, to get a lip of uniform thickness ⑫. Trim off any excess pastry by rolling the rolling pin over the top of the ring ⑬. Then take the lip between your thumbs and fingertips and, rotating the ring as you work around the *tarte* shell, raise the lip to form an even rim around the top ⑭.

You can now flute the rim if you wish. There are several methods. One is to hold the rim between the fingertips of one hand to support it while you press down against it on the diagonal with the dull edge of a paring knife, repeating at ¼ inch (6 mm) intervals around the rim. Another is to pinch the rim between your fingertips ⑮.

Slide the pastry-lined ring onto a heavy baking sheet. Prick the bottom of the *tarte* shell all over with a fork to prevent trapped air bubbles from deforming the shell as it bakes ⑯.

TARTES CARRÉES (SQUARE TARTES): For square *tarte* shells you will need to roll out a square sheet of *spéciale* (see page 5), *sablée* (see page 7), or *rognures* (see page 24) for the base and strips of *feuilletage* (see page 18) for the rim. You will need only a very small quantity of *feuilletage*, so we recommend preparing these *tartes* on the same day as you prepare some pastry requiring a larger quantity of *feuilletage* (see Chapter Six on *feuilletés*).

Depending on your skill, you will need about 10½ to 14 ounces (300 to 400 g) of *spéciale, sablée,* or *rognures* for the base of a 9½-inch (24 cm) square *tarte* shell. For other sizes, decrease or increase the quantity accordingly.

Roll out the pastry dough for the base into a rough square a little larger than the size you want. Using a straightedge as a guide, cut from it a precise square of dough with your chef's knife ⑰. Prick the square all over with a fork.

Brush a heavy baking sheet with cold water. Fold the square in half and lift it from your countertop. Center it on the baking sheet and unfold it. The water makes the square stick to the baking sheet while you assemble the rim of the *tarte* shell.

Roll out some *feuilletage* into a sheet about ⅛ inch (3 mm) thick. Fold this sheet in half (so you can make a short cut to get a long strip) and, using a straightedge as a guide, cut it perpendicular to the fold to get four strips, each about ¾ inch (2 cm) wide and at least as long as the square base. Use the rest of the *feuilletage* for another purpose or for *rognures*.

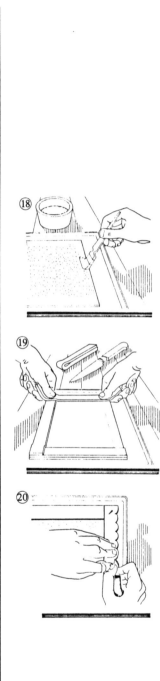

Unfold the strips of *feuilletage* and cut them to the precise length of the square base. Brush a band ¾ inch (2 cm) wide around the perimeter of the base with a little water or beaten egg ⑱. Starting at one corner and working around the square, lay the *feuilletage* strips on the brushed edge of the square ⑲. Brush the end of each strip with water or beaten egg before you add the next strip, and press the corner gently with your thumb so the overlapping strips will adhere. Pierce all of the finished corners with the tip of a paring knife.

Chiqueter the edge of the pastry. That is, make a toothlike pattern around the outside edge by gently pressing the tips of the index and middle fingers of one hand on top of the *feuilletage* strip at the edge to hold it in place while you press the dull edge of a paring knife against the edge of the pastry between your fingertips ⑳. Work around the outside edge of the *tarte* shell, separating the indentations by about 1 inch (2½ cm).

Brush the tops (but not the sides) of the *feuilletage* strips with a little beaten egg.

BANDES DE TARTE (TARTE STRIPS): This variant of the square *tarte* is easier to cut into serving pieces.

The size *bande de tarte* you can make is determined by the length of your baking sheet. For a *bande* 15 inches (38 cm) long you will need about 10½ to 14 ounces (300 to 400 g) of *spéciale* (see page 5), *sablée* (see page 7), or *rognures* (see page 24) for the base.

Roll out the pastry dough into a rough rectangle the length of your baking sheet and 6 to 7 inches (15 to 18 cm) wide. Using a straight edge as a guide, cut from it a rectangle 5 to 6 inches (13 to 15 cm) wide and about 1 inch (2½ cm) shorter than the baking sheet. Prick it all over with a fork. Brush your baking sheet with cold water. Fold the rectangle in half and lift it from your countertop. Place it on the baking sheet and unfold it.

Roll out some *feuilletage* into a sheet about ⅛ inch (3 mm) thick, fold it in half, and cut from it two strips, each about ¾ inches (2 cm) wide and at least as long as the baking sheet. Unfold the strips and cut them to the precise length of the rectangular base.

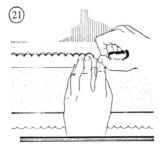

Brush a strip ¾ inch (2 cm) wide on each long side of the base with a little water or beaten egg and lay the *feuilletage* strips on top. The short ends of the *bande* are left open.

Chiqueter the sides (but not the ends) of the *bande* as for square *tartes* ㉑, and brush the tops of the *feuilletage* strips with a little beaten egg.

The Rest Before Baking (*Repos*)

Depending on which fruit and filling you are using, you can bake the *tarte* shell before filling *(cuisson à blanc),* or you can fill the raw *tarte* shell and bake the fruit in the shell. In either case, let the *tarte* shell rest in the refrigerator for at least 30 minutes after it is formed and before baking or filling so that the gluten in the flour will relax and the pastry will not shrink while baking.

About Tarte Sizes

We have given the recipes in this chapter for 9½-inch (24 cm) round or square *tartes* or 15-inch (38 cm) long *bandes de tarte*. The quantities of filling, fruit, and topping for these are approximately the same. For other sizes, a good general rule is that an 8-inch (20 cm) round or square *tarte* requires about 30 percent less of all components than the 9½-inch (24 cm) size, whereas an 11-inch (28 cm) round or square *tarte* requires about 35 percent more of all components than the 9½-inch (24 cm) size. For a 19-inch (48 cm) *bande de tarte,* expect to use 30 percent more of all components than for a 15-inch (38 cm) *bande.*

For other sizes and for special shapes, use the thickness of the pastry and filling, the appearance of the fruit on the *tarte,* and your own judgment, rather than measuring weights and volumes, to determine how much to use. With experience, you will find this faster and more convenient even for sizes where we provide accurate measures.

STORAGE

Fruit *tartes* are fresh pastries that should be eaten soon after they are made. As a general rule, they should be kept uncovered at room temperature for no longer than 12 hours, and less if the fruit is juicy or if the crust is made from *pâte sablée.* Do not refrigerate fruit *tartes* or keep them longer, or they will become soggy. Some *tartes*—notably *tarte Tatin* and fruit *tartes* with *pâte sucrée* bases—are even more perishable, while, on the other hand, almond cream *tartes* can be covered with waxed paper and refrigerated for up to 2 or 3 days before glazing. Before filling, prebaked *tarte* shells can be stored, uncovered, at room temperature and in a dry place for 2 or 3 days.

Fruit Tartes in Prebaked Shells

Tarte shells are prebaked (baked blind, or *à blanc* in French) when they will be filled with fruits that would suffer in taste or appearance if baked in the shell. These include bananas, pineapples, grapes, red currants, and most berries. Some fresh fruits, such as lemons, can be baked or not, according to your preference.

When using canned fruits, choose fruits in heavy syrup (those in light syrup aren't sweet enough). The ones we find most successful are pineapples and peaches. Drain the fruits thoroughly so the syrup doesn't soak the *tarte* shell.

General Recipe

For 6 to 8 people

INGREDIENTS

An unbaked 9½-inch (24 cm) round or square *tarte* shell or a 15-inch (38 cm) *bande de tarte* (see pages 135–139)

Lightly beaten egg for brushing

1 cup (270 g) *crème pâtissière* (see page 83), or other filling

1 tablespoon (1½ cL) kirsch, dark rum, or other liqueur

Fruit (quantities and treatments specified below)

3½ to 5 tablespoons (70 to 100 g) red currant jelly or strained apricot jam

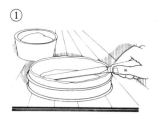

1 Preheat the oven to 450° F (230° C).

2 Line the inside of the *tarte* shell with tissue paper and fill it with rice, dried beans, or fruit stones to prevent the pastry dough from rising unevenly.

3 Place the *tarte* shell in the oven and reduce the heat to 425° F (220° C). Bake until the rim is light brown, 15 to 20 minutes.

4 Take the *tarte* shell from the oven and remove the tissue paper and rice. The inside of the shell will still be a pale cream color. Brush the inside of the shell with just enough beaten egg to coat it lightly and seal it.

5 Return the *tarte* shell to the oven until the inside is a uniform light brown, dry, crisp, and shiny, about 3 to 5 minutes.

6 Slide the *tarte* shell onto a cooling rack. If the shell was formed in a flan ring, carefully remove the ring. Let cool to room temperature.

7 Flavor the *crème pâtissière* with kirsch or dark rum.

8 Spread a layer of *crème pâtissière* ¼ inch (6 mm) thick over the bottom of the *tarte* shell ①.

9 Arrange the fruit over the *crème pâtissière*. Place whole fruits adjacent to each other ②. For sliced fruits in round *tarte* shells, arrange the slices in concentric circles, starting from the outside and overlapping the slices as you go ③; in square *tarte* shells or *bandes de tarte,* start from one corner and arrange the slices in alternating diagonal rows, like fish scales ④.

10 For red or dark-colored fruits, pass the red currant jelly through a fine sieve. For other fruits, warm the apricot jam over low heat, stirring occasionally, until melted.

141

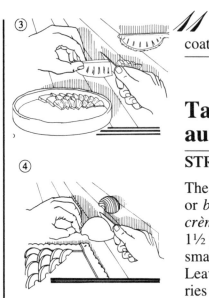

③

④

Brush the fruits with the jam or jelly until lightly coated and glistening.

Tarte aux Fraises and Tarte aux Framboises

STRAWBERRY AND RASPBERRY

These are especially nice in a thin square *tarte* shell or *bande de tarte* with a *rognures* base. Flavor the *crème pâtissière* with kirsch. You will need about 1½ pints (600 g) of strawberries or raspberries, and small strawberries are preferable to large ones. Leave small strawberries whole. Cut large strawberries in half and arrange them cut side down.

Tarte aux Raisins

GRAPE

Flavor the *crème pâtissière* with Cognac or other grape brandy. You will need about 1 pound (450 g) of grapes, preferably seedless. Glaze the grapes with apricot jam or red currant jelly, depending on color.

Tarte aux Groseilles

RED CURRANT

Fill a round *pâte sablée* shell with a layer ¾ inch (2 cm) thick of *crème chiboust* (about 3 cups, or 375 g, see page 93), omitting the liqueur flavoring. You will need about 2 cups (300 g) of red currants to cover the *crème chiboust*. If you like, you can omit the glaze of red currant jelly and instead dust the currants with about 2 tablespoons (20 g) of confectioners sugar just before serving.

Tarte aux Myrtilles

BLUEBERRY

Same as strawberry and raspberry *tartes* above. If you prefer, you can glaze the fruits with blueberry jelly instead of red currant jelly. You can also treat blueberries in the same way as red currants, especially if the blueberries are very tart.

Tarte aux Bananes

BANANA

Flavor the *crème pâtissière* with dark rum. Peel 4 ripe bananas and slice them ¼ inch (6 mm) thick. If the bananas aren't quite ripe enough, poach the slices in *sirop léger* (see page 422) for a few minutes until they are no longer hard; then cool in the syrup and drain well before proceeding.

Tarte aux Ananas

PINEAPPLE

Flavor the *crème pâtissière* with dark rum or kirsch. Peel and core one pineapple. Quarter it lengthwise and cut each quarter into slices ¼ inch (6 mm) thick. Unless the pineapple is extremely ripe and sweet, poach the slices in *sirop léger* (see page 422) until tender, 10 to 15 minutes; then cool in the syrup and drain well before proceeding.

Tarte au Citron

LEMON

To balance the tartness of the lemon, use a round *pâte sablée* shell. Fill it almost to the rim with a mixture of equal parts *crème pâtissière* and lemon curd (see page 91), and omit the liqueur flavoring. You will need about 2½ to 3 cups (675 to 800 g) of filling. For this *tarte* the fruit is used only as decoration. Arrange 8 candied lemon slices (see page 424)—one for each serving—in a circle on top of the *tarte*. Do not overlap the slices or the *tarte* will be difficult to cut at serving time. Omit the jam glaze and dust the *tarte* with 2 tablespoons (20 g) of confectioners sugar just before serving.

Tarte aux Kiwis

KIWI

Flavor the *crème pâtissière* with Grand Marnier. Peel 6 to 8 kiwis, cut them in half lengthwise, and slice them ¼ inch (6 mm) thick. Kiwis are very decorative in combination with other fruits (such as pineapples or bananas).

Fruit Tartes Baked in the Shell

Fresh apples, pears, cherries, apricots, plums, and peaches are always baked in the shell. You can also bake fresh oranges and lemons. Canned pears, peaches, apricots, and cherries in light syrup work well when good fresh ones are unavailable, but drain them thoroughly so the syrup doesn't soak the *tarte* shell. Canned fruits in heavy syrup should never be baked because their high sugar content makes them brown too much.

General Recipe

For 6 to 8 people

INGREDIENTS

1 cup (270 g) *crème pâtissière*, (see page 83), *crème d'amandes* (see page 87), or other filling

An unbaked 9½-inch (24 cm) round or square *tarte* shell or a 15-inch (38 cm) *bande de tarte* (see pages 135–139)

Fruit (quantities and treatments specified below)

2 tablespoons to ½ cup (25 to 100 g) superfine sugar

3½ to 5 tablespoons (70 to 100 g) red currant jelly or strained apricot jam

1 Preheat the oven to 425° F (220° C).

2 Spread a layer of *crème pâtissière* or other filling ¼ inch (6 mm) thick over the bottom of the *tarte* shell ①.

3 Arrange the fruit over the filling. Place whole fruits adjacent to each other ②. Arrange half fruits cut side up, in concentric circles for round *tartes* ③ or alternating rows for square *tartes* or *bandes de tarte*; tilt the fruit halves and overlap them. For sliced fruits in round *tarte* shells, arrange the slices in concentric circles, starting from the outside and overlapping the slices as you go ④; in square *tarte* shells or *bandes de tarte,* start from one corner and arrange the slices in overlapping diagonal rows like fish scales ⑤.

4 Dust the superfine sugar over the fruit. Adjust the amount of sugar according to the sweetness of the fruit. For most fruits, the minimum 2 tablespoons (25 g) is about right.

5 Place the *tarte* in the oven, and reduce the temperature to 400° F (200° C). Bake until the rim of the *tarte* shell browns lightly, 20 to 25 minutes. Reduce the oven to 350° F (180° C) and continue baking at least 20 minutes longer. When the *tarte* has been in

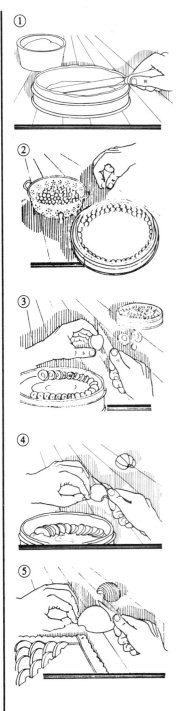

the oven for 40 minutes, carefully lift one side of the *tarte* off the baking sheet, using a wide dough scraper or pancake turner, so you can check the color of the bottom of the crust. The *tarte* is done when the crust is a uniform light brown and any juice that has been exuded by the fruit has evaporated so the top of the *tarte* is dry. The total baking time may be as short as 40 minutes or, if the fruit is very juicy, as long as 1½ hours. If the fruit cooks before the bottom of the crust is browned, place a sheet of buttered kitchen parchment on top to prevent the fruit from burning.

6 Remove the *tarte* from the oven. If juice from the fruit has overflowed the shell and the crust sticks to the ring or baking sheet, carefully separate the crust from the flan ring with the tip of a paring knife or from the baking sheet with a dough scraper or pancake turner. Slide the *tarte* onto a cooling rack. If it was formed in a ring, carefully remove the ring. Let cool to room temperature.

7 For cherries, pass the red currant jelly through a sieve. For other fruits, warm the strained apricot jam over low heat, stirring occasionally, until it is melted.

8 Brush the fruit with the jam or jelly until lightly coated and glistening.

Tarte aux Cerises

CHERRY

Sour cherries are best for baking. You will need about 1 pound 6 ounces (600 g) of them. You can bake them raw; or you can poach them first for 5 to 10 minutes in *sirop léger* (see page 422), allowing them to cool in the syrup and draining thoroughly before proceeding. Poached cherries do not exude as much liquid during baking as raw ones, but they are less flavorful and have less color.

Pit the cherries with a hair pin or cherry pitter. Use about ¼ cup (50 g) of superfine sugar to dust raw cherries before baking, and less for poached cherries.

Tarte aux Pommes

APPLE

According to your preference, you can fill the *tarte* with *crème pâtissière, compôte de pommes* (see page 88), or *crème d'amandes*. Peel and core 4 or 5 tart medium cooking apples. Cut them in half and then cut each half into slices or wedges ¼ inch (6 mm) thick with a paring knife. Arrange the slices over the filling. If you are making a round *tarte*, save half of a small apple for the center and slice it thin, perpendicular to the core, without separating the slices. Leave a space in the center when you arrange the other slices over the filling, then finish by placing the reserved sliced apple half in the middle and pressing it gently to fan out the slices like a deck of cards.

Bake the *tarte* until the apples are tender and lightly browned, about 45 minutes. It can be served either hot or cold. If you want to eat the *tarte* hot, dust the top with 2 tablespoons (20 g) of confectioners sugar after you have removed it from the oven and omit the jam glaze. Otherwise, cool and glaze as usual.

Tarte aux Poires

PEAR

Make a round *pâte sablée* shell with a filling of *crème d'amandes*. Peel and core 4 or 5 firm, unblemished ripe pears. Bartletts are best, then Comice and d'Anjou pears. If the pears are hard, poach them in *sirop léger* (see page 422) until they can be pierced easily with a skewer, 5 to 15 minutes; then cool in the syrup and drain well before proceeding.

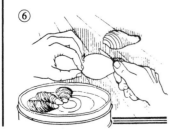

Cut the pears in half lengthwise if you have not already done so, and cut each half crosswise (perpendicular to the core) into slices ¼ inch (6 mm) thick, without separating the slices. Arrange the sliced pear halves on the *crème d'amandes* filling, radiating out from the center like the spokes of a wheel, with the stem ends nearest the center of the *tarte* ⑥. Place a small sliced pear half that is close to round in shape in the center. Press down gently on the top of each pear half to fan out the slices like a deck of cards.

As the *tarte* bakes, the pears will sink down into the *crème d'amandes*. It is ready when the tops of the pears and the *crème d'amandes* are lightly browned. The total baking time should be about 45 minutes, or a little longer if the pears are especially ripe and juicy.

Tarte aux Pêches

PEACH

Choose 4 to 6 firm, ripe, unblemished freestone peaches. If they are hard, poach them in *sirop léger* (see page 422) until they can be pierced easily with a skewer, 5 to 15 minutes; then cool in the syrup and drain well before proceeding.

Peel the peaches, cut them in half, and remove the pits. Cut each half into wedges or slices 1/4 inch (6 mm) thick with a paring knife. Arrange the slices over a *crème pâtissière* or *crème d'amandes* filling.

Tarte aux Abricots

APRICOT

Cut 15 to 20 apricots in half and remove the pits. Arrange the apricot halves, cut side up, over the *crème pâtissière*, tilting and overlapping them. Unless the apricots are exceptionally sweet, use the maximum 1/2 cup (100 g) of superfine sugar to dust them before baking.

Tarte aux Prunes

PLUM

Small plums, such as Italian prune plums or blood plums, are best, and you will need about 30 of them. Since plums are extremely juicy, it is a good idea to poach them in *sirop léger* (see page 422) for about 10 minutes; then cool them in the syrup and drain thoroughly. If the plums are not poached, the *tarte* will have to be baked much longer to dry them.

Cut the plums in half and remove the pits. Arrange the plum halves, cut side up, over the *crème pâtissière*, tilting and overlapping them. Use about 1/4 cup (50 g) of superfine sugar to dust the plums before baking. Omit the jam glaze, and just before serving, dust the *tarte* with 2 tablespoons (20 g) of confectioners sugar.

Tarte aux Oranges

ORANGE

You will need 4 to 6 large navel oranges. Grate the aromatic zest from the outside of one of the oranges. Flavor the *crème pâtissière* with the grated zest and about 2 tablespoons (3 cL) of curaçao or other orange liqueur. Peel the oranges, removing all of the bitter white pith. Cut each orange in half through the core. Then slice each half, perpendicular to the core, about ¼ inch (6 mm) thick. Arrange the slices over the *crème pâtissière* in the *tarte* shell, making sure there are no ragged edges sticking up that will burn.

After the *tarte* has baked and cooled, glaze the top with apricot jam. Or, if you have a salamander omit the jam glaze. Heat the salamander. Dust the oranges with about ¼ cup (50 g) of superfine sugar and the rim of the *tarte* with a little confectioners sugar, and caramelize the sugar on top of the oranges by ironing with the salamander. Leave the rim white. This makes an especially handsome *tarte*.

Tarte aux Mandarines

TANGERINE

Large Mineola tangerines and mandarins can be treated in the same way as oranges, above. Substitute Mandarine for the orange liqueur.

Tarte au Citron

LEMON

Mix 1 to 1¼ cups (270 to 335 g) of lemon curd (see page 91) with an equal amount of *crème pâtissière* and 1 tablespoon (8 g) of cornstarch. Fill a round *tarte* shell with a ½- to ⅝-inch (12 to 16 mm) layer of this mixture. Cut 8 very thin slices from a small lemon. Arrange the slices, one for each serving, in a circle on top of the *tarte*. Do not overlap them or the *tarte* will be difficult to cut at serving time. Bake until the *tarte* shell is a uniform light brown on the bottom, about 40 minutes altogether. Glaze with apricot jam.

Opposite: Mille-feuilles (Napoleons), page 180. Following page: Pithiviers, page 167.

Tartes Alsaciennes

For these very decorative flower-shaped *tartes*, *pâte à choux* forms the rim and divides the *tarte* into petal-shaped compartments. By placing different fruits in separate compartments, you can get spectacular effects. However, if the fruits are baked in the shell, you must choose combinations that have similar baking times—for example, apples with pears or cherries with apricots. Do not mix juicy with nonjuicy fruits or thick fruits with thin ones.

Tarte Alsacienne

For 6 people

INGREDIENTS

12 to 14 ounces (350 to 400 g) *rognures* (see page 24)

1 cup (240 g) *pâte à choux spéciale* or *ordinaire* (see page 78)

Lightly beaten egg for brushing

6 tablespoons (100 g) *crème pâtissière* (see page 83)

Fruit, prepared as for ordinary fruit tartes (see pages 141–148)

2½ to 4 tablespoons (50 to 80 g) red currant jelly or strained apricot jam

FRUITS BAKED IN THE SHELL

1 to 2 tablespoons (12 to 25 g) superfine sugar

1 Roll out the *rognures* into a rough circle about 13 inches (33 cm) in diameter and ⅛ inch (3 mm) thick.

2 Center an 8-inch (20 cm) flan ring, *vol-au-vent* disc, or round mold on the sheet of *rognures* and press it gently to mark a circle on the dough. Then mark six circles around the perimeter with a 4-inch (10 cm) flan ring or *vol-au-vent* disc ①. The 4-inch (10 cm) circles should be centered on the perimeter and adjacent to each other, with the outer perimeters of the small circles forming a six-petaled flower. Cut out this flower-shaped base from the sheet of dough with the tip of a paring knife, using the small flan ring as a guide so you don't stretch the dough.

3 Brush a heavy baking sheet with a damp pastry brush to moisten it lightly. Fold the *rognures* base in half, then in half a second time. Carefully lift it without stretching, place on the baking sheet, and unfold. Let rest in the refrigerator for 20 minutes.

4 Preheat the oven to 425° F (220° C).

5 Prepare the *pâte à choux*.

6 Lightly brush a band ½ inch (12 mm) wide around the perimeter of the base with beaten egg. Brush egg wash over the lines connecting each corner where the petals intersect with the opposite corner ②.

149

Opposite: Flaky pastry cookies: Palmier, page 183; Papillon, page 185; Sacristains, page 186. Preceding page: Chaussons aux pommes, page 177.

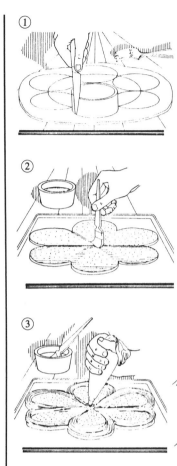

7 Transfer the *pâte à choux* to a pastry bag fitted with a medium fluted pastry tube (Ateco 5B). Starting from the center of the *rognures* base, pipe a ½-inch (12 mm) thick rope of *pâte à choux* out to the edge, around the border of one petal, and back to the center. Then reverse direction and pipe more *pâte à choux* back out to the edge and around the next petal. Continue around the base until you have outlined all of the petals with *pâte à choux* ③. Be careful not to pipe too much *pâte à choux* at the center of the base or in the compartment divisions.

8 If you are baking the *tarte* shell blind, go to step 11. Otherwise spread about 1 tablespoon (16 g) of *crème pâtissière* over the *rognures* base in each compartment, using a small palette knife.

9 Arrange the fruit over the *crème pâtissière* in the compartments. For sliced or halved fruits, start at the tip of each petal and overlap them like fish scales. Place whole cherries adjacent to each other.

10 Dust the superfine sugar over the fruit. Adjust the amount of sugar according to the sweetness of the fruit.

11 Lightly brush the *pâte à choux* border with beaten egg.

12 Place the *tarte* in the preheated oven and reduce the temperature to 400° F (200° C). Bake until the *pâte à choux* puffs up and begins to brown, 15 to 20 minutes. Reduce the oven to 350° F (180° C) and continue baking at least 20 to 25 minutes longer. When the *tarte* has been in the oven for 30 minutes, carefully lift one side of the *tarte* off the baking sheet, using a wide dough scraper or pancake turner, so you can check the color of the bottom of the crust. When the *tarte* is done, the *pâte à choux* will be a medium golden brown. If it is baked blind, the *rognures* base should be evenly browned on top and bottom. If it is filled, the bottom of the *rognures* base should be a uniform light brown, and any juice that has been exuded by the fruit should have evaporated. The total baking time may be as short as 30 minutes if the *tarte* is baked blind or as long as 1 hour, 20 minutes if it is filled with a very juicy fruit. If the *pâte à choux* seems to be browning too much, cover the top of the *tarte* with buttered kitchen parchment to protect it while the *tarte* continues to bake.

13 Slide the *tarte* onto a cooling rack and let cool to room temperature.

14 If the fruit was baked in the shell, proceed to step 16. Otherwise, spread about 1 tablespoon (16 g) of *crème pâtissière* over the *rognures* base in each compartment.

15 Arrange the fruit over the *crème pâtissière* in the compartments. Place whole fruits adjacent to each other. For sliced fruits, start at the tip of each petal and overlap the slices like fish scales.

16 For red or dark-colored fruits, pass the red currant jelly through a sieve. For other fruits, warm the strained apricot jam over low heat, stirring occasionally, until melted.

17 Brush the fruits with the jam or jelly until lightly coated and glistening.

Some Special Apple and Pear Tartes

Apple *tartes* are undoubtedly the most popular fruit *tartes* in both France and the United States. Apples, and to a lesser extent pears, lend themselves to a greater range of specialized variations than do other fruits.

Tarte aux Pommes Caramélisée

This is one of the première specialties of Pâtisserie Clichy. The top of the *tarte* is caramelized with a salamander (see page 349) after it is baked.

For 6 to 8 people

INGREDIENTS

An unbaked round
tarte shell, 9½
inches (24 cm) in
diameter and 1 inch
(2½ cm) deep,
made with *pâte à
foncer spéciale* (see
page 5)

6 to 8 tart medium
cooking apples

7 tablespoons (100 g)
butter

1 cup (200 g)
superfine sugar

1 Preheat the oven to 450° F (230° C).

2 Peel and core the apples and cut each apple into
about a dozen wedges ¾ inch (2 cm) thick.

3 Melt the butter in a 4-quart saucepan. Add the
apple wedges and turn them in the butter with a
wooden spoon. Add half of the sugar, mix it with the
apples, and cook gently for about 5 minutes, turning
frequently with a wooden spoon.

4 Remove the apples from the heat, drain thoroughly, and transfer to the *tarte* shell with a slotted
spoon.

5 Bake until the apples begin to brown on top,
about 30 minutes.

6 Slide the *tarte* onto a cooling rack, remove the
ring, and let rest for 10 to 15 minutes at room temperature to allow the apples to settle.

7 Heat your salamander. Sprinkle the remaining
sugar over the apples, and caramelize it by ironing
with the salamander.

8 Serve hot. Or let cool to room temperature, then
reheat in a 250° F (120° C) oven for 10 to 15
minutes. Serve within 2 hours or the caramel on top
will dissolve in the juice from the apples.

Tarte Tatin

This is the classic caramelized apple *tarte*, which is baked upside down in a
layer-cake pan. The only trick is in the unmolding. Use a heavy-gauge layer-
cake pan, preferably aluminum.

For 6 people

INGREDIENTS

5 to 7 tart medium
cooking apples

½ cup (115 g) butter

6 tablespoons (75 g)
sugar

1 Peel and core the apples. Cut them into wedges
¼ inch (6 mm) thick.

2 Melt 5 tablespoons (75 g) of the butter in a 4-
quart saucepan. Add the apples and turn them in the
butter with a wooden spoon. Add the sugar, mix it
with the apples, and cook gently for about 5 minutes,
turning frequently with the wooden spoon.

¾ cup (150 g)
  superfine sugar
5 ounces (150 g)
  rognures (see page
  24)

3 Remove from the heat and transfer the apples to a colander to drain and cool.

4 Heavily brush the inside of a layer-cake pan 8 inches (20 cm) in diameter with melted butter. Spread the superfine sugar about ¼ inch (6 mm) thick over the bottom of the layer-cake pan. Cut the remaining butter into bits and scatter it over the sugar.

5 Arrange the apples over the sugar, remembering that the *tarte* will be baked upside down. Place a few wedges at the center like the petals of a flower. Then, working outward from the center, arrange the apple wedges in concentric circles, overlapping them slightly. When you have covered the bottom of the mold with one layer of apples, add the remaining wedges to almost fill the mold. Since these will be on the inside of the *tarte,* they do not have to be arranged as carefully as the first layer. Gently press the apples down in the mold. (You can prepare the *tarte* to this point up to 2 hours in advance.)

6 Roll out the *rognures* into a rough circle slightly larger than the layer-cake pan and about ⅛ inch (3 mm) thick. Prick the *rognures* all over with a fork. Place it on a baking sheet and let it rest in the refrigerator for 30 minutes.

7 Meanwhile preheat the oven to 400° F (200° C).

8 Drape the circle of *rognures* over the filled layer-cake pan and trim off the excess with your rolling pin.

9 Bake until the pastry is browned and crisp and the apples are lightly caramelized, about 1½ hours. Tilt the layer-cake pan to check the color of the syrup at the bottom; it should be a pale to medium amber. If the pastry seems to be browning too much before the apples are cooked, cover it with kitchen parchment.

10 Dip the bottom of the layer-cake pan in ice water to stop the cooking and cool the *tarte*. Refrigerate the *tarte* for 1 to 2 hours to chill it and set the apples, so the *tarte* will hold together when it is unmolded.

11 Briefly heat the layer-cake pan on your cooktop to melt the caramel on the inside surface of the mold. Place a heatproof plate upside down on top of the mold, and, holding plate and mold together, invert them to unmold the *tarte*. If the *tarte* does not slide out easily, heat the layer-cake pan a little longer until the *tarte* slips freely in the mold, and unmold it onto the plate. Serve within 2 hours after unmolding.

12 When ready to serve, reheat the *tarte* in a 250° F (120° C) oven for 10 to 15 minutes.

Tarte aux Pommes Normande, Tarte aux Pommes Anglaise, and Tarte Bourdaloue

For these *tartes* the apples or pears are covered with *crème anglaise* before baking. They are best served hot out of the oven.

For 6 to 8 people

INGREDIENTS

¾ cup (200 g) *crème pâtissière* (see page 83)

An unbaked 9½-inch (24 cm) round *tarte* shell (see page 135) made with *rognures* or *pâte à foncer spéciale*

TARTE AUX POMMES NORMANDE OR ANGLAISE

3 or 4 tart medium cooking apples

1 Preheat the oven to 425° F (220° C).

2 Spread the *crème pâtissière* over the bottom of the *tarte* shell.

3 Peel and core the apples or pears. If the pears are hard, poach them in *sirop léger* (see page 422) until they can be pierced easily with a skewer, 5 to 15 minutes; then cool in the syrup and drain well before proceeding.

4 Cut the apples or pears into wedges ½ inch (12 mm) thick ①.

5 Arrange the wedges in concentric circles over the *crème pâtissière* in the *tarte* shell, starting from the outside and overlapping them as you go ②. Finish with a few wedges in the center like the petals of a flower.

6 Pour the *crème anglaise* over the apples or pears to nearly cover them.

TARTE BOURDALOUE

3 or 4 unblemished
  ripe pears

1⅓ to 1½ cups (3¼
  to 3½ dL) *crème
  anglaise* (see page
  126), made with the
  maximum number
  of yolks

TARTE AUX POMMES NORMANDE

2 tablespoons (3 cL)
  calvados

TARTE AUX POMMES ANGLAISE OR TARTE BOURDALOUE

¼ cup (50 g)
  superfine sugar

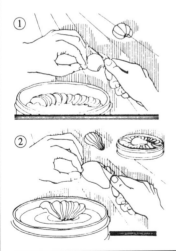

7 Place in the oven and reduce the temperature to 400° F (200° C). Bake until the rim of the *tarte* shell begins to brown, 20 to 25 minutes. Reduce the oven to 350° F (180° C) and continue baking until the apples or pears are tender and the *crème anglaise* is set, 15 to 20 minutes longer.

8 Slide the *tarte* onto a serving platter. Let the custard and the apples or pears settle for 10 to 15 minutes. (If necessary, let rest at room temperature for up to 4 hours, then reheat in a 250° F or 120° C oven.)

9 For *tarte aux pommes normande:* Flambé the *tarte* with calvados by warming the calvados, igniting it, and pouring it flaming over the *tarte.*

For *tarte aux pommes anglaise* or *tarte bourdaloue:* Heat your salamander. Sprinkle the sugar over the top of the *tarte* and caramelize it by ironing with the salamander.

Tarte Paysanne

For this pear *tarte* the shell is made of *brioche.*

For 6 to 8 people

INGREDIENTS

3 or 4 unblemished
 ripe pears
¾ pound (340 g)
 pâte à brioche (see
 page 37)
Melted butter for
 brushing mold
1½ cups (400 g)
 crème d'amandes
 (see page 87)
2 to 3 tablespoons
 (40 to 60 g) strained
 apricot jam

1 If the pears are hard, peel and core them and poach them in *sirop léger* (see page 422) until they can be pierced easily with a skewer, 5 to 15 minutes. Let cool in the syrup.

2 Roll out the *pâte à brioche* into a rough circle about 14 inches (35 cm) in diameter and ⅛ inch (3 mm) thick. Brush the inside of a 9-inch (23 cm) layer-cake pan with melted butter and line it with *pâte à brioche*. Drape the excess dough over the edge of the mold and trim it by rolling your rolling pin over the top.

3 Spread the *crème d'amandes* evenly over the bottom of the *pâte à brioche*–lined mold, filling the mold to about one third of its height.

4 If you have poached the pears, drain thoroughly. If not, peel and core them. Cut the pears in half.

5 Arrange the pear halves over the *crème d'amandes,* radiating them out from the center like the spokes of a wheel, with the stem ends at the center.

6 Let rise in a warm place until the *brioche* has doubled in volume, about 1½ hours.

7 Preheat the oven to 425° F (220° C). Place a heavy baking sheet on the middle shelf.

8 Place on the hot baking sheet in the oven, and bake until the top of the *brioche* dough changes from a pale, creamy yellow to a deeper, golden yellow, 5 to 10 minutes. Reduce the oven to 350° F (180° C) and continue baking until the top of the *brioche* is firm to the touch and golden brown and the *crème d'amandes* is lightly browned and solid but not dry, 40 to 60 minutes longer. If the *brioche* colors too quickly, drape a sheet of kitchen parchment over the *tarte*.

9 Transfer the *tarte* to a cooling rack, and let cool to room temperature in the mold. Then carefully unmold it.

10 Warm the apricot jam over low heat, stirring occasionally, until melted. Brush the top of the *tarte* with jam until lightly coated and glistening.

Almond Cream Tartes

These *tartes* turn the usual relationship between fruit and filling upside down. Here you place some preserved fruits on the bottom of a raw *pâte sucrée tarte* shell, fill with *crème d'amandes,* and bake. You can finish the *tarte* by either brushing with jam or dusting with confectioners sugar.

We give three examples, plus suggestions to get you started on other variations.

Tarte St.-Germain

For 6 to 8 people

INGREDIENTS

An unbaked round *pâte sucrée tarte* shell, 9½ inches (24 cm) in diameter and 1 inch (2½ cm) deep, trimmed to the height of the flan ring (see pages 135–137)

¾ cup (240 g) raspberry jam

About 2⅔ cups (700 g) *crème d'amandes* (see page 87)

2½ to 3½ tablespoons (50 to 70 g) strained apricot jam

1 teaspoon (½ cL) kirsch

Red food coloring

1 Preheat the oven to 350° F (180° C).

2 Spread a layer of raspberry jam ¼ inch (6 mm) thick over the bottom of the pastry shell, leaving a band ¾ inch (2 cm) wide around the edge free from jam.

3 Fill the shell with *crème d'amandes,* using a palette knife to smooth the surface level with the top of the ring, and make a slight depression in the center so it won't form a dome when baked.

4 Bake until the *crème d'amandes* is a uniform light brown and firm to the touch but not dry, about 45 minutes.

5 Slide the *tarte* onto a cooling rack, remove the ring and let cool to room temperature.

6 Warm the apricot jam over low heat, stirring occasionally, until melted. Stir in the kirsch to flavor the jam and a few drops of food coloring to tint it red.

7 Brush the top of the *tarte* with jam until lightly coated and glistening. Sprinkle chopped almonds on

1 tablespoon (10 g) chopped almonds

top in a decorative pattern—for example, a few bits in the center and the rest in a 6-inch (15 cm) circle around it.

Variations: 1. You can make a simpler version by omitting the raspberry jam and dusting the top of the *tarte* with about 2 to 3 teaspoons (5 to 8 g) of confectioners sugar instead of brushing it with apricot jam. In this case, scatter about 2 tablespoons (15 g) of sliced almonds over the top of the *tarte* before baking.

2. Replace the raspberry jam with a *salpicon* of candied fruits (for a *tarte St.-Germain aux fruits*) or canned pineapple in heavy syrup (for a *tarte St.-Germain aux ananas*). To make the *salpicon,* cut about 5 ounces (140 g) of candied fruits or canned pineapple into ¼- to ⅜-inch (6 to 10 mm) dice. Thoroughly drain the pineapple dice on a paper towel. Mix the candied fruits or pineapple with about 6 tablespoons (120 g) of strained apricot jam. Flavor this *salpicon* with a little rum for candied fruits or kirsch for pineapple. After baking, decorate the top of the *tarte* with candied fruits (cherries cut in half, other fruits sliced and cut into triangles and diamonds) or canned pineapple (cut into wedge-shaped slices). Brush the top of the *tarte* with strained apricot jam, flavored with rum for candied fruits or kirsch for pineapple. Omit the chopped almonds.

Tarte Danoise

For 6 to 8 people

INGREDIENTS

An unbaked round *pâte sucrée tarte* shell, 9½ inches (24 cm) in diameter and 1 inch (2½ cm) deep, trimmed to the height of the

1 Preheat the oven to 350° F (180° C).

2 Scatter the brandied cherries over the bottom of the unbaked *tarte* shell.

3 Fill the shell with *crème d'amandes,* using your palette knife to smooth the surface level with the top of the ring and make a slight depression in the center so it won't form a dome when baked.

flan ring (see pages 135–137)

1½ cups (260 g) brandied cherries (stoned), thoroughly drained

About 2⅔ cups (700 g) *crème d'amandes* (see page 87)

2½ to 3½ tablespoons (50 to 70 g) strained apricot jam

1 teaspoon (½ cL) kirsch

Red food coloring

1 tablespoon (10 g) chopped pistachios, or substitute chopped almonds tinted pale green with a small drop of food coloring

4 Bake until the *crème d'amandes* is a uniform light brown and firm to the touch but not dry, about 45 minutes.

5 Slide the *tarte* onto a cooling rack, remove the ring, and let cool to room temperature.

6 Warm the apricot jam over low heat, stirring occasionally, until melted. Stir in the kirsch to flavor the jam and a few drops of food coloring to tint it red.

7 Brush the top of the *tarte* with jam until lightly coated and glistening. Sprinkle the chopped pistachios on top in a decorative pattern—for example, sprinkle most of the chopped pistachios over 2 perpendicular diameters to divide the top into quadrants, and sprinkle the remaining chopped pistachios in the center of each quadrant.

Variation: Substitute fresh blueberries for the brandied cherries, brush the top of the *tarte* with black currant jelly (pass it through a fine sieve rather than melting it) instead of apricot jam, and use chopped almonds instead of pistachios for decoration.

Tarte Catalane

For this very deep *tarte*, the shell must be formed in an entremet ring.

For 8 to 10 people

INGREDIENTS

An unbaked round *pâte sucrée tarte* shell, 9½ inches (24 cm) in diameter and 1⅜ inches (3½ cm) deep, trimmed to the height of the entremet ring (see pages 135–137)

1 cup (270 g) *crème*

1 Preheat the oven to 350° F (180° C).

2 Spread a layer of *crème pâtissière* ¼ inch (6 mm) thick evenly over the bottom of the *tarte* shell.

3 Split the apricots in half and remove the stones. Arrange the apricot halves cut side down over the *crème pâtissière*.

4 Warm the apricot jam over low heat, stirring occasionally, until melted. Brush the apricots with jam.

159

pâtissière (see page 83)

Two 7-ounce (482 g) cans of apricots in heavy syrup

1 to 1½ tablespoons (20 to 30 g) strained apricot jam

About 2⅔ cups (700 g) *crème d'amandes* (see page 87)

2 tablespoons (15 g) sliced almonds

2 to 3 teaspoons (5 to 8 g) confectioners sugar

5 Fill the *tarte* shell with the *crème d'amandes*, using your palette knife to smooth the surface level with the top of the ring and make a slight depression in the center so it won't form a dome when baked.

6 Scatter the sliced almonds over the *crème d'amandes*.

7 Bake until the *crème d'amandes* is a uniform light brown and firm to the touch but not dry, about 1 hour.

8 Slide the *tarte* onto a cooling rack, remove the ring, and let cool to room temperature.

9 Before serving, dust the top of the *tarte* with confectioners sugar.

Chapter Six

FEUILLETÉS
(FLAKY PASTRIES)

Feuilletés are the pastries made from the *pâtes feuilletées,* or flaky pastry doughs. They fall into three distinct groups.

First are the *feuilletage* and *rognures* desserts. Except for the rather austere *galette des rois,* these are always filled. The most common fillings are *crème d'amandes* and cooked apples (both of which are baked inside of the pastry) and *crème pâtissière* (which is added after baking). Regardless of the filling, these desserts have in common the exceptional flakiness of the *feuilletage* and *rognures.*

Feuilletage can also be used to make cookies, the most familiar of which are *palmiers.* For these the *feuilletage* is sometimes given its final turns on sugar rather than flour, and the sugar caramelizes when the pastries are baked.

Croissants and *pains au chocolat* are made from *pâte à croissant.* These two breakfast pastries combine a flaky exterior with a soft, breadlike interior, setting them apart from the other *feuilletés* as well as from the leavened pastries in the brioche and *baba* families.

TOURS DE MAIN

The Final Turns *(Tourage)*

In the initial preparation of the *pâte feuilletée* the dough is given four turns (for *feuilletage*) or two turns (for *pâte à croissant*). Depending on how it will be used, it will now be given one and a half or two additional turns. Of course *rognures* does not get any turns.

Ideally you should do the final turns while the dough is cold, immediately after removing from the refrigerator. *Feuilletage* will be very firm, and if it is too firm to roll you can soften it first by striking the *paton* firmly several times with your rolling pin. If necessary, let it rest briefly at room temperature before rolling to warm and soften it, but do not let it warm much above 50° F (10° C) or it will become too soft and sticky. In any case, remember that *feuilletage* is a very strong dough, and the best way to roll it is to put as much pressure on your rolling pin as you can.

Pâte à croissant is much softer than *feuilletage,* so you should have no difficulty rolling the cold dough. Also, since it contains yeast it should never be allowed to soften at room temperature before rolling.

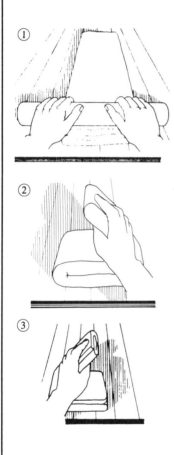

If the *pâte feuilletée* will eventually be rolled into a rectangular sheet, then give it two final turns before the final rolling and shaping ①-②.

On the other hand, if you will be rolling *feuilletage* into large circles, give the dough only one and a half final turns to make five and a half turns altogether. The half turn is given last by rolling the dough out to double its size in the direction perpendicular to the fifth turn ① and then folding it in half (rather than thirds as for a full turn) ③.

Whether you give the *feuilletage* one and a half or two final turns, dust the counter and the dough with flour as needed to prevent the dough from sticking to counter or rolling pin. Or, if you are making a cookie recipe that requires it, dust the counter and dough with sugar instead of flour. Dusting with sugar is easiest with a dredge. The sugar will extract moisture from the dough, so in this case the turns and the subsequent rolling and shaping of the dough should be done as quickly as possible.

After completing the final turns, let the *paton* rest in the refrigerator for 20 to 30 minutes to relax the gluten in the *détrempe*.

Rolling out Pâtes Feuilletées (*Abaissage*)

To make a rectangular sheet of dough, lightly dust your countertop and the *paton* of *pâte feuilletée* with flour (or sugar for some cookies), and start rolling the dough in the direction perpendicular to the last turn. Pressing down firmly and evenly, roll your rolling pin from the end of the dough nearest you to

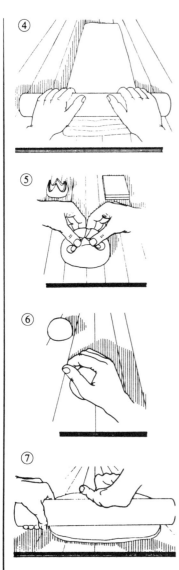

the far end of the dough ④. Reverse direction and roll the rolling pin back to the near edge. Repeat until the *paton* has increased to one and a half to two times its original length. Then you can roll it in the other direction as well, widening as well as lengthening the dough. Continue rolling the dough, pressing down as firmly and as evenly as you can, until you reach the required size and thickness. Dust the counter and the dough with flour (or sugar) as needed to prevent sticking.

To make circular sheets of *feuilletage* first roll out the dough in the direction perpendicular to the last turn to flatten and lengthen it. Cut the dough in roughly square pieces of the size required. Form each square into a ball by folding the edges underneath ⑤, placing it on your countertop, and rolling the dough in a circle under your palms ⑥ in the same way you would a ball of *pâte à brioche* (see page 37 for more details). This gives the dough equal strength in all directions so it won't shrink unevenly when baked. Be sure the ball is tightly formed. Flatten the ball into a thick, round pad with the heel of your hand. Then dust your countertop lightly with flour, place the pad of dough on the counter with the folded edges underneath, and dust the pad with flour. Roll out the pad of dough into a circle. Start with your rolling pin at the edge of the dough nearest you. Pressing down with as much weight as you can, roll your rolling pin from the near edge of the pad to the far edge ⑦. Reverse direction and roll the rolling pin back to the near edge. Rotate the pad of dough and repeat. Continue rolling the dough, rotating it after each forward and backward motion, until you get a rough circle of the size required. Dust your countertop and the dough with flour as needed to prevent sticking.

Whether you are rolling rectangular sheets or circles, the process of rolling the dough will activate the gluten in the flour, making the dough elastic. Do not try to fight the dough. If it begins to get elastic, place the dough on a baking sheet and let it rest in the refrigerator for 20 minutes to relax the gluten in the *détrempe*. Then continue rolling the dough. If you do not heed this advice, the dough will repeatedly shrink throughout the rolling, shaping, and baking process, and the finished pastry will be tough.

Whenever you lift a sheet of *pâte feuilletée,* fold it in half or in quarters first so you can support it on your outstretched hand. Otherwise, the dough can stretch under its own weight, making it more elastic and more likely to shrink unevenly later.

Cutting the Pâte Feuilletée (*Détaillage*)

Before cutting the sheet of dough, place it on a baking sheet and let it rest in the refrigerator for 20 minutes. Otherwise, no matter how careful you have been the dough will shrink and deform the shapes you cut.

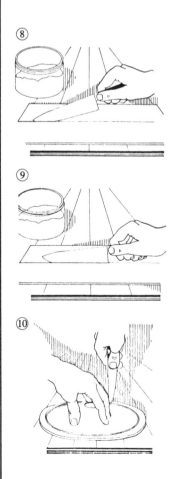

Lay the sheet of *pâte feuilletée* on your countertop. There are three ways to cut it, depending on the sizes and shapes you need:

If you are making straight line cuts, place the tip of your chef's knife on the counter ⑧ and cut the dough by pressing down on the handle, pivoting the blade from the tip ⑨. Do not drag the tip of the blade through the dough or you will stretch and deform it.

To cut circles, place a *vol-au-vent* disc, a flan ring, or a round mold or bowl on top of the sheet of dough, and, using it as a guide, cut through the dough with the tip of a paring knife ⑩. The *vol-au-vent* disc will hold the dough in place so you won't stretch it.

There are special pastry cutters made for cutting small circles and decorative shapes. To use these, place the cutter on top of the dough and press down firmly to cut all the way through the dough.

Trimmings from *feuilletage* rolled on flour are saved to make *rognures.* However, trimmings from sugared *feuilletage* or from *pâte à croissant* cannot be saved. If you are rolling out a second *paton* right away, enclose these trimmings in the center of the new *paton* when you fold it during the next to last turn; otherwise discard the trimmings.

Shaping and Brushing with Egg Wash *(Fonçage et Dorage)*

Depending on which pastry you are making, it will be assembled either on your countertop or on a baking sheet. In either case, before placing the pastry on your baking sheet, brush the baking sheet with a damp pastry brush to moisten it lightly. There should be tiny droplets of water all over the baking sheet. This prevents the pastry from sliding on the baking sheet. However, for *feuilletage* cookies that were rolled on sugar, the baking sheet should not be moistened because sugar on the outside of the cookies would dissolve in the water and then burn in the oven.

If no topping is applied to the pastry and the dough was not rolled on sugar, then brush the top with lightly beaten egg to prevent it from drying and forming a crust. Use the egg wash sparingly. Just paint on enough to coat the surface lightly and make it glisten.

The Final Rest for Feuilletage and Rognures *(Repos)*

The baking sheet with the assembled pastry (or pastries) should now be placed in the refrigerator for 20 minutes to 1 hour. This rest serves several purposes. First, it allows the gluten to relax, so that the pastry will not shrink in the oven. This is the reason for the 20-minute minimum. Between 20 minutes and 1 hour, the longer the pastry rests, the more the gluten will relax, and correspondingly the more evenly the *feuilletage* or *rognures* will bake and the less it will rise. (But, in any case, it will rise quite well!)

Second, if there is egg wash sealing layers of *feuilletage* or *rognures* together or *glace royale* on top of the pastry, it needs 20 to 60 minutes to dry.

Third, if there is a *crème d'amandes* filling, it must be very cold and firm before baking to prevent it from leaking out before the outside edge of the pastry sets in the oven. This usually requires about 1 hour in the refrigerator.

The rest times given here are minimums. The pastry can rest in the refrigerator for 2 or 3 hours without significant change. If the pastry is going to be frozen, it must have at least 20 to 30 minutes rest before freezing.

Scoring Feuilletage *(Rayage)*

If the top of the pastry was brushed with egg wash, it is usually scored in a decorative pattern with the point of a paring knife before baking. This scoring serves more than a decorative purpose. It helps heat get inside the pastry more quickly and makes the *feuilletage* rise more quickly and evenly—provided the scoring is done evenly.

Before scoring, lightly brush the top of the pastry a second time with egg wash. Then hold the blade of your paring knife at an angle of 60° with respect to the surface of the pastry and score the pastry in the recommended pattern with the tip of the blade, cutting down into but not through the top layer of *feuilletage* ⑪.

The Second Rise for Pâte à Croissant *(La Deuxième Pousse)*

Place the baking sheet of pastries in a warm place (75° to 85° F or 25° to 30° C) and let the pastries rise until doubled in volume, about 1½ to 2 hours. If they are too warm, the butter in them will melt onto the baking sheet; and, if they rise for too long, they will soften too much and loose their shape.

After the croissants or *pains au chocolat* have risen, lightly brush them a second time with beaten egg to dissolve the dried egg wash on the surface and moisten them so that the *pâte à croissant* will rise evenly and brown nicely in the oven.

Baking *(Cuisson)*

Pâtes feuilletées require a high initial heat to make them rise quickly, then a lower heat to cook and dry out the inside of the pastry without burning the outside. After baking transfer the pastries to a cooling rack.

STORAGE

After baking, *feuilletage* and *rognures* desserts are best kept at room temperature, with the length of time determined by the filling: 12 hours for *crème pâtissière*, 24 hours for apple fillings or no filling, and 2 days for *crème d'amandes*. Those filled with *crème d'amandes* or apples should be covered airtight with plastic wrap, while others should be left uncovered. *Feuilletage* cookies can be kept in a dry place, loosely covered (for example in a cookie jar) for up to 3 days.

Feuilletage and *rognures* desserts and cookies can also be frozen for up to 1 month before baking. Before freezing, complete all of the preliminary steps in the preparation, including allowing the pastry to rest, brushing with egg wash and scoring, or topping with *glace royale*. Freeze the unbaked pastry on the baking sheet, then transfer it to a plastic bag. When ready to bake, place the pastry on a moistened (except for cookies) baking sheet and bake immediately without first defrosting.

You can keep croissants and *pains au chocolat* wrapped in a paper bag at room temperature for up to 12 hours. Leave them in the bag when you reheat them in a 250° F (120° C) oven. If you want to keep them longer, there are two methods for freezing. Best is to form the pastries and brush them with beaten egg, then freeze on the baking sheet immediately. Transfer the frozen pastries to a plastic bag and keep frozen for up to 1 week. The day before you want to bake them, return the pastries to a moistened baking sheet and defrost in the refrigerator overnight. Then put them in a warm place to rise, brush a second time with egg wash, and bake. Alternatively, bake the croissants or *pains au chocolat* first, then while still warm (but not hot) seal airtight in a plastic bag and place in the freezer for up to 2 weeks. When ready to eat, place the frozen pastries on a baking sheet, cover with kithen parchment or aluminum foil, and reheat for 5 to 10 minutes in a 300° F (150° C) oven.

Feuilletage and Rognures Desserts

Pithiviers

Located about fifty miles (82 km) south of Paris, the tiny town of Pithiviers has given birth to several gastronomic delicacies. Most famous is this *crème d'amandes*–filled, dome-shaped *"gâteau."*

For 10 to 12 people

INGREDIENTS

Half of a *paton* of
feuilletage (4 turns;
see page 18)
1½ cups (400 g) cold
crème d'amandes
(see page 87)
Lightly beaten egg
for brushing
1½ teaspoons (5 g)
confectioners sugar

1 Give the *feuilletage* one turn. Then roll it out to about double its size in the perpendicular direction and fold it in half. This makes a total of five and a half turns.

2 Let the *paton* rest in the refrigerator for 20 to 30 minutes.

3 Roll out the dough into a rectangle about 5 × 10 inches (13 × 26 cm). Cut it in half. Form each half into a ball by wrapping the edges underneath and rolling it in a circle under your palms. Flatten each ball into a thick, round pad with the heel of your hand.

4 Roll each pad into a circular sheet about 12 inches (30 cm) in diameter and ⅛ inch (3 mm) thick. Lightly dust the counter and the dough with flour as needed to prevent sticking.

5 Place the sheets of *feuilletage* on a baking sheet, and let rest in the refrigerator for 20 minutes.

6 Return the sheets of *feuilletage* to your counter, and cut from each a circle 11 inches (28 cm) in diameter.

7 Brush a heavy baking sheet with a damp pastry brush to moisten it. Place one of the circles of *feuilletage* on the baking sheet, and prick it all over with a fork. Brush a border 1½ inches (4 cm) wide around the outside of the circle with beaten egg. Place the *crème d'amandes* in the center of the circle and smooth it into a mound ¾ inch (2 cm) thick, inside the egg-wash border ①.

8 Drape the second circle of *feuilletage* over the mound of *crème d'amandes*. Press down with your fingertips all around the edge to seal the two circles with the egg wash. Center a flan ring or round mold 8 inches (20 cm) in diameter around the mound in the center and press it to seal the *crème d'amandes* inside. Remove the ring. *Chiqueter* the edge of the pastry—that is, decorate the edge in a toothlike pattern by pressing the back edge of a paring knife against it at 1½- to 2-inch (4 to 5 cm) intervals ②.

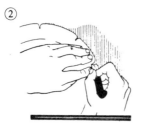

9 Lightly brush the top of the pastry with beaten egg. Place in the refrigerator and let rest until the *crème d'amandes* is firm and the egg wash dry, about 1 hour.

10 Meanwhile, preheat the oven to 450° F (230° C).

11 Lightly brush the top of the *pithiviers* a second time with beaten egg. Decorate the top by drawing arcs from the center of the pastry to the outside edge with the tip of a paring knife ③. Hold the blade at an angle, and cut into but not through the top layer of *feuilletage*. Space the arcs evenly around the top of the *pithiviers*.

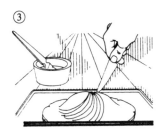

12 Place the *pithiviers* in the oven and reduce the temperature to 425° F (220° C). Bake until the pastry rises and the top is lightly browned, about 15 to 20 minutes. Then reduce the oven temperature to 325° F (160° C) and continue baking until the top of the *pithiviers* is a deep, uniform golden brown and the edge is light brown with no streaks of yellow, about 45 minutes to 1 hour 15 minutes longer.

13 Remove from the oven and turn on the broiler. Evenly dust the top of the *pithiviers* with the confectioners sugar. Return it to the oven, on the second shelf from the top, until the sugar melts and glazes the top, 30 to 90 seconds longer. If the sugar seems to be melting unevenly, rotate the baking sheet; and if it looks like it is about to burn, remove the *pithiviers* from the oven immediately, even if some white spots remain.

14 Transfer the *pithiviers* to a cooling rack. Serve warm; or let cool to room temperature and reheat in a 250° F (120° C) oven before serving.

Pithiviers Hollandais

Here is a richer and heavier version of *pithiviers*. It is also called *pain complet*.

For 10 to 12 people

INGREDIENTS

Half of a *paton* of *feuilletage* (4 turns; see page 18)

1½ cups (400 g) cold *crème d'amandes* (see page 87)

Lightly beaten egg for brushing

1 egg white

1 tablespoon (20 g) strained apricot jam

1¼ cups (190 g) *TPT blanc* (see page 413)

1½ teaspoons (5 g) confectioners sugar

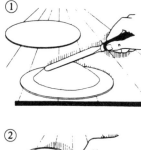

1 Give the *feuilletage* one turn. Then roll it out to about double its size in the perpendicular direction and fold it in half. This makes a total of five and a half turns.

2 Let the *paton* rest in the refrigerator for 20 to 30 minutes.

3 Roll out the dough into a rectangle about 5 × 10 inches (13 × 25 cm). Cut it into 2 pieces, one about 5½ inches (14 cm) long and the other 4½ inches (11 cm) long. Form each piece into a ball by wrapping the edges underneath and rolling it in a circle under your palms. Flatten each ball into a thick, round pad with the heel of your hand.

4 Roll each pad into a circular sheet, the larger one 13 inches (33 cm) in diameter, the smaller one 11 inches (28 cm) in diameter, and both about ⅛ inch (3 mm) thick. Lightly dust the countertop and the dough with flour as needed to prevent sticking.

5 Place the circles of *feuilletage* on a baking sheet and let rest in the refrigerator for 20 minutes.

6 Place the sheets of *feuilletage* on your counter, and cut from each a circle, the larger one 12 inches (30 cm) in diameter, and the smaller one 10 inches (25 cm) in diameter.

7 Place the *crème d'amandes* in the center of the larger circle and smooth it into a mound ¾ inches (2 cm) thick, leaving uncovered a border of pastry 1½ inches (4 cm) wide around the outside of the circle ①. Drape the second circle over the mound of *crème d'amandes,* centering it on the larger circle. Brush a band 1 inch (2½ cm) wide around the edge of the smaller circle with beaten egg ②. The border of the bottom circle extends beyond the smaller top circle; fold it over and press it down with your fingertips all the way around to seal the edge with the egg wash ③.

8 Brush a heavy baking sheet with a damp pastry brush to moisten it. Invert the *pithiviers hollandais* and place it on the baking sheet. Press the edge of the pastry again to be sure it is well sealed, and shape the pastry into a symmetrical mound with your hands. Chill until firm, about 1 hour.

9 Preheat the oven to 450° F (230° C).

10 Stir together the egg white and apricot jam, then stir in the *TPT blanc* to form a thick almond paste or *pâte d'amandes crue*.

11 Using your palette knife, spread the *pâte d'amandes crue* in a thin even layer over the top of the *pithiviers hollandais* ④. Dust the confectioners sugar over the *pâte d'amandes crue*. Press the edge of your palette knife down on the *pâte d'amandes crue* to make lines through the center of the circle and divide the top surface of the *pithiviers hollandais* into eight wedges ⑤. Pierce the top of the pastry in three or four places with the tip of your paring knife to let steam escape.

12 Place the *pithiviers hollandais* in the oven and reduce the temperature to 425° F (220° C). Bake until the pastry rises and the top just begins to brown, 7 to 12 minutes. Then reduce the oven temperature to 325° F (160° C) and continue baking until the almond paste on top is dark brown and firm to the touch, about 1 hour to 1 hour 20 minutes longer. The inside of the *pithiviers hollandais* must be solid so that it doesn't jiggle when you move it. The confectioners sugar will still be white. If the almond paste looks like it is browning too much, cover with a sheet of kitchen parchment to prevent burning.

13 Slide the *pithiviers hollandais* onto a cooling rack and let cool to room temperature.

Storage Note: If you want to freeze the *pithiviers hollandais,* do so after step 8. When ready to bake, proceed with the rest of the recipe, without allowing the pastry to defrost.

Galette des Rois

This is the Twelfth Night cake served for Epiphany in the French provinces north of the Loire. While it is rather austere—just an unfilled circle of *feuilletage* embellished only by decorative scoring and a sugar glaze—it has long been the favorite of Parisians for that occasion. The name *galette* refers to its shape—like a pancake.

For about 10 people

INGREDIENTS

Half of a *paton* of *feuilletage* (4 turns; see page 18)

Lightly beaten egg for brushing

2 teaspoons (6 g) confectioners sugar

1 Give the *feuilletage* one turn. Then roll it out to double its size in the perpendicular direction and fold it in half. This makes a total of five and a half turns.

2 Let the *paton* rest in the refrigerator for 20 to 30 minutes.

3 Roll out the dough into a rough circle or square about 6 inches (15 cm) in diameter. Form the dough into a ball by wrapping the edges underneath and rolling it in a circle under your palms. Flatten the ball into a thick, round pad with the heel of your hand.

4 Roll the pad into a circle about 13 inches (33 cm) in diameter and ⅜ inch (1 cm) thick. Lightly dust the counter and the dough with flour as needed to prevent sticking.

5 Place the sheet of *feuilletage* on a baking sheet and let rest in the refrigerator for 20 minutes.

6 Return the sheet of *feuilletage* to your countertop, and from it cut a circle 12 inches (30 cm) in diameter.

7 Hold the fingertips of one hand on the circle of *feuilletage,* about ¾ inch (2 cm) in from the edge. Take your paring knife in the other hand and hold it at an angle of about 30° with respect to the countertop. Press the dull edge of the blade against the edge of the pastry at ⅛ inch (3 mm) intervals to make a fine toothlike pattern (this is a variation of the *chiqueter* technique) and raise a small rim by pressing the pastry up against your fingertips ①. Rotate the pastry as you work your way around the edge.

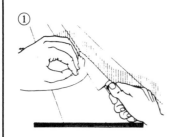

8 Brush a heavy baking sheet with a damp pastry brush to moisten it. Place the circle of *feuilletage* on the baking sheet. Lightly brush the top with beaten egg. Then place in the refrigerator and let rest for 20 to 30 minutes.

9 Meanwhile, preheat the oven to 450° F (230° C).

10 Lightly brush the top of the *galette* a second time with beaten egg. Decorate the top by scoring it with the tip of a paring knife, as follows. Holding the blade at an àngle, draw parallel lines about 1¼ inches (3 cm) apart across the *galette,* and then make a chevron pattern by drawing diagonal lines about ¾ inch (2 cm) apart between every other pair of parallel lines ②. Cut down about ⅛ inch (3 mm) into the pastry to score it deeply.

②

11 Place the *galette* in the oven and reduce the temperature to 425° F (220° C). Bake until the pastry rises and the top of the *galette* just begins to brown, 10 to 15 minutes. Reduce the oven temperature to 350° F (180° C) and continue baking until the top is a deep, uniform golden brown and the sides are light brown with no streaks of yellow, about 45 minutes to 1 hour longer.

12 Remove from the oven and turn on the broiler. Evenly dust the top of the *galette* with the confectioners sugar. Return it to the oven, on the second shelf from the top, until the sugar melts and glazes the top, 30 to 90 seconds. If the sugar seems to be melting unevenly, rotate the baking sheet; and if it looks like it is about to burn, remove the *galette* from the oven immediately, even if some white spots remain.

13 Slide the *galette* onto a cooling rack. Serve warm; or let cool to room temperature and reheat in a 250° F (120° C) oven before serving.

Conversation

This very elegant variation of the *pithiviers* is baked in a flan ring.

For 10 to 12 people

INGREDIENTS

About 1 pound 5 ounces (600 g) *rognures* (see page 24)

Melted butter for brushing flan ring

About 2 cups (540 g) *crème d'amandes* (see page 87)

¼ cup (115 g) *glace royale* (see page 104)

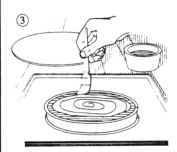

1 Cut the *rognures* into two pads, one about 12 ounces (350 g) and the other 9 ounces (250 g). Roll out the larger pad of dough into a circle about 12 inches (30 cm) in diameter and ⅛ inch (3 mm) thick. Roll out the second pad into a circle about 10 inches (25 cm) in diameter and ⅛ inch (3 mm) thick. Lightly dust your countertop and the *rognures* with flour as needed to prevent sticking.

2 Brush the inside of a flan ring 9½ inches (24 cm) in diameter and ¾ inch (2 cm) deep with melted butter. Line the ring with the larger circle of *rognures* ①. Bend and fold a double thickness of dough about ¼ inch (6 mm) wide extending over the inside edge of the *tarte* shell. Pinch this lip between the fingertips of one hand and the thumb of the other to get a lip of uniform thickness all around the circumference ②.

3 Prick the bottom of the pastry all over with a fork. Slide the pastry-lined ring onto a heavy baking sheet.

4 Fill the *rognures*-lined flan ring almost to the rim with *crème d'amandes*, leaving about ³⁄₁₆ inch (5 mm) at the top.

5 Brush the lip of pastry around the top of the ring with beaten egg ③. Prick the second circle of *rognures* all over with a fork, and drape it over the ring. Roll your rolling pin over the top to trim off the excess *rognures* and seal the edge ④. Gather the excess *rognures* into a ball and flatten it into a pad. Wrap the pad in waxed paper.

6 Refrigerate the *conversation* and the pad of excess *rognures* until the filling is firm, about 1 hour.

7 Lightly dust your counter and the pad of excess *rognures* with flour. Roll out the *rognures* into a rectangular sheet about 12 inches (30 cm) long and ³⁄₃₂ inch (2 mm) thick. Fold the sheet in half to get a rectangle 6 inches (15 cm) long and trim the three open edges to straight lines with your chef's knife.

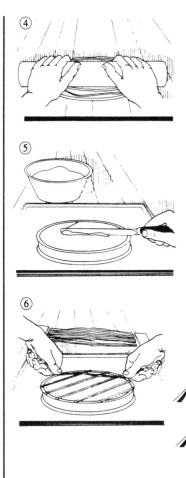

Cut through the folded edge parallel to the sides of the rectangle, to make strips ⅛ inch (3 mm) wide, stopping ½ inch (1 cm) from the opposite, open side of the rectangle. Unfold the rectangle, then cut off the ends to separate the strips.

8 Spread the *glace royale* over the top of the *conversation* in an even layer with your palette knife ⑤. One at a time, carefully lift strips of *rognures,* without stretching them, and drape them over the top of the *conversation* ⑥. Trim off the ends of the strips by pressing down on the rim of the flan ring with your thumbs. Arrange the strips parallel and about 1½ inches (4 cm) apart. Then drape more strips of *rognures* over the *conversation* on the diagonal with respect to the first set of strips to form a lozenge or diamond pattern. Prick the top of the *conversation* in three or four places with the tip of a paring knife.

9 Let the *conversation* rest in the refrigerator until the *glace royale* dries and forms a crust, about 1 hour.

10 Meanwhile, preheat the oven to 425° F (220° C).

11 Place the *conversation* in the oven and reduce the temperature to 400° F (200° C). Bake until the top just begins to brown, 10 to 15 minutes. Then reduce the oven to 325° F (160° C) and continue baking until the filling is set and the top is a medium beige, 40 to 60 minutes longer.

12 Slide the *conversation* onto a cooling rack. Remove the flan ring and let cool to room temperature.

Jalousie de Pommes

This apple-filled band of *feuilletage* gets its name from the parallel slits across its top which make it look like a venetian blind.

For 8 to 10 people

INGREDIENTS

Half of a *paton* of *feuilletage* (4 turns; see page 18)

Lightly beaten egg for brushing

Either 1½ cups (450 g) *pommes sautées au beurre* (see page 88); *or* ¾ cup (225 g) *pommes sautées au beurre* mixed with ¾ cup (225 g) *compote de pommes* (see page 88)

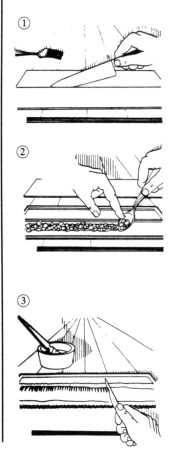

1 Give the *feuilletage* two final turns.

2 Let the *paton* rest in the refrigerator for 20 to 30 minutes.

3 Roll out the dough into a rough rectangle about 13 × 20 inches (32 × 50 cm). Lightly dust the counter and the dough with flour as needed to prevent sticking.

4 From the sheet of *feuilletage*, cut two rectangular bands 18 inches (45 cm) long (or as long as your baking sheet), one 5¼ inches (13½ cm) wide and the other 5¾ inches (14½ cm) wide ①.

5 Brush a heavy baking sheet with a damp pastry brush to moisten it. Place the narrower of the two bands of *feuilletage* on the baking sheet and prick it all over with a fork. Brush a border 1 inch (2½ cm) wide around the edge of this rectangle with beaten egg. Spoon the apple filling down the center of the band of *feuilletage* ② and smooth it into a mound surrounded by the egg wash border. Drape the second band of *feuilletage* over the apples so it just covers the first band of *feuilletage*. Press it down all around the edge to seal the two layers together with the egg wash.

6 *Chiqueter* the edge of the *jalousie*—that is, decorate the edge in a toothlike pattern by pressing the dull edge of a paring knife against it at ½-inch (12 mm)—fingertip width—intervals.

7 Lightly brush the top of the pastry with beaten egg. Place it in the refrigerator and let it rest for 20 to 30 minutes, to dry the egg wash and firm the pastry.

8 Meanwhile, preheat the oven to 450° F (230° C).

9 Lightly brush the top of the *jalousie* a second time with beaten egg. Pierce the top with the tip of a paring knife to make a series of parallel crosswise slits about ½ inch (1 to 1½ cm) apart ③. Cut through the pastry over the apples, but not the border around the outside.

10 Place the *jalousie* in the oven and reduce the temperature to 425° F (220° C). Bake until the pastry rises and the top is lightly browned, 15 to 20 minutes. Then reduce the oven temperature to 350° F (180° C) and continue baking until the top is golden brown and firm to the touch and the sides are light brown with no streaks of yellow, 40 to 60 minutes longer.

11 Slide the *jalousie* onto a cooling rack and let cool to room temperature.

Chaussons aux Pommes

APPLE TURNOVERS

Chausson means "slipper," and refers to the shape of these pastries. Our less poetic "turnover" derives from the method of preparation.

For 12 to 15 turnovers

INGREDIENTS

One *paton* of *feuilletage* (4 turns; see page 18)

Lightly beaten egg for brushing

Either 2 cups (600 g) *pommes sautées au beurre* (see page 88); *or* 1 cup (300 g) *pommes sautées au beurre* mixed with 1 cup (300 g) *compote de pommes* (see page 88)

7 teaspoons (15 g) confectioners sugar

1 Give the *feuilletage* two final turns.

2 Let the *paton* rest in the refrigerator for 20 to 30 minutes.

3 Roll out the dough into a rough rectangle about 18 × 34 inches (45 × 85 cm) and ⅛ inch (3 mm) thick. Lightly dust the countertop and the dough with flour as needed to prevent sticking.

4 Cut from the sheet of *feuilletage* twelve to fifteen circles, each 6 inches (15 cm) in diameter.

5 Brush a band 1 inch (2½ cm) wide around the bottom half edge of each circle with beaten egg.

6 Spoon 2½ to 3 tablespoons (40 to 50 g) of the apple filling onto the center of each circle ① and fold the top half of the circle over the apple mixture and onto the egg-brushed bottom edge. Press the pastry down around the edge with your fingertips to seal it. Press the edge of a flan ring or bowl 4 inches (10 cm) in diameter, or the side of your cupped hand, down on the pastry border around the enclosed apples to seal the filling tightly inside ②.

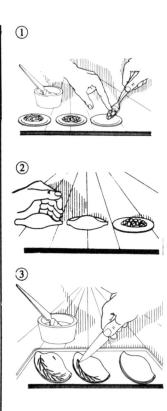

① ② ③

7 Brush one or two heavy baking sheets with a damp pastry brush to moisten them. Invert the *chaussons* onto the sheets, spacing them at least 1 inch (2½ cm) apart.

8 Lightly brush the top of each *chausson* with beaten egg. Let rest in the refrigerator for 20 to 30 minutes.

9 Preheat the oven to 450° F (230° C).

10 Lightly brush the tops of the *chaussons* a second time with beaten egg. Draw an arc down the center of each with the tip of a paring knife ③. Then draw lines extending out from the arc on both sides to make a leaflike pattern. The second brushing and the decorating should be done just before you bake the turnovers, so, if you can bake only one sheet of pastries at a time, wait to decorate the pastries on the second sheet until the first sheet comes out of the oven.

11 Place the *chaussons* in the oven and reduce the temperature to 425° F (220° C). Bake until the pastry rises and the tops of the *chaussons* are lightly browned, 10 to 15 minutes. Reduce the oven to 350° F (180° C) and continue baking until the tops are golden brown and firm to the touch and the sides are light brown with no streaks of yellow, 25 to 35 minutes longer.

12 Remove from the oven and turn on the broiler. Dust the tops of the *chaussons* with confectioners sugar. Return to the oven, on the second shelf from the top, until the sugar melts and glazes the tops, 30 to 90 seconds longer. If the sugar seems to be melting more quickly at one side of the oven than the other, rotate the baking sheet. If some of the *chaussons* are done before the others, remove them; and take all of the *chaussons* from the oven before the sugar starts to burn, even if some white spots remain. (If you have not yet baked all of the *chaussons*, reset the oven temperature at 450° F, or 230° C, and go back to step 10 to decorate and bake the remaining pastries.)

13 Slide the *chaussons* onto a cooling rack. Serve warm, or let cool to room temperature and reheat in a 250° F (120° C) oven before serving.

Alumettes

The name *alumettes*, which means "matchsticks" in French, derives from the shape of these pastries.

For 36 individual pastries

INGREDIENTS

Half of a *paton* of *feuilletage* (4 turns; see page 18)

6 to 8 tablespoons (175 to 230 g) *glace royale* (see page 104)

2¼ cups (600 g) *crème pâtissière* (see page 83)

2 tablespoons (3 cL) kirsch)

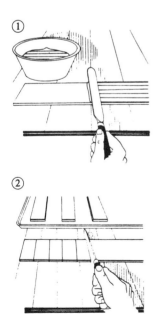

1 Give the *feuilletage* two final turns.

2 Let the *paton* rest in the refrigerator for 20 to 30 minutes.

3 Roll the *feuilletage* out into a rough rectangle a little larger than 10 × 27 inches (24 × 72 cm). Lightly dust the countertop and the dough with flour as needed to prevent sticking.

4 Cut from the sheet of *feuilletage* two 5 × 27 inch (12 × 72 cm) rectangles.

5 Spread the *glace royale* in a thin even layer on top of each rectangle of *feuilletage* with your palette knife ①.

6 Cut each rectangle of *feuilletage* into eighteen strips, each 5 inches (12 cm) long × 1½ inches (4 cm) wide ②.

7 Brush two (or more) heavy baking sheets with a damp pastry brush to moisten them. Place the strips of *feuilletage* on the baking sheets, separating them by about 1 inch (3 cm). Let them rest in the refrigerator until the *glace royale* dries and forms a crust on top, 1 to 2 hours.

8 Preheat the oven to 450° F (230° C).

9 Place a baking sheet of *alumettes* in the oven and reduce the temperature to 425° F (220° C). Bake until the tops just begin to brown, about 5 minutes. Reduce the oven to 350° F (180° C) and continue baking until the tops are a medium beige and the sides are light brown with no streaks of yellow, about 15 to 25 minutes longer.

③

10 Remove the pastries from the oven and slide them onto a cooling rack. Let cool to room temperature.

11 If you have not yet baked all the *alumettes,* raise the oven temperature to 450° F (230° C) and go back to step 9.

12 When all of the *alumettes* have baked and cooled, cut each in half horizontally with a bread knife ③. Flavor the *crème pâtissière* with the kirsch, and spread about 1 tablespoon (17 g) of pastry cream on the bottom half of each pastry with a small palette knife. Place the other half on top, like a sandwich.

Mille-Feuilles

NAPOLEONS

Of all the *feuilletés, mille-feuilles* are probably the most familiar in the United States. The name means "thousand layers." The only trick to making them is to use *rognures* rather than *feuilletage,* because the latter rises too high and results in an overly thick and heavy dessert.

For a small pastry serving 6 people or a large pastry serving 8

SMALL PASTRY

14 ounces (400 g)
  rognures (see page 24)

1⅔ cups (450 g)
  crème pâtissière
  (see page 83)

Optional: 4 teaspoons
  (2 cL) dark rum, or
  other liqueur

Either confectioners
  sugar for dusting; *or*
  2½ to 3 tablespoons
  (50 to 60 g) strained
  apricot jam and 6
  tablespoons (50 g)

1 You will need a 12 × 16-inch (30 × 40 cm) baking sheet for a small *mille-feuilles,* or a 13 × 20-inch (33 × 50 cm) baking sheet for a large *mille-feuilles.* Roll out the *rognures* into a rectangle a little larger than the baking sheet and about ³⁄₃₂ inch (2 mm) thick. Dust the countertop and the dough with flour as needed to prevent sticking.

2 Brush your baking sheet with a damp pastry brush to moisten it. Fold the rectangle of *rognures* in half, then in half again. Lift it from the counter onto the baking sheet and unfold it, centering it on the baking sheet with the edges overhanging on all sides. Run the dull edge of a chef's knife over the dough on the edge of the baking sheet to trim off the excess ①. Thoroughly prick the dough all over with a fork.

Opposite: Assorted brioche, pages 200–205. Following page: Brioche polonaise, page 217.

confectioners sugar; *or* about 1 tablespoon (15 g) *pâte à écrire* (see page 120) and ⅔ cup (225 g) fondant (see page 105) and *sirop à trente* (see page 398) for thinning fondant

LARGE PASTRY

1 pound 5 ounces (600 g) *rognures* (see page 24)

2½ cups (675 g) *crème pâtissière* (see page 83)

Optional: 2 tablespoons (3 cL) dark rum, or other liqueur

Either confectioners sugar for dusting; *or* 3½ to 4 tablespoons (70 to 80 g) strained apricot jam and ½ cup (65 g) confectioners sugar; *or* about 1 tablespoon (15 g) *pâte à écrire* (see page 120) and 1 cup (340 g) fondant (see page 105) and *sirop à trente* (see page 398) for thinning fondant

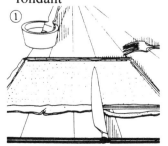

3 Let rest in the refrigerator for 30 to 40 minutes.

4 Preheat the oven to 425° F (220° C).

5 Place the baking sheet in the oven and reduce the temperature to 400° F (200° C). Bake until the pastry rises and just begins to brown on top, 15 to 20 minutes. Then reduce the oven to 350° F (180° C) and continue baking until the top of the pastry is a uniform medium brown and firm to the touch, 5 to 15 minutes longer.

6 Remove from the oven and transfer the baked sheet of pastry to a cooling rack. Let cool to room temperature.

7 Using a bread knife, trim the edges from the baked sheet of *rognures*. Cut it into three equal rectangles, each as long as the original sheet was wide ②. If there are any uneven bumps on top of the rectangles of *rognures*, shave them off with your bread knife. The most even of the three rectangles should be used as the top layer of the *mille-feuilles*.

8 Flavor the *crème pâtissière* with the optional rum. Spread half of the *crème pâtissière* over one of the rectangles of pastry using your palette knife or pastry corne ③. Bevel the edges of the layer of pastry cream so that, when you cut the *mille-feuilles*, it won't be pressed out the sides. Place a second layer of *rognures* on top and spread the remaining *crème pâtissière* over it, beveling the edges again. Invert the third rectangle of *rognures* and place it on top.

9 The top of the *mille-feuilles* can be finished in one of three ways:

Dusting with confectioners sugar: Dust the sugar heavily over the top of the pastry. To be more fancy, burn a lozenge pattern into the confectioners sugar using a wire or skewer heated to red hot on your cooktop ④.

Glazing with apricot jam and glace à l'eau: Warm the apricot jam over low heat, stirring occasionally, until melted. Brush the top of the pastry with the apricot jam. Prepare a *glace à l'eau* by stirring cold

Opposite: Savarin aux pêches (peach savarin), page 231. Preceding page: Assorted babas, pages 224–230.

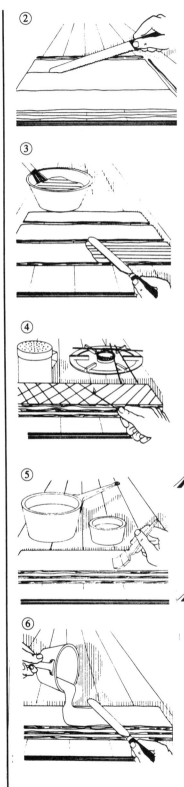

water (or, if you have flavored the *crème pâtissière* with rum, use half rum and half water) into the confectioners sugar until smooth, creamy, and just liquid enough to spread easily with a pastry brush. Brush this *glace à l'eau* over the apricot jam on top of the pastry to coat it evenly ⑤. Allow the *glace à l'eau* to set.

Glazing with fondant: Gently warm the *pâte à écrire* until melted, and prepare a parchment cornet (see page 118). Warm the fondant over low heat, stirring with a wooden spoon until melted. Stir in just enough *sirop à trente* to thin the fondant to the consistency of heavy cream. Pour the fondant over the top of the *mille-feuilles* and spread it evenly with the edge of your palette knife ⑥, letting the excess flow off the edges. Transfer the *pâte à écrire* to the cornet. Cut the tip of the cornet, and, while the fondant is still moist, pipe parallel lines of *pâte à écrire* lengthwise over the top of the *mille-feuilles,* separating the lines by about ¾ inch (2 cm) ⑦. Drag the tip of your paring knife crosswise over the fondant at 1-inch (2½ cm) intervals, wiping it off after each stroke and alternating direction from one stroke to the next to form a "marbled" pattern ⑧. The blade should just touch the surface of the fondant. Allow the fondant to set.

10 Trim about ¼ to ⅜ inch (6 to 10 mm) off each edge of the *mille-feuilles* to give it clean, straight sides. First saw through the top layer of pastry with a bread knife. Then cut through the remaining layers with your chef's knife, pressing down quickly and firmly.

11 To serve the *mille-feuilles,* divide it crosswise into 6 or 8 equal strips, sawing through the top layer of pastry with a bread knife and then cutting through the remaining layers with a chef's knife ⑨.

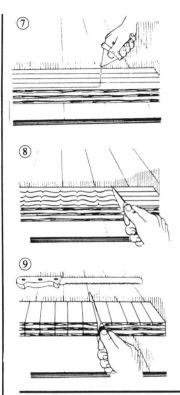

Variation: You can, if you like, fill the bottom layer of the *mille-feuilles* with kirsch-flavored *crème pâtissière* and the second layer with 4 to 6 tablespoons (80 to 120 g) of raspberry jam. Glaze the *mille-feuilles* with pink-tinted fondant, and marble it with *pâte à écrire*.

Feuilletage Cookies

Palmiers

These *feuilletage* cookies are shaped like palm leaves.

For 15 to 20 cookies

INGREDIENTS

One *paton* of *feuilletage* (4 turns; see page 18)

About 1½ cups (300 g) sugar for dusting

Lightly beaten egg for brushing

1 Give the *feuilletage* two final turns, dusting your countertop and the dough with sugar to sweeten it and prevent it from sticking to counter or rolling pin.

2 Let the *paton* rest in the refrigerator for 20 to 30 minutes.

3 Roll out the *feuilletage* into a rough rectangle a little larger than 12 × 16 inches (30 × 40 cm) and about ⅜ inch (1 cm) thick ①. Dust your countertop

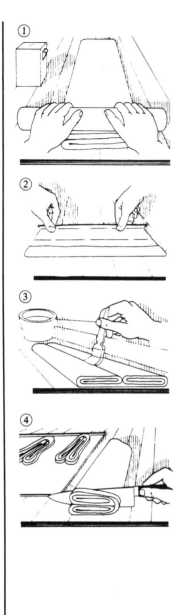

and the dough with sugar as needed to prevent the dough from sticking to counter or rolling pin.

4 Trim the sheet of dough to a 12 × 16-inch (30 × 40 cm) rectangle. Press the side of your rolling pin on the center of the rectangle to make a crosswise indentation. Fold each short edge of the dough a little less than half way to the center ②. Brush the strip down the center between the folded edges with egg wash. Then fold the short edges a second time so that they meet in the center. Press your rolling pin on the line down the center to seal the folds together. You will now have a folded band of dough about 12 inches (30 cm) long and 5 inches (13 cm) wide. Brush one side of the band with beaten egg ③, then fold it in half along the center line. Dust the band with sugar; and roll your rolling pin over it to press the layers together and seal the final fold with egg wash, and to flatten and elongate the band of dough. Press the side of your rolling pin lengthwise on the folded band of dough and rock it back and forth to make a slight indentation in the band down the center.

5 Using your chef's knife, cut the band into slices ⅝ inch (1½ cm) thick ④. Place the slices on one or two heavy baking sheets, spacing them about 3 inches (8 cm) apart.

6 Let rest for 30 to 40 minutes in the refrigerator.

7 Meanwhile, preheat the oven to 425° F (220° C).

8 Place a baking sheet of *palmiers* in the oven and reduce the temperature to 400° F (200° C). Bake until the bottoms begin to turn a light caramel color, 10 to 15 minutes. Turn the cookies, reduce the oven to 350° F (180° C), and continue baking until they are a medium caramel color with the centers golden, 10 to 20 minutes longer.

9 Transfer the cookies to your countertop, and let cool to room temperature.

10 If you have not yet baked all of the cookies, raise the oven to 425° F (220° C) and repeat steps 8 and 9.

Papillons

BUTTERFLIES

When these cookies are baked, the *feuilletage* expands to form butterfly-like shapes. Actually they look more like bow ties (*noeud-papillons* in French).

For about 14 cookies

INGREDIENTS

Half of a *paton* of *feuilletage* (4 turns; see page 18)

About ¾ cup (150 g) sugar for dusting

Lightly beaten egg for brushing

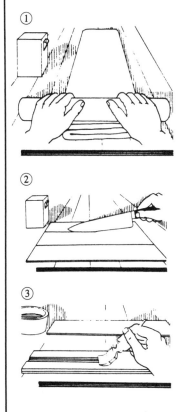

1 Give the *feuilletage* two final turns, dusting your countertop and the dough with sugar to sweeten it and prevent it from sticking to counter or rolling pin.

2 Let the *paton* rest in the refrigerator for 20 to 30 minutes.

3 Roll out the *feuilletage* into a rough rectangle a little larger than 6 × 18 inches (15 × 45 cm) and about ⁵⁄₁₆ inch (8 mm) thick ①. Dust your countertop and the dough with sugar as needed to prevent the dough from sticking to counter or rolling pin.

4 Trim the edges from the sheet of dough to a 6 × 18-inch (15 × 45 cm) rectangle. Cut the rectangle into three squares, each 6 × 6 inches (15 × 15 cm) ②. Press the side of your rolling pin on the center of one square to make a lengthwise indentation in the dough. Brush the indentation with a little beaten egg ③. Place a second square of dough on top of the first one, then press your rolling pin on the center to make an indentation and seal the squares together. Place the third square on top and press the rolling pin on the center to seal all three layers of dough together. Dust the pile of squares with a little more sugar and gently roll your rolling pin over it in the direction parallel to the indentation to thin it slightly. The pile of *feuilletage* rectangles should now be about 7 inches (18 cm) long by 6 inches (15 cm) wide and ¾ inch (2 cm) thick.

5 Using your chef's knife, cut the pile of *feuilletage* rectangles perpendicular to the indentation into strips about 6 inches (15 cm) long and ½ inch (12 mm) wide ④.

185

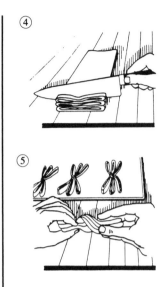

④

⑤

6 Pinch the center of each strip; then take the ends of the strip and give it a half twist ⑤. Place the twisted strip on a heavy baking sheet, with the center of the strip flat on the baking sheet. Press the center of the strip down on the baking sheet with your fingertip, and gently push the three layers of each end of the strip together. Repeat with the remaining strips, spacing them about 2 inches (5 cm) apart on the baking sheet. You will need two baking sheets.

7 Let rest for 20 to 30 minutes in the refrigerator.

8 Meanwhile, preheat the oven to 425° F (220° C).

9 Place a baking sheet of *papillons* in the oven and reduce the temperature to 400° F (200° C). Bake until the bottoms begin to turn a light caramel color, 8 to 12 minutes. Turn the cookies, reduce the oven to 350° F (180° C), and continue baking until the cookies are a medium caramel color at the ends and centers and the areas immediately adjacent to the centers have changed from pale cream to golden, 10 to 20 minutes longer.

10 Transfer the cookies to your countertop and let cool to room temperature.

11 If you have not yet baked all of the cookies, raise the oven to 425° F (220° C) and repeat steps 9 and 10.

Sacristains

These almond-coated *feuilletage* twists earned their ecclesiastical name by their resemblance to a corkscrew, a mundane but necessary adjunct to the sacramental vessels.

For about 24 cookies

INGREDIENTS

Half of a *paton* of

1 Give the *feuilletage* two final turns, dusting your countertop and the dough with flour to prevent it from sticking to counter or rolling pin.

feuilletage (4 turns;
see page 18)

Lightly beaten egg
for brushing

½ cup (75 g)
chopped blanched
almonds

6 tablespoons (75 g)
crystallized sugar
(see page 397)

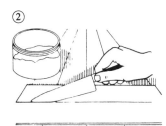

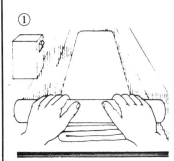

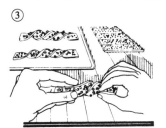

② Let the *paton* rest in the refrigerator for 20 to 30 minutes.

③ Roll out the *feuilletage* into a rough rectangle a little larger than 10 × 14 inches (26 × 36 cm) and about ¼ inch (6 mm) thick ①. Dust your countertop and the dough with flour as needed to prevent the dough from sticking to counter or rolling pin.

④ Trim the sheet of dough to a 10 × 14-inch (26 × 36 cm) rectangle. Cut the rectangle into two bands, each 5 × 14 inches (13 × 36 cm) ②. Generously brush the top of each band with beaten egg. Mix the almonds and crystallized sugar, and sprinkle half of the mixture over the bands. Gently roll your rolling pin over the bands to make the almonds and sugar adhere. Turn the bands over, brush them with egg wash on the second side, and sprinkle with the remaining almonds and crystallized sugar. Gently roll your rolling pin over each band.

⑤ Cut each band into 12 strips, each 5 inches (13 cm) long and 1¼ inches (3 cm) wide. One at a time, take each small strip by the ends and twist it one full turn, stretching it slightly ③. Place the twisted strip on a heavy baking sheet and press the ends on the baking sheet with your fingertips to anchor them firmly in place. Repeat with the remaining strips, spacing them about 1 inch (2½ cm) apart on the baking sheet. You will need two baking sheets.

⑥ Let rest for 20 to 30 minutes in the refrigerator.

⑦ Meanwhile, preheat the oven to 425° F (220° C).

⑧ Place a baking sheet of *sacristains* in the oven and reduce the temperature to 400° F (200° C). Bake until they begin to brown on top and bottom, 8 to 12 minutes. Turn the cookies, reduce the oven to 350° F (180° C), and continue baking until they are a medium brown with the twisted edges golden, 10 to 20 minutes longer.

⑨ Transfer the *sacristains* to your countertop and let cool to room temperature.

10 If you have not yet baked all of the cookies, raise the oven to 425° F (220° C) and repeat steps 8 and 9.

Arlettes

Arlette is a girl's name.

For about 20 cookies

INGREDIENTS

Half of a *paton* of *feuilletage* (4 turns; see page 18)

About 1 cup (200 g) sugar for dusting

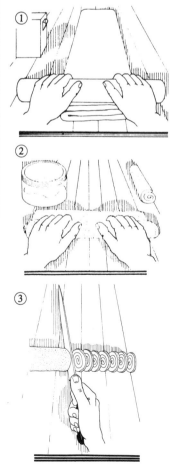

1 Give the *feuilletage* two final turns, dusting your countertop and the dough with flour for the fifth turn and sugar for the sixth to sweeten it and prevent it from sticking to counter or rolling pin.

2 Let the *paton* rest in the refrigerator for 20 to 30 minutes.

3 Roll out the *feuilletage* into a rough rectangle a little larger than 10 × 24 inches (25 × 60 cm) and about 3/16 inch (5 mm) thick ①. Dust your countertop and the dough with sugar as needed to prevent the dough from sticking to counter or rolling pin.

4 Trim the sheet of dough to a 10 × 24 inch (25 × 60 cm) rectangle. Roll up this rectangle into a cylinder 10 inches (25 cm) long ②. Press the side of your rolling pin on the cylinder to flatten it slightly and make the rolled dough adhere to itself. Using your chef's knife, cut the cylinder into slices ½ inch (12 mm) thick ③.

5 One at a time, place a slice of the cylinder on your sugar-dusted countertop, tucking the free end of the spiral underneath. Dust the slice with sugar and roll it out with your rolling pin into a circular disc about ⅛ inch (3 mm) thick ④. Place this thin circle on a heavy baking sheet. Repeat with the remaining slices, dusting your counter with more sugar to prevent the dough from sticking, and separating the slices by about 1 inch (2½ cm) on the baking sheet. You will need several baking sheets.

6 Let rest for 20 to 30 minutes in the refrigerator.

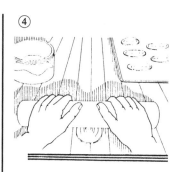

④

7 Meanwhile, preheat the oven to 425° F (220° C).

8 Place a baking sheet of *arlettes* in the oven and reduce the temperature to 400° F (200° C). Bake until the bottoms begin to turn a light caramel color, 10 to 15 minutes. Turn the cookies, reduce the oven to 350° F (180° C), and continue baking until the cookies are a medium caramel color with the centers golden to light caramel, about 10 minutes longer.

9 Transfer the *arlettes* to your countertop, and let cool to room temperature.

10 If you have not yet baked all of the cookies, raise the oven to 425° F (220° C) and repeat steps 8 and 9.

Breakfast Pastries

Croissants

Croissants take their crescent shape from the emblem on the Ottoman flag. In 1686, the Turks lay siege to Budapest and tried to tunnel into the city. The attempt failed because bakers working in their basement kitchens heard the digging. The bakers were honored with the exclusive privilege of making the croissant, which was later adopted by the French as a breakfast pastry.

For about 36 croissants

INGREDIENTS

1 *paton* of *pâte à croissant* (2 turns; see page 25)
Lightly beaten egg for brushing

1 Give the *pâte à croissant* two final turns.

2 Let the *paton* rest in the refrigerator for 20 minutes.

3 Roll out the *pâte à croissant* into a rough rectangle about 14 × 35 inches (35 × 90 cm) and ³⁄₁₆ inch (5 mm) thick. Dust the countertop and the dough with flour as needed to prevent the dough from sticking to counter or rolling pin.

4 Dust the dough very lightly with flour. Fold the sheet in half lengthwise ①. Trim the ends and the side opposite the fold to form a precise rectangle

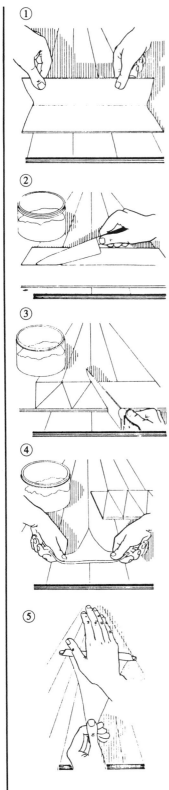

about 6 inches (16 cm) wide. Unfold the sheet and cut it in half along the crease ②.

5 Place one band of dough on top of the other so you can cut them simultaneously. Using a large chef's knife, cut the bands of dough into identical triangles, each about 6 inches (16 cm) high and 3½ inches (9 cm) along the base ③.

6 Take one of the triangles of dough and pull it gently on the lateral corners to stretch the base of the triangle ④. Then stretch the wide half of the triangle down the center a little in the long direction. This will ensure that the croissant will not be too fat in the center.

7 Roll up each triangle, on a marble slab if you have one. There are two methods—pulling and pushing. In either case, brush any excess flour from your countertop and the dough so that the triangles won't slide on the counter.

Pulling: Place a triangle of dough on the counter with the base at the top. Press your fingertips down on the base of the triangle to make it stick to the counter. Hold the tip of the triangle with one hand, and place your other hand palm down, with the base of your index finger on the center of the base of the triangle. Move the base of your index finger back and forth over the base of the triangle, pressing gently, until the dough begins to roll up ⑤. Roll the dough one or two revolutions by pulling your hand toward you, pushing down on the base of your index finger to flatten the center of the roll slightly so the center of the croissant will be tight. Then place both hands, palms down, on the ends of the partially rolled croissant ⑥. Starting from below the base of your thumbs, roll up the croissant by pulling your hands toward you in one smooth motion until the ends of the rolled triangle reach the tips of your index fingers.

Pushing: Place a triangle of dough on the countertop with the base at the bottom. Press your fingertips down on the base of the triangle to make it stick to the counter. Place your fingertips on the base of the triangle and begin rolling it up by pushing your hands away from you. When you have gotten the roll

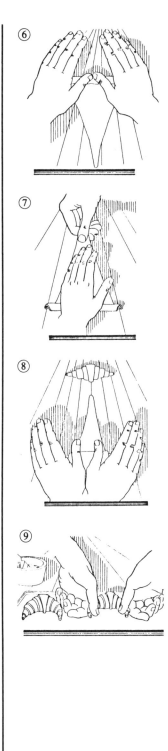

started, take the tip of the triangle in one hand. Place your other hand palm down, with the base of your index finger on the center of the base of the triangle; and roll up the base of the triangle by pushing this hand away from you as you gently pull on the tip of the triangle with the other hand to stretch the triangle so the center of the croissant will be tight ⑦. When you have made about two rotations, place both hands palms down, with the tips of your index fingers on the ends of the partially rolled triangle. Finish rolling up the triangle by pushing your hands away from you in one continuous motion, finishing with the ends of the rolled triangle at the bases of your thumbs ⑧.

8 Brush two or three heavy baking sheets with a damp pastry brush to moisten them. One at a time, transfer the rolled croissants to the baking sheets. Place the tip of the rolled triangle under the body of the croissant and pointing away from you, and bend the ends of the rolled triangle toward you to make a crescent shape ⑨. Twist the corners a little to tighten the roll, and gently press them onto the baking sheet with your thumbs to anchor the croissant. Do not, however, press the corners too thin, or they will burn when baked. Space the croissants about 1½ inches (4 cm) apart on the baking sheet.

9 Lightly brush the tops of the croissants with beaten egg, and let them rise in a warm place until doubled in volume, about 1½ to 2 hours.

10 Preheat the oven to 425° F (220° C).

11 When the croissants have risen, brush those on one baking sheet again with a little beaten egg.

12 Place this baking sheet of croissants in the preheated oven and reduce the temperature to 400° F (200° C). Bake until they are a uniform golden brown and firm to the touch, 15 to 20 minutes.

13 Slide the croissants onto a cooling rack. Serve warm; or let cool to room temperature and reheat in a 250° F (120° C) oven before serving.

14 If you have not yet baked all of the croissants, raise the oven to 425° F (220° C) and repeat steps 11 through 13.

Pains au Chocolat

Hot out of the oven, with a melted bar of bittersweet chocolate down the center, these are a great favorite among French children and a delightful alternative to croissants for anyone who enjoys chocolate.

For about 36 pastries

INGREDIENTS

1 *paton* of *pâte à croissant* (2 turns; see page 25)

36 *batons au chocolat* (see page 194)

Lightly beaten egg for brushing

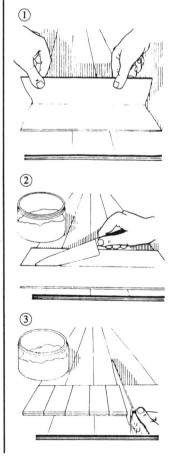

1 Give the *pâte à croissant* two turns, making four turns altogether.

2 Let the *paton* rest in the refrigerator for 20 minutes.

3 Roll out the *pâte à croissant* into a rough rectangle about 18 × 32 inches (45 × 80 cm) and ³/₁₆ inch (5 mm) thick. Dust the countertop and the dough with flour as needed to prevent the dough from sticking to counter or rolling pin.

4 Dust the dough very lightly with flour. Fold the sheet in half lengthwise ①. Trim the ends and the side opposite the fold to form a precise rectangle about 8 inches (20 cm) wide. Unfold the sheet and cut in half along the crease ②. Fold each band of dough in half lengthwise to mark the center, then unfold and cut in half along the crease. You should now have four identical rectangular bands, each about 4 × 30 inches (10 × 76 cm).

5 Pile the bands of dough one on top of the other so you can cut all four simultaneously. Using a *baton au chocolat* as a guide to measure the width, cut them into identical rectangles, each about 4 inches (10 cm) long and 3¼ inches (8½ cm) wide ③.

6 Take one of the rectangles of dough and lay a *baton au chocolat* across it horizontally, a little below the center. Using both hands, fold the near end of the rectangle over the *baton*, then press down gently on this end of the rectangle with your fingertips to tightly enclose the *baton* ④. Fold the near, double layer of dough (which includes the *baton au chocolat*) up over the far end of the rectangle. The

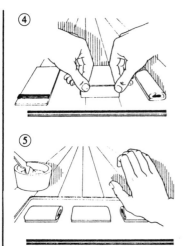

far end of the rectangle should now extend about two thirds of the way under the package. Press down on the top of the folded package of dough to close it tightly ⑤. Repeat with the remaining rectangles of dough and *batons au chocolat*.

7 Brush two or three heavy baking sheets with a damp pastry brush to moisten them. One at a time, place the *pains au chocolat* on the baking sheets, with the free end of the rectangle of dough underneath so that the weight of the *pain au chocolat* will prevent it from opening while baking. Press each *pain au chocolat* with the heel of your hand to flatten it slightly. Space the *pains au chocolat* about 1½ inches (4 cm) apart on the baking sheet.

8 Lightly brush the tops of the *pains au chocolat* with beaten egg, and let them rise in a warm place until doubled in volume, about 1½ to 2 hours.

9 Preheat the oven to 425° F (220° C).

10 When the *pains au chocolat* have risen, brush those on one baking sheet again with a little beaten egg.

11 Place this baking sheet of *pains au chocolat* in the oven and reduce the temperature to 400° F (200° C). Bake until they are a uniform golden brown and firm to the touch, 10 to 20 minutes.

12 Slide the *pains au chocolat* onto a cooling rack. Serve warm; or let cool to room temperature and reheat in a 250° F (120° C) oven before serving.

13 If you have not yet baked all of the *pains au chocolat*, raise the oven to 425° F (220° C) and repeat steps 10 through 12.

Batons au Chocolat

These are little sticks of semisweet chocolate that are baked inside *pains au chocolat*. You can form them easily by molding the chocolate in a 1-pint plastic freezer storage container with a 3¼-inch (8½ cm) square bottom.

For 36 batons

INGREDIENTS

9 ounces (250 g)
  semisweet chocolate

1 Temper the chocolate as follows: Melt the chocolate. Dip the bottom of the pot of chocolate in cold water and stir until it begins to thicken. Immediately return it to the heat and gently warm the chocolate a second time, stirring constantly, until just melted again.

2 Pour the melted chocolate into six 1 pint freezer storage containers, dividing the chocolate equally.

3 Let the chocolate cool and set. Then briefly chill it in the refrigerator so it will be firm and won't melt when you unmold it.

4 Invert each container and press on the bottom to unmold the 3¼-inch (8½ cm) squares of chocolate.

5 Dip the blade of your chef's knife in boiling water. Wipe it dry and carefully cut each square of chocolate into six *batons* 3¼ inches (8½ cm) long and ½ inch (13 mm) wide.

6 Separate the cut *batons* and let the melted edges set.

Storage: Covered airtight, in a cool place for up to 1 year.

Chapter Seven

BRIOCHES

The principal subject of this chapter is brioche itself, a bread so rich in butter and eggs that it is one of the *grande luxe* pillars of French gastronomy. We have included pastries made from *brioche aux fruits* and *pâte à kugelhopf* with those made from *pâte à brioche* because the doughs and the pastries produced from them are very similar. In contrast to the rest of this book, the majority of these pastries are constructed from pastry doughs alone, with no fillings or toppings, and only a few of them are eaten for dessert.

TOURS DE MAIN

The French have devised dozens of ways to use *brioche,* all based on a handful of methods for shaping, molding, and baking the dough. *Brioche aux fruits* differs from *pâte à brioche* in proportions and flavorings but is handled by the same techniques. Both are refrigerated before they are shaped, making them relatively firm. *Pâte à kugelhopf* is not refrigerated and is rather soft and sticky when it is molded, so the general shaping and molding techniques described below do not apply to it.

Deflating the Dough (*Rabattage*)

After the brioche dough has rested overnight in the refrigerator, turn it out onto a lightly floured countertop. Dust your hands lightly with flour and deflate and flatten the dough by patting it down with your palms ①.

The side of the dough that was on top in the refrigerator will have a slight crust, and the dough will be easier to shape if you first enclose the crust in the center of the dough. Arrange the dough, crust side up, on the countertop. Press and stretch it into a rough square. Fold over two opposite sides so they meet in the center. Then fold the dough in half along the line where the two edges meet. Pat the dough lightly, pressing it together so it will not open up when the dough is shaped.

Cut the dough into pieces of the size required with a dough scraper. The dough must be cold when it is shaped, so any dough you will not form right away should be returned to the refrigerator, in a bowl covered with a damp kitchen towel.

Shaping the Dough *(Boulage)*

Each piece of brioche dough must now be formed into one of six shapes. This step must be executed quickly and precisely, because if the dough is warmed too much or is not symmetrically shaped before molding, then the finished pastry will suffer in appearance. Shape the dough on a chilled marble slab, if you have one.

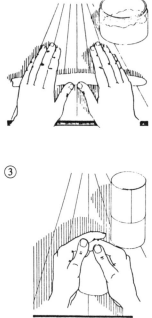

CYLINDERS: Cut a thick, roughly rectangular piece of *pâte à brioche*. Dust your hands and the countertop or marble slab with just enough flour to prevent the dough from sticking. Place both hands palms down on the dough and roll it back-and-forth to thin and lengthen it into a uniform cylinder ②.

LARGE BALLS: The lump of dough you start with should be at least 5 ounces (150 g) — if smaller, use the method for small balls below. Place the dough on an unfloured countertop or marble slab. Dust your hands lightly with flour and cup them around the dough, with the sides of both hands on the counter and your thumbs on top of the dough. Pressing down at first to make it stick to the counter, roll the dough in a circle under your palms and use your thumbs on top to control the shape of the ball ③. Keeping the sides of your hands on the counter, continue rolling the dough in a circle and gradually raise the incline of your hands until your palms are perpendicular to the counter and the dough is shaped into a tight, symmetrical sphere.

SMALL BALLS: This is the method to use for rolling a lump of dough weighing less than 5 ounces (150 g). Place the dough on an unfloured countertop or marble slab. Dust one hand lightly with flour and cup it over the dough, with the side of your hand, your fingertips, and the side of your thumb on the counter. Pressing down at first to make it stick to the counter, roll the lump of dough in a circle (counter-clockwise for your right hand, or clockwise for your left) under your palm, dragging the lump toward you with the side of your hand and pushing back with your thumb ④. Continue rolling the dough in the circular motion, gradually raising the incline of your hand with the counter and pulling in your thumb to raise the lump into a tight, symmetrical sphere ⑤.

CIRCLES: First roll the dough into a ball as described in the method for large balls, above. Dust the countertop or marble slab and the ball of dough with flour and press the ball with the heel of your hand to flatten it into a thick, round pad. Place the center of your rolling pin on the end of the pad nearest you and roll it in a smooth forward motion to the far end of the dough ⑥. Reverse direction and roll it back over the dough to the end nearest you. Rotate the dough 90° and repeatedly roll the pad and rotate it after each forward and backward motion to make a rough circle about ⅛ to ³⁄₁₆ inch (3 to 5 mm) thick. Occasionally lift the dough from the counter and dust both the counter and dough with flour to prevent the dough from sticking to counter or rolling pin.

RECTANGLES: Cut a rectangular pad of *pâte à brioche;* or press each side of a piece of *brioche* against the countertop to give it a roughly rectangular shape. With your rolling pin, roll out the pad into a rectangular sheet about ⅛ to ³⁄₁₆ inch (3 to 5 mm) thick by the same method (omitting, of course, the first step of forming a ball) as for circles. Trim the dough to a neat rectangle of the required dimensions with your chef's knife. To avoid stretching the dough out of shape, make each cut by placing the tip of the blade on the counter and then, pivoting from the tip of the blade, pressing down on the handle until the entire length of the blade has cut through the dough in a straight line.

RINGS: There are two ways to form the dough into a ring or crown shape. The easiest is to first roll the dough into a cylinder, about 1 inch (2½ cm) in diameter, as described above. Then moisten the ends of the cylinder with a little water or beaten egg and press ends of cylinder together ⑦.

197

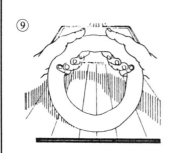

The second method requires more finesse but produces a ring with no seams. First roll the dough into a large ball, as described above. Make a hole in the center of the dough with a floured index finger ⑧. Turn the dough around on your finger to enlarge the hole. When the hole is large enough, grasp the ring with both hands and gradually rotate the ring and squeeze it to thin and enlarge the ring ⑨. The dough should be about 1 inch (2½ cm) thick.

Molding, Egg Wash, and the Second Rise *(Moulage, Dorage, et La Deuxième Pousse)*

Brush the inside of your mold with melted butter, and mold the shaped dough in it following the instructions for the form of brioche you are making. For most forms, the top of the brioche is brushed with a little beaten egg to prevent it from drying out and forming a crust. Brush it sparingly, using only as much beaten egg as required to coat the surface lightly and make it glisten.

Let the molded brioche rise in a warm place (75° to 85° F, or 25° to 30° C) until doubled or tripled in volume, 1 to 2 hours. How much the brioche dough should be allowed to rise depends on the shape of the dough. For example, *brioche mousseline* has a straight-sided mold and a high collar to control the expansion of the dough, so it can rise until tripled in volume with no risk of losing its shape. On the other hand, *brioche couronne* has no mold at all to contain it, and, if it were allowed to rise until tripled in volume it would become too soft and lose its shape. So *brioche couronne* should be allowed to rise until only doubled in volume. Other shapes fall between these two extremes. Since the magnitude of the rise in this step is critical in determining how much the brioche will rise in the oven, *brioche mousseline* is the lightest form of brioche and *brioche couronne* is the heaviest.

After the brioche has risen, lightly brush it a second time with egg wash to dissolve the dried egg on the surface and moisten it so that the brioche will rise

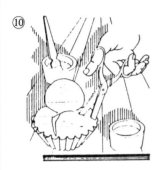

evenly and brown nicely in the oven. For some large forms of brioche, you must make deep incisions into the brioche. If the form you are making requires it, dip a scissors in cold water and then simultaneously snip and plunge the scissors into the top of the brioche in the locations specified by the instructions for that shape ⑩. The scissors should be dipped in cold water before making each incision to prevent the dough from sticking to it. The brioche will fall when you cut it, but these incisions help heat penetrate the center of the brioche quickly, making it rise better in the oven.

Baking the Brioche *(Cuisson)*

Have the oven preheated to 425° F (220° C) with a heavy baking sheet on the middle shelf (or on a lower shelf if the *brioche* requires more height). The hot baking sheet helps the *brioche* rise by providing a quick initial bottom heat and distributes the heat more uniformly.

Place the molded brioche on the hot baking sheet in the oven and bake until the surface begins to color, turning from a pale, creamy yellow to a deeper, golden yellow and just beginning to brown. Then reduce the oven to 400° F (200° C)—except for *petites brioches* and *pains aux raisins* which are cooked at 425° F (220° C) from start to finish—and continue baking until the brioche is golden brown and firm to the touch. If there are incisions, the scars should be golden yellow.

When the brioche has finished baking, remove it from the oven and unmold it immediately onto a cooling rack. *Petites brioches* can be served hot out of the oven or allowed to cool on the rack. Large brioches are difficult to slice when fresh from the oven, so they should be allowed to cool on the rack before slicing. If you want to eat the brioche warm, reheat it in a 250° F (120° C) oven before serving.

STORAGE

After baking, brioche can be kept at room temperature, uncovered, for up to 1 day.

If you want to keep brioche longer, there are two methods for freezing. Best is to mold the dough and brush it with beaten egg, then freeze it immediately. Unmold the frozen brioche, seal airtight in a plastic bag, and keep frozen for up to 1 week. The day before you want to bake it, return the frozen brioche to the (buttered) mold and let it defrost in the refrigerator overnight. Then let it rise in a warm place, brush with egg wash and bake.

Alternatively, bake the brioche first, then while still warm (but not hot), seal airtight in a plastic bag and place it in the freezer for up to 2 weeks. When ready to eat, place the frozen brioche on a baking sheet, cover the top with kitchen parchment or aluminum foil, and reheat in a 300° F (150° C) oven for 5 to 15 minutes, depending on the size of the brioche.

The Classic Brioche Shapes

Brioche has innumerable uses, from forming *tarte* shells (see *tarte paysanne* on page 155, for example) to enclosing meats and pâtés, but it plays its most important role as the partner of croissants at the French breakfast table and with coffee or tea in the morning and afternoon. While brioche can appear there in many guises, there are seven that are so ancient, distinctive, and ubiquitous that they have come to be regarded as the classic brioche shapes.

Brioche Mousseline

This tall cylinder is the easiest brioche to make, and also the lightest.

For 4 to 6 people

INGREDIENTS

Melted butter for
  brushing mold
7 or 12 ounces (200
  or 350 g) *pâte à
  brioche* (page 37)
Lightly beaten egg
  for brushing brioche

1 Clean and dry an empty 16- or 29-ounce (454 or 822 g) fruit can, depending on the quantity of *pâte à brioche*. Brush the inside of the can with melted butter.

2 Cut a strip of brown wrapping paper 4 inches (10 cm) wide and either 12 inches (30 cm) long for a 7-ounce (200 g) brioche or 15 inches (38 cm) long

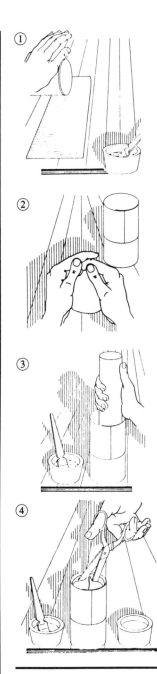

for a 12-ounce (350 g) brioche. Brush one short and one long edge of the strip of paper with beaten egg. Wrap it around the outside of the can to form a collar extending about 2 inches (5 cm) above the top of the can, with the egg wash sticking the bottom edge of the paper to the can and sealing the outer end of the paper in place ①.

3 Place the *pâte à brioche* on the countertop and form it into a tight ball by rolling it in a circle under your palm ②. Drop the ball of brioche into the can and tamp it down with the end of a French-style rolling pin to give it the shape of the mold ③. Lightly brush the top with beaten egg.

4 Let the brioche rise in a warm place until it reaches the top of the can, about 1½ to 2 hours.

5 Place a heavy baking sheet on the lowest shelf of the oven and remove the upper shelf. Preheat the oven to 425° F (220° C).

6 Brush the brioche again with egg wash. Dip a scissors in cold water and make two deep incisions by plunging the scissors into the top of the brioche, forming a cross ④.

7 Place the mold on the hot baking sheet in the oven and bake until the top of the brioche changes from a pale, creamy yellow to a deeper, golden yellow and just begins to brown, 10 to 15 minutes. Reduce the oven to 400° F (200° C) and continue baking until the top is firm to the touch and golden brown, with the scars golden yellow, 30 to 45 minutes longer.

8 Unmold the brioche onto a cooling rack and let cool to room temperature.

Brioche Parisienne

For this distinctive shape, with its flared body and high round head, you will need a fluted brioche mold.

For 4 to 6 people

INGREDIENTS

Melted butter for
brushing mold

7 to 10½ ounces
(200 to 300 g) *pâte
à brioche* (see page
37)

Lightly beaten egg
for brushing brioche

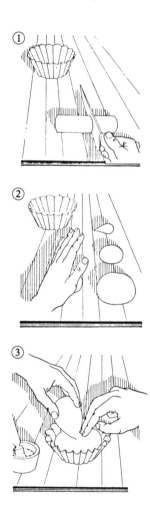

1 Choose a brioche mold 6¼ to 7 inches (16 to 18 cm) in diameter, depending on the quantity of *pâte à brioche*. Brush the inside of the mold with melted butter.

2 Divide the dough into two parts, two thirds in one piece and one third in the other ①. The large piece will become the body of the *brioche parisienne*, and the small piece the head. Place each piece of dough on the countertop and roll it (using both hands for the large piece and one hand for the small one) in a circle to form a tight ball.

3 Place the large ball in the center of the mold, and press it down firmly with your fingertips to give it the shape of the mold and make a depression in the center.

4 Roll the smaller ball under your palm to give it a teardrop shape ②. Place it on top of the larger piece of dough in the mold with the point of the teardrop in the center of the depression ③. Dust the index and middle fingers of one hand with flour so they won't stick to the dough. Gently guide the top of the head with your other hand, and anchor the head by firmly pushing the point of the teardrop down into the depression with your floured index and middle fingers until your fingertips touch the bottom of the mold. Repeat five or six times, working around in a circle, until the head is well anchored and straight.

5 Lightly brush the brioche with beaten egg, and let it rise in a warm place until at least doubled in volume, about 1½ to 2 hours.

6 Preheat the oven to 425° F (220° C). Place a heavy baking sheet on the middle shelf of the oven.

7 Brush the brioche again with egg wash. Dip a scissors in cold water and make four deep cuts in the body of the brioche, spacing the incisions evenly around the circumference ④.

8 Place the mold on the hot baking sheet in the oven and bake until the top of the brioche changes

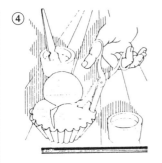

④ from a pale, creamy yellow to a deeper, golden yellow and just begins to brown, 5 to 10 minutes. Reduce the oven to 400° F (200° C) and continue baking until the top is firm to the touch and golden brown, with the scars golden yellow, 15 to 30 minutes longer.

9 Unmold the brioche onto a cooling rack, and let cool to room temperature.

Petites Brioches

These small brioches have the same shape as *brioche parisienne*. For this recipe, you need fluted brioche molds 2¾ inches (7 cm) in diameter. You can also bake slightly larger individual brioches in cupcake pans 2¾ inches (7 cm) diameter, using 14 ounces (400 g) of dough for eight pastries.

For 8 individual brioches

INGREDIENTS

Melted butter for
  brushing molds

9 ounces (250 g) *pâte
à brioche* (see page
37)

Lightly beaten egg
  for brushing brioche

①

②

1 Brush the inside of each mold with melted butter.

2 Lightly dust your hands and countertop with flour. Place the dough on the counter and roll it under your palms into an even cylinder about 8 inches (20 cm) long. Cut the cylinder in half, then cut each half in half, and finally cut each quarter in half to get eight equal pieces.

3 Roll each lump of dough into a small, tight ball under your palm ①. Then roll the side of your hand back and forth over each ball to divide it into a head and body connected by a thick neck ②.

4 Dust your fingertips with flour. Lift one of the pieces of dough by the neck and, centering it carefully, press the body down in one of the molds ③. Gently guide the top of the head with the index finger of one hand; and using the floured index finger of the other hand, firmly press the base of the neck down to the bottom of the mold three or four times ④, working around in a circle, to give the body the shape of the mold and anchor the head ⑤. Gently

③

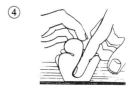

④

⑤

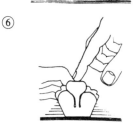

⑥

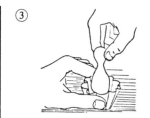

press the tip of your index finger on top of the head to center it more perfectly and flatten it slightly ⑥. Repeat with the remaining pieces of dough.

5 Brush the brioches with a little beaten egg, and let them rise in a warm place until at least doubled in volume, about 1 hour.

6 Preheat the oven to 425° F (220° C). Place a heavy baking sheet on the middle shelf of the oven.

7 Brush the brioches again with egg wash. Place the molds on the hot baking sheet in the oven and bake until the tops of the brioches are golden brown and firm to the touch, 10 to 15 minutes.

8 Unmold the brioches onto a cooling rack. Serve hot, or let cool on the rack.

Brioche Nanterre

Baked in a rectangular loaf pan, this brioche is almost as light as *brioche mousseline*.

For 4 to 8 people

INGREDIENTS

Melted butter for brushing mold

7 to 14 ounces (200 to 400 g) *pâte à brioche* (see page 37)

Lightly beaten egg for brushing brioche

1 Choose a 3- to 6-cup (¾ to 1½ L) loaf pan, depending on the quantity of *pâte à brioche*. Brush the inside with melted butter.

2 Lightly dust your hands and countertop with flour. Place the dough on the counter and roll it under your palms into an even cylinder about 6 inches (15 cm) long ①. Cut the cylinder into five equal pieces.

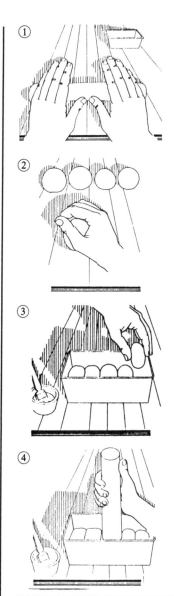

3 Roll each piece of dough into a small, tight ball, under the palm of your hand ②.

4 Place the balls in a row in the bottom of the loaf pan, pressing them together to flatten them slightly so they will all fit in a straight line ③. Gently press each ball with the end of a French-style rolling pin or your knuckles to flatten it against the bottom of the mold ④.

5 Brush the brioche with a little beaten egg, and let it rise in a warm place until it reaches almost to the top of the mold, about 1½ to 2 hours.

6 Preheat the oven to 425° F (220° C). Place a heavy baking sheet on the middle shelf of the oven.

7 Brush the brioche again with egg wash. Dip a scissors in cold water and snip the top of each ball. Orient the incisions on the diagonal with respect to the sides of the mold, and reverse directions from ball to ball to form a zigzag pattern.

8 Place the mold on the hot baking sheet in the oven and bake until the top of the brioche changes from a pale, creamy yellow to a deeper, golden yellow and just begins to brown, 5 to 10 minutes. Reduce the oven to 400° F (200° C) and continue baking until the top is firm to the touch and golden brown, with the scars golden yellow, 15 to 30 minutes longer.

9 Unmold the brioche onto a cooling rack, and let cool to room temperature.

Brioche Couronne

This brioche, shaped like a ring or crown *(couronne),* is baked without any mold.

For 6 to 12 people

INGREDIENTS

Melted butter for
brushing baking
sheet

10½ ounces to 1
pound 5 ounces
(300 to 600 g) *pâte
à brioche* (see page
37)

Lightly beaten egg
for brushing brioche

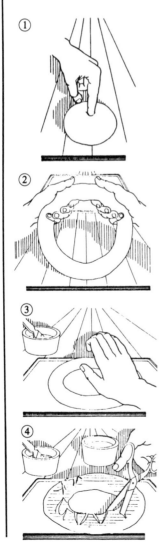

1 Brush a heavy baking sheet with melted butter.

2 Form the dough with your hands into a ring about 1 inch (2½ cm) thick with a hole 4 to 8 inches (10 to 20 cm) in diameter in the center ①-②.

3 Place the ring on the buttered baking sheet, and pat the top gently with your palm to flatten it slightly ③.

4 Brush the brioche with a little beaten egg, and let it rise in a warm place until doubled in volume, 1 to 1½ hours.

5 Preheat the oven to 425° F (220° C). Place a second heavy baking sheet on the middle shelf of the oven.

6 Brush the brioche again with egg wash. Dip a scissors in cold water and make a series of cuts in the top of the brioche, following a zigzag path around the ring ④.

7 Place the brioche on the hot baking sheet in the oven, and bake until the top changes from a pale, creamy yellow to a deeper, golden yellow and just begins to brown, 5 to 10 minutes. Reduce the oven to 400° F (200° C) and continue baking until the top is firm to the touch and golden brown, with the scars golden yellow, 15 to 30 minutes longer.

8 Transfer the brioche to a cooling rack and let cool to room temperature.

Pains aux Raisins

These raisin buns are excellent as snacks with tea or coffee, as well as for breakfast.

For 16 individual raisin buns

INGREDIENTS

2½ ounces (70 g), or about ½ cup, seedless raisins

2 tablespoons plus 2 teaspoons (4 cL) dark rum

¾ pound (350 g) *pâte à brioche* (see page 37)

1 cup (270 g) *crème pâtissière* (see page 83)

2 to 3 tablespoons (40 to 60 g) strained apricot jam

¼ cup plus 2 tablespoons (50 g) confectioners sugar

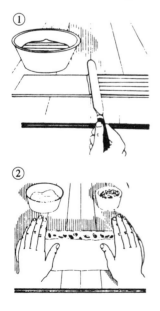

1 Place the raisins in a strainer and steam them over simmering water until they just begin to soften, about 5 minutes. Transfer the raisins to a bowl and pour the rum over them. Cover and let soak in the rum for at least 2 hours and preferably overnight. Then drain thoroughly and reserve any rum that has not been absorbed.

2 Dust your countertop and the dough with flour, and roll out the dough with your rolling pin into a sheet a little larger than 12 inches (32 cm) square and about ⅛ inch (3 mm) thick. Trim the sheet to a 12-inch (32 cm) square.

3 Spread the *crème pâtissière* over the sheet of brioche dough in a thin, even layer with your palette knife ①. Scatter the raisins over the *crème pâtissière*. Roll up this sheet into a cylinder 12 inches (32 cm) long, enclosing the *crème pâtissière* and raisins in a spiral of brioche dough ②. Cut the roll into sixteen slices, each ¾ inch (2 cm) thick, with a bread knife, being careful not to press the roll out of shape ③.

4 Brush a heavy baking sheet with a damp pastry brush to moisten it. Place the slices on it, spacing them about 2 inches (5 cm) apart. Gently pat each slice with the palm of your hand to flatten it slightly.

5 Let rise in a warm place until doubled in volume, about 1 hour.

6 Preheat the oven to 425° F (220° C). Place a second heavy baking sheet on the middle shelf of the oven.

7 Put the baking sheet of *pains aux raisins* on the hot baking sheet in the oven, and bake until the brioche is golden brown, while the *crème pâtissière* is

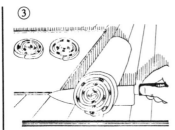

still yellow, 10 to 15 minutes. The *pains aux raisins* must be firm to the touch, but still soft inside.

8 Transfer the *pains aux raisins* to a cooling rack and let cool to room temperature.

9 Warm the apricot jam over low heat, stirring occasionally, until melted. Brush the tops of the *pains aux raisins* with jam until lightly coated and glistening.

10 Raise the oven temperature to 450° F (230° C).

11 Prepare a *glace à l'eau* by adding 1 teaspoon (½ cL) of the reserved rum to the confectioners sugar and stirring in enough water to make it smooth, creamy, and just liquid enough to spread easily with a pastry brush. Brush this *glace à l'eau* over the jam on top of the *pains aux raisins*.

12 Transfer the *pains aux raisins* to a baking sheet and place them in the oven until the sugar melts and the glaze turns from opaque white to almost transparent, 1 to 2 minutes. If the *glace à l'eau* starts to bubble, remove from the oven immediately.

Brioche Bordelaise

In France, this sweet brioche cake is considered a dessert, but, for American tastes, it would be an excellent coffee cake or breakfast pastry. It is made by baking several *pains aux raisins* in a brioche-lined layer-cake pan.

For an 8-inch (20 cm) cake, to serve 8 to 10 people

INGREDIENTS

1½ ounces (40 g), or about 5 tablespoons, seedless raisins

2 ounces (60 g) candied fruits, cut into ¼-inch (6 mm) dice

3½ tablespoons (½ dL) dark rum

1 Place the raisins in a strainer and steam them over simmering water until they just begin to soften, about 5 minutes. Transfer the raisins to a bowl, add the diced candied fruits, and pour the rum over them. Cover and let soak in the rum for at least 2 hours and preferably overnight. Then drain thoroughly and reserve any rum that has not been absorbed.

2 Brush the inside of an 8-inch (20 cm) layer-cake pan with melted butter.

Melted butter for brushing mold

1 pound 10 ounces (750 g) *pâte à brioche* (see page 37)

1¼ cups (340 g) *crème d'amandes* (see page 87), or substitute *crème pâtissière* (see page 83)

About 2½ to 3 tablespoons (50 to 60 g) strained apricot jam

¼ cup (35 g) confectioners sugar

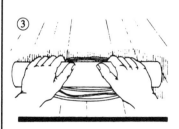

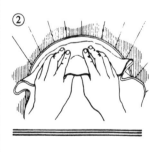

3 Place half of the brioche dough on your countertop and roll it under your palms into a tight ball. Flatten the ball into a thick, round pad with the heel of your hand. Dust your countertop and the dough with flour and roll it out into a circle 12 to 13 inches (30 to 33 cm) in diameter with your rolling pin. Fold the circle in half, then fold it a second time. Lift the quarter circle from the counter to the layer-cake pan, center and unfold it, and gently ease it down to line the bottom and sides of the mold ①. Fold the far side of the pastry back away from the side of the mold and press down on the fold with your fingertips to pinch it and press it into the corner where the bottom and side of the mold meet ②. Then press the pastry back against the side of the mold. Work around the circumference, rotating the mold as you go. Drape the excess brioche dough over the top edge of the mold and trim it off by rolling your rolling pin over the top of the mold ③. Combine the trimmings with the remaining dough.

4 Spread about ½ cup (135 g) of the *crème d'amandes* or *crème pâtissière* in an even layer over the bottom of the brioche-lined layer-cake pan. Place the mold in the refrigerator.

5 Dust your countertop and the remaining dough with flour, and roll out the dough into a sheet a little larger than 10 inches (25 cm) square and about ³⁄₁₆ inch (5 mm) thick. Trim the sheet to a 10-inch (25 cm) square.

6 Spread the remaining *crème d'amandes* or *crème pâtissière* over the sheet of brioche dough in a thin, even layer with your palette knife ④. Scatter the raisins and candied fruits over the pastry cream. Roll up this sheet into a cylinder 10 inches (25 cm) long, enclosing the pastry cream, raisins, and candied fruits in a spiral of brioche ⑤. Cut the roll into seven equal slices with a bread knife, being careful not to press it out of shape.

7 Take the brioche-lined layer-cake pan from the refrigerator. Place one slice in the center of the mold, and arrange the other six in a circle around it ⑥. Gently pat each slice with the palm of your hand to flatten it slightly.

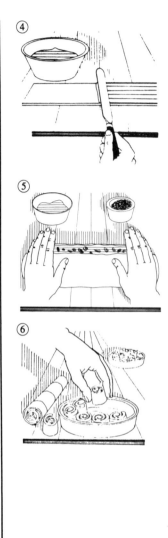

8 Let rise in a warm place until doubled in volume and the slices press against each other and the brioche lining the sides of the mold, about 1½ hours.

9 Preheat the oven to 425° F (220° C). Place a heavy baking sheet on the middle shelf of the oven.

10 Put the *brioche bordelaise* on the hot baking sheet in the oven and bake until the top changes from a pale, creamy yellow to a deeper, golden yellow and begins to brown, 5 to 10 minutes. Reduce the oven to 350° F (180° C) and continue baking until the top of the brioche is firm to the touch and golden brown, while the pastry cream is still yellow, about 30 to 45 minutes longer. If the brioche colors too quickly, place a piece of kitchen parchment over the top.

11 Remove the *brioche bordelaise* from the oven and place it, still in the mold, on a rack to cool. Do not unmold while hot, or it will fall apart.

12 When cooled to room temperature, unmold the brioche.

13 Warm the apricot jam over low heat, stirring occasionally, until melted. Brush the top of the brioche with jam until lightly coated and glistening.

14 Preheat the oven to 450° F (230° C).

15 Prepare a *glace à l'eau* by adding ½ teaspoon (¼ cL) of the reserved rum to the confectioners sugar and stirring in enough water to make it smooth, creamy, and just liquid enough to spread easily with a pastry brush. Brush this *glace à l'eau* over the jam on top of the *brioche bordelaise*.

16 Transfer the brioche to a baking sheet and place it in the preheated oven until the sugar melts and the glaze turns from opaque white to almost transparent, 1 to 2 minutes. If the *glace à l'eau* starts to bubble, remove from the oven immediately.

Related Cakes

Brioche aux fruits and *pâte à kugelhopf* are closely related to *pâte à brioche*, both in the method of preparing the doughs and the pastries that are produced from them. *Brioche aux fruits* is shaped into rings to make *gâteau des rois;* and, as its name implies, *pâte à kugelhopf* is used only for the cake called kugel-hopf.

Gâteau des Rois

This aromatic brioche, baked in the form of a crown studded with jewel-like candied fruits and crystallized sugar, is the traditional Twelfth Night cake in the south of France. A favor is usually baked inside, and the guest who gets it is the king or queen for the day.

For 6 to 12 people

INGREDIENTS

Melted butter for brushing baking sheet

10½ ounces to 1 pound 5 ounces (300 to 600 g) *brioche aux fruits* (see page 41)

Lightly beaten egg for brushing brioche

1 to 1½ ounces (30 to 45 g) candied fruits

2 to 4 teaspoons (8 to 15 g) crystallized sugar (see page 397)

1 Brush a heavy baking sheet with melted butter.

2 Form the *brioche aux fruits* with your hands into a ring, about 1 inch (2½ cm) thick, with a hole 4 to 8 inches (10 to 20 cm) in diameter in the center ①-②.

3 Place the ring on the buttered baking sheet, and pat the top gently with your palm to flatten it slightly ③.

4 Brush the top of the crown with a little beaten egg, and let it rise in a warm place until doubled in volume, 1 to 1½ hours.

5 Preheat the oven to 425° F (220° C). Place a second heavy baking sheet on the middle shelf of the oven.

6 Brush the brioche again with egg wash. Cut the candied fruits into wedges, triangles, or diamonds (except cherries—cut them in half), and arrange them around the top of the crown like jewels. Then sprinkle the crystallized sugar over the ring.

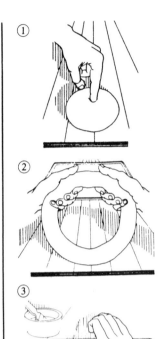

7 Place the baking sheet with the *gâteau des rois* on the hot baking sheet in the oven, and bake until the top changes from a pale, creamy yellow to a deeper, golden yellow and begins to brown, 10 to 15 minutes. Reduce the oven to 350° F (180° C) and continue baking until the top is firm to the touch and golden brown, 15 to 30 minutes longer.

8 Transfer the *gâteau des rois* to a cooling rack, and let cool to room temperature.

Storage: Same as for brioches (see page 200).

Kugelhopf

Kugelhopf is typically served with coffee. Since it is quite dry, some people like it sauced with *crème anglaise*, while others prefer to wash it down with a good Alsatian riesling or gewürztraminer.

For 8 to 12 people

INGREDIENTS

Melted butter for brushing mold
12 to 15 blanched almonds
1 pound 15 ounces to 2 pounds 14 ounces (875 to 1300 g) *pâte à kugelhopf* (see page 45)

1 Choose a 1½- to 2½-quart (1½ to 2½ L) kugelhopf mold, depending on the quantity of dough. Brush the inside of the kugelhopf mold with melted butter. Place one almond in each indentation in the bottom of the mold.

2 Lift the dough in one piece with both hands. Make a hole in the center of the dough with your fingers, and enlarge it so that it will fit over the tube in the mold. Drop this ring of dough into the mold and press it down to distribute the dough evenly①.

Opposite: Grand Marnier, page 259. Following page: Moka Café, page 252.

Confectioners sugar for dusting top of kugelhopf

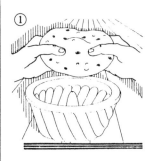

3 Let rise in a warm place until the dough reaches the top of the mold, 1¼ to 2 hours.

4 Preheat the oven to 350° F (180° C). Place a heavy baking sheet on the middle shelf of the oven.

5 Place the kugelhopf on the hot baking sheet in the oven and bake until the top begins to brown, 15 to 20 minutes. Drape a sheet of kitchen parchment over the top to prevent it from browning too much, reduce the oven to 325° F (160° C), and continue baking 30 to 45 minutes longer. The kugelhopf is done when a skewer inserted in the cake comes out clean.

6 Unmold the *kugelhopf* onto a cooling rack and let cool to room temperature.

7 Dust the top of the kugelhopf with confectioners sugar.

Storage: Same as for brioches (see page 200).

Desserts Made from Leftover Brioche

Because brioche is such a luxurious commodity, French pastry chefs have devised some beautiful desserts to use up the leftovers. *Diplomate, bostock,* and *brioche polonaise* are three classics.

Diplomate

For this elegant bread pudding you can use leftovers of any brioche except *pain aux raisins* and *brioche bordelaise*. It is baked in a charlotte mold or other deep, round mold with steeply sloping sides.

Opposite: Fromage, page 255. Preceding page: Noëlla, page 249.

For 8 to 10 people

INGREDIENTS

Melted butter for brushing mold

Superfine sugar for dusting mold

1 pound to 1 pound 5 ounces (450 to 600 g) leftover brioche

2 ounces (60 g) candied fruits, cut into ¼-inch (6 mm) dice

6 cups (1½ L) *appareil à diplomate* (see page 215)

½ cup (160 g) strained apricot jam

About 1 ounce (30 g) candied fruits for decoration

1 Preheat the oven to 425° F (220° C).

2 Brush the inside of a 2-quart (2 L) charlotte mold with melted butter and dust it with superfine sugar.

3 Trim off and discard the crust from the brioche. Cut the crumb into ½-inch (12 mm) dice. If you run short of brioche, you can add some white bread.

4 Fill the mold halfway with brioche dice. Scatter the diced candied fruits over the brioche. Then fill the mold to the top with brioche dice, and press the brioche down gently with your palm. Pour the *appareil à diplomate* over the brioche dice to cover and soak them.

5 Place the filled mold in a deep baking dish, and pour enough water into the baking dish to fill it to half the height of the mold.

6 Bake, uncovered, until browned and firm on top and the custard has set, about 45 minutes.

7 Place the charlotte mold on a cooling rack and let cool to room temperature. Then chill in the refrigerator before unmolding.

8 When the *diplomate* is cold, trim off any burned pieces on top with a bread knife. Cut a cardboard cake-decorating circle (see pages 383 and 433 for details and sources) slightly smaller than the base of the *diplomate*. Unmold the *diplomate* onto the cake decorating circle, and place it on a wire rack. Warm the jam over low heat, stirring occasionally, until melted. Pour the jam on top of the *diplomate*, smooth it over the top with your palette knife, and let it run down the sides, tilting the *diplomate* to coat the top and sides evenly.

9 Cut the remaining candied fruits into wedges, triangles, or diamonds (except cherries—cut them in half), and arrange them in a ring around the top of the *diplomate*.

Storage: Tightly covered for up to 1 week in the refrigerator, *before* unmolding. After unmolding and decorating, serve the *diplomate* within a few hours.

Appareil à Diplomate

CUSTARD FOR DIPLOMATE

This variation of *crème anglaise* calls for whole eggs rather than egg yolks.

INGREDIENTS

For 6 cups (1½ L)

3½ cups (8½ dL) milk

7 large eggs

1¼ cups (250 g) sugar

¼ cup plus 3 tablespoons (1 dL) dark rum

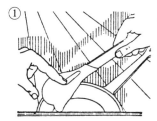

1 Bring the milk just to a simmer in a 3-quart (3 L) saucepan.

2 Meanwhile, beat together the eggs and sugar with a wire whisk until smooth.

3 Slowly pour about one third of the hot milk into the egg yolk–sugar mixture, stirring constantly. Pour this mixture back into the saucepan with the remaining milk and stir until thoroughly blended.

4 Place the saucepan over low heat and cook it gently, stirring constantly with a wooden spoon, until lightly thickened. The custard is sufficiently cooked when it coats the back of the wooden spoon lightly ①.

5 Remove the custard from the heat immediately, quickly strain it into a bowl, and stir in the rum.

Storage: None. Use the custard while it is still hot.

Bostock

These almond pastries are made from slices of leftover *brioche mousseline*.

For 12 individual pastries

INGREDIENTS

A leftover *brioche mousseline* (see page 200)

¾ to 1 cup (about 2 dL) *sirop d'amandes* (see below)

1 large egg white

1 tablespoon (20 g) strained apricot jam

1¼ cups (190 g) *TPT blanc* (see page 413)

½ tablespoon (4 g) confectioners sugar

1 Preheat the oven to 450° F (230° C).

2 Trim the ends from the brioche, and cut it into 12 slices, each ⅜ to ½ inch (10 to 12 mm) thick.

3 Place the *sirop d'amandes* in a shallow bowl or a small layer-cake pan. Dip one side of each slice in the syrup, then place it, dry side down, on a wire rack.

4 Stir together the egg white and apricot jam, then stir in the *TPT blanc* to form a thick almond paste or *pâte d'amandes crue*. Spoon about 1 tablespoon (20 g) of this *pâte d'amandes crue* onto the center of each slice of brioche. Smooth it down from the center of each slice to the edges with your palette knife to cover the entire slice, with the almond paste slightly thicker at the center than at the edge.

5 Dust the top of each slice with confectioners sugar.

6 Place the slices on a heavy baking sheet, and place this baking sheet on a second heavy baking sheet to prevent the bottoms of the slices from burning. Bake in the preheated oven until a crust forms on top of the almond paste and the pastries are lightly and evenly browned on top and bottom, 5 to 10 minutes. Some of the confectioners sugar on top will melt, but most of it will remain white.

7 Transfer the pastries to a cooling rack and let cool to room temperature.

Storage: Uncovered, at room temperature for up to 1 day. Or you can keep them standing on their sides in an airtight plastic or tin storage container for 2 or 3 days.

Sirop d'Amandes

ALMOND SYRUP FOR BOSTOCK

INGREDIENTS

**For about 1¾ cups
  (4 dL)**

2 ounces (60 g)
  blanched almonds

1 cup (2.4 dL) water

1½ cups (300 g)
  sugar

2 teaspoons (1 cL)
  orange flower water

1 tablespoon (1½ cL)
  amaretto liqueur

1 Purée the almonds with the water in a food processor or electric blender.

2 Drape a kitchen towel over a bowl and pour in the almond–water mixture. Gather the edges of the towel together and twist it tightly to extract a white liquid, called ''almond milk.'' Then discard the ground almonds, and add enough water to the almond milk to make 1 cup (2.4 dL).

3 Combine the almond milk, sugar, orange flower water, and amaretto liqueur in a small saucepan. Bring to a boil and skim off any foam that comes to the surface. Then remove from the heat.

4 Allow the syrup to cool before using.

Storage: Covered airtight, at room temperature for up to 4 weeks. If sugar crystals form on the bottom of the container, add a little water and bring to a boil, then cool again before using.

Brioche Polonaise

This is a very luxurious beehive–shaped *gâteau* made by filling a *brioche parisienne* with *crème pâtissière* and candied fruits and topping it with *meringue italienne*.

For a small cake serving 6 to 8 people or a large cake serving 8 to 10

SMALL CAKE

1½ ounces (45 g)
  candied fruits

¼ cup (6 cL) kirsch

One 7-ounce (200 g)
  brioche parisienne
  (see page 201)

⅓ cup (8 cL) *sirop à
  trente* (see page
  398)

1 Cut the candied fruits into ¼- to ⅜-inch (6 to 10 mm) dice and place them in a small bowl. Pour one third of the kirsch over the candied fruits, cover airtight, and let steep in the kirsch for at least 2 hours and preferably overnight.

2 Cut the head off the *brioche parisienne,* and trim the crust from both head and body. Cut the head and body horizontally into slices ¾ to 1 inch (2 to 2½ cm) thick, making 4 or 5 slices altogether. Rearrange the slices in a beehive shape, and trim the slices to make the beehive more even.

⅓ cup (8 cL) boiling water

½ cup (135 g) *crème pâtissière* (see page 83), flavored with 1½ teaspoons (¾ cL) kirsch

1½ cups (90 g) *meringue italienne* (see page 101)

4 teaspoons (8 g) sliced almonds

Confectioners sugar

LARGE CAKE

2½ ounces (70 g) candied fruits

¼ cup plus 2 tablespoons (9 cL) kirsch

One 10½-ounce (300 g) *brioche parisienne* (see page 201)

½ cup (12 cL) *sirop à trente* (see page 398)

½ cup (12 cL) boiling water

¾ cup (200 g) *crème pâtissière* (see page 83), flavored with 2 teaspoons (1 cL) kirsch

2¼ cups (135 g) *meringue italienne* (see page 101)

2 tablespoons (13 g) sliced almonds

Confectioners sugar

3 Drain the candied fruits, and combine the kirsch in which they were soaked with the *sirop à trente*, boiling water, and the remaining kirsch. Place this kirsch syrup in a shallow bowl or a small layer-cake pan. Dip the largest slice of brioche in the warm syrup, then place it on a wire rack to drain. Dip the next largest slice in the syrup and place it on top of the first slice. Continue dipping the slices in the syrup and piling them one on top of the other, finishing with the smallest slice.

4 Cut a cardboard cake-decorating circle about ½ inch (12 mm) larger in diameter than the largest slice of brioche.

5 Place the largest slice of brioche on the cake-decorating circle and spread a layer ⅛ inch (3 mm) thick of *crème pâtissière* over it. Scatter some diced candied fruits over the *crème pâtissière*. Add the second largest slice of brioche, spread with *crème pâtissière*, and scatter candied fruits over the pastry cream. Continue adding layers to build the beehive shape, finishing with the smallest slice on top.

6 Preheat the oven to 500° F (260° C).

7 Scoop the *meringue italienne* from the mixing bowl onto the top of the brioche beehive. Spread the meringue down over the sides of the beehive with your palette knife. Slide the blade of your palette knife under the cake-decorating circle and lift the beehive from the countertop. Transfer it to the fingertips of one hand, and smooth the meringue with the edge of your palette knife, working from top to bottom. Slide the beehive onto a baking sheet.

8 Sprinkle the sliced almonds over the *meringue italienne* on the outside of the beehive, and dust with confectioners sugar until the almonds on top are almost white.

9 Place in the oven until a crust forms on the outside of the meringue and it browns lightly on top, 2 to 3 minutes.

10 Slide the *brioche polonaise* onto a cooling rack and let cool to room temperature.

Storage: Uncovered, in refrigerator for up to 1 day.

Chapter Eight

BABAS (RUM-SOAKED PASTRIES)

*T*his is the dessert side of the family of leavened pastries. Legend has it that they were derived from kugelhopf by King Stanislas Leczinski, who flamed that tea cake with rum. Being a devotee of the *Thousand and One Nights,* the king named his favorite dessert after Ali Baba. In the early nineteenth century, a chef named Sthorer introduced this pastry at his shop in Paris and shortened the name to *baba.*

Today *pâte à baba* is baked in several shapes, and the baked cakes are soaked in a rum-flavored syrup. The *bouchon,* or champagne-cork shape, is referred to as a "rum baba" in the United States, but we use the word *babas* more generally for all pastries made from *pâte à baba.*

TOURS DE MAIN

Pâte à baba is a very sticky and elastic dough. It is molded immediately after it is prepared, then allowed to rise, and baked. After baking, the pastries are always soaked in *sirop à baba* (see page 221), which gives them their distinctive taste and texture.

Molding Babas *(Moulage)*

Brush the insides of the molds thoroughly with melted butter.

If the *pâte à baba* was prepared in a food processor, transfer it to a large pastry bag fitted with an $^{11}/_{16}$-inch (18 mm) plain pastry tube (Ateco 9) and pipe the *pâte à baba* into the buttered molds. Otherwise, mold it by hand following the instructions below.

SMALL MOLDS (for *bouchons,* *marignans,* and *petites savarins*): Take a handful of dough in one hand, without disconnecting it from the bulk of the dough in your bowl ①. It will form an elastic rope. With your hand wrapped around the dough in a loose

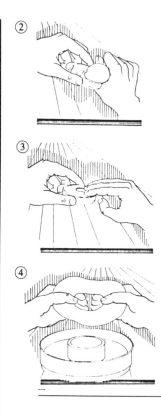

fist, manipulate the dough in your palm to get a lump of dough extending above your fist, between thumb and index finger. Try to get a lump of the size required to fill your mold about halfway. Take a mold in your other hand. Press the lump of *pâte à baba* into the mold and simultaneously cut it off by constricting your thumb and index finger ②. (You can also use the edge of the mold to help cut the dough.) Press the *pâte à baba* down into the mold so that it is distributed evenly and there is no air under it ③. Continue filling the buttered molds, pulling up more of the rope of *pâte à baba* from the mixing bowl as you need it.

RING MOLDS (for large *savarins*): Take the piece of *pâte à baba* in both hands. Press your thumbs through the center to make a hole and enlarge the hole to make a ring. Drop this ring of dough into the mold ④. Press it into the mold with your fingertips to line the bottom and distribute it uniformly. The dough should fill the mold to about half of its height.

The Second Rise (*La Deuxième Pousse*)

Let the molded *babas* rise in a warm place (75° to 85° F, or 25° to 30° C) until doubled in volume, about 45 minutes to 1½ hours. For most shapes the dough should rise to the top of the mold, or puff just above the top of the mold. Never let it rise more than that, because it is fragile and deflates easily if it has risen too much. Unlike most other *pâtes levées, pâte à baba* is never brushed with egg wash.

Baking the Babas (*Cuisson*)

Preheat the oven to 400° F (200° C). Place a heavy baking sheet on the middle shelf. The hot baking sheet helps the *babas* rise by providing a quick initial bottom heat and distributes the heat more evenly.

Place the *babas* on the hot baking sheet in the oven and reduce the temperature to 375° F (190° C). Bake until the *babas* are a deep uniform brown on top and firm to the touch. They should shrink from the sides of the molds, and a skewer inserted in the centers of the cakes should come out clean.

When the *babas* have finished baking, remove them from the oven and unmold them onto a cooling rack. Let them cool to room temperature.

Soaking *(Imbibage)*

After baking, the *babas* must be soaked in rum-flavored syrup. They will be less fragile and will absorb the syrup better if they are first allowed to rest, uncovered, at room temperature for 1 day; but if necessary they can be soaked as soon as they are cool.

Sirop à Baba

INGREDIENTS

For about 5½ cups (1¼ L)

1 quart (1 L) water
3 cups (600 g) sugar
1 tablespoon (1½ cL) dark rum
1 tablespoon (1½ cL) Curaçao, or juice of one-half orange

1 Combine the water and sugar in a saucepan and bring to a boil, stirring occasionally to dissolve the sugar.

2 Remove from the heat and add the rum and the Curaçao or orange juice.

3 Let the syrup cool to about 120° F (50° C).

Storage: Use the *sirop à baba* right away, while still hot. Or let cool to room temperature, cover airtight, and keep for up to 1 week in the refrigerator. If the syrup begins to bubble or look oily, indicating that it is fermenting, discard it. When ready to soak the *babas,* return the syrup to a boil and let it cool to about 120° F (50° C).

Place the hot *sirop à baba* in a wide, flat-bottomed bowl or layer-cake pan. After soaking, the *babas* will be very fragile, so, to lift them out of the syrup, you should have either a large skimmer or a wire rack that will fit inside the bowl on the bottom. The bowl should be just large enough to easily accommodate at least three or four small *babas* or one large *baba* and to allow you to remove them easily with the skimmer or wire rack. (If the bowl is too wide, you will have to use much more syrup.)

Place the *babas* in the syrup with the dark, crusty side down. Soak three or four small *babas* simultaneously; soak large *babas* one at a time. There should be enough syrup to come at least halfway up the sides of the *babas*. Gently press them down occasionally, until the crusty bottoms begin to soften. Then, using a bulb baster or spoon, baste the tops of the *babas* with the syrup to soak the upper halves as well. Continue basting until they are moistened all the way through and the tops, bottoms, and sides are moist and tender. (Do not, however, let them soak so long that they become soggy and begin to fall apart.) Then remove them from the syrup, lifting them with either a skimmer or the rack at the bottom of the bowl. Transfer the *babas* to a cooling rack and let them drain over a jelly-roll pan. When you are finished, return the syrup that has accumulated in the jelly-roll pan to the bowl with the remaining syrup, and strain the syrup for later use.

Sprinkle the *babas* with a little dark rum. Pour the rum directly from the bottle, reducing the flow of rum to a trickle by covering the opening with your thumb. Be sure to sprinkle the rum slowly enough that it is all absorbed.

The *babas* are now ready to be garnished or filled.

STORAGE

After baking and before soaking, the *babas* can be stored at room temperature, uncovered for 1 day, or in an airtight tin cookie box or plastic bag for up to 3 days. Alternatively, after baking and while the *babas* are still warm (but not hot), you can wrap them airtight in a plastic bag and freeze for up to 3 weeks. If frozen, remove from the plastic bag and defrost at room temperature before soaking. After soaking, the *babas* can be kept in the refrigerator, preferably covered in an airtight plastic container, for 1 day. Serve as soon as possible after garnishing and filling. If necessary, *babas* filled with *crème pâtissière* can be kept in the refrigerator for up to 12 hours, those filled with *crème chantilly* or fresh fruits for up to 6 hours.

Individual Pastries

Bouchons

Bouchons are baked in small timbale molds to give them their familiar champagne cork shape. The size you need for this recipe is 2¼ inches (5½ cm) wide and holds 7 tablespoons (11 cL).

For 8 individual pastries

INGREDIENTS

Melted butter for brushing molds

¼ cup (35 g) seedless raisins

14 ounces (400 g) *pâte à baba* (see page 48)

About 4 cups (1 L) *sirop à baba* (see page 221)

3 tablespoons (4½ cL) dark rum

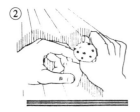

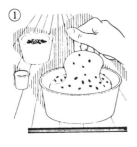

1 Brush the insides of eight timbale molds with melted butter.

2 Mix the raisins with the *pâte à baba* ①.

3 If the *pâte à baba* was made by hand or electric mixer, press about 1¾ ounces (50 g) of the dough into each mold ②; if it was made in a food processor, pipe the dough from a pastry bag fitted with an ¹¹/₁₆-inch (18 mm) plain pastry tube (Ateco 9). The dough should fill the mold about halfway.

4 Let the *pâte à baba* rise in a warm place until it reaches the tops of the molds, 45 minutes to 1 hour 15 minutes.

5 Preheat the oven to 400° F (200° C). Place a heavy baking sheet on the middle shelf.

6 Place the molds on the hot baking sheet in the oven and reduce the temperature to 375° F (190° C). Bake until the tops of the *bouchons* are a deep uniform brown and firm to the touch, 20 to 30 minutes.

7 Unmold the *bouchons* onto a cooling rack and let cool to room temperature.

8 Prepare a *sirop à baba*, or, if you have prepared it in advance, bring it to a boil. Let cool to about 120° F (50° C).

9 Three or four at a time, place the *bouchons* in the *sirop à baba*. Turn them occasionally and baste them with the syrup until they are moistened all the way through and all sides of the *bouchons* are moist and tender. Transfer them to a wire rack and let drain while you soak the remaining *bouchons*.

10 Strain and reserve the excess *sirop à baba*.

11 Sprinkle the dark rum over the *bouchons*.

Marignans

These boat-shaped pastries are filled with *crème chantilly*. Marignan was the name of a battle that King François I won in Italy in 1515.

For 8 individual pastries

INGREDIENTS

Melted butter for brushing molds

7 ounces (200 g) *pâte à baba* (see page 48)

About 3 cups (¾ L) *sirop à baba* (see page 221)

3 tablespoons (4½ cL) dark rum

1 to 1½ cups (125 to 200 g) *crème chantilly* (see page 82)

1½ to 2 tablespoons (30 to 40 g) strained apricot jam

2 candied cherries

1 Brush the insides of eight barquette molds 4¼ inches (11 cm) long with melted butter.

2 If the *pâte à baba* was made by hand or electric mixer, press about ⅞ ounce (25 g) of the dough into each mold ①; if it was made in a food processor, pipe the dough from a pastry bag fitted with an ¹¹⁄₁₆-inch (18 mm) plain pastry tube (Ateco 9). The dough should fill about three fourths of the mold.

3 Let the *pâte à baba* rise in a warm place until it doubles in volume and bulges above the tops of the molds, 45 minutes to 1 hour.

4 Preheat the oven to 400° F (200° C). Place a heavy baking sheet on the middle shelf.

5 When the dough has risen, place the molds on the hot baking sheet in the oven and reduce the temperature to 375° F (190° C). Bake until the tops of the *marignans* are a deep and uniform brown and firm to the touch, about 15 minutes.

6 Unmold the *marignans* onto a cooling rack and let cool to room temperature.

7 Prepare a *sirop à baba,* or, if you have prepared it in advance, bring it to a boil. Let cool to about 120° F (50° C).

8 Three or four at a time, place the *marignans* in the *sirop à baba* with the dark, crusty side down. Let them soak in the syrup until the bottoms begin to soften. Then baste the tops with the syrup until they are moistened all the way through and both tops and bottoms are moist and tender. Transfer them to a wire rack and let drain while you soak the remaining *marignans*.

9 Strain and reserve the excess *sirop à baba*.

10 Sprinkle the dark rum over the *marignans*.

11 Slit each *marignan* lengthwise, parallel to the base, like a hot dog bun.

12 Transfer the *crème chantilly* to a pastry bag fitted with a medium star tube (Ateco 5). Hold the pastry bag in one hand. One at a time, take a *marignan* in the other hand and, holding the *marignan* open, pipe 2 to 3 tablespoons (15 to 25 g) of *crème chantilly* in a spiral down the center ②. The *marignan* should be open about 30°, with the *crème chantilly* showing down the center of the opening.

13 Warm the apricot jam over low heat, stirring occasionally, until melted. Brush the top of each *marignan* with jam until lightly coated and glistening.

14 Cut the candied cherries into quarters and place a piece of candied cherry on top of each *marignan*.

Petits Savarins

These round pastries have a shallow depression in the center. Depending on how the depression is filled, they become either *savarins chantilly* or *savarins crème pâtissière*.

For 8 individual pastries

INGREDIENTS

Melted butter for
  brushing molds

1 Brush the insides of eight individual Mary Ann or *savarin* molds (about 3¼ inches, or 8 cm, in diameter) with melted butter.

2 If the *pâte à baba* was made by hand or electric mixer, press about 1½ ounces (43 g) of dough into

¾ pound (350 g) *pâte à baba* (see page 48)

About 4 cups (1 L) *sirop à baba* (see page 221)

3 tablespoons (4½ cL) dark rum

3 to 4 tablespoons (60 to 80 g) strained apricot jam

SAVARINS CHANTILLY

1½ to 2 cups (200 to 250 g) *crème chantilly* (see page 82)

Optional: 8 crystallized violets

SAVARINS CRÈME PÂTISSIÈRE

1½ to 2 cups (400 to 540 g) *crème pâtissière* (see page 83) flavored with 1½ to 2 tablespoons (2 to 3 cL) dark rum

2 candied cherries, cut into quarters

each mold ①; if it was made in a food processor, pipe the dough from a pastry bag fitted with an ¹¹⁄₁₆-inch (18 mm) plain pastry tube (Ateco 9). The dough should just cover the depression in the center of the bottom of the mold and almost fill the ring around the depression.

3 Let the *pâte à baba* rise in a warm place until it doubles in volume and fills the Mary Ann molds to about two thirds of their height; or, if you use individual *savarin* molds ⅞ inch (2.2 cm) deep, the dough should rise to the tops of the molds. The rising time should be about 45 minutes to 1 hour.

4 Preheat the oven to 400° F (200° C). Place a heavy baking sheet on the middle shelf.

5 Place the molds on the hot baking sheet in the oven and reduce the temperature to 375° F (190° C). Bake until the tops of the *savarins* are a deep uniform brown and firm to the touch, 15 to 25 minutes.

6 Unmold savarins onto a cooling rack and let cool to room temperature.

7 Prepare a *sirop à baba,* or, if you have prepared it in advance, bring it to a boil. Let cool to about 120° F (50° C).

8 Three or four at a time, place the *savarins* in the *sirop à baba* with the dark, crusty side down. Let soak in the syrup until the bottoms begin to soften. Then baste the tops with the syrup until they are moistened all the way through and tops, bottoms, and sides are moist and tender. Transfer them to a wire rack and let drain while you soak the remaining *savarins*.

9 Strain and reserve the excess *sirop à baba*.

10 Sprinkle the dark rum over each *savarin*.

11 Warm the apricot jam over low heat, stirring occasionally, until melted. Brush the sides and the rim around the depression in the center of each *savarin* with apricot jam until lightly coated and glistening.

②

12 Transfer the *crème chantilly* or *crème Pâtissière* to a pastry bag fitted with a medium star tube (Ateco 5). Pipe the filling into the depression in the center of each *savarin*, moving the pastry tube in an upward spiral motion to make a fluted mound and terminating the mound by releasing the pressure on the pastry bag and moving the pastry tube to the center of the *savarin* and up ②.

13 Place a crystallized violet or a quarter of a candied cherry on the center of each *savarin*.

Petits Ali Babas and Punchs

These are made from upside down *petits savarins* filled with *crème pâtissière*.

For 8 individual pastries

INGREDIENTS

Melted butter for brushing molds

¾ pound (340 g) *pâte à baba* (see page 48)

¼ cup plus 2 tablespoons (9 cL) dark rum

About 4 cups (1 L) *sirop à baba* (page 221)

1 cup (270 g) *crème pâtissière* (see page 83) flavored with 1 tablespoon (1½ cL) dark rum

4 to 5 tablespoons (80 to 100 g) strained apricot jam

¼ cup plus 2 tablespoons (50 g) confectioners sugar

1 Mold and bake the *pâte à baba* following steps 1 through 6 of the recipe for *petits savarins*.

2 If you are making *ali babas*, place the raisins in a strainer and steam them over simmering water until they just begin to soften, about 5 minutes.

3 Place the steamed raisins or diced candied fruits in a bowl and pour ¼ cup (6 cL) of the rum over them. Cover and let soak in the rum for at least 2 hours and preferably overnight. Then drain thoroughly and reserve any rum that has not been absorbed.

4 Prepare a *sirop à baba,* or, if you have prepared it in advance, bring it to a boil. Let cool to about 120° F (50° C).

5 Three or four at a time, place the *savarins* in the *sirop à baba* with the dark, crusty side down. Let them soak in the syrup until the bottoms begin to soften. Then baste the tops with the syrup until they are moistened all the way through and tops, bottoms, and sides are moist and tender. Transfer them to a wire rack and let them drain while you soak the remaining *savarins*.

ALI BABAS

⅔ cup (85 g)
  seedless raisins

PUNCHS

3 ounces (85 g)
  candied fruits, cut
  into ¼ inch (6 mm)
  dice

6 Strain and reserve the excess *sirop à baba*.

7 Sprinkle 2 tablespoons (3 cL) of dark rum over the *savarins*.

8 Invert the *savarins,* putting the flat sides on top, and cut them in half horizontally, a little above the indentations in the bottoms. Spread about 2 table-spoons (35 g) of *crème pâtissière* on the bottom half of each, and sprinkle some raisins or diced candied fruits on the *crème pâtissière*. Place the other half of the *savarin* on top.

9 Warm the apricot jam over low heat, stirring occasionally, until melted. Brush the top and sides of each pastry with jam until lightly coated and glistening.

10 Preheat the oven to 450° F (230° C).

11 Prepare a *glace à l'eau* by adding 1 teaspoon (½ cL) of the reserved rum to the confectioners sugar and stirring in enough cold water to make it smooth, creamy, and just liquid enough to spread easily with a pastry brush. Brush this *glace à l'eau* over the jam on top of the *ali babas* or *punchs*.

12 Transfer the pastries to a baking sheet, and place in the oven until the sugar melts and the glaze turns from opaque white to almost translucent, about 1 or 2 minutes. If the *glace à l'eau* starts to bubble, remove the pastries from the oven immediately.

Large Pastries

Les Grands Savarins

These crown or ring-shaped *babas* are named for Jean Anthelme Brillat-Savarin, the great nineteenth-century French gastronomic writer. *Savarins* can be served accompanied by a *crème anglaise;* or the center can be filled with *crème chantilly, crème pâtissière,* or fresh fruits. *Savarin chantilly* can also be enhanced by adding fresh strawberries, raspberries, or blueberries to the *crème chantilly* filling.

For 8 to 10 people

INGREDIENTS

Melted butter for
  brushing mold
¾ pound (350 g)
  pâte à baba (see
  page 48)
About 5½ cups (1¼
  L) *sirop à baba* (see
  page 221)
2 tablespoons (3 cL)
  dark rum
3 to 4 tablespoons
  (60 to 80 g) strained
  apricot jam
A few candied fruits
  for decorating

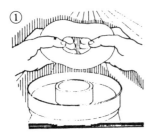

SAVARIN
CHANTILLY

Either 3 cups (375 g)
crème chantilly (see
page 82); *or* 2 cups
(250 g) *crème
chantilly* and ½ pint
(225 g) fresh
strawberries,
raspberries, or
blueberries

1 Brush the inside of a 3-cup (¾ L) *savarin* mold with melted butter.

2 If the *pâte à baba* was made by hand or electric mixer, take it in both hands and press your thumbs through the center to make a hole. Enlarge the hole and drop this ring into the mold ①. Press the dough into the mold so that it is evenly distributed. If the *pâte à baba* was made in a food processor, pipe it into the mold from a pastry bag fitted with an ¹¹⁄₁₆-inch (18 mm) plain pastry tube (Ateco 9). In either case, the dough should fill the mold to half its height.

3 Let the *pâte à baba* rise in a warm place until it reaches the top of the mold, 45 minutes to 1 hour 15 minutes.

4 Preheat the oven to 400° F (200° C). Place a heavy baking sheet on the middle shelf.

5 Place the molded *savarin* on the hot baking sheet in the oven and reduce the temperature to 375° F (190° C). Bake until the top of the *savarin* is a deep, uniform brown and firm to the touch, 20 to 35 minutes.

6 Unmold the *savarin* onto a cooling rack and let cool to room temperature.

7 Prepare a *sirop à baba,* or, if you have prepared it in advance, bring it to a boil. Let cool to about 120° F (50° C).

8 Place the *savarin* in the *sirop à baba* with the dark, crusty side down. Let the *savarin* soak in the syrup, gently pressing it down occasionally, until it sinks and the bottom begins to soften. Then baste the top with the syrup until the *savarin* is moistened all the way through and the top, bottom, and sides are moist and tender. Transfer the *savarin* to a wire rack and let it drain.

9 Strain and reserve the excess *sirop à baba.*

10 Sprinkle the dark rum over the top of the *savarin*.

SAVARIN CRÈME PÂTISSIÈRE

3 cups (800 g) *crème pâtissière* (see page 83) flavored with 3 tablespoons (4½ cL) dark rum

UNFILLED SAVARIN

Optional: 2 cups (½ L) *crème anglaise* (see page 126)

11 Warm the apricot jam over low heat, stirring occasionally, until melted. Brush the top and sides of the *savarin* with jam until lightly coated and glistening.

12 Place the *savarin* on a serving plate. If you are making an unfilled *savarin*, proceed to step 13. Otherwise, spoon about two thirds of the filling into the center of the *savarin*, mounding it slightly; and, if you are including fresh berries in *savarin chantilly*, scatter the berries over alternating layers of *crème chantilly* as you fill the *savarin*. Transfer the remaining filling to a pastry bag fitted with a medium star tube (Ateco 5). For *savarin chantilly*, cover the mound of *crème chantilly* in the center with large rosettes of *crème chantilly* ②. For *savarin crème pâtissière*, finish the mound in the center by piping a spiral of *crème pâtissière* on top, starting from the outside of the mound and ending at the center.

13 Decorate the top of the *savarin* with candied fruits. Cut candied cherries into halves. Cut larger candied fruits into triangular or diamond-shaped slices.

Savarin aux Fruits

For many fruits, kirsch is a more suitable alcohol than rum. This *savarin* is soaked in a neutral, unflavored *sirop à baba* and then flavored by sprinkling with kirsch.

For 8 to 10 people

INGREDIENTS

Melted butter for brushing mold

¾ pound (350 g) *pâte à baba* (see page 48)

About 5½ cups (1¼ L) *sirop à baba* (see page 221), with the rum and orange liqueur omitted

1 Follow steps 1 through 9 of the previous recipe for *savarins*, leaving the *sirop à baba* unflavored in step 7.

2 Slowly sprinkle the kirsch over the top and sides of the *savarin*.

3 Warm the apricot jam over low heat, stirring occasionally, until melted. Brush the top and sides of the *savarin* with jam until lightly coated and glistening.

3 tablespoons (4½ cL) kirsch

3 to 4 tablespoons (60 to 80 g) strained apricot jam

1½ pints (675 g) fresh strawberries, raspberries, and/or blueberries, *or* mixed fresh fruits such as sliced peaches, orange segments, pineapple wedges, and sliced bananas

Some *crème chantilly* (see page 82) for decorating *savarin*

4 Place the *savarin* on a serving plate. Fill the center with the fruit.

5 Place the *crème chantilly* in a pastry bag fitted with a small star tube (Ateco 3). Decorate the *savarin* by piping a few rosettes of *crème chantilly* around the top of the ring.

Savarin aux Pêches

For this dessert, the *pâte à baba* is baked in a layer-cake pan. Then, after soaking in *sirop à baba,* a circle is cut from the top center of the cake to make an indentation, which is filled with *crème chantilly* and fruit. The circle that was removed becomes a lid.

This method produces an especially elegant and refreshing result with peaches, but you can use the same method for other fruits. Choose the liquor for soaking and flavoring the *savarin* depending on the fruit—for example, kirsch with peaches, strawberries, or raspberries; or rum for bananas, oranges, or pineapple.

For 10 to 12 people

INGREDIENTS

Melted butter for brushing mold

1 pound 5 ounces (600 g) *pâte à baba* (see page 48)

1 Brush the inside of an 8-inch (20 cm) layer-cake pan with melted butter.

2 If the *pâte à baba* was made by hand or electric mixer, press it into the layer-cake pan and smooth the surface. If the *pâte à baba* was made in a food processor, scrape it out of the food processor and

About 5½ cups (1¼ L) *sirop à baba* (see page 221), with the rum and orange liqueur omitted

¼ cup plus 1 tablespoon (7½ cL) kirsch

4 to 5 tablespoons (80 to 100 g) strained apricot jam

2 or 3 medium ripe freestone peaches, or substitute canned peaches in heavy syrup

2 cups (250 g) *crème chantilly* (see page 82)

into the layer-cake pan, using your pastry corne or rubber spatula. Press the dough into the mold and smooth the surface.

3 Let the *pâte à baba* rise in a warm place until it doubles in volume and reaches the top of the mold, about 1 to 1½ hours.

4 Preheat the oven to 400° F (200° C). Place a heavy baking sheet on the middle shelf.

5 Place the molded *baba* on the hot baking sheet in the oven and reduce the temperature to 375° F (190° C). Bake until the top of the *savarin* is a deep, uniform brown and firm to the touch, 25 to 40 minutes.

6 Unmold the *baba* onto a cooling rack and let cool to room temperature.

7 Prepare a *sirop à baba*, or, if you have prepared it in advance, bring it to a boil. Let cool to about 120° F (50° C).

8 Place the *baba* in the *sirop à baba* with the dark, crusty side down. Let the *baba* soak in the syrup, gently pressing it down occasionally, until it sinks in the syrup and the bottom begins to soften. Then baste the top with the syrup until the *baba* is moistened all the way through and the top, bottom, and sides are moist and tender. Transfer the *baba* to a wire rack and let it drain.

9 Strain and reserve the excess *sirop à baba*.

10 Slowly sprinkle the kirsch over the *baba*.

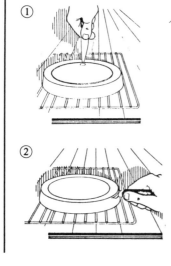

11 With a 6-inch (15 cm) *vol-au-vent* disc or flan ring as a guide, use the tip of a paring knife to make a circular incision in the top of the *baba* about ¾ inch (2 cm) deep and parallel to the edge of the cake ①. This will leave a rim about ¾ inch (2 cm) wide around the outside of the *baba*. Then insert a slicing knife into the side of the *baba*, parallel to and about ¾ inch (2 cm) below the top of the cake. Slide the blade back and forth to detach the circle you have cut in the top of the *baba*, while leaving the rim attached ②. Remove this ''lid'' and place it on the rack while you fill the *baba*.

12 Warm the apricot jam over low heat, stirring occasionally, until melted. Brush the top of the lid and the top and sides of the *baba* with jam until lightly coated and glistening.

13 Peel and pit the peaches. Cut them into wedges ¼ inch (6 mm) thick. Dip the wedges in acidulated water to prevent them from discoloring.

14 Place the *baba* on a serving plate. Transfer the *crème chantilly* to a pastry bag fitted with a medium star tube (Ateco 4). Pipe a ¼-inch (6 mm) thick layer of *crème chantilly* over the cut-out center of the cake ③. Arrange the peach slices in a circle on top of the *crème chantilly*, overlapping the slices like the blades of a fan ④. Pipe *crème chantilly* over the peach slices to cover them and fill the *baba* to just above the rim, and pipe a circle of adjacent rosettes of *crème chantilly* around the inside edge of the rim. You should have a little *crème chantilly* left to decorate the lid.

15 Place the lid on top of the *baba*, with the rosettes of *crème chantilly* showing around its base.

16 To decorate the lid, first pipe a rosette of *crème chantilly* on the center. Then enlarge the decoration into a starlike design by piping about six teardrop-shaped *rosaces* of *crème chantilly* radiating out from the rosette in the center.

Ali Baba and Punch

For these two desserts, the *pâte à baba* is baked in layer-cake pans. After soaking with *sirop à baba*, they are cut in half horizontally and filled with rum-flavored *crème pâtissière*. The tops of the cakes are glazed with apricot jam and *glace à l'eau*.

For 8 to 10 people

INGREDIENTS

Melted butter for
brushing mold

1 Follow steps 1 through 6 of the previous recipe for *savarin aux pêches*.

1 pound 5 ounces (600 g) *pâte à baba* (see page 48)

¼ cup plus 2 tablespoons (9 cL) dark rum

5½ cups (1¼ L) *sirop à baba* (see page 221)

1¼ cups (340 g) *crème pâtissière* (see page 83), flavored with 1 tablespoon (1½ cL) dark rum

5 to 6 tablespoons (100 to 120 g) strained apricot jam

½ cup plus 2 tablespoons (85 g) confectioners sugar

Candied fruits for decoration

ALI BABA

¼ cup plus 3 tablespoons (60 g) seedless raisins

PUNCH

2 ounces (60 g) candied fruits, cut into ¼-inch (6 mm) dice

2 If you are making *ali baba,* place the raisins in a strainer and steam them over simmering water until they just begin to soften, about 5 minutes.

3 Place the steamed raisins or diced candied fruit in a bowl and pour 2 tablespoons (3 cL) of the rum over them. Cover and let soak in the rum for at least 2 hours and preferably overnight. Then drain thoroughly and reserve any rum that has not been absorbed.

4 Prepare a *sirop à baba,* or, if you have prepared it in advance, bring it to a boil. Let cool to about 120° F (50° C).

5 Place the *baba* in the *sirop à baba* with the dark, crusty side down. Let the *baba* soak in the syrup, gently pressing it down occasionally, until it sinks in the syrup and the bottom begins to soften. Then baste the top with the syrup until the *baba* is moistened all the way through and the top, bottom, and sides are moist and tender. Transfer the *baba* to a wire rack and let it drain.

6 Strain and reserve the excess *sirop à baba.*

7 Sprinkle 4 tablespoons (6 cL) of dark rum over the *baba.*

8 Slice the *baba* in half horizontally ①. Cut a cardboard cake-decorating circle (see pages 383 and 433 for details and sources) slightly smaller than the base of the cake and place the bottom layer on it, cut side up. Spread the *crème pâtissière* on the bottom layer ②. Sprinkle the rum-soaked raisins or candied fruit over the *crème pâtissière* ③. Place the other half of the cake, cut side down, on top.

9 Warm the apricot jam over low heat, stirring occasionally, until melted. Brush the top and sides of the cake with jam until lightly coated and glistening ④.

10 Preheat the oven to 450° F (230° C).

11 Prepare a *glace à l'eau* by adding 1 teaspoon (½ cL) of the reserved rum to the confectioners sugar and stirring in enough cold water to make it smooth, creamy, and just liquid enough to spread easily with a pastry brush. Brush this *glace à l'eau*

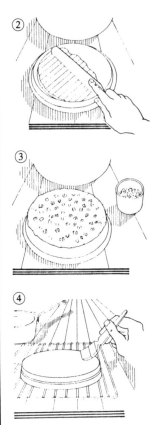

over the jam on the top and sides of the *ali baba* or *punch*. Transfer the cake to a baking sheet and place it in the oven until the sugar melts and the glaze turns from opaque white to almost transparent, 1 to 2 minutes. If the *glace à l'eau* starts to bubble, remove the cake from the oven immediately.

12 Decorate the top of the *ali baba* or *punch* with some candied fruit. If possible, use two different colors—for example, peaches or pears with red-tinted pineapple. Slice the candied fruits ⅛ inch (3 mm) thick, and cut the slices into wedge shapes. Arrange the wedges on the center of the dessert in a pinwheel of alternating colors.

Chapter Nine

GATEAUX (CAKES)

âteaux are the elegant French counterparts to the pedestrian American layer cake. They are nearly always either round or rectangular in shape, and to a large extent the shape determines how they are assembled and decorated.

This is one of the areas of French pastry that leaves the greatest room for creativity. Our methods can be used with many different combinations of cake layers, fillings, and toppings to generate a wide variety of desserts. And once you have mastered the basic techniques you can concentrate on the art of decorating your *gâteaux* with ever increasing finesse and individuality.

TOURS DE MAIN

Round *gâteaux* can be assembled in two ways. In the classical method you spread the topping over the outside of the *gâteau* with a long, flexible palette knife. This technique requires practice, but once mastered it is quick and versatile. The alternative is to assemble the *gâteau* in an *entremet* ring. Then the ring does the work of smoothing the sides and serves as a guide for smoothing the top with your palette knife. We explain both techniques in detail below. In most of our recipes we use the classical method, but you can nearly always assemble the same *gâteau* in an *entremet* ring.

Assembling rectangular *gâteaux* is much more straightforward, and most of the techniques are completely explained in the recipes. At the end of this section we touch on a few aspects of rectangular *gâteaux* in more detail.

Cake Sizes, and Trimming and Slicing Cake Rounds

The cake layers used for these *gâteaux* are primarily *génoise, dijonnaise,* and *succès,* and there are usually two cake layers in the *gâteau.* If there is a third layer, it is likely to be a round of *meringue ordi-*

naire, sandwiched between two of the others to add lightness.

We have taken a 9-inch (23 cm) round *gâteau* as the standard and given our recipes for this size. If you prefer to make another size, you can easily adjust our recipes. For an 8-inch (20 cm) round *gâteau,* decrease the quantities of all ingredients by 20 percent. Or, for a 10-inch (25 cm) round *gâteau,* increase the quantities of all ingredients by 25 percent.

If the foundation you are using is *génoise,* you will need a single round 1½ inches (4 cm) thick. If the *gâteau* will be assembled in an *entremet* ring, slice off the bottom crust (the side which was on top in the oven) of the *génoise* with a bread knife, and trim the crust from the sides to make a straight-sided round ⅛ to ¼ inch (3 to 6 mm) smaller in diameter than the ring.

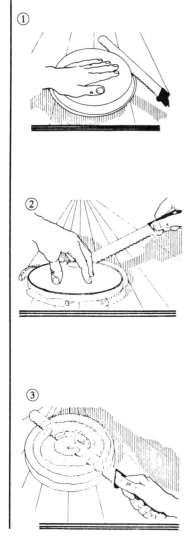

Slice the *génoise* round in half horizontally ①. To help guide the blade of your knife, hold one hand, palm down, on top of the *génoise* so you can feel the blade moving through the cake and detect any deviation from a straight horizontal cut.

Rounds of *dijonnaise, succès,* and *meringue ordinaire* must be trimmed to circles of identical size. If the *gâteau* will be assembled in an *entremet* ring, the circles should be about ⅜ inch (1 cm) smaller in diameter than the ring. In any case, use a flan ring, a *vol-au-vent* disc, or a round mold as a guide, and carefully cut the circles with a bread knife so you don't crack them ②. If one of the rounds does crack, piece it back together—the filling in the *gâteau* will eventually hold the pieces in place.

Dijonnaise, succès, and *meringue ordinaire* also have a tendency to rise a bit unevenly, with some arcs of the spiral you piped to form them bulging up above the rest. To make the rounds more even in thickness, shave the top of each with the bread knife, taking off just a little at a time ③. Shave off only the tops of the highest bumps. If you shave off too much, you may uncover large air pockets in the round, making it less rather than more even.

Save the trimmings from *dijonnaise* and *succès,* and store them airtight in a plastic bag for up to 1 month. Pulverize them in an electric blender, a food processor, or a mortar and pestle to use for decorating or in place of chopped nuts to finish the bases of *gâteaux*. Pulverized *succès* trimmings can also be used in place of part of the *TPT blanc* the next time you make *succès* (see page 75).

Cardboard Cake-Decorating Circles

To properly assemble and decorate a round *gâteau*, you must have a cardboard cake-decorating circle. The American corrugated cardboard variety is simply not appropriate, and we advise using the lids for foil take-out containers (made from a single layer of white cardboard with foil on top; see pages 383 and 433 for details and sources).

The cake-decorating circle must be cut to size, depending on how the outside of the *gâteau* will be finished. If the *gâteau* will simply be brushed with strained apricot jam, then the circle should be slightly smaller than the base of the *gâteau* so it won't show around the edge. On the other hand, if the outside of the *gâteau* will be spread with a frosting, such as *crème au beurre,* then the circle should be cut slightly larger than the base of the *gâteau* in a near perfect circle . It then serves as a guide and support for spreading and smoothing the topping around the sides of the *gâteau*. For *crème au beurre* or *ganache,* the circle should be about ¼ inch (6 mm) larger in diameter than the base of the *gâteau*; and for lighter toppings, such as *crème chantilly, mousse à paris,* and *meringue italienne,* which are spread thicker than *crème au beurre,* the circle should be cut about ⅜ inch (1 cm) larger in diameter than the base. However, if the *gâteau* will be assembled in an *entremet* ring, the circle must always be cut to fit inside the ring.

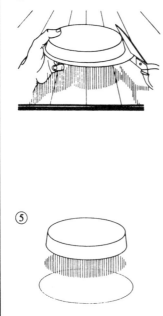

When you have cut the cake decorating circle, place the bottom cake layer on it ⑤. For *génoise,* this will be the half that was on top in the oven, and it should be cut side up. For *dijonnaise* or *succès,* choose the less perfect or less even layer for the bottom, and place it flat side (the side that was on the baking sheet) down.

Brushing with Syrup

Génoise is always brushed with a syrup to make it more moist and add flavor to the *gâteau*. *Succès* may also be brushed with syrup, but *dijonnaise* and *meringue ordinaire* are never brushed because the syrup would destroy their dry, crisp texture.

The syrup used is always *sirop à trente* diluted with an equal quantity of liqueur or coffee. Part of the liqueur may be replaced with water if the liqueur is only a flavor accent (such as rum in a chocolate *gâteau*). Diluting the *sirop à trente* makes it soak into the cake layers more easily and enables you to adjust the flavor to suit the *gâteau*.

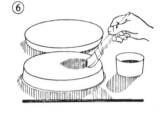

For *génoise*, brush the cut faces of both layers with most of the syrup ⑥. For *succès*, brush the tops of both layers with most of the syrup, being careful not to make the *succès* soggy.

Assembling with a Palette Knife

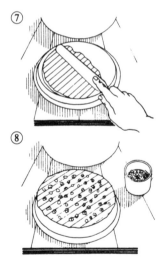

Spread the filling in an even layer over the bottom cake layer of the *gâteau* with a palette knife ⑦. Scatter any candied fruits, raisins, or chopped nuts called for in the recipe over the filling ⑧.

If there are three cake layers in the *gâteau*, place the second layer (usually *meringue ordinaire*) on top and press it down gently. Spread this layer with filling, and scatter candied fruit, raisins, or chopped nuts over it, if required.

Place the final cake round on top. If it is *génoise*, it must be cut side down. For *dijonnaise* or *succès*, invert the final cake round to get a flat top surface. Press gently on the top of the *gâteau* to eliminate any gaps between the layers and to be sure that it is even.

For *génoise* or *succès*, lightly brush the top of the *gâteau* with the flavored syrup. Do not brush it too much, or, when you spread the topping over it, the topping will not adhere well.

The most versatile technique for topping the *gâteau* is that of covering the outside surface with a frosting such as *crème au beurre*, *ganache*, *crème chantilly*, or *mousse à paris*. This is done in three stages:

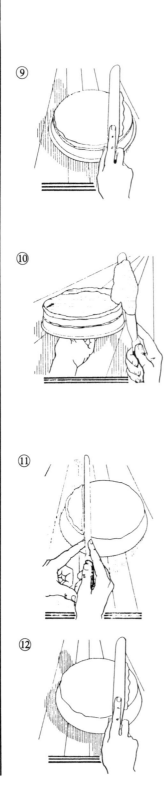

⑨

⑩

⑪

⑫

spreading the topping over the entire outside of the *gâteau*, smoothing the top, and smoothing the sides.

First spread an even layer of topping over the top of the *gâteau* ⑨. Slide your palette knife under the cake-decorating circle, lift the *gâteau* from the countertop, and transfer it to the fingertips of one hand. Scoop up some of the topping with the tip of your palette knife and scrape it off on the rim of the bowl. Slide the edge of your palette knife under some of this topping to pick it up about three quarters of the way up the face of the blade. Spread this topping on the side of the *gâteau* by moving the face of the palette knife down and around the side, and leave a small rim of the topping extending above the top edge of the *gâteau* ⑩. Rotate the *gâteau* on your fingertips (use the tip of your palette knife as an aid to avoid dropping it, if necessary), and repeat until you have covered all sides of the *gâteau* with the topping and made a rim of topping extending up around the entire top edge. Slide your palette knife under the *gâteau* and return it to the counter.

The second stage is to smooth the top surface of the *gâteau*. Start with your palette knife at the right side of the *gâteau*, with the face of the blade at an angle of 30° relative to the top surface. Sweep the blade a little more than halfway across the top ⑪, keeping the edge of the blade at a fixed height and turning the face of the blade. When you have passed the center of the *gâteau* and lift the blade off the surface, the face of the blade should have rotated through about 90°. This motion spreads the rim of topping across the *gâteau* and smooths half of the surface. Clean off your palette knife on the rim of the bowl, and place the edge of the blade on the left side of the *gâteau*, with the face of the blade at an angle of 30° relative to the top surface. Sweep the blade from left to right across the left half of the *gâteau* ⑫, again keeping the edge of the blade at a fixed height and turning the face of the blade through about 90°. You should now have finished spreading the rim of topping and the top of the *gâteau* should be almost smooth. Clean off your blade on the rim of the bowl again. To finish smoothing the top surface, grasp the ends of the blade of the palette knife between the thumb and the

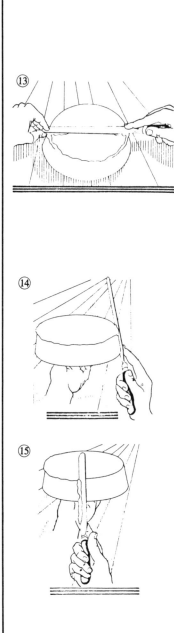

index and middle fingers of each hand and place the edge of the blade on the far side of the *gâteau*. Start with the face of the blade angled toward you. Pull the edge of the blade across the *gâteau*, sweeping the entire top surface in one smooth, continuous motion ⑬. As you do so, keep the edge of the blade at a fixed height and gradually turn the edge first under and then up, so when it reaches the near edge of the *gâteau*, the blade is angled away from you. Take off just enough topping to get a level surface.

Now you are ready to sweep the sides of the *gâteau*. Slide your palette knife under the cake-decorating circle and lift the *gâteau* from the countertop. Transfer the *gâteau* to the fingertips of one hand. Place the bottom third of the blade of the palette knife against the side of the *gâteau*, with the face of the blade nearly parallel to the surface ⑭. Using the cake-decorating circle as a guide, sweep the edge of the blade around the side of the *gâteau* to smooth the surface and clean off the excess topping. As you do so, draw the blade downward and turn the face of the blade toward you ⑮. Clean off the blade on the rim of the bowl, rotate the *gâteau* on your fingertips, and repeat until you have smoothed the entire outside surface of the *gâteau*. Return the *gâteau* to the counter.

This completes the spreading and smoothing procedure. Do not expect to use all of the topping, because a necessary part of the smoothing is sweeping excess topping off the surface of the *gâteau*.

The method for coating the surface of a *gâteau* with *meringue italienne* is essentially the same. However, *meringue italienne* is more sticky and viscous than the other toppings, and when you smooth it, you should keep the face of your palette knife nearly perpendicular to the surface of the meringue. That way, you will cut it cleanly, rather than having the meringue that clings to the blade dragging the meringue on the surface of the *gâteau*.

Assembling in an Entremet Ring

Do not use this method if the *gâteau* has more than 2 cake layers or if the topping is *meringue italienne*. Scoop up some of the topping on the tip of your palette knife, and spread it on part of the bottom half of the inside of the entremet ring ⑯. Rotate the ring and repeat until the entire bottom half of the ring is coated with topping about ¼ inch (6 mm) thick. Center the ring over the bottom layer of cake, and press the ring down on the counter. The cake layer should be surrounded by topping on all sides.

Now spread the filling over the cake layer in the ring ⑰. Spread the topping about ¼ inch (6 mm) thick over the upper half of the inside of the ring ⑱. If the recipe calls for it, scatter candied fruits, raisins, or chopped nuts over the filling.

Center the second cake layer over the filling and press it down into the ring. If it is *génoise*, put it in cut side down and compress the sides by pressing it in toward the center to make it fit inside the surrounding topping. If the cake layer is *dijonnaise* or *succès*, invert it to get a flat top surface before pressing it straight down into the ring, being careful not to crack it.

Whatever the cake layers, the top round must be pressed down below the top of the ring so there is room for a final layer of topping.

For *génoise* or *succès*, lightly brush the top of the cake with flavored syrup.

Spread the remaining topping over the second cake layer and smooth it with your palette knife to make it level with the top of the ring and take off any excess topping ⑲.

Carefully slide the *gâteau* onto a wire rack or baking sheet. Refrigerate for at least 1 hour to make the topping firm. Place the chilled *gâteau* on an inverted layer-cake pan slightly smaller in diameter and taller than the ring. Dip a kitchen towel in hot water, then wring it out. Briefly wrap the hot towel around the outside of the ring to just melt the topping touching the inside of the ring. Wipe the ring dry and carefully slip it down off the *gâteau* ㉑. If the ring doesn't slip off easily, warm it a little more and try again.

Glazing with Fondant or Pâte à Glacé

Fondant or *pâte à glacé* can be used as a glaze over *crème au beurre* or *ganache*.

First slide your palette knife under the cake-decorating circle, lift the *gâteau* from the countertop, and transfer it to a wire rack. Refrigerate for at least 1 hour to make the *crème au beurre* or *ganache* firm.

If you are using *pâte à glacé,* temper it to get the right consistency for glazing.

If you are glazing with fondant, gently warm it, stirring constantly until melted. The temperature should be about 100° to 105° F (38° to 40° C) and the fondant should be fluid, with about the same body as heavy cream or a light *crème anglaise*. If necessary, add *sirop à trente,* a little at a time, until the fondant is thinned to the proper consistency.

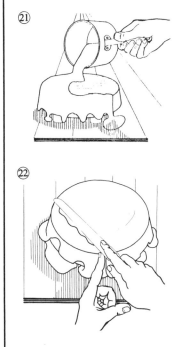

Pour the fondant or *pâte à glacé* on top of the *gâteau* in a circle just inside the perimeter so it flows naturally down the sides ㉑. Quickly smooth the top surface with the edge of your palette knife to cover the top with a thin, even layer of glaze and push the excess glaze over the edges ㉒. Try to make the fondant or *pâte à glacé* flow evenly down all sides of the *gâteau*. If there are any bare or uneven spots around the sides, smooth the glaze over them with the edge of your palette knife. Work as quickly as you can, because, once the fondant or *pâte à glacé* begins to thicken, you will no longer be able to spread it smoothly. When you have finished, clean off any excess glaze clinging to the rack around the base of the *gâteau* with a paring knife.

The fondant or *pâte à glacé* must be allowed to set before serving. However, if the base of the *gâteau* is to be coated with chopped nuts or chocolate sprinkles, this must be done before it sets so that they will adhere to the surface.

Enrobing in Pâte d'Amandes

A thin sheet of *pâte d'amandes* is sometimes used instead of a glaze over *crème au beurre* on the outside of a *gâteau*.

First transfer the *gâteau* to a wire rack and refrigerate for at least 1 hour to make the *crème au beurre* firm.

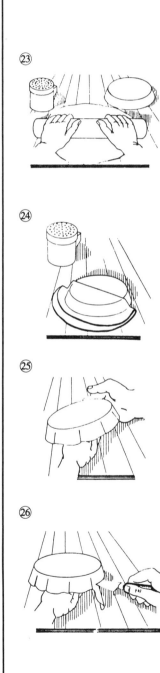

Work the *pâte d'amandes* on the countertop with the heel of your hand to smooth and soften it. Roll out the *pâte d'amandes* in a circle with your rolling pin ㉓. Lightly dust the counter and the *pâte d'amandes* with confectioners sugar as needed to get an even, smooth sheet which doesn't stick to counter or rolling pin; and wipe the sheet gently with the palm of your hand to spread the confectioners sugar and eliminate any white blotches of sugar. Roll out the *pâte d'amandes* into a sheet about 1/16 inch (1½ mm) thick and at least 4 inches (10 cm) larger in diameter than the *gâteau*.

Carefully roll or drape the sheet of *pâte d'amandes* over your rolling pin so it doesn't tear when you lift it. (Or fold it in half and lift it with your hands.) Then unroll (or unfold) it on the *gâteau* ㉔, centering the circle so that the edges hang over all sides and the sheet is flat against the top. Cup your hands around the sides of the *gâteau* and gently press the sheet of *pâte d'amandes* to make it lie flat against the sides with no folds or creases ㉕.

Trim the sheet of *pâte d'amandes* about ¼ to ⅜ inch (6 to 10 mm) above the bottom of the *gâteau* to leave a strip of *crème au beurre* exposed around the base ㉖. This strip of *crème au beurre* will be coated with chopped nuts or chocolate sprinkles.

Opposite: Napolitain, page 266. Following page: Paris, page 281.

Finishing the Base of a Gâteau

The bases of many *gâteaux* are coated with chopped nuts or chocolate sprinkles. This must be done while the topping or glaze on the *gâteau* is soft, so that the nuts or sprinkles will adhere.

Slide your palette knife under the cake-decorating circle and lift the *gâteau* from the countertop. Support it on the fingertips of one hand. If the *gâteau* was glazed with fondant or *pâte à glacé*, be careful to hold it straight so that cracks don't form in the glaze. Take the nuts or chocolate sprinkles in the palm of your other hand, and have more ready so you can refill your palm as you go along. Press the base of the *gâteau* against the nuts or sprinkles in your palm so that they adhere to the *gâteau* ㉗. Rotate the *gâteau* on your fingertips and press it against the nuts or sprinkles in your palm again. Continue until the entire base of the *gâteau* is coated with nuts or sprinkles.

For most *gâteaux*, you should coat the base with an even band of nuts or sprinkles about ⅜ to ½ inch (10 to 12 mm) high. Sometimes you can be more fancy and make high arcs of chocolate sprinkles around the base by taking more sprinkles in your hand and rotating the *gâteau* a little more between each time you press it against the sprinkles ㉘. You can also coat the entire side of the *gâteau* with chopped nuts or sprinkles by taking a handful of them at a time, tilting the *gâteau*, and pressing the side of the *gâteau* against the nuts or sprinkles in your hand. And you can substitute fine *copeaux en chocolat* (chocolate shavings, see page 122) for chocolate sprinkles, provided you work quickly so they don't melt in your hand.

Another related technique is to decorate the sides of the *gâteau* with chocolate petals (like *feuilles à noëlla*, but larger—see page 124). Chill the *gâteau* and form the petals directly on the side of the *gâteau* using the tip of an 8-inch (20 cm) palette knife. The petals should be uniform in size and about three quarters of the height of the *gâteau*. You might try this on our *Grand Marnier gâteau*, for example.

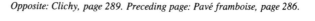
Opposite: Clichy, page 289. Preceding page: Pavé framboise, page 286.

Dusting the Outside of a Gâteau

One of the simplest ways to finish a *gâteau* that has been covered with, say, *crème au beurre* is to dust the top and sides with sliced almonds, chocolate sprinkles, *dijonniase* or *succès* crumbs, or confectioners sugar. You should use a light, even dusting or sprinkling, and the only trick is in coating the sides of the *gâteau*.

To coat the sides easily, first slide your palette knife under the cake-decorating circle, lift the *gâteau* from your countertop, and support it on the fingertips of one hand. Tilt the *gâteau* away from you and dust or sprinkle it with the other hand, so the sliced almonds or whatever will coat the side more effectively.

On the other hand, if you want to dust only the top of the *gâteau* and not the sides, you should lift the *gâteau* and tilt it toward you ㉙. That way, when you dust the *gâteau* with the other hand, nothing will land on the sides.

About Decorating Gâteaux

There are many ways to decorate the top of a *gâteau*. They include *pâte d'amandes* garnishes (leaves, twigs, and berries for example); writing in *pâte à écrire, glace royale,* or excess *pâte à glacé;* piping decorative patterns in *crème au beurre* or *crème chantilly;* and stenciling designs in confectioners sugar. The decoration depends on both the flavors and the topping in the *gâteau,* and the tastes and preferences of the cook.

One presentation can be used for different flavors. For example, whether it is flavored with coffee or *praliné,* a *mascotte* is always sprinkled with sliced almonds. On the other hand, varying the way a particular *gâteau* is finished can produce strikingly different results. *Moka café, mascotte café, grenoblois,* and *moulin* are all *gènoise*-based *gâteau* filled and topped with coffee *crème au beurre,* but they differ dramatically in presentation.

For each *gâteau,* we give the presentation we like best. However, you can vary the decoration to suit

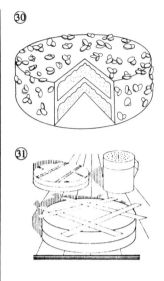

your own tastes, the materials you have on hand, and the time available.

Keep in mind that if the surface of your *gâteau* has been swept perfectly smooth, it will look good no matter how simply you decorate it. A light sprinkling of roasted sliced almonds over *crème au beurre* or a geometric pattern made from a few strips of paper and stenciled in confectioners sugar can be the perfect touch on a wide variety of *gâteaux* ③⓪–③①.

Finally, Mies van der Rohe's dictum that "less is more" is as valid in French pastry as it is in architecture. The one sure way to spoil the appearance of any *gâteau* is to cover it with an excess of piped flowers, *pâte d'amandes* fruits, or the like. So whatever you do, keep it simple!

Rectangular Gâteaux

Thin sheets of *russe, génoise,* and *joconde* are used in rectangular *gâteaux.* These include some of the most elegant desserts in the French pastry chef's repertoire; yet they are relatively easy to assemble because the sides of these *gâteaux* are not coated with topping. Instead, the sides are simply trimmed to reveal the multilayered structure of the *gâteau.*

For all of our rectangular *gâteaux,* we give recipes using both 13 × 20-inch (33 × 50 cm) and 12 × 16-inch (30 × 40 cm) sheets of cake. Most baking sheets and jelly-roll pans are close enough to one of these standard sizes that sheet cakes baked on them can be used in our recipes without altering the quantities of ingredients.

The sheet of cake is cut into two, three, or four rectangles, depending on the number of layers in the *gâteau* you are making. Always cut the cakes with a bread knife and use a straightedge as a guide ③②.

Assembling the *gâteau* ③③ on a cardboard base will make it easier to decorate and move without damage. If you have a supply of cardboard take-out lids (a single layer of white cardboard with foil on top— see pages 383 and 433 for details and sources), cut one about 1 to 2 inches (2½ to 5 cm) smaller in length and width than the rectangles of cake so it won't extend beyond the sides of the *gâteau.*

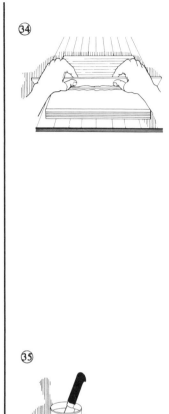

To smooth the topping on the *gâteau*, use either a long palette knife or a metal straightedge ㉞. After spreading the topping, grasp the ends of the blade between the thumb and the index and middle fingers of each hand. Start with the edge of the blade on the far side of the *gâteau* and the face of the blade angled toward you. In one continuous motion, pull the edge of the blade toward you across the surface of the *gâteau*, gradually turning the face of the blade so that when it reaches the near side of the *gâteau* the face of the blade is angled away from you. Keep the edge of the blade at a fixed height as you sweep it across the *gâteau*, and take off just enough topping to get a level surface.

Before trimming the *gâteau*, it must be refrigerated until the filling is firm so the edges can be cut evenly. About ½ hour before serving, remove the *gâteau* from the refrigerator and place it on a flat cutting surface. Cut a slice ¼ to ⅜ inch (6 to 10 mm) thick from each side of the *gâteau* using a bread knife. If the *gâteau* is glazed with fondant or *pâte à glacé*, warm the blade by dipping it in hot water before making each cut so the blade will melt through the glaze without cracking it ㉟. In any case, all four sides of the *gâteau* should be perfectly flat. If there are any gaps in the layers of filling, you didn't trim off enough of the edge.

STORAGE

Gâteaux that are filled and topped with *crème au beurre, ganache,* or *fruit mousse* can be kept uncovered in the refrigerator for up to 2 days. These *gâteaux* can also be frozen before glazing, dusting with confectioners sugar, chocolate sprinkles, nuts, etc, or decorating. When the *gâteau* has frozen, cover it airtight with plastic wrap or in a plastic bag and store in the freezer for up to 3 weeks. The day before serving, remove the plastic wrap and defrost the *gâteau* overnight in the refrigerator, then finish the preparation.

Gâteaux that contain *crème pâtissière* or *mousse à paris,* or are topped with *meringue italienne* or brushed with jam, can be kept, uncovered, in the refrigerator for up to 1 day. They cannot be frozen. Those containing *crème chantilly* should be kept in the refrigerator for no longer than 12 hours, and they are best eaten within 2 to 4 hours.

Regardless of the filling and topping, *génoise* goes stale quickly when exposed to air. So for *génoise*-based *gâteaux*, these storage times are applicable only if the *génoise* is completely coated with topping.

Round Gâteaux

Moka Chocolat and Noëlla

These two génoise *gâteaux* are filled and covered with chocolate *crème au beurre*. They differ only in the way they are finished. For *moka chocolat*, which is also called *décor chocolat*, *crème au beurre* is piped in a decorative pattern on top. *Noëlla* is topped with concentric circles of chocolate petals.

For 8 people

INGREDIENTS

1½ ounces (43 g) unsweetened chocolate

2¼ cups (400 g) *crème au beurre* (see page 85)

2 tablespoons (3 cL) *sirop à trente* (see page 398)

Either 1 tablespoon (1½ cL) dark rum; *or* ¼ teaspoon (1 mL) vanilla extract

One 9-inch (23 cm) round of *génoise* or *génoise chocolat* (see page 59)

¼ cup (35 g) chocolate sprinkles

1 Melt the chocolate and mix it with the *crème au beurre*.

2 Mix the *sirop à trente* with either the rum and 1 tablespoon (1½ cL) of water or the vanilla extract and 2 tablespoons (3 cL) of water.

3 Cut a cardboard cake-decorating circle about ¼ inch (6 mm) larger in diameter than the base of the *génoise* round.

4 Slice the *génoise* in half horizontally. Place the bottom layer on the cake-decorating circle, cut side up, and brush the cut faces of both layers with most of the syrup. Spread ½ to ⅔ cup (90 to 110 g) of *crème au beurre* over the bottom layer. Add the second layer of *génoise*, cut side down, and lightly brush the top with syrup.

5 Spread the top and sides of the *gâteau* with *crème au beurre*. Sweep first the top and then the sides with the edge of your palette knife to smooth the surface. Save at least ¼ cup (45 g) of excess *crème au beurre* for decorating the *gâteau*.

NOËLLA

About 100 *feuilles à noëlla* (see page 124)

Confectioners sugar for dusting

6 Lift the *gâteau* from the countertop and support it on the fingertips of one hand. Take the chocolate sprinkles in the palm of your other hand. Decorate the bottom edge of the *gâteau* with arcs of sprinkles by pressing it against the sprinkles in your palm, then rotating the *gâteau* and repeating until the entire base is covered with adjacent arcs.

7 Transfer the excess *crème au beurre* to a small pastry bag fitted with a fluted decorating tube (such as the Ateco 17 open star tube).

For *Moka Chocolat:* Pipe the *crème au beurre* on the top of the *gâteau* in a decorative pattern ①. For example, make a lozenge pattern by piping one set of parallel lines separated by about 1 inch (2½ cm) and a second set of parallel lines on the diagonal with respect to the first set. Pipe tiny rosettes of *crème au beurre* on the intersections.

For *noëlla:* Pipe four concentric circles of *crème au beurre* on top of the *gâteau*, starting on the outside rim and separating the circles by about 1 inch (2½ cm) Then arrange the *feuilles à noëlla* on the *gâteau* in concentric pinwheel-like circles, propping them up against the *crème au beurre* circles and overlapping them slightly. Use the largest *feuilles à noëlla* for the outer circle and the smallest ones for the inner circle. Pipe a rosette of *crème au beurre* in the center of the *gâteau*, and dust the top of the finished *gâteau* very lightly with confectioners sugar.

Thermidor

In the French revolutionary calendar, the eleventh month is *Thermidor*. We assemble this *gâteau* in an *entremet* ring.

For 10 to 12 people

INGREDIENTS

2 tablespoons (3 cL) dark rum

1 Mix the dark rum with the *sirop à trente*.

2 tablespoons (3 cL) *sirop à trente* (see page 398)

One 10-inch (25 cm) round of *génoise* or *génoise chocolat* (see page 59)

2 cups (500 g) *ganache au rhum* (see page 89)

Either 12 ounces (340 g) *pâte à glacé* (see page 110); *or* 9 ounces (250 g) semisweet chocolate, 6 tablespoons (85 g) barely melted butter, and 1½ tablespoons (2¼ cL) water

3 tablespoons (35 g) chocolate sprinkles

2 Trim the bottom crust of the *génoise* round with a bread knife to make it flat. Trim the sides to make it about ⅛ to ¼ inch (3 to 6 mm) smaller in diameter than a 9½-inch (24 cm) *entremet* ring. Slice the *génoise* in half horizontally, and brush the cut faces of both layers with most of the rum syrup.

3 Cut a cardboard cake-decorating circle to just fit inside the *entremet* ring.

4 Place the bottom layer of *génoise*, cut side up, on the cake-decorating circle. Using the tip of your palette knife, coat the bottom half of the inside of the ring with *ganache*. Center the ring over the bottom layer of *génoise*, and press the ring down on the counter. Spread about 1 cup (250 g) of *ganache* over the bottom layer of *génoise* and the top half of the inside of the ring. Center the second layer of *génoise*, cut side down, over the *ganache* and press it down and into the ring. Lightly brush the top with rum syrup. Spread the remaining *ganache* over the *génoise* and smooth it level with the top of the ring, using your palette knife.

5 Carefully slide the *gâteau* onto a wire rack or a baking sheet. Refrigerate until the *ganache* is firm, at least 1 hour.

6 Place the *gâteau* on an inverted 9-inch (23 cm) layer-cake pan. Dip a kitchen towel in hot water, then wring it out. Briefly wrap the hot towel around the outside of the ring to just melt the *ganache* touching the inside of the ring. Wipe the ring dry and carefully slip it down off the *gâteau*. Return the *gâteau* to a wire rack and chill it in the refrigerator again until the *ganache* on the outside is firm.

7 If you have *pâte à glacé* on hand, temper it to get the right consistency for coating the *gâteau*. Otherwise, prepare a *pâte à glacé* as follows: Melt the chocolate and stir in the butter. When smooth, stir in the water. Dip the bottom of the pot of chocolate in cold water and stir until it begins to thicken. Return this *pâte à glacé* to the heat and gently warm it a second time until just melted.

8 Pour the *pâte à glacé* over the top of the *gâteau* and spread it with the edge of your palette knife, smoothing the top surface and making it flow evenly down the sides. Touch up any uneven areas around the sides with the edge of your palette knife, and clean off any excess *pâte à glacé* around the base.

9 Before the *pâte à glacé* sets, lift the *gâteau* from the wire rack and support it on the fingertips of one hand. Take the chocolate sprinkles in the palm of your other hand. Finish the bottom edge of the *gâteau* by pressing it against the sprinkles in your palm to make a strip of sprinkles ⅜ to ½ inch (10 to 12 mm) high around the base. Place the *gâteau* on a serving plate and let the *pâte à glacé* set.

10 Prepare a parchment cornet (see page 118 for details).

11 Collect the excess *pâte à glacé* and temper it again. Transfer some of it to the parchment cornet and write ''Thermidor'' across the top of the *gâteau*. Then pipe a scroll pattern around the rim.

Note: An alternative way to finish this *gâteau* is to glaze only the top (not the sides) with *pâte à glacé* before unmolding. Then after unmolding coat the entire side of the *gâteau* with chocolate sprinkles, or better yet fine *copeaux en chocolat* (chocolate shavings, see page 122).

Mascotte Café, Moka Café, Grenoblois, and Moulin

Here are four classic ways to finish *génoise gâteaux* filled and topped with coffee *crème au beurre*. *Mascotte café* is sprinkled with sliced almonds. *Moka café* (or *décor café*) is decorated with piped *crème au beurre*. *Grenoblois* has chopped walnuts inside and is glazed with fondant. And *moulin* has a windmill-inspired garnish of *nougatine* triangles on top.

For 8 people

INGREDIENTS

3⅓ tablespoons (5 cL) very strong

1 Flavor the *crème au beurre* with 4 teaspoons (2 cL) of the coffee. Mix the *sirop à trente* with the remaining coffee.

black coffee (see page 416)

2¼ cups (400 g) *crème au beurre* (see page 85)

2 tablespoons (3 cL) *sirop à trente* (see page 398)

One 9-inch (23 cm) round of *génoise* or *génoise aux amandes* (see page 59)

MASCOTTE CAFÉ

⅓ cup (35 g) roasted sliced almonds

MOKA CAFÉ

3 tablespoons (30 g) roasted chopped almonds

MOULIN

3 tablespoons (30 g) roasted chopped almonds

About 7 ounces (200 g) *nougatine* (see page 115)

2 Cut a cardboard cake-decorating circle about ¼ inch (6 mm) larger in diameter than the base of the *génoise* round.

3 Slice the *génoise* in half horizontally. Place the bottom layer on the cake-decorating circle, cut side up, and brush the cut faces of both layers with most of the coffee syrup. Spread ½ to ⅔ cup (90 to 110 g) of *crème au beurre* over the bottom layer. For *grenoblois*, sprinkle about 3 tablespoons (25 g) of the chopped walnuts over this layer of *crème au beurre*. Add the second layer of *génoise*, cut side down, and lightly brush the top with coffee syrup.

4 Spread the top and sides of the *gâteau* with *crème au beurre*. Sweep first the top and then the sides with the edge of your palette knife to smooth the surface. For *moka café, grenoblois*, or *moulin*, save about ¼ cup (45 g) of *crème au beurre* for decorating.

5 For *mascotte café:* Scatter the roasted sliced almonds over the top and sides of the *gâteau*.

For *moka café* and *moulin:* Lift the *gâteau* from the countertop and support it on the fingertips of one hand. Take the chopped almonds in the palm of your other hand. Decorate the bottom edge of the *gâteau* by pressing it against the chopped almonds in your palm to make a strip of chopped nuts ⅜ to ½ inch (10 to 12 mm) high around the base.

For *moka café:* Transfer the excess *crème au beurre* to a small pastry bag fitted with a fluted decorating tube (such as the Ateco 17 open star tube). Pipe the *crème au beurre* on the top of the *gâteau* in a decorative pattern. For example, divide the top into quadrants by piping lines of *crème au beurre* along two perpendicular diameters; then pipe a scroll pattern or a cloudlike pattern of *rosaces* in one quandrant, and repeat the same pattern in each of the other three quadrants ①.

For *moulin:* Warm the nougatine in a 250° F (120° C) oven until very soft. Lightly oil your countertop and rolling pin, and roll out the *nougatine* into a rough circle about 9 inches (23 cm) in diameter and ⅛ inch (3 mm) thick. Cut a precise circle of *nougatine* the size of the top of the *gâteau*. Then cut the

GRENOBLOIS

¼ cup plus 2 tablespoons (50 g) finely chopped walnuts

1⅓ cup (450 g) fondant (see page 105)

1 tablespoon (1½ cL) caramel food coloring (see page 431)

1 tablespoon (1½ cL) very strong black coffee (see page 416)

Sirop à trente for thinning fondant

8 walnut halves

Optional: About 1 tablespoon (15 g) *pâte à écrire* or *glace royale* (see page 120 or 104)

circle into eight equal wedges. While the *nougatine* cools, transfer the excess *crème au beurre* to a small pastry bag fitted with a small fluted pastry tube (Ateco 2). Pipe eight ½-inch (12 mm) high rosettes of *crème au beurre* around the perimeter of the top of the *gâteau,* spacing them equally. Refrigerate until the *crème au beurre* is firm, then arrange the wedges of *nougatine* on top like the blades of a windmill, propping each wedge up with a rosette of *crème au beurre* ②. Finally, pipe a rosette of *crème au beurre* in the center.

For *grenoblois:* Place the *gâteau* on a wire rack and refrigerate at least 1 hour to make the *crème au beurre* firm. Warm the fondant over low heat, stirring constantly until melted. Mix in the caramel and the coffee to color and flavor the fondant, and stir in just enough *sirop à trente* to thin the fondant to the consistency of heavy cream. Pour the fondant over the top of the *gâteau* and spread it with the edge of your palette knife, smoothing the top surface and making it flow evenly down the sides. Touch up any uneven areas around the sides with the edge of your palette knife, and clean off any excess fondant around the base. Before the fondant starts to set, lift the *gâteau* from the wire rack and support it on the fingertips of one hand. Take the remaining chopped walnuts in the palm of your other hand. Decorate the bottom edge of the *gâteau* by pressing it against the chopped walnuts in your palm to make a strip of chopped nuts ⅜ to ½ inch (10 to 12 mm) high around the base. Place the *gâteau* on a serving plate and let the fondant set. Transfer the excess *crème au beurre* to a small pastry bag fitted with a small fluted pastry tube (Ateco 1). Pipe eight rosettes of *crème au beurre* in a circle around the circumference of the top of the *gâteau.* Place a walnut half on each rosette. If you like, you can pipe ''Grenoblois'' on the center of the *gâteau* in *pâte à écrire* or *glace royale,* using a parchment cornet.

Mascotte Praliné, Fromage, and Noisettier

These are *génoise*-based *gâteaux* filled and topped with *praliné*-flavored *crème au beurre*. *Mascotte praliné* is sprinkled with sliced almonds; *fromage* is decorated with *dijonnaise, russe,* or *succès* crumbs, pistachio nuts, and confectioners sugar to look like a Camembert cheese; and *noisettier* is glazed with fondant.

For 8 people

INGREDIENTS

2 cups (360 g) *crème au beurre* (page 85)

¼ cup (75 g) *praliné* (see page 414)

2 tablespoons (3 cL) *sirop à trente* (see page 398)

2 tablespoons (3 cL) kirsch

3 tablespoons (25 g) chopped hazelnuts

One 9-inch (23 cm) round of *génoise* or *génoise aux amandes* (page 59)

MASCOTTE PRALINÉ

⅓ cup (35 g) roasted sliced almonds

1 Beat the *crème au beurre* into the *praliné* with a wooden spoon, adding the *crème au beurre* gradually to be sure there are no lumps of *praliné*.

2 Mix the *sirop à trente* with the kirsch.

3 Cut a cardboard cake-decorating circle about ¼ inch (6 mm) larger in diameter than the base of the *génoise* round.

4 Slice the *génoise* in half horizontally. Place the bottom layer on the cake-decorating circle, cut side up, and brush the cut faces of both layers with most of the kirsch syrup. Spread ½ to ⅔ cup (90 to 110 g) of *crème au beurre* over the bottom layer. Scatter the chopped hazelnuts or *nougatine* over the *crème au beurre,* and add the second layer of *génoise,* cut side down. Lightly brush the top with kirsch syrup.

5 Spread the top and sides of the *gâteau* with *crème au beurre*. Sweep first the top and then the sides with the edge of your palette knife to smooth the surface. For *noisettier,* save about ¼ cup (45 g) of *crème au beurre* for decorating.

6 For *mascotte praliné:* Scatter the roasted sliced almonds over the top and sides of the *gâteau* ①.

For *fromage:* Dust the top and sides of the *gâteau* with the *dijonnaise, succès,* or *russe* trimmings. Lightly dust the top and sides with confectioners sugar; and sprinkle the chopped pistachio nuts in a few spots on top of the *gâteau* to simulate mold. Make a series of parallel lines on top of the *gâteau* by gently pressing the edge of your palette knife on

FROMAGE

About ¼ cup (30 g)
pulverized
dijonnaise, russe, or
succès trimmings
About 1 teaspoon (4
g) chopped pistachio
nuts or chopped
almonds tinted a
pale green
Confectioners sugar
for dusting

NOISETTIER

1⅓ cup (450 g)
fondant (page 105)
4 teaspoons (2 cL)
caramel food
coloring (page 431)
Sirop à trente for
thinning fondant
3 tablespoons (25 g)
finely chopped
hazelnuts
12 to 15 whole
blanched or raw
hazelnuts

the surface of the *crème au beurre*. Then make two pairs of lines in the perpendicular direction. This is intended to look like the straw mats used on farmhouse cheeses.

For *noisettier:* Place the *gâteau* on a wire rack and refrigerate at least 1 hour to make the *crème au beurre* firm. Warm the fondant over low heat, stirring constantly until melted. Mix in the caramel to color the fondant, and stir in just enough *sirop à trente* to thin the fondant to the consistency of heavy cream. Pour the fondant over the top of the *gâteau* and spread it with the edge of your palette knife, smoothing the top surface and making the fondant flow evenly down the sides. Touch up any uneven areas around the sides with the edge of your palette knife, and clean off any excess fondant around the base. Before the fondant starts to set, lift the *gâteau* from the wire rack and support it on the fingertips of one hand. Take the chopped hazelnuts in the palm of your other hand. Decorate the bottom edge of the *gâteau* by pressing it against the chopped hazelnuts in your palm to make a strip of chopped nuts ⅜ to ½ inch (10 to 12 mm) high around the base. Place the *gâteau* on a serving plate and let the fondant set. Transfer the excess *crème au beurre* to a small pastry bag fitted with a fluted decorating tube (such as the Ateco 17 open star tube). Pipe about a dozen small rosettes of *crème au beurre* around the circumference of the top of the *gâteau* and one in the center. Pipe four teardrop-shaped *rosaces* pointing out from the center of the gateau. Top each rosette with a whole hazelnut.

Ardechois

The Ardeche region in southeastern France is famous for chestnuts. This *gâteau* is filled and topped with *crème de marrons,* and glazed with *pâte à glacé.*

Classically, it is flavored with rum, but we recommend bourbon as an even better choice to accent the flavor of the chestnuts.

For 8 people

INGREDIENTS

2 tablespoons (3 cL) bourbon (preferably) or dark rum

2 tablespoons (3 cL) *sirop à trente* (see page 398)

One 9-inch (23 cm) round of *génoise* (see page 59)

2 cups (360 g) *crème de marrons* flavored with bourbon (preferably) or dark rum (see page 92)

Either 12 ounces (340 g) *pâte à glacé* (see page 110); *or* 9 ounces (250 g) semisweet chocolate, 6 tablespoons (85 g) barely melted butter, and 1½ tablespoons (2¼ cL) water

3 tablespoons (35 g) chocolate sprinkles

1 Mix the bourbon or dark rum with the *sirop à trente*.

2 Cut a cardboard cake-decorating circle about ¼ inch (6 mm) larger in diameter than the base of the *génoise* round.

3 Slice the *génoise* in half horizontally. Place the bottom layer on the cake-decorating circle, cut side up, and brush the cut faces of both layers with most of the flavored syrup. Spread ½ to ⅓ cup (90 to 110 g) of *crème de marrons* over the bottom layer. Add the second layer of *génoise*, cut side down, and lightly brush the top with syrup.

4 Spread the top and sides of the *gâteau* with *crème de marrons*. Sweep first the top and then the sides with the edge of your palette knife to smooth the surface.

5 Place the *gâteau* on a wire rack and refrigerate at least 1 hour to make the *crème de marrons* firm.

6 If you have *pâte à glacé* on hand, temper it to get the right consistency for coating the *gâteau*. Otherwise, prepare a *pâte à glacé* as follows: Melt the chocolate, and stir in the butter. When smooth, stir in the water. Dip the bottom of the pot of chocolate in cold water and stir until it begins to thicken. Return this *pâte à glacé* to the heat and gently warm it a second time, stirring until just melted.

7 Pour the *pâte à glacé* over the top of the *gâteau* and spread it with the edge of your palette knife, smoothing the top surface and making the *pâte à glacé* flow evenly down the sides. Touch up any uneven areas around the sides with the edge of your palette knife, and clean off any excess *pâte à glacé* around the base.

8 Before the *pâte à glacé* sets, lift the *gâteau* from the wire rack and support it on the fingertips of one hand. Take the chocolate sprinkles in the palm of your other hand. Finish the bottom edge of the *gâteau* by pressing it against the sprinkles in your palm to make a strip of sprinkles ⅜ to ½ inch (10 to 12 mm) high around the base. Place the *gâteau* on a serving plate and let the *pâte à glacé* set.

9 Prepare a parchment cornet (see page 118 for details).

10 Collect the excess *pâte à glacé* and temper it again. Transfer some of it to the parchment cornet and write "Ardechois" across the top of the *gâteau*. You can also pipe some decorative scrolls of *pâte à glacé* around the rim.

Romeo

Raisins and rum make a perfect marriage in this *gâteau*.

For 8 people

INGREDIENTS

10 tablespoons (80 g) seedless raisins

⅓ cup (8 cL) dark rum

2 tablespoons (3 cL) *sirop à trente* (see page 398)

2 cups (360 g) *crème au beurre* (see page 85)

One 9-inch (23 cm) round of *génoise* (see page 59)

1⅓ cups (450 g) fondant (see page 105)

Sirop à trente for thinning fondant

2 tablespoons (35 g) chocolate sprinkles

1 Place ½ cup (70 g) of the raisins in a strainer and steam them over simmering water until they just begin to soften, about 5 minutes. Transfer the raisins to a bowl and pour 2 tablespoons (3 cL) of rum over them. Cover airtight and let steep in the rum for at least 2 hours and preferably overnight. Then drain the raisins thoroughly.

2 Combine the *sirop à trente* with 2 tablespoons (3 cL) of rum. Flavor the *crème au beurre* with the remaining 4 teaspoons (2 cL) of rum.

3 Cut a cardboard cake-decorating circle about ¼ inch (6 mm) larger in diameter than the base of the *génoise* round.

4 Slice the *génoise* in half horizontally. Place the bottom layer on the cake decorating circle, cut side up, and brush the cut faces of both layers with most of the rum syrup. Spread ½ to ⅓ cup (90 to 110 g) of the *crème au beurre* over the bottom layer. Scatter the rum-soaked raisins over the *crème au beurre* and add the second layer of *génoise,* cut side down. Lightly brush the top with rum syrup.

Optional: About 1 tablespoon (15 g) *pâte à écrire* (see page 120)

5 Spread the top and sides of the *gâteau* with *crème au beurre*. Sweep first the top and then the sides with the edge of your palette knife to smooth the surface. Arrange the remaining (unsoaked) raisins in a circle on top of the *gâteau*, and gently press them into the *crème au beurre*.

6 Place the *gâteau* on a wire rack and refrigerate at least 1 hour to make the *crème au beurre* firm.

7 Warm the fondant over low heat, stirring constantly until melted. Stir in just enough *sirop à trente* to thin the fondant to the consistency of heavy cream. Pour the fondant over the top of the *gâteau* and spread it with the edge of your palette knife, smoothing the top surface and making it flow evenly down the sides. Touch up any uneven areas around the sides with the edge of your palette knife, and clean off any excess fondant around the base.

8 Before the fondant starts to set, lift the *gâteau* from the wire rack and support it on the fingertips of one hand. Take the chocolate sprinkles in the palm of your other hand. Decorate the bottom edge of the *gâteau* with arcs of sprinkles by pressing it against the sprinkles in your palm, then rotating the *gâteau* and repeating until the entire base is covered with adjacent arcs. Place the *gâteau* on a serving plate and let the fondant set. If you like, you can write ''Romeo'' on the top center of the *gâteau* in *pâte à écrire* using a parchment cornet.

Grand Marnier

A sheet of *pâte d'amandes* draped in gently flowing asymmetrical folds gives this *gâteau* a very contemporary look.

For 8 people

INGREDIENTS

3 ounces (85 g) candied fruits

1 Cut the candied fruits into ¼- to ⅜-inch (6 to 10 mm) dice and place them in a bowl. Pour 2 tablespoons (3 cL) of Grand Marnier over them, cover airtight, and let steep at least 2 hours and preferably overnight.

¼ cup plus 1 tablespoon (7½ cL) Grand Marnier

2 tablespoons (3 cL) *sirop à trente* (see page 398)

2 cups (300 g) *crème au beurre* (see page 85)

Red food coloring

One 9-inch (23 cm) round of *génoise* (see page 59)

3 tablespoons (35 g) chocolate sprinkles

3½ ounces (100 g) *pâte d'amandes* (see page 111)

Confectioners sugar for dusting

2 Drain the candied fruits. Combine the Grand Marnier in which they were soaked with the *sirop à trente* and an additional 2 teaspoons (1 cL) of Grand Marnier.

3 Flavor the *crème au beurre* with the remaining 4 teaspoons (2 cL) of Grand Marnier, and tint it a pale peach color with a couple of drops of red food coloring.

4 Cut a cardboard cake-decorating circle about ¼ inch (6 mm) larger in diameter than the base of the *génoise* round.

5 Slice the *génoise* in half horizontally. Place the bottom layer on the cake decorating circle, cut side up, and brush the cut faces of both layers with most of the Grand Marnier syrup. Spread 8 to 10 tablespoons (90 to 110 g) of the *crème au beurre* over the bottom layer. Scatter the candied fruits over the *crème au beurre* and add the second layer of *génoise*, cut side down. Lightly brush the top with Grand Marnier syrup.

6 Spread the top and sides of the *gâteau* with *crème au beurre*. Sweep first the top and then the sides with the edge of your palette knife to smooth the surface.

7 Lift the *gâteau* from the countertop and support it on the fingertips of one hand. Take the chocolate sprinkles in the palm of your other hand. Decorate the bottom edge of the *gâteau* with arcs of chocolate sprinkles by pressing it against the sprinkles in your palm, then rotating the *gâteau* and repeating until the entire base is covered with adjacent arcs.

8 Place the *gâteau* on a serving plate, and chill it in the refrigerator.

9 On your countertop, work the *pâte d'amandes* with the heel of your hand to make it smooth, and then work in a drop or two of red food coloring to tint it a pale pink. Dust your countertop and the *pâte d'amandes* with confectioners sugar and roll it into a rough circle about 10 inches (25 cm) in diameter. Cut a 9-inch (23 cm) circle from the sheet of *pâte d'amandes*. Carefully lift the circle and drape it over the top of the *gâteau* in gentle, natural folds.

10 Lightly dust the top of the *gâteau* with confectioners sugar.

Framboisine

The raspberry brandy *framboise* gives this *gâteau* a special flavor.

For 8 people

INGREDIENTS

1½ cups (270 g) *crème au beurre* (see page 85)

3 tablespoons (4½ cL) *eau de vie de framboise* (preferably) or kirsch

2 tablespoons (3 cL) *sirop à trente* (see page 398)

One 9-inch (23 cm) round of *génoise* (see page 59)

½ cup plus 1 tablespoon (180 g) raspberry jam

9 ounces (250 g) *pâte d'amandes* (see page 111)

3 tablespoons (35 g) chocolate sprinkles

Green and yellow food colorings

A few fresh raspberries or German raspberries (raspberry jelly candies) for decoration

1 Flavor the *crème au beurre* with 1 tablespoon (1½ cL) of the *eau de vie*. Mix the remaining *eau de vie* with the *sirop à trente*.

2 Cut a cardboard cake decorating circle about ¼ inch (6 mm) larger in diameter than the base of the *génoise* round.

3 Slice the *génoise* in half horizontally. Place the bottom layer on the cake-decorating circle, cut side up, and brush the cut faces of both layers with most of the syrup. Spread the raspberry jam over the bottom layer, and add the second layer cut side down. Lightly brush the top with syrup.

4 Spread the top and sides of the *gâteau* with *crème au beurre*. Sweep first the top and then the sides with the edge of your palette knife to smooth the surface.

5 Place the *gâteau* on a wire rack and refrigerate at least 1 hour to make the *crème au beurre* firm.

6 On your countertop, work the *pâte d'amandes* with the heel of your hand to make it smooth. Take about two thirds of the *pâte d'amandes*, dust it and your countertop with confectioners sugar, and roll it out into a rough circle about 12 to 13 inches (30 to 33 cm) in diameter. Place the *gâteau* on your countertop. Carefully roll the sheet of *pâte d'amandes* over your rolling pin, then unroll it onto the *gâteau*, centering it so that the edges hang over the sides of the *gâteau* and the sheet is flat against the top. Gently press the *pâte d'amandes* against the sides so that it covers the entire surface of the *gâteau*, with no creases. Using the tip of a paring knife, trim off the

261

Optional: About 1
tablespoon (15 g)
pâte à écrire (see
page 120)

excess *pâte d'amandes*, leaving a strip of *crème au beurre* ¼ to ⅜ inch (6 to 10 mm) high showing around the base. Combine the trimmings with the remaining *pâte d'amandes*.

7 Lift the *gâteau* from the counter and support it on the fingertips of one hand. Take the chocolate sprinkles in the palm of your other hand. Decorate the bottom edge of the *gâteau* by pressing it against the sprinkles in your palm to coat the exposed strip of *crème au beurre*.

8 Work a drop each of green and yellow food colorings into the remaining *pâte d'amandes* to tint it a pale green. Take half of this *pâte d'amandes* and roll it under your palms into a long thin rope, about ³⁄₁₆ inch (5 mm) in diameter. Arrange this rope in a meandering, vine-like decoration around the top of the *gâteau*. Roll out the remaining *pâte d'amandes* into a sheet about ³⁄₃₂ inch (2 mm) thick, and cut from it small leaf shapes. Arrange the leaves with the vine on the *gâteau*. Finally, add a few fresh raspberries or German raspberries around the vine to complete the motif.

9 If you like, you can write "Framboisine" on the top center of the *gâteau* in *pâte à écrire,* using a parchment cornet.

Cherry

The French word for cherries is *cerises*. Nonetheless, the name of this classic *gâteau* is *cherry*.

For 8 people

INGREDIENTS

1½ ounces (43 g)
candied cherries
¼ cup (6 cL)
maraschino liqueur
(preferably) or
Cointreau

1 Cut the candied cherries in half and place them in a bowl. Pour 1 tablespoon plus 2 teaspoons (2½ cL) of the maraschino over them, and cover airtight. Let steep at least 2 hours and preferably overnight.

2 When you are ready to assemble the *gâteau*, drain the cherries. Combine the liqueur in which

2 tablespoons (3 cL) *sirop à trente* (see page 398)

2 cups (360 g) *crème au beurre* (see page 85)

One 9-inch (23 cm) round of *génoise* (see page 59)

7 ounces (200 g) *pâte d'amandes* (see page 111)

3 tablespoons (35 g) chocolate sprinkles

Green and yellow food colorings

2 or 3 candied cherries for decoration

1 tablespoon (15 g) sugar

About 1 tablespoon (15 g) *pâte à écrire* (see page 120)

they were soaked with the *sirop à trente* and an additional 1 tablespoon (1½ cL) of maraschino.

3 Flavor the *crème au beurre* with the remaining 4 teaspoons (2 cL) of maraschino.

4 Cut a cardboard cake-decorating circle about ¼ inch (6 mm) larger in diameter than the base of the *génoise* round.

5 Slice the *génoise* in half horizontally. Place the bottom layer on the cake-decorating circle, cut side up, and brush the cut faces of both layers with most of the syrup. Spread ½ to ⅓ cup (90 to 110 g) of the *crème au beurre* over the bottom layer. Scatter the candied cherries over the *crème au beurre* and add the second layer of *génoise,* cut side down. Lightly brush the top with syrup.

6 Spread the top and sides of the *gâteau* with *créme au beurre.* Sweep first the top and then the sides with the edge of your palette knife to smooth the surface.

7 Place the *gâteau* on a wire rack and refrigerate at least 1 hour to make the *crème au beurre* firm.

8 On your countertop, work the *pâte d'amandes* with the heel of your hand to make it smooth. Dust your countertop and the *pâte d'amandes* with confectioners sugar and roll it out into a rough circle about 12 to 13 inches (30 to 33 cm) in diameter. Place the gâteau on your countertop. Carefully roll the sheet of *pâte d'amandes* over your rolling pin, then unroll it onto the *gâteau,* centering it so that the edges hang over the sides of the *gâteau* and the sheet is flat against the top. Gently press the *pâte d'amandes* against the sides so that it covers the entire surface of the *gâteau,* with no creases. Using the tip of a paring knife, trim off the excess *pâte d'amandes,* leaving a strip of *crème au beurre* ¼ inch (6 mm) high showing around the base.

9 Lift the *gâteau* from the counter and support it on the fingertips of one hand. Take the chocolate sprinkles in the palm of your other hand. Decorate the bottom edge of the *gâteau* by pressing it against the sprinkles in your palm to coat the exposed strip of *crème au beurre.*

10 Work a drop each of green and yellow food colorings into the trimmings of *pâte d'amandes* to color the *pâte d'amandes* a pale green. Roll out this *pâte d'amandes* about ³⁄₃₂ inch (2 mm) thick and cut from it a few small leaf shapes. Roll two or three candied cherries in sugar to give them a frosted look.

① *11* Gently warm the *pâte à écrire* until melted and transfer it to a parchment cornet (see page 118). Cut the tip of the cornet and pipe a few stems in *pâte à écrire* around the center of the *gâteau*. Arrange a few *pâte d'amandes* leaves and the frosted candied cherries with the stems to complete the motif ①.

Marquis

Filled and topped with *crème chantilly* and fresh peaches, this is a delightful *gâteau* for late summer, at the height of the peach season. If you like, you can substitute fresh raspberries for the peaches.

For 6 to 8 people

INGREDIENTS

3 to 4 ripe medium freestone peaches, or canned peaches in heavy syrup

2 tablespoons (3 cL) *sirop à trente* (see page 398)

2 tablespoons (3 cL) kirsch

One 9-inch (23 cm) round of *génoise* or *génoise chocolat* (see page 59)

4 cups (500 g) *crème chantilly,* flavored with vanilla (see page 82)

3 tablespoons (35 g) chocolate sprinkles

1 If the peaches are not quite ripe, poach them in *sirop léger* (see page 422) until they can be pierced easily with a skewer. Then cool in the syrup and drain thoroughly.

2 Peel and stone the peaches and cut them into slices ¼ inch (6 mm) thick. If the peaches have not been poached, dip the slices in acidulated water to prevent discoloration.

3 Mix the *sirop à trente* with the kirsch.

4 Cut a cardboard cake-decorating circle about ³⁄₈ inch (1 cm) larger in diameter than the base of the *génoise* round.

5 Slice the *génoise* in half horizontally. Place the bottom layer on the cake-decorating circle, cut side up, and brush the cut faces of both layers with most of the kirsch syrup. Spread about ½ cup plus 2 tablespoons (80 g) of *crème chantilly* over the bottom layer. Starting from the outside, arrange the peach slices over the *crème chantilly* in concentric circles, overlapping the slices slightly like the blades of a fan. Save eight of the slices for decorating the top of the *gâteau*. Spread another 10 tablespoons (80 g) of *crème chantilly* over the cut face of the second layer of *génoise*, and place this layer on the peaches, cut side down. Lightly brush top with kirsch syrup.

6 Spread the top and sides of the *gâteau* with *crème chantilly*. Sweep first the top and then the sides with the edge of your palette knife to smooth the surface. Save about ½ cup (65 g) of *crème chantilly* for decorating.

7 Lift the *gâteau* from the countertop and support it on the fingertips of one hand. Take the chocolate sprinkles in the palm of your other hand. Decorate the bottom edge of the *gâteau* with arcs of sprinkles by pressing it against the sprinkles in your palm, then rotating the *gâteau* and repeating until the entire base is covered with adjacent arcs.

8 Transfer the remaining *crème chantilly* to a pastry bag fitted with a small star tube (Ateco 1). Pipe a circle of teardrop-shaped *rosaces* around the rim of the gateau. Pipe a large rosette of *crème chantilly* in the center and arrange the reserved peach slices around it like a pinwheel ①. Pipe a rosette of *crème chantilly* between each pair of peach slices.

Abricotine

Filled and glazed with apricot jam, *abricotine* is especially easy to make.

For 6 to 8 people

INGREDIENTS

2 tablespoons (3 cL) *sirop à trente* (see page 398)

2 tablespoons (3 cL) kirsch

1 Mix the *sirop à trente* with the kirsch.

2 Cut a cardboard cake-decorating circle slightly smaller than the base of the *génoise* round.

3 Slice the *génoise* in half horizontally. Place the bottom layer on the cake-decorating circle, cut side up, and brush the cut faces of both layers with most of the kirsch syrup. Spread the whole apricot jam

One 9-inch (23 cm)
round of *génoise*
(see page 59)

8 ounces (225 g)
whole apricot jam

4 to 5 tablespoons
(80 to 100 g)
strained apricot jam

3 tablespoons (30 g)
roasted chopped
almonds

1 ounce (30 g) *pâte
d'amandes* (see
page 111)

Green and yellow
food colorings

1 candied apricot

over the bottom layer. Add the second layer, cut side down, and lightly brush the top with kirsch syrup.

4 Warm the strained apricot jam over low heat, stirring occasionally, until melted. Brush the top and sides of the *gâteau* with jam until lightly coated and glistening.

5 Lift the *gâteau* from the countertop and support it on the fingertips of one hand. Take the chopped almonds in the palm of your other hand. Decorate the bottom edge of the *gâteau* by pressing it against the chopped almonds in your palm to make a strip of chopped nuts ⅜ to ½ inch (10 to 12 mm) high around the base.

6 On your countertop, work the *pâte d'amandes* with the heel of your hand to make it smooth. Then work in a drop each of green and yellow food colorings to tint it a pale green. Dust your countertop and the *pâte d'amandes* with confectioners sugar. Take half of the *pâte d'amandes* and roll it under your palms into a thin string about ⅛ inch (3 mm) in diameter. Cut the string into short stems. Roll out the remaining *pâte d'amandes* with your rolling pin into a sheet about ³⁄₃₂ inch (2 mm) thick, and cut from it a few leaf shapes. Slice the candied apricot in half horizontally to make two thin round slices. Arrange the *pâte d'amandes* leaves and stems and the candied apricot halves (cut side down) on the center of the *gâteau*.

Napolitain

The name of this *gâteau* is French for Neapolitan. It should come as no surprise that it is covered with *meringue italienne*.

For 8 people

INGREDIENTS

One 8-ounce (225 g)
can of pineapple
slices or chunks in
heavy syrup

1 Drain the canned pineapple. Cut it into ¼- to ⅜-inch (6 to 10 mm) dice and place the dice on a paper towel to drain off as much moisture as possible. Mix the dice with 6 tablespoons (120 g) of apricot jam to make a *salpicon*.

½ cup plus 1 to 2 tablespoons (180 to 200 g) strained apricot jam

2 tablespoons (3 cL) *sirop à trente* (see page 398)

2 tablespoons (3 cL) kirsch

One 9-inch (23 cm) round of *génoise* (see page 59)

About 3 cups (180 g) *meringue italienne* (see page 101)

3 tablespoons (30 g) roasted chopped almonds

3 to 4 candied cherries

Candied angelica

2 Mix the *sirop à trente* with the kirsch.

3 Cut a cardboard cake-decorating circle about ¼ inch (6 mm) larger in diameter than the base of the *génoise* round.

4 Slice the *génoise* in half horizontally. Place the bottom layer on the cake-decorating circle, cut side up, and brush the cut faces of both layers with most of the kirsch syrup. Spread the *salpicon* over the bottom layer and add the second layer, cut side down. Lightly brush the top with kirsch syrup.

5 Spread a layer of *meringue italienne* 1 inch (2½ cm) thick over the top of the *gâteau*, and spread the sides with a thin layer of the meringue. Holding the face of your palette knife almost perpendicular to the surface of the *gâteau*, sweep first the top and then the sides to smooth the surface.

6 Put the *gâteau* in a warm place (ideally, 125° to 175° F, or 50° to 80° C.) and let the *meringue* dry until it is crusty outside but still soft inside, 2 to 3 hours.

7 Heat a steel wire or skewer on your cooktop until red hot. Draw it over the top of the *gâteau* in a straight line, caramelizing the sugar in the meringue. Heat it again and draw a second line, separated from the first by about ¼ inch (6 mm). Continue heating the wire and drawing pairs of parallel lines, separating each pair by about 1½ inches (4 cm). Then draw a second set of pairs of parallel lines, on the diagonal with respect to the first set, to make a lozenge pattern on the top of the *gâteau*. Finally, continue the lines about one quarter of the way down the sides.

8 Warm the remaining apricot jam over low heat, stirring occasionally, until melted. Brush the top and sides of the *gâteau* with jam until lightly coated and glistening.

9 Lift the *gâteau* from the countertop and support it on the fingertips of one hand. Take the chopped almonds in the palm of your other hand. Decorate the bottom edge of the *gâteau* by pressing it against the almonds in your palm to make a strip of chopped nuts ⅜ to ½ inch (10 to 12 mm) high around the base.

10 Cut the candied cherries in half. Slice some angelica about ⅛ inch (3 mm) thick, and cut it into ½-inch (12 mm) diamonds. Arrange alternating rows of half cherries and angelica diamonds in the large lozenges on top of the *gâteau.*

Succulent

A round of meringue between two layers of *génoise* adds lightness to this kirsch-flavored *gâteaux.*

For 10 to 12 people

INGREDIENTS

5 ounces (145 g) candied fruits

¼ cup plus 1 tablespoon (7½ cL) kirsch

2 tablespoons (3 cL) *sirop à trente* (see page 398)

3 cups (540 g) *crème au beurre* (see page 85)

One 9-inch (23 cm) round of *génoise* (see page 59)

One 9- to 9½-inch (23 to 24 cm) round of *meringue ordinaire* (see page 72)

¼ cup plus 2 tablespoons (40 g) roasted sliced almonds

1 Cut the candied fruits into ¼- to ⅜-inch (6 to 10 mm) dice and place them in a bowl. Pour 3 tablespoons (4½ cL) of the kirsch over them, cover airtight, and let steep at least 2 hours and preferably overnight.

2 Drain the candied fruits. Combine the kirsch in which they were soaked with the *sirop à trente.* Flavor the *crème au beurre* with the remaining 2 tablespoons (3 cL) of kirsch.

3 Cut a cardboard cake-decorating circle about ¼ inch (6 mm) larger in diameter than the base of the *génoise* round.

4 Carefully trim the round of *meringue ordinaire* to a circle the size of the top of the *génoise* round, using a bread knife. Shave the top of the meringue to eliminate any large bumps.

5 Slice the *génoise* in half horizontally. Place the bottom layer on the cake-decorating circle, cut side up, and brush the cut faces of both layers with most of the kirsch syrup. Spread ½ to ⅓ cup (90 to 110 g) of *crème au beurre* over the bottom layer. Scatter half of the candied fruits over the *crème au beurre.* Add the circle of meringue, spread it with ½ to ⅓ cup (90 to 110 g) of *crème au beurre,* and scatter the remaining candied fruits over it. Add the second layer of *génoise,* cut side down, and lightly brush the top with kirsch syrup.

OPTIONAL

1 ounce (25 g) *pâte d'amandes* (see page 111)

Green food coloring

About 1 tablespoon (15 g) *pâte à écrire* (see page 120)

6 Spread the top and sides of the *gâteau* with *crème au beurre*. Sweep first the top and then the sides with the edge of your palette knife to smooth the surface.

7 Scatter the roasted sliced almonds over the top and sides of the *gâteau*.

8 If you want to decorate the *gâteau* more elaborately, work the *pâte d'amandes* with the heel of your hand to make it smooth and work in a drop of green food coloring to tint it a pale green. Dust your countertop and the *pâte d'amandes* with confectioners sugar and roll it out about 3/32 inch (2 mm) thick with your rolling pin. Cut from the sheet of *pâte d'amandes* a small writing card about 2 × 4 inches (5 × 10 cm) and place it on the center of the *gâteau*. Melt the *pâte à écrire* and transfer it to a parchment cornet (see page 118). Cut the tip of the cornet and pipe the word "Succulent" in *pâte à écrire* on the *pâte d'amandes* ①.

Délicieux

The flavors of Grand Marnier and chocolate mingle in this very rich *gâteau*.

For 10 to 12 people

INGREDIENTS

3 tablespoons plus 1 teaspoon (5 cL) Grand Marnier

2 tablespoons (3 cL) *sirop à trente* (see page 398)

2⅓ cups (420 g) *crème au beurre* (see page 85)

Red food coloring

One 9-inch (23 cm) round of *génoise* (see page 59)

1 Combine 2 tablespoons (3 cL) of Grand Marnier with the *sirop à trente*. Flavor the *crème au beurre* with the remaining Grand Marnier, and tint it a pale peach color with a couple of drops of red food coloring.

2 Cut a cardboard cake-decorating circle about ¼ inch (6 mm) larger in diameter than the base of the *génoise* round.

3 Carefully trim the round of *meringue ordinaire* to a circle the size of the top of the *génoise* round, using a bread knife. Shave the top of the *meringue* to eliminate any large bumps.

4 Slice the *génoise* in half horizontally. Place the bottom layer on the cake-decorating circle, cut side

One 9- to 9½-inch (23 to 24 cm) round of *meringue ordinaire* (see page 72)

⅔ cup (160 g) *ganache au Grand Marnier* (see page 89)

Either 12 ounces (340 g) *pâte à glacé* (see page 110); *or* 9 ounces (250 g) semisweet chocolate, 6 tablespoons (85 g) barely melted butter, and 1½ tablespoons (2¼ cL) water

3 tablespoons (35 g) chocolate sprinkles

1 ounce (30 g) *pâte d'amandes* (see page 111)

up, and brush the cut faces of both layers with most of the Grand Marnier syrup. Spread the *ganache* over the bottom layer. Add the circle of *meringue* and spread it with ½ to ⅓ cup (90 to 110 g) of the *crème au beurre*. Add the second layer of *génoise*, cut side down, and lightly brush the top with Grand Marnier syrup.

5 Spread the top and sides of the *gâteau* with the *crème au beurre*. Sweep first the top and then the sides with the edge of your palette knife to smooth the surface.

6 Place the *gâteau* on a wire rack and refrigerate at least 1 hour to make the *crème au beurre* firm.

7 If you have *pâte à glacé* on hand, temper it to get the right consistency for coating the *gâteau*. Otherwise, prepare a *pâte à glacé* as follows: Melt the chocolate and stir in the butter. When smooth, stir in the water. Dip the bottom of the pot of chocolate in cold water and stir until it begins to thicken. Return this *pâte à glacé* to the heat and gently warm it a second time, stirring until just melted.

8 Pour the *pâte à glacé* over the top of the *gâteau* and spread it with the edge of your palette knife, smoothing the top surface and making the *pâte à glacé* flow evenly down the sides. Touch up any uneven areas around the sides with the edge of your palette knife, and clean off any excess *pâte à glacé* around the base.

9 Before the *pâte à glacé* sets, lift the *gâteau* from the wire rack and support it on the fingertips of one hand. Take the chocolate sprinkles in the palm of your other hand. Finish the bottom edge of the *gâteau* by pressing it against the sprinkles in your palm to make a strip of chocolate sprinkles ⅜ to ½ inch (10 to 12 mm) high around the base. Place the *gâteau* on a serving plate and let the *pâte à glacé* set.

10 Prepare a parchment cornet (see page 118).

11 Collect the excess *pâte à glacé* and temper it again. Transfer some of it to the parchment cornet and write ''Delicieux'' across the top of the *gâteau*.

12 On your countertop, work the *pâte d'amandes* with the heel of your hand to make it smooth, and then work in a drop of red food coloring to tint it a very pale pink. Roll the *pâte d'amandes* under your palms into a long thin rope, about ¼ inch (6 mm) in diameter. Arrange the rope in a circle around the rim of the *gâteau* and cut the ends so they meet.

Succès Kirsch

For 8 people

INGREDIENTS

3 ounces (85 g) candied fruits

¼ cup (6 cL) kirsch

2 tablespoons (3 cL) *sirop à trente* (see page 398)

2 cups (360 g) *crème au beurre* (see page 85)

Two 9- to 9½-inch (23 to 24 cm) rounds of *succès* (see page 75)

1⅓ cups (450 g) fondant (see page 105)

Sirop à trente for thinning fondant

3 tablespoons (30 g) roasted chopped almonds

Candied fruits for decoration

1 tablespoon (15 g) sugar

1 Cut the candied fruits into ¼- to ⅜-inch (6 to 10 mm) dice and place them in a small bowl. Pour 2 tablespoons (3 cL) of the kirsch over them, cover airtight, and let steep for at least 2 hours and preferably overnight.

2 Drain the candied fruits. Combine the kirsch in which they were soaked with the *sirop à trente* and an additional 2 teaspoons (1 cL) of kirsch. Flavor the *crème au beurre* with the remaining 4 teaspoons (2 cL) of kirsch.

3 Carefully trim each round of *succès* into a 9-inch (23 cm) circle with a bread knife. Shave the tops of both circles of *succès* to eliminate any large bumps.

4 Cut a cardboard cake-decorating circle about ¼ inch (6 mm) larger in diameter than the circles of *succès*.

5 Place one circle of *succès* on the cake-decorating circle. Brush the tops of both layers with kirsch syrup. Spread the bottom layer with ½ to ⅓ cup (90 to 110 g) of the *crème au beurre*, and scatter the candied fruits over it. Invert the second circle of *succès*, and place it on the *crème au beurre*. Lightly brush the top with kirsch syrup.

6 Spread the top and sides of the *gâteau* with *crème au beurre*. Sweep first the top and then the sides with the edge of your palette knife to smooth the surface.

7 Place the *gâteau* on a wire rack and refrigerate at least 1 hour to make the *crème au beurre* firm.

8 Warm the fondant over low heat, stirring constantly until melted. Stir in just enough *sirop à trente* to thin the fondant to the consistency of heavy cream. Pour the fondant over the top of the *gâteau* and spread it with the edge of your palette knife, smoothing the top surface and making it flow evenly down the sides. Touch up any uneven areas around the sides with the edge of your palette knife, and clean off any excess fondant around the base.

9 Before the fondant starts to set, lift the *gâteau* from the wire rack and support it on the fingertips of one hand. Take the chopped almonds in the palm of your other hand. Decorate the bottom edge of the *gâteau* by pressing it against the chopped almonds in your palm to make a strip of chopped nuts ⅜ to ½ inch (10 to 12 mm) high around the base.

10 Cut the candied fruits into slices and toss them in the sugar to give them a frosted look. Arrange slices in a floral pattern on the center of the *gâteau*.

11 Allow the fondant to set before serving.

Café Noix

For 8 people

INGREDIENTS

3 cups (540 g) *crème au beurre* (see page 85)

¼ cup plus 1 tablespoon (3½ cL) very strong black coffee (see page 416)

2 tablespoons (3 cL) *sirop à trente* (see page 398)

1 Flavor the *crème au beurre* with 2 tablespoons (3 cL) of coffee. Mix 2 tablespoons (3 cL) of coffee with the *sirop à trente*.

2 Trim each round of *succès* to a circle about ⅜ inch (1 cm) smaller in diameter than the inside of a 9½-inch (24 cm) *entremet* ring using a bread knife. Shave the top of each circle of *succès* to eliminate any large bumps.

3 Cut a cardboard cake-decorating circle to just fit inside the *entremet* ring.

4 Brush the top of each circle of *succès* with coffee syrup.

Two 9½-inch (24 cm) rounds of *succès* (see page 75)

¼ cup plus 2 tablespoons (50 g) chopped walnuts

1⅓ cup (450 g) fondant (see page 105)

1 tablespoon (1½ cL) caramel food coloring (page 431)

Sirop à trente for thinning fondant

3 to 4 walnut halves

5 Place one layer of *succès* on the cake-decorating circle. Using the tip of your palette knife, coat the bottom half of the inside of the ring with *crème au beurre.* Center the ring over the bottom layer of *succès,* and press the ring down on the countertop. Spread about 1 cup (180 g) of *crème au buerre* over the bottom layer of *succès* and the top half of the inside of the ring. Scatter 3 tablespoons (25 g) of the chopped walnuts over the *crème au beurre.* Invert the second circle of *succès,* center it over the *crème au beurre,* and press it down into the ring. Lightly brush the top with coffee syrup. Spread the remaining *crème au beurre* over the *succès* and smooth it level with the top of the ring, using your palette knife.

6 Carefully slide the *gâteau* onto a wire rack. Refrigerate the *gâteau* until the *crème au beurre* is firm, at least 1 hour.

7 Place the *gâteau* on an inverted 9-inch (23 cm) layer-cake pan. Dip a kitchen towel in hot water, then wring it out. Briefly wrap the hot towel around the outside of the ring to just melt the *crème au beurre* touching the inside of the ring. Wipe the ring dry and carefully slip it down off the *gâteau.* Return the *gâteau* to the wire rack and refrigerate again until the *crème au beurre* on the outside is firm.

8 Warm the fondant over low heat, stirring constantly until melted. Color and flavor the fondant with the caramel and the remaining 1 tablespoon (1½ cL) coffee, and stir in just enough *sirop à trente* to thin the fondant to the consistency of heavy cream. Pour the fondant over the top of the *gâteau* and spread it with the edge of your palette knife, smoothing the top surface and making it flow evenly down the sides. Touch up any uneven areas around the sides with the edge of your palette knife, and clean off any excess fondant around the base.

9 Before the fondant starts to set, lift the *gâteau* from the wire rack and support it on the fingertips of one hand. Take the remaining chopped walnuts in the palm of your other hand. Decorate the bottom edge of the *gâteau* by pressing it against the chopped walnuts in your palm to make a strip of chopped nuts ⅜ to ½ inch (10 to 12 mm) high around the base.

Place the *gâteau* on a serving plate, and arrange the walnut halves round the center to finish decorating it.

10 Let the fondant set before serving.

Progrès

This *gâteau* is made by sandwiching *praliné*-flavored *crème au beurre* between two layers of the *appareil meringuée* called *progrès*.

For 8 people

INGREDIENTS

2¼ cups (400 g)
  crème au beurre
  (see page 85)
¼ cup (75 g) *praliné*
  (see page 414)
Two 9- to 9½-inch
  (23 to 24 cm)
  rounds of *progrès* or
  succès (see page
  75)
Confectioners sugar
  for dusting

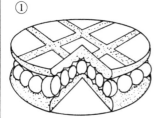

1 Beat the *crème au beurre* into the *praliné* with a wooden spoon, adding the *crème au beurre* gradually to be sure there are no lumps of *praliné*.

2 Using a flan ring, a round mold, or a *vol-au-vent* disc as a guide, carefully trim each round of *progrès* into a circle 9 inches (23 cm) in diameter with a bread knife. Shave the tops of both circles of *progrès* to eliminate any large bumps.

3 Cut a cardboard cake-decorating circle slightly smaller than the circles of *progrès*.

4 Place one circle of *progrès* on the cake-decorating circle. Transfer the *crème au beurre* to a pastry bag fitted with a ⁷⁄₁₆- to ½-inch (11 to 12 mm) plain pastry tube (Ateco 5 or 6). Starting from the center, pipe a continuous spiral of *crème au beurre* over the bottom layer, leaving a border 1 inch (2½ cm) wide around the outside uncovered. Fill the border by piping 1-inch (2½ cm) diameter balls of *crème au beurre* around the circumference. Pipe the balls adjacent to each other and about ½ inch (12 mm) thick.

5 Invert the second circle of *progrès*, place it on the *crème au beurre*, and press down very gently.

6 Cut some strips of paper about ⅜ inch (1 cm) wide and arrange them on top of the *gâteau* in a decorative geometric pattern—for example, a lozenge pattern ①. Dust the top heavily with confectioners sugar. Then carefully remove the paper strips.

Janou and Michounnet

Janou-Michou was a pastry shop in the Parisian suburb Asnières. The owner named the shop and these two *gâteaux* after his twin sons. Paul's father, Marcel Bugat, obtained the recipes when he purchased that shop many years ago, then took them with him when he went to Pâtissière Clichy in 1955. Paul took over Clichy in 1970 and is still making *janou* and *michounnet*.

For 8 people

INGREDIENTS

Two 9- to 9½-inch (23 to 24 cm) rounds of *dijonnaise* (see page 74)

2 cups (360 g) *crème au beurre* (see page 85)

JANOU

1½ ounces (43 g) unsweetened chocolate

¼ cup (50 g) chocolate sprinkles, or *copeaux en chocolat* (see page 122)

MICHOUNNET

4 teaspoons (2 cL) very strong black coffee (see page 416)

⅓ cup (35 g) roasted sliced almonds

1 Using a flan ring, a round mold, or a *vol-au-vent* disc as a guide, carefully trim each round of *dijonnaise* into a 9-inch (23 cm) circle with a bread knife. Shave the tops of both circles of *dijonnaise* to eliminate any large bumps.

2 For *janou*, gently melt the unsweetened chocolate and stir it into the *crème au beurre*. For *michounnet*, flavor the *crème au beurre* with the coffee.

3 Cut a cardboard cake-decorating circle about ¼ inch (6 mm) larger in diameter than the circles of *dijonnaise*.

4 Place one circle of *dijonnaise* on the cake decorating circle. Spread ½ to ⅓ cup (90 to 110 g) of the *crème au beurre* over it. Invert the second circle, and place it on the *crème au beurre*.

5 Spread the top and sides of the *gâteau* with *crème au beurre*. Sweep first the top and then the sides with the edge of your palette knife to smooth the surface.

6 Sprinkle the top and sides of the *gâteau* with the chocolate sprinkles or roasted sliced almonds.

Chanteclair

The classic decoration for this *gâteau* is a rooster (*chanteclair* in French) stenciled on top in confectioners sugar.

For 8 people

INGREDIENTS

½ cup (70 g) seedless raisins

2 tablespoons (3 cL) dark rum

2 cups (360 g) *crème au beurre* (see page 85)

¼ cup (75 g) *praliné* (see page 414)

Two 9- to 9½-inch (23 to 24 cm) rounds of *dijonnaise* (see page 74)

Confectioners sugar for stenciling

1 Place the raisins in a strainer and steam them over simmering water until they just begin to soften, about 5 minutes. Transfer the raisins to a bowl and pour the rum over them. Cover airtight and let steep for at least 2 hours and preferably overnight. Then drain thoroughly.

2 Beat the *crème au beurre* into the *praliné* with a ly to be sure there are no lumps of *praliné*.

3 Using a flan ring, a round mold, or a *vol-au-vent* disc as a guide, carefully trim each round of *dijonnaise* into a 9-inch (23 cm) circle with a bread knife. Shave the tops of both circles of *dijonnaise* to eliminate any large bumps. Pulverize the *dijonnaise* trimmings in a blender, food processor, or mortar and pestle.

4 Cut a cardboard cake-decorating circle about ¼ inch (6 mm) larger in diameter than the circles of *dijonnaise*.

5 Place one circle of *dijonnaise* on the cake-decorating circle. Spread ½ to ⅓ cup (90 to 110 g) of the *crème au beurre* over it. Scatter the rum-soaked raisins over the *crème au beurre*. Invert the second circle of *dijonnaise* and place it on top.

6 Spread the top and sides of the *gâteau* with *crème au beurre*. Sweep first the top and then the sides with the edge of your palette knife to smooth the surface.

7 Sprinkle the top and sides of the *gâteau* with about ¼ cup (25 g) of the pulverized *dijonnaise* trimmings.

8 If you don't already have a stencil, cut one from a piece of paper. Make a rooster or a design of your

Opposite: Bûche de Noël (Yule log), page 291. Following page: Vacherin, page 300.

choice ①. Place the stencil on top of the *gâteau* and dust it heavily with confectioners sugar ②. Then carefully remove the stencil.

Stanislas

For 10 to 12 people

INGREDIENTS

2⅓ cups (420 g) *crème au beurre* (see page 85)

4 teaspoons (2 cL) very strong black coffee (see page 416)

Two 9- to 9½-inch (23 to 24 cm) rounds of *dijonnaise* (see page 74)

One 9- to 9½-inch (23 to 24 cm) round of *meringue ordinaire* (see page 72)

⅔ cup (160 g) *ganache clichy* (see page 89)

Either 12 ounces (340 g) *pâte à glacé* (see page 110); *or* 9 ounces (250 g) semisweet chocolate, 6 tablespoons (85 g) barely melted butter, and 1½ tablespoons (2¼ cL) water

3 tablespoons (35 g) chocolate sprinkles

1 Flavor the *crème au beurre* with the coffee.

2 Using a flan ring, a round mold, or a *vol-au-vent* disc as a guide, carefully trim each round of *dijonnaise* and *meringue ordinaire* into a 9-inch (23 cm) circle with a bread knife. Shave the tops of the circles to eliminate any large bumps.

3 Cut a cardboard cake decorating circle about ¼ inch (6 mm) larger in diameter than the *dijonnaise* and *meringue* circles.

4 Place one circle of *dijonnaise* on the cake-decorating circle, and spread ½ to ⅓ cup (90 to 110 g) of the *crème au beurre* over it. Add the circle of *meringue* and spread the *ganache* over it. Invert the second circle of *dijonnaise* and place it on top.

5 Spread the top and sides of the *gâteau* with *crème au beurre*. Sweep first the top and then the sides with the edge of your palette knife to smooth the surface.

6 Place the *gâteau* on a wire rack and refrigerate for at least 1 hour to make the *crème au beurre* firm.

7 If you have *pâte à glacé* on hand, temper it to get the right consistency for coating the *gâteau*. Otherwise, prepare a *pâte à glacé* as follows: Melt the chocolate and stir in the butter. When smooth, stir in the water. Dip the bottom of the pot of chocolate in cold water and stir until it begins to thicken. Return this *pâte à glacé* to the heat and gently warm it a second time, stirring until just melted.

Opposite: Paris-brest, page 317. Preceding page: Assorted cream puff pastries, pages 306–312.

8 Pour the *pâte à glacé* over the top of the *gâteau* and spread it with the edge of your palette knife, smoothing the top surface and making the *pâte à glacé* flow evenly down the sides. Touch up any uneven areas around the sides with the edge of your palette knife, and clean off any excess *pâte à glacé* around the base.

9 Before the *pâte à glacé* sets, lift the *gâteau* from the wire rack and support it on the fingertips of one hand. Take the chocolate sprinkles in the palm of your other hand. Finish the bottom edge of the *gâteau* by pressing it against the sprinkles in your palm to make a strip of sprinkles ⅜ to ½ inch (10 to 12 mm) high around the base. Place the *gâteau* on a serving plate and let the *pâte à glacé* set.

10 Prepare a parchment cornet (see page 118 for details).

11 Collect the excess *pâte à glacé* and temper it again. Transfer some of it to the parchment cornet, and write "Stanislas" across the top of the *gâteau*. Then pipe a scroll pattern in *pâte à glacé* around the rim.

Chocolatine and Noisettine

These are two of the simplest *gâteaux* to assemble. For both, a single round of *dijonnaise* is covered with a thick layer of a very light butter cream. They are formed in *entremet* rings which do all the work, and the only decorations are chocolate sprinkles or the pulverized *dijonnaise* trimmings scattered over the top.

For 8 people

INGREDIENTS

One 9½-inch (24 cm) round of *dijonnaise* (see page 74)

⅔ cup (150 g) butter, softened

1 Trim the round of *dijonnaise* with a bread knife so it just fits inside a 9½-inch (24 cm) *entremet* ring. Shave the top of the *dijonnaise* to eliminate any large bumps. For *noisettine,* pulverize the *dijonnaise* trimmings in an electric blender, food processor, or mortar and pestle.

2 Place the softened butter in a bowl and beat it with a wooden spoon until very soft, warming it over

5 cups (300 g)
meringue italienne
(see page 101)

CHOCOLATINE

1½ ounces (43 g)
unsweetened
chocolate

3 tablespoons (35 g)
chocolate sprinkles,
or *copeaux en
chocolat* (see page
122)

NOISETTINE

⅓ cup (35 g) *praliné*
(see page 414)

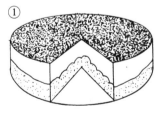

low heat if necessary. For *noisettine,* gradually beat
the butter into the *praliné* with a wire whisk to make
it smooth, with no lumps of *praliné*. For *chocolatine,* melt the chocolate.

3 Add about one third of the *meringue italienne* to
the butter (or butter and *praliné)*, and mix thoroughly with a rubber spatula. Then gently fold in the
remaining meringue. For *chocolatine,* add the
melted chocolate when the mixture is almost
smooth. Continue folding until completely mixed
and homogeneous. The result is a very light butter-
cream.

4 Cut a cardboard cake-decorating circle to just fit
inside the *entremet* ring.

5 Place the *dijonnaise* round inside the *entremet*
ring, with the cake-decorating circle underneath.
Spoon the butter cream into the ring and sweep the
surface level with the rim, using your palette
knife.

6 Sprinkle the chocolate sprinkles or 2 tablespoons (15 g) of the pulverized *dijonnaise* trimmings
over the top of the *gâteau*.

7 Carefully slide the *gâteau* onto a baking sheet or
wire rack, and refrigerate until the filling is set, at
least 1 hour.

8 Place the *gâteau* on an inverted 9-inch (23 cm)
layer-cake pan. Dip a kitchen towel in hot water,
then wring it out. Briefly wrap the hot towel around
the outside of the ring to just melt the filling touching
the inside of the ring. Wipe the ring dry and carefully
slip it down off the *gâteau*. Transfer the *gâteau* to a
serving plate ①.

Marie Stuart

This is an extravagently rich *gâteau* based on *crème de marrons*.

For 8 people

INGREDIENTS

3½ ounces (100 g) whole *marrons glacés*

¼ cup (6 cL) bourbon

One 8½-inch (22 cm.) round of *dijonnaise* (see page 74)

3 cups (540 g) *crème de marrons* flavored with bourbon (see page 92)

Either 4 ounces (115 g) *pâte à glacé* (see page 110); *or* 3 ounces (85 g) semisweet chocolate, 2 tablespoons (30 g) barely melted butter, and 1½ teaspoon (¾ cL) water

1 Set aside one *marron glacé* to decorate the top of the *gâteau*. Place the remaining *marrons glacés* in a bowl, pour the bourbon over them, and cover airtight. Let steep overnight, then drain thoroughly.

2 Trim the round of dijonnaise with a bread knife so it just fits inside an 8-inch (20 cm) *entremet* ring. Shave the top of the *dijonnaise* to eliminate any large bumps.

3 Cut a cardboard cake-decorating circle to just fit inside the *entremet* ring.

4 Place the *dijonnaise* round inside the ring, with the cake-decorating circle underneath. Spread a thin layer of *crème de marrons* over the *dijonnaise*, and arrange the bourbon-soaked *marrons glacés* on it. Fill the ring with the remaining *crème de marrons*, covering the *marrons glacés*, and smooth the surface level with the rim, using your palette knife.

5 Carefully slide the *gâteau* onto a wire rack and refrigerate for at least 1 hour to make the *crème de marrons* firm.

6 If you have *pâte à glacé* on hand, temper it to get the right consistency for coating the *gâteau*. Otherwise, prepare a *pâte à glacé* as follows: Melt the chocolate and stir in the butter. When smooth, stir in the water. Dip the bottom of the pot of chocolate in cold water and stir until it begins to thicken. Return this *pâte à glacé* to the heat and gently warm it a second time, stirring until just melted.

7 Pour the *pâte à glacé* over the top of the *gâteau* and spread it with your palette knife, smoothing the top surface and making the excess flow down the sides of the ring. Place the reserved *marron glacé* on the center of the *gâteau*, and allow the *pâte à glacé* to set.

8 Place the *gâteau* on an inverted 7-inch (18 cm) layer cake pan or other mold of similar size. Dip a kitchen towel in hot water, then wring it out. Briefly wrap the hot towel around the outside of the ring to just melt the *crème de marrons* and *pâte à glacé*

touching the inside of the ring. Wipe the ring dry and carefully slip it down off the *gâteau*. Transfer the *gâteau* to a serving plate.

Paris

This *gâteau* is one of the specialties at Patisserie Clichy. With a sheet of *chocolat plastique* draped in undulating folds on top, it looks like a striking piece of abstract sculpture.

For 8 people

INGREDIENTS

One 9½-inch (24 cm) round of *dijonnaise* (see page 74)

4 cups (500 g) *mousse à Paris* (see page 90)

About ⅓ pound (150 g) *chocolat plastique* (see page 113)

Confectioners sugar for dusting

1 Trim the *dijonnaise* round to a circle about ⅜ inch (1 cm) smaller in diameter than the inside of a flan ring 9½ inches (24 cm) in diameter and ¾ inch (2 cm) deep, using a bread knife. Shave the top of the *dijonnaise* to eliminate any large bumps.

2 Cut a cardboard cake-decorating circle to just fit inside the ring.

3 Place the *dijonnaise* round on the cake-decorating circle. With the tip of your palette knife, coat the inside of the ring with *mousse à paris*. Center the ring over the *dijonnaise* round, and press the ring down on the counter. Spoon the remaining *mousse à paris* over the *dijonnaise* and smooth it into a low conical mound with your palette knife.

4 Carefully slide the *gâteau* onto a wire rack or baking sheet. Allow the *mousse* to set, either in a cool place or in the refrigerator.

5 Place the *gâteau* on an inverted 9-inch (23 cm) layer-cake pan. Dip a kitchen towel in hot water, then wring it out. Briefly wrap the hot towel around the ring to just melt the *mousse* touching the inside of the ring. Wipe the ring dry and carefully slip it down off the *gâteau*.

6 On your countertop, work the *chocolat plastique* with the heel of your hand to soften it. Roll out the *chocolat plastique* with your rolling pin into a round sheet about 11 to 12 inches (27 to 30 cm) in diameter. Lightly dust the counter and the *chocolat plastique* with confectioners sugar as needed, and wipe the sheet gently with the palm of your hand to spread the powder and eliminate any blotches.

7 Carefully lift the sheet of *chocolat plastique* and drape it over the top of the *paris,* arranging it in natural, flowing folds. Press the sheet against the side of the *gâteau* with the side of your hand ①, and trim the sheet at the base of the *gâteau* with the tip of your paring knife.

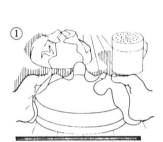

8 Lightly dust the top of the *paris* with confectioners sugar.

Note: Chilling in the refrigerator tends to make the *mousse à paris* heavier, so, if possible, keep it in a cool place before serving.

Alternative presentation: Instead of topping the *paris* with the sheet of *chocolate plastique,* you can, if you wish, decorate it with chocolate shavings. You need about 1 ounce (30 g) of *copeaux en chocolat* (see page 122), and you can also include some *cigarettes en chocolat.* Sprinkle them over the *mousse à paris* and then dust lightly with confectioners sugar.

Rectangular Gâteaux

Russe au Chocolat

For a small cake serving 6 to 8 people or a large cake serving 8 to 10

SMALL CAKE

One 12 × 16-inch (30 × 40 cm) sheet of *russe* (page 77)

1 cup (180 g) *crème au beurre* (page 85)

⅔ ounce (20 g) unsweetened chocolate

1 Trim the short ends from the sheet of *russe* and cut it in half crosswise to make two equal rectangles.

2 If the *russe* is too dry and cracks easily, then brush both rectangles of *russe* with a mixture of equal parts *sirop à trente* (page 398) and water to soften them.

3 Melt the chocolate and mix it with the *crème au beurre.* Fold in the *meringue italienne.*

1½ cups (90 g)
meringue italienne
(see page 101)

LARGE CAKE

One 13 × 20-inch
(33 × 50 cm) sheet
of *russe* (page 77)

1⅓ cups (240 g)
crème au beurre
(see page 85)

1 ounce (30 g)
unsweetened
chocolate

2 cups (120 g)
meringue italienne
(see page 101)

4 Spread about two thirds of this chocolate butter-cream over one rectangle of *russe*. Add the second rectangle and spread the remaining butter cream in a thin, even layer on top.

Decoration: Scatter ⅓ to ½ ounce (10 to 15 g) *copeaux en chocolat* (see page 122) and some *cigarettes en chocolat* (see page 122) over the top of the *gâteau*. Refrigerate until 30 minutes before serving. Then lightly dust the top of the *gâteau* with confectioners sugar. Cut a thin slice from each edge of the *gâteau* so the sides will be flat ①.

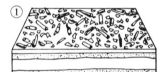

Russe Praliné

For a small cake serving 6 people or a large cake serving 8

SMALL CAKE

One 12 × 16-inch
(30 × 40 cm) sheet
of *russe* (page 77)

1¼ cups (225 g)
crème au beurre
(see page 85)

2½ tablespoons
(45 g) *praliné*
(page 414)

Confectioners sugar

1 Trim the short ends from the sheet of *russe* and cut it crosswise into three equal rectangles.

2 If the *russe* is too dry and cracks easily, then brush the rectangles of *russe* with a mixture of equal parts *sirop à trente* (see page 398) and water to soften them. The rectangle that will be the top of the finished *gâteau* should be brushed on the under side, but the other two rectangles should be brushed on top.

LARGE CAKE

One 13 × 20-inch
(33 × 50 cm) sheet
of *russé* (page 77)

1⅔ cups (300 g)
crème au beurre
(see page 85)

3 tablespoons plus 1
teaspoon (60 g)
praliné (page 414)

Confectioners sugar

3 Beat the *crème au beurre* into the *praliné* with a wooden spoon, adding the *crème au beurre* gradually to be sure there are no lumps of *praliné*.

4 Spread half of the *crème au beurre* over one rectangle of *russe*. Add a second rectangle and spread the remaining *crème au beurre* over it. Place the third layer of *russe* on top.

5 Refrigerate until 30 minutes before serving. Then lightly dust the top of the *gâteau* with confectioners sugar. Cut a thin slice from each edge of the *gâteau* so the sides will be flat.

Dauphinois

This is a coffee *russe* with chopped walnuts inside. It gets its name from the Dauphiné, the province in France which is famous for its walnuts.

For a small cake serving 6 people or a large cake serving 8

SMALL CAKE

One 12 × 16-inch
(30 × 40 cm) sheet
of *russe* (page 77)

2 teaspoons (1 cL)
sirop à trente (see
page 398)

4 teaspoons (2 cL)
very strong black
coffee (page 416)

1¼ cups (225 g)
crème au beurre
(see page 85)

3 tablespoons (25 g)
chopped walnuts

Confectioners sugar

1 Trim the short ends from the sheet of *russe* and cut it crosswise into three equal rectangles.

2 Mix the *sirop à trente* with half of the coffee and brush the tops of all three rectangles of *russe* with this syrup.

3 Flavor the *crème au beurre* with the remaining coffee.

4 Spread half of the *crème au beurre* over one rectangle of *russe*. Scatter half of the chopped walnuts over the *crème au beurre*. Add a second rectangle, spread the remaining *crème au beurre* over it, and scatter the remaining chopped walnuts over the *crème au beurre*. Invert the third rectangle of *russe* and place it on top.

5 Refrigerate the *gâteau* until 30 minutes before serving.

6 Cut some strips of paper about ½ inch (12 mm) wide and arrange them on top of the *gâteau* in a

LARGE CAKE

One 13 × 20-inch
(33 × 50 cm) sheet
of *russe* (page 77)

1 tablespoon (1½ cL)
sirop à trente (see
page 398)

2 tablespoons (3 cL)
very strong black
coffee (page 416)

1⅔ cups (300 g)
crème au beurre
(see page 85)

¼ cup (32 g)
chopped walnuts

Confectioners sugar

decorative geometric pattern—for example, diagonal stripes, lozenges, or a sunburst. Dust the top of the *gâteau* with confectioners sugar. Then carefully remove the paper strips.

7 Cut a thin slice from each edge of the *gâteau* so the sides will be flat ①.

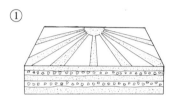

①

Russe Grand Marnier

For a small cake serving 6 people or a large cake serving 8

SMALL CAKE

5 ounces (150 g)
candied fruits

3 tablespoons (4½
cL) Grand Marnier

One 12 × 16-inch
(30 × 40 cm) sheet
of *russe* (see page
77)

2 teaspoons (1 cL)
sirop à trente (see
page 398)

1¼ cup (225 g)
crème au beurre
(see page 85)

2¼ teaspoon (1.2 cL)
Grand Marnier

Red food coloring

Confectioners sugar

1 Cut the candied fruits into ¼- to ⅜-inch (6 to 10 mm) dice and place them in a bowl. Pour the Grand Marnier over them, cover, and let steep for at least 2 hours and preferably overnight.

2 Trim the short ends from the sheet of *russe* and cut it crosswise into three equal rectangles.

3 Drain the candied fruits. Mix the *sirop à trente* with an equal quantity of the Grand Marnier in which the fruits were soaked. Brush the tops of all three rectangles of *russe* with this syrup.

4 Flavor the *crème au beurre* with the remaining Grand Marnier, and tint it a pale peach color with a couple of drops of red food coloring.

5 Spread half of the *crème au beurre* over one rectangle of *russe*. Scatter half of the candied fruits over the *crème au beurre*. Add a second rectangle, spread the remaining *crème au beurre* over it, and scatter the remaining candied fruits over the *crème*

285

LARGE CAKE

7 ounces (200 g)
  candied fruits
¼ cup (6 cL) Grand
  Marnier
One 13 × 20-inch
  (33 × 50 cm) sheet
  of *russe* (see page
  77)
1 tablespoon (1½ cL)
  sirop à trente (see
  page 398)
1⅔ cups (300 g)
  crème au beurre
  (see page 85)
1 tablespoon (1½ cL)
  Grand Marnier
Red food coloring
Confectioners sugar

au beurre. Invert the third rectangle of *russe* and place it on top.

6 Refrigerate the *gâteau* until 30 minutes before serving.

7 Cut some strips of paper about ½ inch (12 mm) wide and arrange them on top of the *gâteau* in a decorative geometric pattern—for example, diagonal stripes, lozenges, or a sunburst. Dust the top of the *gâteau* with confectioners sugar. Then carefully remove the paper strips.

8 Cut a thin slice from each edge of the *gâteau* so the sides will be flat.

Pavé Framboise

Russe can be filled with a fruit mousse rather than *crème au beurre* to get a lighter, fruit-flavored *gâteau*. We think the flavor and color of raspberries are especially good in this *gâteau*, and give the recipe with *mousse aux framboises*. The name *pavé* means paving stone and refers to the rectangular shape.

For a small cake serving 6 to 8 people or a large cake serving 8 to 10

SMALL CAKE

One 12 × 16-inch
  (30 × 40 cm) sheet
  of *russe* (page 77)
2 teaspoons (1 cL)
  sirop à trente (see
  page 398)
2 teaspoons (1 cL)
  *eau de vie de
  framboise*

1 Trim the short ends from the sheet of *russe* and cut it crosswise into three equal rectangles.

2 Mix the *sirop à trente* with the *eau de vie*.

3 Chill the mousse until it is almost about to set so it will have a good spreading consistency for the next step.

4 Brush one rectangle of *russe* with some *eau de vie*–flavored syrup and spread half of the *mousse* over it. Scatter about half of the optional fresh rasp-

3 cups (¾ L) *mousse aux framboises* (see page 97)

Optional: ¼ pint (120 g) fresh raspberries

1⅓ cups (170 g) *crème chantilly* (see page 82)

LARGE CAKE

One 13 × 20-inch (33 × 50 cm) sheet of *russe* (page 77)

1 tablespoon (1½ cL) *sirop à trente* (see page 398)

1 tablespoon (1½ cL) *eau de vie de framboise*

4 cups (1 L) *mousse aux framboises* (see page 97)

Optional: ⅓ pint (160 g) fresh raspberries

2 cups (250 g) *crème chantilly* (page 82)

berries over the mousse. Add a second rectangle of *russe*, brush it with syrup, and spread the remaining mousse over it. Set aside eight to twelve raspberries to use for decoration and scatter the remaining raspberries over the mousse. Invert the third layer of *russe* and place it on top. Brush the top with syrup.

5 Place the *gâteau* in the freezer so the mousse will be firm when you trim the edges. If you will not be cutting it the same day, cover the frozen *gâteau* airtight in plastic wrap.

6 Cut a thin slice from each edge of the *gâteau* so the sides will be flat. Then defrost in the refrigerator for several hours or overnight.

7 Spread half of the *crème chantilly* on top of the *gâteau* in a layer ¼ inch (6 mm) thick and smooth it with your palette knife so the top is perfectly flat. Transfer the remaining *crème chantilly* to a pastry bag fitted with a small fluted pastry tube (Ateco 1). Pipe a swath of *crème chantilly* 2 inches (5 cm) wide lengthwise down the center of the *pavé*, using a back-and-forth figure-eight motion. Pipe a row of teardrop-shaped *rosaces* down the center of the swath, then pipe a row of teardrop-shaped *rosaces* down each long edge of the *pavé*. Arrange the reserved fresh raspberries between the *rosaces* down the center.

Ray Ventura

Ray Ventura was a French bandleader who was very popular right after World War II. This *gâteau* is also called *fraiser,* for the strawberries *(fraises)* that give it its distinctive appearance.

For a small cake serving 8 to 10 people or a large cake serving 12 to 15

SMALL CAKE

One 12 × 16-inch
(30 × 40 cm) sheet
of *génoise* (page 59)

2 tablespoons (3 cL)
sirop à trente (see
page 398)

¼ cup (6 cL) kirsch

3⅓ cups (600 g)
crème au beurre
(see page 85)

1⅓ pints (600 g)
small to medium
fresh strawberries

1 cup (340 g) fondant
(see page 105)

LARGE CAKE

One 13 × 20 inch
(33 × 50 cm) sheet
of *génoise* (page 59)

3 tablespoons (4½
cL) *sirop à trente*
(see page 398)

¼ cup plus 2
tablespoons (9 cL)
kirsch

5 cups (900 g) *crème
au beurre* (page 85)

2 pints (900 g) small
to medium fresh
strawberries

1⅓ cups (450 g)
fondant (page 105)

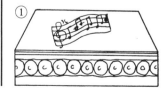

1 Trim the short ends from the sheet of *génoise* and cut it in half crosswise to make two equal rectangles.

2 Mix the *sirop à trente* with half of the kirsch and brush both rectangles of *génoise* with this syrup.

3 Flavor the *crème au beurre* with the remaining kirsch.

4 Hull the strawberries. If they are small, leave them whole. Otherwise cut them in half.

5 Spread a thin layer of *crème au beurre* over one rectangle of *génoise.* Arrange the strawberries over the *crème au beurre,* with a row of strawberries in a straight line down each edge of the cake. Spread *crème au beurre* over the strawberries to fill the gaps between them and just cover them. Place the second layer of *génoise* on top, spread a thin layer of *crème au beurre* over it, and smooth the *crème au beurre* with your palette knife to give the *gâteau* a flat top surface.

6 Place the *gâteau* on a wire rack and refrigerate at least 1 hour to make the *crème au beurre* firm.

7 Warm the fondant over low heat, stirring until melted. Tint it a very pale green with a drop of green food coloring, and stir in just enough *sirop à trente* to thin the fondant to the consistency of heavy cream. Pour the fondant over the top of the *gâteau* and sweep it smooth with the edge of your palette knife, letting the excess flow off the edges of the *gâteau.* Let the fondant set.

8 Gently warm the *pâte à écrire* until melted, and transfer it to a parchment cornet (see page 118). Cut the tip of the cornet and decorate the top of the *gâteau* by piping a couple of bars of a musical score.

9 Refrigerate the *gâteau* until 30 minutes before serving. Then trim the edges of the *gâteau.* Cut through the center of the row of strawberries on each edge, so that the sides of the *gâteau* are flat, with the

DECORATION

Green food coloring

Sirop à trente for thinning fondant

About 1 tablespoon (15 g) *pâte à écrire* (see page 120)

cut strawberries showing down the center ①. Before making each cut, warm the blade of your bread knife in hot water so it will cut through the fondant without cracking.

Clichy

The signature cake of Pâtisserie Clichy is composed of four layers of *joconde* separated by coffee *crème au beurre* and *ganache*. The top is glazed with *pâte à glacé*.

For a small cake serving 6 to 8 people or a large cake serving 8 to 10

SMALL CAKE

One 12 × 16-inch (30 × 40 cm) sheet of *joconde* (page 70)

1 tablespoon (1½ cL) *sirop à trente* (see page 398)

1 tablespoon plus 2 teaspoons (2½ cL) very strong black coffee (see page 416)

1 cup (180 g) *crème au beurre* (see page 85)

⅓ cup (85 g) *ganache clichy* (see page 89)

Either 4 ounces (115 g) *pâte à glacé* (see page 110); *or* 3 ounces (85 g) semisweet chocolate, 2

1 Trim the edges from the sheet of *joconde* and cut it in half crosswise and lengthwise to make four equal rectangles.

2 Mix the *sirop à trente* with an equal amount of the coffee and brush the tops of all four rectangles of *joconde* with this syrup. Flavor the *crème au beurre* with the remaining coffee.

3 Spread one third of the *crème au beurre* over one rectangle of *joconde*. Add a second rectangle of *joconde* and spread the *ganache* over it. Add a third rectangle of *joconde* and spread it with half of the remaining *crème au beurre*. Place the fourth layer of *joconde* on top and spread the remaining *crème au beurre* over it. Carefully smooth the top of the *gâteau* with your palette knife so it is perfectly flat.

4 Place the *gâteau* on a wire rack and refrigerate for at least 1 hour to make the *crème au beurre* firm.

5 If you have *pâte à glacé* on hand, temper it to get the right consistency for coating the *gâteau*. Otherwise, prepare a *pâte à glacé* as follows: Melt the chocolate and stir in the butter. When smooth, stir in

tablespoons (30 g)
barely melted
butter, and 1½
teaspoons (¾ cL)
water

LARGE CAKE

One 13 × 20-inch
(33 × 50 cm) sheet
of *joconde* (see page
70)

1½ tablespoons (2.3
cL) *sirop à trente*
(see page 398)

2½ tablespoons (3.8
cL) very strong
black coffee (see
page 416)

1½ cups (270 g)
crème au beurre
(see page 85)

½ cup (125 g)
ganache clichy (see
page 89)

Either 6 ounces (170
g) *pâte à glacé* (see
page 110); *or* 4½
ounces (130 g)
semisweet
chocolate, 3
tablespoons (40 g)
barely melted
butter, and 2
teaspoons (1 cL)
water

the water. Dip the bottom of the pot of chocolate in cold water and stir until it begins to thicken. Return this *pâte à glacé* to the heat and gently warm it a second time, stirring until just melted.

6 Pour the tempered *pâte à glacé* over the top of the *gâteau* and sweep it smooth with the edge of your palette knife, letting the excess flow over the edge of the *gâteau*. Let the *pâte à glacé* set.

7 Prepare a parchment cornet (see page 118 for details).

8 Collect the excess *pâte à glacé* and temper it again. Transfer some of it to the parchment cornet and write ''Clichy'' on the diagonal across the top of the *gâteau*.

9 Refrigerate the *clichy* until 30 minutes before serving. Then cut a thin slice from each edge of the *gâteau* so the sides will be flat. Before making each cut, warm the blade of a bread knife in hot water so it will cut through the *pâte à glacé* without cracking.

Bûche de Noël (Yule Log)

This is the traditional French Christmas *gâteau*. It can be made by baking *génoise* in a special trough-shaped *bûche de Noël* mold, cutting it horizontally and filling it just like a round *gâteau;* or by spreading the filling on a sheet of *génoise* and rolling it into a long cylinder. Either way, the outside of the *gâteau* is piped with strips of *crème au beurre* to simulate bark on a log and decorated with meringue mushrooms and *pâte d'amandes* holly leaves and berries.

We prefer the molded *bûche* because it requires less *crème au beurre* and is therefore less rich. The *bûche de Noël* mold we use is 20×3×2 inches (50×7×5 cm). Butter the mold and fill it with *génoise* batter to three quarters of its height. It requires the same amount of batter and about the same baking time as a 9-inch (23 cm) layer-cake pan.

The rolled *bûche* has the advantage that it requires no special mold. We give the recipe using a 13×20-inch (33×50 cm) sheet of *génoise*. For a 12×16-inch (30×40 cm) sheet, reduce the amounts of all ingredients in our recipe by about one third.

You can assemble the *bûche* on a long serving platter. Or, if you prefer, you can cut a heavy piece of cardboard a little larger than the base of the *bûche* and cover it with aluminum foil to make a base to support the *gâteau*.

Bûche de Noël

For 10 to 15 people

MOLDED BÛCHE

2⅓ cups (420 g) *crème au beurre* (see page 85)

Either 3 tablespoons (4½ cL) very strong black coffee (see page 416); *or* 1¼ ounces (35 g) unsweetened chocolate and 1 tablespoon (1½ cL) each dark rum and water

1 Set aside ½ cup (90 g) of the *crème au beurre*.

For a coffee-flavored *bûche:* Flavor the remaining *crème au beurre* with 1 tablespoon (1½ cL) of coffee for a molded *bûche* or 5 teaspoons (2½ cL) of coffee for a rolled *bûche*.

For a chocolate-flavored *bûche:* Melt the chocolate and stir it into the remaining *crème au beurre*.

2 Mix the *sirop à trente* with either the remaining coffee or the dark rum and water.

2 tablespoons (3 cL) *sirop à trente* (see page 398)

One 3×20-inch (7 by 50 cm) log of *génoise* (see page 59), baked in a *bûche de Noël* mold

ROLLED BÛCHE

3⅓ cups (600 g) *crème au beurre* (see page 85)

Either 5⅔ tablespoons (8½ cL) very strong black coffee (see page 416); *or* 2 ounces (55 g) unsweetened chocolate and 2 tablespoons (3 cL) each dark rum and water

¼ cup (6 cL) *sirop à trente* (see page 398)

One 13×20-inch (33×50 cm) sheet of *génoise* (see page 59)

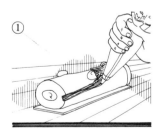

3 For a molded *bûche:* Slice the *génoise* in half horizontally. Place the bottom layer on a long serving platter, and brush the cut faces of both layers with syrup. Spread ½ cup (90 g) of *crème au beurre* over the bottom layer. Add the second layer, cut side down, and lightly brush the top with syrup. Transfer the *gâteau* to a serving platter.

For a rolled *bûche:* Place the sheet of *génoise* on your counter, with the paper on which it was baked underneath. Neatly trim the edges of the *génoise*. Brush it with syrup. Spread about 1 cup (180 g) of the *crème au beurre* over the *génoise* with your palette knife. Then use the end of the paper under the *génoise* to lift the long edge of the *génoise* and begin rolling it up. Once the roll is started, let go of the paper and continue rolling the *génoise* into a log approximately 19 inches (48 cm) long. Lightly brush the outside of the log with syrup, and carefully roll it onto a long serving platter.

4 Transfer the unflavored *crème au beurre* to a pastry bag fitted with a ⁷⁄₁₆-inch (12 mm) plain pastry tube (Ateco 5). Pipe a circle of *crème au beurre* ½ inch (12 mm) thick on each end of the log. Pipe four or five mounds of *crème au beurre* 1 inch (2½ cm) in diameter on the upper half of the log. Each mound will become a "knot."

5 Transfer the coffee or chocolate *crème au beurre* to a pastry bag fitted with a small fluted pastry tube (Ateco 0). Pipe some of this *crème au beurre* in the center of the circle of plain *crème au beurre* on each end of the log. Then, starting at the bottom of one side of the log, pipe continuous strips of *crème au beurre* back and forth over the length of the log ①. After the first two or three strips, pipe some strips only part of the length before reversing direction so you make an irregular pattern like the bark on a tree. Stop when you reach the top of the log, rotate the *gâteau*, and pipe the *crème au beurre* over the other side in the same fashion. Cover the entire surface of the log, including the knots, with the flavored *crème au beurre*.

②

DECORATION

1 to 2 tablespoons
(10 to 20 g)
chopped pistachios,
or chopped almonds
tinted pale green
with food coloring

8 to 10 *champignons
en meringue* (see
page 298)

2 ounces (50 g) *pâte
d'amandes* (see
page 111)

Red, green, and
yellow food
coloring

6 Refrigerate for at least 30 minutes to make the *crème au beurre* firm.

7 Dip the blade of a paring knife in boiling water ②. Then cut off each end of the *gâteau* with the hot blade, slicing through the *crème au beurre* to get a bull's-eye pattern. Dipping the blade in boiling water before each cut, slice off the tops of the knots, giving them a slightly concave surface and exposing the plain *crème au beurre* in the center.

8 Sprinkle some chopped pistachios in a few spots on the log to simulate moss. Arrange the *champignons en meringue* on the log.

9 On your countertop, work the *pâte d'amandes* with the heel of your hand to make it smooth. Tint about one tenth of the *pâte d'amandes* a rich red with food coloring, and form it into six to eight ''holly berries.'' Add a drop each of green and yellow food colorings to the remaining *pâte d'amandes* to tint it a pale green. Roll about one quarter of the *pâte d'amandes* under your palm into a thin string, and cut it into two or three twigs. Roll out the rest of the green *pâte d'amandes* into a sheet ³⁄₃₂ inch (2 mm) thick with your rolling pin. Cut from it four to six holly leaves and score the top of each leaf with the tip of your paring knife to simulate the veins of the leaf.

10 Place the *pâte d'amandes* twigs on the log. Bend each holly leaf in a gentle arch and arrange the leaves around the twigs. Place a bunch of three or four holly berries next to each twig.

293

Chapter Ten

MERINGUES

Meringues are light, crisp, and sweet. With the exception of *vacherins,* they are either individual serving-size desserts or decorations.

STORAGE

Meringues filled with *crème au beurre* can be kept, uncovered, in the refrigerator (or better yet, a cool dry place) for 1 or 2 days, but those filled with *crème chantilly* should be eaten with 2 to 4 hours after filling.

The only meringues that can—and must—be frozen are those filled with ice cream. Covered airtight, these can be kept for up to 1 month before decorating with *crème chantilly.* However, filling a *vacherin* is so easy that we recommend filling and decorating shortly before serving so that the *chantilly* will be tender, the ice cream soft and creamy, and the meringue crisp.

Truffes Praliné and Truffes Chocolat

These meringue truffles are made by sandwiching two domes of *meringue ordinaire* together with chocolate- or *praliné*-flavored *crème au beurre* and coating the outside with *crème au beurre* and either chocolate shavings or roasted sliced almonds.

For 10 truffles

INGREDIENTS

Twenty 2½-inch (6 cm) domes of

1 For *truffes chocolat,* melt the chocolate and stir it into the *crème au beurre.* For *truffes praliné,* gradually stir the *crème au beurre* into the *praliné* to be sure there are no lumps; then separate 1 cup (180 g)

meringue ordinaire
(see page 72)

2½ cups (450 g)
crème au beurre
(see page 85)

Confectioners sugar

TRUFFES PRALINÉ

⅓ cup (95 g) *praliné*
(see page 414)

¼ cup (25 g) crushed
nougatine
(see page 115)

2½ cups (300 g)
roasted sliced
almonds

TRUFFES CHOCOLAT

2 ounces (55 g)
unsweetened
chocolate

9 ounces (250 g)
copeaux en chocolat
(page 122)

of the *praliné*-flavored butter cream and mix in the crushed *nougatine*.

2 Spread about 5 teaspoons (20 g) of the chocolate or *praliné*-and-*nougatine crème au beurre* on the center of the flat side of one of the meringue domes, and press a second dome against it back to back, cementing the two together with the *crème au beurre* to make a rough sphere ①. Repeat with the remaining domes of meringue.

3 Warm the remaining *crème au beurre* over direct heat, stirring constantly with a wooden spoon, until it is soft enough to spread easily with a pastry brush.

4 Place the sliced almonds or *copeaux en chocolat* in a bowl. Thoroughly brush the outside of a meringue sphere with *crème au beurre* ②, place it in the bowl of almonds or chocolate shavings, and shake the bowl back and forth to roll the sphere around and coat it with almonds or shavings on all sides. Repeat wih the remaining spheres of meringue.

5 Lightly dust the top of each *truffe* with confectioners sugar ③.

Meringues Chantilly

For 10 meringues

INGREDIENTS

4 cups (500 g) *crème chantilly* flavored with vanilla (see page 82)

Twenty 3½-inch (9 cm) fingers of *meringue ordinaire* (see page 72)

10 crystallized violets or 5 candied cherries

1 Transfer the *crème chantilly* to a pastry bag fitted with a medium fluted pastry tube (Ateco 4). Pipe a thick strip of *crème chantilly* down the center of the flat side of one of the meringue fingers ①. Press a second finger against it back to back, cementing the two together with the *crème chantilly*.

2 Place this pair of meringue fingers on its side and cover the crack between the two fingers by piping *crème chantilly* down the center, using a repeated back-and-forth figure-eight motion as you move from one end to the other. Pipe a rosette of *crème chantilly* on the center, and top it with a crystallized violet or half of a candied cherry. Repeat with the remaining meringue fingers.

Meringues Café and Meringues Chocolat

Meringue italienne can be flavored with coffee or chocolate and baked just like *meringue ordinaire* in finger shapes to make crisp individual desserts that are left unfilled. Or the same batter can be baked on a damp sheet of plywood to produce a soft interior, and the fingers sandwiched together in pairs.

For about 16 crisp meringue fingers or 8 soft-centered pairs of fingers

INGREDIENTS

Melted butter for brushing baking sheet

1 *For crisp meringues:* Brush a large, heavy baking sheet with melted butter and dust it with flour. *For soft meringues:* Get a sheet of plywood ⅜ inch (1 cm) thick, about the size of a large baking sheet, and soak the plywood in cold water until thoroughly

Flour for dusting
  baking sheet
  4½ cups (270 g)
  meringue italienne
  (see page 101)
½ cup (70 g)
  confectioners sugar

MERINGUES
CHOCOLAT

⅔ ounces (20 g)
  unsweetened
  chocolate

MERINGUES
CAFÉ

4 teaspoons (2 cL)
  very strong black
  coffee (see page
  416)

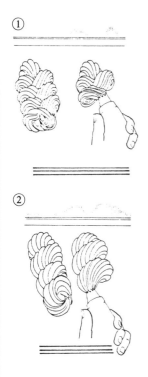

moistened. Cover the top side of the damp plywood with a sheet of newsprint and place the plywood on a baking sheet.

2 Preheat the oven to 275° F (135° C) for crisp meringues or 300° F (150° C) for soft meringues.

3 Prepare the *meringue italienne*.

4 For meringues café: Mix half of the confectioners sugar with the coffee.

For meringues chocolat: Melt the chocolate.

5 Sift the remaining confectioners sugar over the *meringue italienne* and gently fold it into the meringue. When almost completely incorporated, add the coffee or chocolate and continue folding until smooth and thoroughly mixed.

6 Transfer the batter to a pastry bag fitted with a medium-size fluted pastry tube (Ateco 4). Hold the tip of the pastry tube about ¼ inch (6 mm) above the baking sheet or plywood. Press on the pastry bag, and when the batter starts to spread around the tip of the pastry tube, draw the pastry tube toward you in a repeated side-to-side figure 8 (for crisp meringues) ① or spiral (for soft meringues) ② motion to pipe a finger of meringue 1½ inches (4 cm) wide and 3½ inches (9 cm) long. Terminate the finger by releasing the pressure on the bag and cutting the meringue with a quick flick of the tip of the pastry tube through the final loop of the figure 8 or spiral. Pipe about 16 fingers in staggered rows, separating them by about 1 inch (2½ cm).

7 For crisp meringues: Bake until set, dry, and firm to the touch, 40 to 60 minutes.

For soft meringues: Bake until dry and crusty outside but still soft inside, 20 to 30 minutes.

8 Remove from the oven and place the baking sheet or plywood on a cooling rack.

For crisp meringues: Let cool to room temperature on the baking sheet.

For soft meringues: When the meringues have cooled to luke warm and you can lift them without breaking, remove the fingers from the plywood and place them back to back in pairs. The bottoms and insides will be soft and sticky, and they will stick together. Place the finished meringues on a wire rack and let cool to room temperature.

Storage Note: The soft-centered meringues can be kept uncovered at room temperature for up to 2 days.

Champignons en Meringue (Meringue Mushrooms)

Meringue mushrooms are used for decorating *bûches de Noël* (see page 291). You probably won't need more than a dozen or so mushrooms for the entire Christmas season, and this requires only a fraction of a recipe of *meringue ordinaire*. So make the mushrooms at the same time as you are preparing another meringue dessert.

There are two methods for piping the mushrooms. The easiest is to pipe the stems and caps separately and stick them together after baking. When you become more expert you can try piping a more stylized mushroom in one piece.

For about 12 mushrooms

INGREDIENTS

Melted butter for brushing baking sheet

Flour for dusting baking sheet

1 cup (105 g) *meringue ordinaire* (see page 72)

Cocoa powder, sweetened with a little confectioners sugar, for dusting

1 Brush a baking sheet with melted butter and dust it with flour.

2 Preheat the oven to 275° F (135° C).

3 Prepare the *meringue ordinaire* and transfer it to a pastry bag fitted with a ³⁄₈-inch (1 cm) plain pastry tube (Ateco 4 or 5).

4 *Method 1:* First pipe the stems ①. Hold the pastry bag vertical, with the tip of the pastry tube just above the baking sheet. Gently press on the pastry bag, and when the meringue batter spreads around the tip of the tube to a width of about ³⁄₄ inch (2 cm), decrease the pressure on the bag, and gradually lift the pastry tube straight up to make a cone-shaped stem about ³⁄₄ inch (2 cm) high. Release the pressure on the pastry bag and lift the pastry tube straight up to make a pointed vertical tail on top of the cone. Pipe more stems than you will need to be sure you

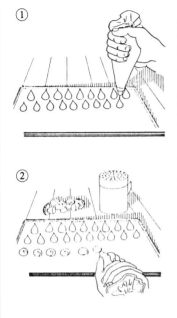

get enough nice-looking ones. For the caps, pipe at least a dozen dome-shaped mounds 1¼ inches (3 cm) in diameter and ¾ inch (2 cm) high on the baking sheet ②.

Method 2: Be sure your batter is very stiff or it won't hold the shape. Hold the pastry bag nearly vertical, with the tip of the pastry tube just above the baking sheet. Gently press on the pastry bag. When the batter spreads around the pastry tube to a width of about ¾ inch (2 cm), decrease the pressure on the pastry bag and slowly lift the pastry tube straight up to make a cone shaped stem about ¾ inch (2 cm) high. Gently increase the pressure on the pastry bag to enlarge the top of the stem and make an hourglass shape. Then drop the tip of the pastry tube slightly, tilt the pastry bag, and press firmly on the bag to inflate the upper part of the hourglass into a cap 1¼ inches (3 cm) wide. The cap will be tilted, with the far side extending barely beyond the stem and the near side resting on the baking sheet. To finish the cap, release the pressure on the pastry bag and cut the batter with a quick, semicircular flick of the tip of the pastry tube.

5 Dust the tops of the mushroom caps very lightly with sweetened cocoa powder.

6 Bake until the mushrooms are set, dry, and firm to touch, about 30 to 40 minutes.

7 Place the baking sheet on a cooling rack and let the mushrooms cool on the baking sheet.

8 If the stems and caps were piped separately, then, when you are ready to use the mushrooms, scrape out a small indentation in the center of the underside of each cap using the tip of a paring knife. Fill the indentation with a little filling or topping (such as *crème au beurre* or *meringue italienne*) from the dessert you are decorating, and insert the tip of the stem into the indentation to cement the stem and cap together.

Vacherins

Vacherins are shells of meringue that are usually filled with ice cream or with *crème chantilly* and fresh fruits. Since *vacherins* require no mold, you can make them in any size you like. We give recipes for a shell 9½ inches (24 cm) in diameter.

Vacherin Glacé, Vacherin Chantilly, and Vacherin Chantilly Glacé

For 10 to 12 people

INGREDIENTS

Melted butter for brushing baking sheet

Flour for dusting baking sheet

4 cups (425 g) *meringue ordinaire* (see page 72)

Either 3 cups (180 g) *meringue italienne* (see page 101); *or* 3 cups (330 g) *meringue ordinaire* (see page 72)

Whole nuts, a few fresh berries, *cigarettes en chocolat* (see page 122), or other garnish, depending on the ice creams or fruits used

1 Brush a large baking sheet with melted butter and dust it with flour. Mark two 9½-inch (24 cm) circles in the flour by tapping the baking sheet with a flan ring, *vol-au-vent* disc, or round mold.

2 Preheat the oven to 275° F (135° C).

3 Prepare the first batch of *meringue ordinaire* and transfer half of it to a pastry bag fitted with a ½-inch (12 mm) plain pastry tube (Ateco 6). Starting at the center of one of the circles marked on the baking sheet, pipe a continuous spiral of meringue that fills the circle.

4 Transfer the remaining *meringue ordinaire* to another pastry bag fitted with a ⅝-inch (16 mm) plain pastry tube (Ateco 8). Pipe a ring of meringue ¾ inch (2 cm) wide on the perimeter of the disc you have already piped. Pipe a ring of meringue ¾ inch (2 cm) wide just inside the second circle marked on the baking sheet ①.

5 Bake until the meringue is set, dry, and firm to the touch, about 40 to 60 minutes.

6 Remove the baking sheet from the oven and place it on a cooling rack. Allow the meringue to cool on the baking sheet.

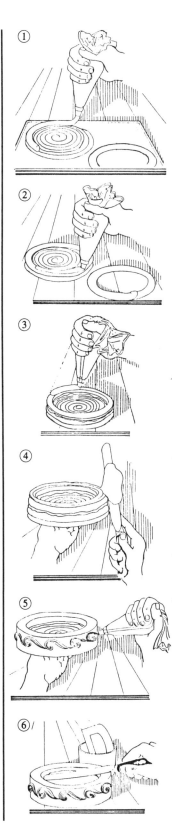

① ② ③ ④ ⑤ ⑥

7 When you are ready to assemble the *vacherin* shell, preheat the oven to 200° F (90° C).

8 Cut a cardboard cake-decorating circle about ¼ inch (6 mm) larger in diameter than the meringue base. Place the base on the cake-decorating circle.

9 Prepare the *meringue italienne* or a second batch of *meringue ordinaire*. Transfer about half of the fresh meringue to a pastry bag fitted with a ½-inch (12 mm) plain pastry tube (Ateco 6). Pipe a strip of meringue on the rim on the meringue base ②. Place the ring of baked meringue on top and pipe a strip of meringue over the top of the ring ③. Using your palette knife, spread the sides of the *vacherin* with meringue ④. Sweep your palette knife over the top of the rim to give the *vacherin* a flat top surface. Then lift the *vacherin* from the countertop, support it on the fingertips of one hand, and sweep the sides with your palette knife to give it a smooth surface.

10 Transfer the remaining fresh meringue to a pastry bag fitted with a medium-small fluted pastry tube (Ateco 3). Pipe a simple scroll pattern around the sides of the *vacherin* ⑤.

11 Place the *vacherin* shell on a baking sheet and bake until the outside of the shell is dry and firm to the touch but still white, about 1 hour or longer if necessary. If it begins to color before it is dry, reduce the temperature to 175° F (80° C).

12 Let cool to room temperature on the baking sheet.

13 For *vacherin glacé:* Soften the ice cream and fill the *vacherin* shell to the rim with it, in two layers if you are using two flavors.

For *vacherin chantilly:* Set aside 2 cups (250 g) of the *crème chantilly* for decorating the *vacherin*. Fill the *vacherin* with alternating layers of fresh berries and the remaining *crème chantilly,* starting and finishing with layers of *crème chantilly* ⑥.

For *vacherin chantilly glacé:* Soften the ice cream and fill the *vacherin* shell about halfway with it. Add the berries and top with *crème chantilly* to fill the *vacherin* to the rim.

VACHERIN GLACÉ

2 quarts (2 L) ice cream, preferably two flavors such as chocolate and coffee, chocolate and butter pecan, or coffee and *praliné*, but not vanilla

2 cups (250 g) *crème chantilly* (page 82)

VACHERIN CHANTILLY

6 cups (750 g) *crème chantilly* (page 82)

1 quart (900 g) fresh strawberries, raspberries, or blueberries

VACHERIN CHANTILLY GLACÉ

1 quart (1 L) vanilla or kirsch ice cream

4 cups (500 g) *crème chantilly* (page 82)

1 pint (450 g) fresh strawberries, raspberries, or blueberries

14 Transfer the reserved *crème chantilly* to a pastry bag fitted with a medium-small fluted pastry tube (Ateco 3). Cover the top of the filling in the *vacherin* with concentric circles of rosettes of *crème chantilly*, starting from the outside and working in to the center. Pipe a large rosette of *crème chantilly* on the center of the *vacherin*. Then pipe a circle of teardrop-shaped *rosaces* of *crème chantilly* on top of the rim of the *vacherin* shell ⑦. (See page 117 for more details on the methods of piping *rosaces*.)

15 Decorate the top of the *vacherin* according to the filling. For example, if you used chocolate and butter pecan ice creams, you might place a single pecan half on the rosette on the center of the *vacherin* and arrange about six chocolate cigarettes (each about 1½ to 2 inches, or 4 to 5 cm, long) radiating out from the center. Or, if you included fresh berries in the filling, you could place one berry on the rosette on the center and eight to twelve berries on rosettes around the perimeter. Or place a single crystallized violet on the center. Keep the garnish to a minimum—just enough to prevent the pure white exterior of the *vacherin* from becoming monotonous.

Chapter Eleven

CHOUX (CREAM PUFFS, ÉCLAIRS, AND RELATED PASTRIES)

*L*es *choux* are the pastries made from *pâte à choux*. In addition to referring to this entire class of desserts, *choux* is also used more specifically for spherically shaped *pâte à choux* pastries, including the ones we call "cream puffs" in English.

The name *choux* derives from the French word for "cabbage." With a little imagination, you can see how the spherical shape and ridged surface of the baked balls of *pâte à choux* inspired the appellation.

TOURS DE MAIN

Once the *pâte à choux* has been piped and baked, all that remains is to fill and glaze the pastries.

Filling *(Fourrage)*

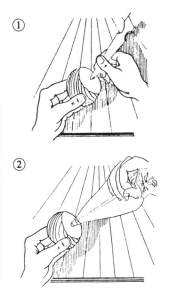

Choux à la crème, salambos, glands, small *choux* for *croquembouche,* and *négus* are filled by a method unique to these pastries. Punch a hole (or several holes for *négus*) in the bottom of each pastry using the tip of a small plain pastry tube, a sharpening steel, or the handle of a slender wooden spoon ①.

Fit a plain pastry tube in a pastry bag, and transfer the filling to the pastry bag. Insert the tip of the pastry tube in the hole in the bottom of the pastry ②. Press gently on the pastry bag until you feel resistance from the pressure building up inside the pastry. The pastry must be completely filled, but, if you pipe in too much filling, the baked *pâte à choux* will burst.

The techniques for filling other *pâte à choux* pastries are not special to *les choux* and are explained in the recipes.

Glazing *(Glaçage)*

Many of these pastries are glazed with fondant or *caramel blond*. In either case, the amount of glaze used is rather small, and the glazing procedure requires dipping the pastry in a much larger quantity of fondant or *caramel blond*. For this reason we do not give quantities for fondant or *caramel blond* in most of our recipes for *choux*.

FONDANT: Choose a saucepan just large enough for you to easily dip the pastry in it. The fondant should be at least ¾ inch (2 cm) deep. Depending on the size of the saucepan, you will need at least ½ to 1 cup (170 to 340 g) of fondant.

Warm the fondant in the saucepan over very low heat, stirring with a wooden spoon until melted. The fondant must have a smooth fluid consistency, similar to a thick *crème anglaise,* for coating the pastries; and it must be warm (about 100° to 105° F or 38° to 40° C) but not hot in order to dry to a shiny surface without dripping. If the fondant is too thick, gradually stir in some *sirop à trente* to thin it and make it more fluid. On the other hand, if the fondant is too thin, stir in some confectioners sugar to thicken it.

When the fondant is fluid, remove it from the heat. You will have to stir it occasionally and possibly warm it again later to keep it at the proper consistency and temperature.

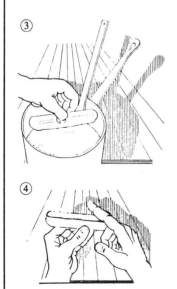

Choux à la creme, éclairs, glands, and *choux* for *religieuses* are glazed with *fondant*. Hold the pastry with the fingertips of one hand and turn it upside down. Dip it in the fondant to coat the top quarter or third of the pastry ③. Lift the pastry up until it is almost out of the fondant; then lower it slightly and raise it again, this time a little higher; finally lower and raise it a third time and lift it clear of the fondant. This technique, called *égoutter à la masse,* makes the mass of fondant in the saucepan pull the excess fondant from the top of the pastry.

Turn the pastry right side up and sweep the side of the index finger of your free hand over the surface of the fondant to smooth it ④. For éclairs and *glands,* sweep the tip of your index finger around the edge of the fondant to make a clean line where the fondant begins. Place the pastry on a rack or plate and let the fondant set while you glaze the remaining pastries.

CARAMEL BLOND: If the *caramel blond* was made in advance, warm it over very low heat, stirring occasionally with a wooden spoon after it begins to melt. Be careful not to let it get too hot, because you don't want it to color any more. Remove the *caramel* from the heat as soon as it is liquid, but warm it again later as needed to keep it fluid.

Salambos and small *choux* for *St.-Honoré* and *croquembouche* are glazed with *caramel blond*. The depth of *caramel* in the pot must be sufficient for dipping the pastries. For *salambos*, you need a depth of at least ¾ inch (2 cm), and the pot must be wide enough to dip the pastries in easily. For small *choux*, place a small mold under one side of the pot to tilt it while glazing so you won't need quite as much *caramel*.

Salambos and small *choux* for *croquembouche* are filled before glazing, and you should hold them with your fingertips just as for glazing with fondant ⑤. For *St.-Honoré,* the *choux* are not filled, and you can insert the tip of a paring knife in the side of each *chou* to hold it while glazing ⑥.

Dip the top of each *salambo* or *chou* in the *caramel* to coat the top quarter of it. Lift it from the *caramel* and sweep off the excess *caramel blond* on the rim of the saucepan or the rim of the pastry you are making ⑦. Then proceed according to the instructions in the recipe you are making.

Always be very careful not to touch the *caramel* until it has cooled to avoid burning your fingers.

STORAGE

Choux filled with *crème pâtissière* can be kept uncovered in a cool place (preferably) or in the refrigerator for up to 12 hours before serving. Those filled with *crème chantilly* should be eaten within 2 to 4 hours and kept in the refrigerator before serving. *Choux praline, négus* and *pont neuf* can be kept refrigerated for up to one day.

Individual Pastries

Choux Chantilly, Choux à la Crème, and Choux Praliné

Depending on how you fill the basic *choux,* you can get three very different looking and tasting desserts.

For 8 individual pastries

INGREDIENTS

8 baked 2¼-inch (6 cm) domes of *pâte à choux spéciale* or *ordinaire* (page 78)

CHOUX PRALINÉ

¾ cup (200 g) *crème pâtissière* (page 83)

1 cup (200 g) *crème au beurre* (page 85)

3 tablespoons (55 g) *praliné* (page 414)

½ teaspoon (4 g) confectioners sugar

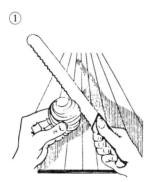

1 For *choux chantilly* and *choux praliné:* Slice off the top of each *chou* at two thirds of its height with a bread knife to form a lid ①. For *choux à la crème:* Punch a hole in the bottom of each *chou* with the tip of a ⅜-inch (1 cm) plain pastry tube (Ateco 4).

2 For *choux chantilly:* Proceed to step 3.

For *choux praliné:* Make a *crème au beurre au lait* by stirring the *crème pâtissière* into the *crème au beurre* with a wooden spoon. Then beat this *crème au beurre au lait* into the *praliné* with the wooden spoon, adding it gradually to be sure there are no lumps of *praliné.*

For *choux à la crème:* Our recipe for *crème pâtissière* includes vanilla, so, for vanilla *choux à la crème,* proceed to step 3. For other flavors, stir the melted chocolate, coffee, or liqueur into the *crème pâtissière.*

3 For *choux chantilly* or *choux praliné:* Transfer the *crème chantilly* or *crème au beurre au lait* to a pastry bag fitted with a medium fluted pastry tube (Ateco 6). Pipe the filling into each *chou,* first filling the hollow in the base and then moving the pastry tube in an upward spiral motion to get a mound about 1½ inches (4 cm) high ②.

For *choux à la crème:* Transfer the *crème pâtissière* to a pastry bag fitted with a ⅜-inch (1 cm) plain pastry tube (Ateco 4). One at a time, insert the tip of the tube in the bottom of each *chou* and pipe in the *crème pâtissière* until the *chou* is filled.

CHOUX CHANTILLY

2 cups (250 g) *crème chantilly* (page 82)

½ teaspoon (2 g) confectioners sugar

CHOUX À LA CRÈME

About 2 cups (540 g) *crème pâtissière* (see page 83)

Optional: 1 ounce (30 g) melted unsweetened chocolate; or 2 tablespoons (3 cL) very strong black coffee (page 416); or kirsch or Grand Marnier

Fondant for glazing, either plain or flavored with chocolate, coffee, kirsch, or Grand Marnier (see pages 105–108)

Sirop à trente (see page 398) for thinning fondant

4 For *choux chantilly* and *choux praliné:* Trim the lid of each *chou* with a fluted pastry cutter 1¾ inches (4½ cm) in diameter. (If you don't have a fluted pastry cutter, use a plain one or trim the lid with the tip of a paring knife.) Dust the top of each lid with confectioners sugar. Then top the mound of filling in each *chou* with a lid.

For *choux à la crème:* Warm the fondant over low heat, stirring until melted. If the fondant is too thick, thin it by gradually stirring in a little *sirop à trente.* Dip the top of each *chou* in the fondant to glaze it, then smooth the fondant with your index finger. Place the *chou* right side up on a plate or rack and let the fondant set.

②

Éclairs

While *éclairs* can be filled with any flavor pastry cream or even *crème chantilly*, we always use either vanilla, chocolate, or coffee *crème pâtissière* and fondant for the filling and topping.

For 8 individual pastries

INGREDIENTS

8 baked 4½-inch (12 cm) long fingers of *pâte à choux spéciale* or *ordinaire* (page 78)

1½ cups (400 g) *crème pâtissière* (see page 83)

Optional: *Either* 1½ ounce (43 g) unsweetened chocolate, melted; *or* 4 teaspoons (2 cL) very strong black coffee (see page 416)

Fondant for glazing, either plain or flavored with chocolate or coffee (see pages 105–108)

Sirop à trente (see page 398) for thinning fondant

1 Using a bread knife, cut each eclair almost in half horizontally, like a hot dog bun ①.

2 Our recipe for *crème pâtissière* includes vanilla, so for vanilla éclairs, proceed to step 3. For other flavors, stir the chocolate or coffee into the *crème pâtissière*.

3 Transfer the *crème pâtissière* to a pastry bag fitted with a ½-inch (12 mm) plain pastry tube (Ateco 6 or 7). One at a time, hold each éclair open with one hand while you pipe in the *crème pâtissière* to fill it with the other ②. The éclairs should close tightly, with none of the filling showing around the edges, but they must also be well filled so that the pastry cream will hold them together.

4 Warm the fondant over low heat, stirring until melted. If the fondant is too thick, thin it by gradually stirring in a little *sirop à trente*. Dip the top of each éclair in the fondant to glaze it ③; then smooth the fondant with your index finger, and sweep your fingertip around the edge of the fondant to make a sharp line ④. Place the éclair right side up on a plate or rack and let the fondant set.

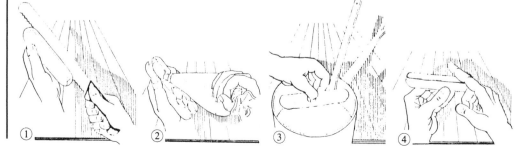

① ② ③ ④

Opposite: St.-Honoré, page 319, and Petits St.-Honorés, page 314. Following page: Croquembouche, page 320.

Salambos and Glands

These oval pastries are half way between *choux* and *éclairs* in shape. They differ from each other in the filling (*crème pâtissière* flavored with kirsch for *salambos* or rum for *glands*) and glaze (*caramel* for *salambos*, pale green fondant for *glands*). For *glands*, the fondant at one end of each pastry is coated with chocolate sprinkles to make them look like acorns, after which they are named.

For 8 individual pastries

INGREDIENTS

8 baked 3½-inch (9 cm) long ovals of *pâte à choux spéciale* or *ordinaire* (see page 78)

1½ cups (400 g) *crème pâtissière* (see page 83)

SALAMBOS

4 teaspoons (2 cL) kirsch

Caramel blond for glazing (see page 108)

1 ounce (30 g) sliced almonds

GLANDS

4 teaspoons (2 cL) dark rum

Fondant for glazing (see page 105)

Sirop à trente (see page 398) for thinning fondant

Green food coloring

3 tablespoons (35 g) chocolate sprinkles

1 Punch a hole in the bottom of each pastry with the tip of a ⅜-inch (1 cm) plain pastry tube (Ateco 4).

2 Flavor the *crème pâtissière* with the kirsch or dark rum.

3 Transfer the *crème pâtissière* to a pastry bag fitted with a ⅜-inch (1 cm) plain pastry tube (Ateco 4). One at a time, insert the tip of the tube in the bottom of each pastry and pipe in the *crème pâtissière* until the pastry is filled.

4 For *salambos:* Sprinkle the sliced almonds on a seasoned baking sheet. Warm the *caramel blond* over very low heat, stirring and being careful not to let it color more. As soon as it is melted, remove it from the heat. Dip the top of each *salambo* in the *caramel*, then press it on the almonds on the baking sheet and let it rest on the baking sheet for 30 seconds. Turn the *salambo* right side up and place it on a plate.

For *glands:* Warm the fondant over low heat, stirring until melted. If the fondant is too thick, thin it by gradually stirring in a little *sirop à trente*. Stir in a drop of green food coloring to tint the fondant a very pale green. Dip the top of each *gland* in the fondant to glaze it, then smooth the fondant with your index finger and sweep your fingertip around the edge of the fondant to make a sharp line. Immediately dip one end of the *gland* in chocolate sprinkles to coat the fondant at that end of the pastry. Place the *gland* right side up on a plate or rack and let the fondant set.

309

Opposite: Charlotte citron, page 337. Preceding page: Charlotte montmorency, page 337.

Religieuses

In the ecclesiastical sense, a *religieuse* is a nun. But, in the culinary world, it is a pastry made from two *choux,* one small and one large. Both *choux* are filled with *crème pâtissière* and glazed with fondant. Then the small *chou* is placed atop the large one, and the base of the small *chou* is decorated with elongated, teardrop-shaped *rosaces.* Butter cream *rosaces* look best, but, if you have none on hand, you can use the same *crème pâtissière* as inside the *choux,* provided it is thick enough to hold its shape.

For 8 individual pastries

INGREDIENTS

8 baked 2½-inch (6 cm) domes and 8 baked 1½-inch (3 cm) domes of *pâte à choux spéciale* or *ordinaire* (see page 78)

Either 2½ cups (675 g) *crème pâtissière* (see page 83); *or* 2 cups (540 g) *crème pâtissière* and ½ cup (100 g) *crème au beurre* (see page 85)

Either 1 ounce (30 g) unsweetened chocolate, melted; *or* 2 tablespoons (3 cL) very strong black coffee (see page 416)

Fondant flavored with chocolate or coffee (see page 107)

Sirop à trente (see page 398) for thinning fondant

1 Punch a hole in the bottom of each *chou* with the tip of a ⅜-inch (1 cm) plain pastry tube (Ateco 4).

2 If you are using the optional *crème au beurre,* flavor it with 1 teaspoon (½ cL) of the coffee or melted chocolate.

3 Flavor the *crème pâtissière* with the (remaining) coffee or melted chocolate.

4 Transfer the *crème pâtissière* to a pastry bag fitted with a ⅜-inch (1 cm) plain pastry tube (Ateco 4). One at a time, insert the tip of the tube in the bottom of each *chou* and pipe in the *crème pâtissière* until the *chou* is filled ①. If you are not using *crème au beurre* for the *rosaces,* then save about ½ cup (135 g) of *crème pâtissière.*

5 Warm the fondant over low heat, stirring until melted. If the fondant is too thick, thin it by gradually stirring in a little *sirop à trente.* Dip the top of each small *chou* in the fondant and smooth the fondant with your index finger. One at a time, dip the top of each large *chou* in the fondant, then smooth the fondant with your index finger. Place the large *chou* right side up on a plate or rack and place a small *chou* on top before the fondant starts to set so the fondant will hold the two *choux* together. Let the fondant set.

6 Transfer the remaining *crème pâtissière* or the optional *crème au beurre* to a pastry bag fitted with a small fluted pastry tube (Ateco 0). Pipe the *crème* in

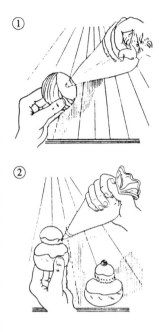

elongated teardrop-shaped *rosaces* up the sides of each *religieuses,* around the base of the small *chou* ②. To pipe each *rosace,* hold the *religieuse* upright on the fingertips of one hand and, with the other hand, hold the pastry bag at a downward 45° angle with the tip of the tube against the large *chou,* just below the base of the small *chou.* Press gently on the pastry bag, then simultaneously flick the tip of the pastry tube upward along the side of the small *chou* and release the pressure on the bag to make a sort of thin, elongated teardrop pointing up. The *rosace* should be about ¾ inch (2 cm) long and extend about halfway up the side of the small *chou.* Rotate the *religieuse* on your fingertips and pipe a second *rosace* adjacent to the first one. Repeat all the way around the *religieuse.* Then decorate the remaining *religieuses* in the same way. Finally pipe a small rosette of *crème au beurre* or *crème pâtissière* on top of each *religieuses.*

Cygnes

These spectacular swans are quite easy to make.

For 8 individual pastries

INGREDIENTS

¾ cup (180 g) *pâte à choux ordinaire* (see page 78)

Lightly beaten egg for brushing

2 cups (250 g) *crème chantilly* flavored with vanilla (see page 82)

½ teaspoon (2 g) confectioners sugar

1 Preheat the oven to 400° F (200° C).

2 Transfer the *pâte à choux* to a pastry bag fitted with a large fluted pastry tube (Ateco 8B). Pipe most of the batter onto a seasoned heavy baking sheet in eight teardrops ①, each 3½ inches (9 cm) long and 1½ inches (4 cm) across at the wide end, separating them by at least 1½ inches (4 cm). These will be used to make the bodies and wings for the swans. Save a little of the *pâte à choux* for the heads and necks (next step).

3 Transfer the remaining *pâte à choux* to a small pastry bag fitted with a ⁵⁄₃₂-inch (4 mm) plain pastry tube (Ateco 0). Pipe the batter onto the baking sheet in *S* shapes about 2 inches (5 cm) high ②. At the

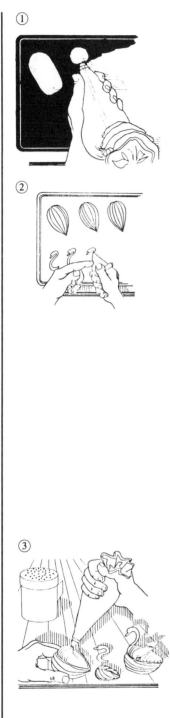

beginning of each *S*, make a head and beak by adjusting the speed at which you move the pastry tube, first quickly piping a narrow beak ¼ inch (6 mm) long, then slowing down almost to a stop to get a wider, rounded head, and finally speeding up to pipe the rest of the *S* in a strip about the width of the tip of the pastry tube. You will need eight *S*s, but pipe a few extra in case some break.

4 Lightly brush the top of each teardrop of *pâte à choux* with beaten egg, but do not brush the *S*s.

5 Using a wooden spoon to hold the oven door ajar, bake until the *S*-shaped necks turn a light brown, 5 to 10 minutes. Carefully slide the necks onto a cooling rack. Continue baking the teardrops, with the oven door ajar, until they have puffed up and turned a medium golden brown with the cracks a pale to medium golden brown, about 15 to 20 minutes longer.

6 Place the baking sheet on a cooling rack and let the teardrops cool on the baking sheet.

7 Slice off the top of each teardrop at two thirds of its height with a bread knife. Trim the top to make a roughly triangular shape with 2 straight sides and one curved end, and cut the triangle in half lengthwise. These will be the wings of the swan.

8 Transfer the *crème chantilly* to a pastry bag fitted with a medium fluted pastry tube (Ateco 5). Pipe the *crème chantilly* into the hollow teardrop bases in a spiral motion, starting at the wide end and ending at the tip of the teardrop ③.

9 Insert the bottom end of one of the *S*-shaped necks in the *crème chantilly* at the wide end of each filled teardrop. Add a pair of wings, pressing the rounded ends of the triangles on the *crème chantilly* at the sides of the neck and positioning the wings around the sides of the *crème chantilly* down the back.

10 Lightly dust the wings and head of each swan with confectioners sugar.

Ponts Neufs

At the end of the sixteenth century the Parisians built a bridge across the Seine; and since it was the newest bridge in town and very modern, they called it Pont Neuf (new bridge). By one of history's ironic twists, the Pont Neuf is now the oldest bridge in Paris.

The pastry called *pont neuf* is unique. To make it, you bake a mixture of *pâte à choux* and *crème pâtissière* in a *rognures*-lined *tartelette* mold.

For 8 individual pastries

INGREDIENTS

Melted butter for brushing molds

9 ounces (250 g) *rognures* (see page 24)

¾ cup (180 g) *pâte à choux spéciale* or *ordinaire* (see page 78)

⅔ cup (180 g) *crème pâtissière* (see page 83)

½ teaspoon (1 cL) orange flower water

1 teaspoon (3 g) confectioners sugar

2 tablespoons (40 g) strained apricot jam

1 Brush the insides of eight 3½-inch (9 cm) plain *tartelette* or *millasson* molds with melted butter.

2 Roll out the *rognures* into a rough rectangle about 10 × 18 inches (25 × 45 cm). Prick the rectangle all over with a fork. If the *rognures* is elastic, fold the sheet in half, place it on a baking sheet, and let it rest in the refrigerator for 20 minutes.

3 Arrange the buttered molds adjacent to each other in two rows of four each on your counter top. Loosely drape the *rognures* over the molds, covering them completely. Trim a little excess *rognures* from one corner of the sheet, form it into a ball, and use it to press the sheet of *rognures* into each mold, eliminating any air gaps. Roll your rolling pin over the tops of the molds to trim off the excess pastry dough. Lift off the excess dough, and cut from it sixteen strips, each at least 4½ inches (12 cm) long and about ⅛ inch (3 mm) wide. Set aside the strips and gather the remaining *rognures* into a pad for another use.

4 Preheat the oven to 400° F (200° C).

5 Mix the *pâte à choux* with the *crème pâtissière* using a wooden spoon. Then mix in the orange flower water.

6 Fill the *rognures*-lined molds with the *pâte à choux–crème pâtissière* mixture and smooth it level with the tops of the molds, using the edge of your

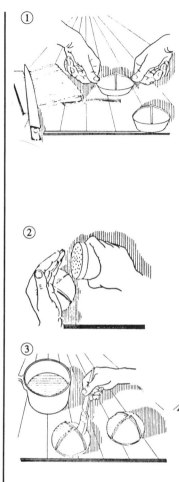

palette knife. Lift a strip of *rognures,* being careful not to stretch it, and drape it over the the center of one of the filled molds. Cut off the ends of the strip by pressing down on the edges of the mold with your fingertips. Drape a second strip of *rognures* across the top of the filled mold perpendicular to the first strip ①, dividing the top surface into quadrants, and cut off the ends of the strip by pressing with your fingertips. Repeat with the remaining filled molds.

7 Transfer the filled molds to a heavy baking sheet and bake, using a wooden spoon to hold the oven door ajar, until the tops of the pastries are well puffed and a uniform medium brown, about 30 to 35 minutes.

8 Transfer the pastries to a cooling rack and let cool in the molds.

9 Unmold the *ponts neufs*. One at a time, dust two opposite quadrants on top of each with confectioners sugar, using the palm of one hand to block the remaining quadrants ②.

10 Warm the strained apricot jam over low heat, stirring occasionally, until melted. Brush the remaining two opposite quadrants of each *pont neuf* with jam until lightly coated and glistening ③.

Puits d'Amour and Petits St.-Honorés

Both of these pastries have a round *rognures* base and a rim of *pâte à choux*. *Puits d'amour,* or "wishing wells," are filled with *crème pâtissière,* sprinkled with sugar, and glazed with a salamander. For *St.-Honorés,* three small caramel-glazed *choux* are placed around the rim of each pastry and the center is filled with *crème chantilly.*

For 8 individual pastries

PUITS D'AMOUR

¾ pound (340 g) *rognures* (page 24)

1 cup (240 g) *pâte à choux spéciale* or *ordinaire* (see page 78)

Lightly beaten egg for brushing

1½ cups (400 g) *crème pâtissière* (see page 83)

3 tablespoons (35 g) superfine sugar

PETITS ST.-HONORÉS

¾ pound (340 g) *rognures* (page 24)

1½ cups (360 g) *pâte à choux spéciale* or *ordinaire* (page 78)

Lightly beaten egg for brushing

3 cups (375 g) *crème chantilly* (page 82) or *crème chiboust* (page 93)

Caramel blond for glazing (page 108)

1 Roll out the *rognures* into a rough rectangle about 11 × 17 inches (28 × 44 cm). Prick the rectangle all over with a fork. If the *rognures* is elastic, fold the sheet in half, place it on a baking sheet, and let it rest in the refrigerator for 20 minutes.

2 Using a *vol-au-vent* disc or *tartelette ring* as a guide, cut eight 4-inch (10 cm) circles from the rectangle with the tip of a paring knife.

3 Preheat the oven to 400° F (200° C).

4 Arrange the circles of *rognures* on a seasoned heavy baking sheet. Transfer the *pâte à choux* to a pastry bag fitted with a ⅜-inch (1 cm) plain pastry tube (Ateco 5). Pipe a rim of *pâte à choux* ⅜ inch (1 cm) wide on the circumference of each circle of *rognures* ①. Pipe a 1¼-inch (3 cm) dome of *pâte à choux* on the center of each circle. For *St.-Honorés*, you should have about one third of the *pâte à choux* left; pipe it directly onto the baking sheet in twenty-four 1¼-inch (3 cm) domes to make small *choux*, spacing them at least 1 inch (3 cm) apart from each other and from the circles of *rognures*. Use a second baking sheet if necessary.

5 Lightly brush the tops of the *pâte à choux* rims and domes with beaten egg.

6 Using a wooden spoon to hold the oven door ajar, bake until the *pâte à choux* puffs up and turns a medium golden brown, with the cracks a pale to medium golden brown, and the *rognures* is evenly browned on top and bottom. The small *choux* for *St.-Honoré* will be done first and should take 15 to 25 minutes; slide them onto a cooling rack and continue baking the *rognures* base, 10 to 20 minutes longer. If the *pâte à choux* seems to be browning too much before the *rognures* is finished, reduce the oven temperature to 350° F (180° C).

7 Place the baking sheet on a cooling rack and let the pastries cool on the baking sheet.

8 For *puits d'amour*: Transfer the *crème pâtissière* to a pastry bag fitted with a medium plain pastry tube

315

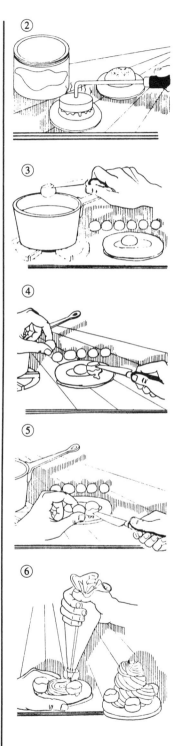

(Ateco 6). Pipe the *crème pâtissière* in a mound inside the rim on each pastry. Heat your salamander. Dust the superfine sugar over the mounds of pastry cream, and caramelize the sugar by ''ironing'' it with the salamander ②.

For *St.-Honorés*: Warm the *caramel blond* over low heat, being careful not to let it color more. As soon as it is melted, remove it from the heat; but briefly return it to low heat later as needed to keep it liquid. One at a time, insert the point of a paring knife in the side of each small *chou* and dip the top in the *caramel* to glaze it ③. Sweep the top of the *chou* across one spot on the rim of one of the *St.-Honorés* to deposit the excess *caramel* there ④. Turn the *chou* right side up and position it on the *caramel* on the rim. Hold the *chou* in place briefly, then pull out the knife ⑤. Repeat with the remaining *choux*, spacing three *choux* evenly around the rim of each pastry. Transfer the *crème chantilly* or *crème chiboust* to a pastry bag fitted with a medium fluted pastry tube (Ateco 5). Using an upward spiral motion with the tip of the pastry tube, pipe a mound of *crème chantilly* or *crème chiboust* in the center of each pastry and about twice as high as the small *choux* on the rim ⑥. Then pipe three large rosettes of *crème chantilly* or *crème chiboust* between the small *choux* on the rim of each pastry, making each rosette about the same size as one of the small *chou*.

Large Pastries

Paris-Brest

For this dessert the *pâte à choux* is baked in the form of a wreath, then filled with either *crème chantilly* (plus strawberries or raspberries in season) or a *praliné*-flavored *crème au beurre au lait*.

For 10 to 12 people

INGREDIENTS

1¼ cups (300 g) *pâte à choux ordinaire* (see page 78)

Lightly beaten egg for brushing

2 tablespoons (40 g) sliced almonds

Half of an 8-inch (20 cm) round of *génoise* (see page 59), or substitute some *biscuit à la cuillère* baked in ladyfinger shapes (see page 68)

4 teaspoons (2 cL) *sirop à trente* (see page 398)

4 teaspoons (2 cL) kirsch

Either 3 cups (375 g) *crème chantilly* (page 82) and (optional) about ¼ pint (100 g) fresh strawberries *or* raspberries; *or* 1 cup plus 2 tablespoons (300 g) *crème pâtissière* (see page 83, 1½ cups (300

1 Preheat the oven to 400° F (200° C).

2 Put some flour on a sheet of waxed paper and dip the edge of a 10-inch (25 cm) flan ring in the flour. Tap the edge of the flan ring on a seasoned heavy baking sheet to mark a circle as a guide for piping the *pâte à choux*.

3 Transfer the *pâte à choux* to a pastry bag fitted with a medium-large fluted pastry tube (Ateco 7B). Pipe a circle of *pâte à choux* the width of the tip of the pastry tube around the inside of the circle on the baking sheet. Pipe a second, concentric circle around the outside of the first circle. Pipe a third circle of *pâte à choux* on top of the intersection of the first two circles ①.

4 Lightly brush the *pâte à choux* circles with beaten egg. Sprinkle the sliced almonds over the *pâte à choux*, making sure that most of them adhere to the egg wash.

5 Using a wooden spoon to hold the oven door ajar, bake until the *pâte à choux* puffs up and turns a medium golden brown with the cracks a pale to medium golden brown. If the almonds seem to be browning too much, reduce the oven to 350° F (180° C). The total baking time should be about 25 to 35 minutes.

6 Place the baking sheet on a cooling rack and let the pastry cool on the baking sheet.

7 Cut off the top of the wreath of baked *pâte à choux* at one half to two thirds of its height with a bread knife. Break or pull out the soft *pâte à choux*

317

g) *crème au beurre* (see page 85), *and* 4½ tablespoons (85 g) *praliné* (see page 414)

Confectioners sugar for dusting

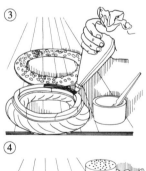

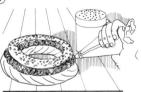

channels inside the bottom of the wreath with your fingertips to make a continuous troughlike depression.

8 Trim the crust from the *génoise* and cut it into strips about 2 to 3 inches (5 to 8 cm) long, ½ inch (12 mm) wide and ½ inch (12 mm) thick. The strips must fit in the trough in the wreath of *pâte à choux*. Mix the *sirop à trente* and the kirsch, and brush the strips of *génoise* with this syrup.

9 If you are using a *crème chantilly* filling and including the optional strawberries, then, depending on the size of the strawberries, leave them whole or cut them in halves, quarters, or slices. If you are using the *praliné*-flavored filling, stir the *crème pâtissière* into the *crème au beurre* with a wooden spoon to make a *crème au beurre au lait*. Then beat this *crème au beurre au lait* into the *praliné* with the wooden spoon, adding it gradually to be sure there are no lumps of *praline*.

10 Transfer the *crème chantilly* or the *crème au beurre au lait* to a pastry bag fitted with a medium fluted pastry tube (Ateco 6). Pipe a thin layer of the filling in the trough in the bottom of the *pâte à choux* wreath ②. Arrange the strips of *génoise* in a continuous circle in the trough and press them down gently on the layer of filling at the bottom. Pipe a layer of filling on top of the *génoise* strips ③. Then place the top of the *pâte à choux* wreath on the *paris-brest* like a lid.

11 Pipe a continuous spiral or swirl of filling over first the inner side and then the outer side of the *génoise* strips, between the base and the lid of the *paris-brest* ④. If you are using the *crème chantilly* filling and including the optional berries, press a row of berries into the swirls of *crème chantilly* around both the inside and outside of the ring.

12 Lightly dust the top of the *paris-brest* with confectioners sugar.

St.-Honoré

This elegant dessert is named for the patron saint of pastry chefs.

For 10 to 12 people

INGREDIENTS

7 ounces (200 g) *rognures* (see page 24)

1 cup (240 g) *pâte à choux ordinaire* (see page 78)

Lightly beaten egg for brushing

Caramel blond for glazing (see page 108)

Either 4 cups (500 g) *crème chantilly* (see page 82); *or* 4 cups (800 g) *crème chiboust,* flavored, if desired, with coffee, dark rum, or kirsch (see page 93)

Optional: A garland of *sucre filé* (see page 121)

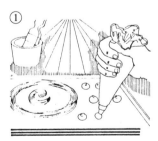

1 Roll out the *rognures* into a rough circle about 11 inches (28 cm) in diameter and ³/₃₂ inch (2 mm) thick. Prick the circle all over with a fork. If the *rognures* is elastic, fold the sheet in half or quarters, place it on a baking sheet, and let it rest in the refrigerator for 20 minutes.

2 Using a flan ring or round mold as a guide, cut a neat 10-inch (25 cm) circle from the sheet of *rognures* with the tip of a paring knife. Place the circle of *rognures* on a heavy baking sheet.

3 Preheat the oven to 400° F (200° C).

4 Transfer the *pâte à choux* to a pastry bag fitted with a large fluted pastry tube (Ateco 8B). Pipe a circle of *pâte à choux* the width of the tip of the pastry tube on the circumference of the circle of *rognures*. Then, starting from the center of the circle and holding the tip of the pastry tube about ⅛ inch (3 mm) above the surface of the *rognures,* pipe a thin strip, ⅝ inch (16 mm) wide, of *pâte à choux* in a spiral out toward the circumference, going through about two full revolutions, and spacing the successive arcs of the spiral about 1 inch (2½ cm) apart. You should have a little more than a quarter of the *pâte à choux* left. Transfer it to a pastry bag fitted with a ⅜-inch (1 cm) plain pastry tube (Ateco 5). Pipe the *pâte à choux* directly onto the baking sheet in ten 1¼-inch (3 cm) domes to make small *choux,* spacing them at least 1 inch (3 cm) apart from each other and from the circle of *rognures* ①.

5 Lightly brush the *pâte à choux* rim and domes with beaten egg.

6 Using a wooden spoon to hold the oven door ajar, bake until the *pâte à choux* puffs up and turns a medium golden brown, with the cracks a light golden brown, and the *rognures* is evenly browned on top and bottom. The small *choux* will be done first and should take 15 to 25 minutes; slide them onto a cooling rack and continue baking the *rognures* base about 10 to 20 minutes longer. If the *pâte à choux* rim seems to be browning too much before the *rognures* is finished, reduce the oven temperature to 350° F (180° C) and continue baking.

7 Place the baking sheet on a cooling rack and let the base cool on the baking sheet.

8 Warm the *caramel blond* over low heat, being careful not to let it color more. As soon as it is melted, remove it from the heat; but briefly return it to low heat later as needed to keep it liquid. One at a time, insert the point of a paring knife in the side of each small *chou* and dip the top in the *caramel* to glaze it. Sweep the top of the *chou* across one spot on the rim of the *St.-Honoré,* to deposit the excess *caramel* there. Turn the *chou* right side up and position it on the caramel on the rim. Hold the *chou* in place briefly, then pull out the knife. Repeat with the remaining *choux,* spacing them evenly around the rim.

②

9 Spoon about 3 cups (375 g) of the *crème chantilly* or *crème chiboust* onto the center of the *rognures* and smooth it into a mound inside the *pâte à choux* rim. Transfer the remaining filling to a pastry bag fitted with a medium fluted pastry tube (Ateco 7B). Pipe rosettes of *crème chantilly* or *crème chiboust* to cover the mound of filling in the center of the *St.-Honoré* ②. Pipe a large rosette of filling between each small *chou* around the rim of the *St.-Honoré.*

10 When ready to serve, place the optional garland of *sucre filé* over the filling in the *St.-Honoré.*

Croquembouche

This tower of small *choux*—each filled with *crème pâtissière,* and held together with *caramel*—is the traditional French wedding cake. The base and the decoration on top are made from *nougatine.* Depending on the number of *choux* and the size of the base, you can make a *croquembouche* of any size you like. We give a recipe for a fairly small one, with only sixty *choux*.

For 12 to 15 people

INGREDIENTS

60 baked 1¼-inch (3 cm) domes of *pâte à choux ordinaire* (see page 78)

1 *nougatine* base molded in an 8-inch (20 cm) layer-cake pan (see page 115)

1 *nougatine* circle 4 inches (10 cm) in diameter and ⅛ inch (3 mm) thick

3 *nougatine* right triangles, each 2½ × 6 inches (6 × 15 cm) and ⅛ inch (3 mm) thick, with the sharpest corner cut off about ½ inch (12 mm) from the tip

2 to 2½ cups (540 to 675 g) *crème pâtissière* (see page 83)

2 tablespoons (3 cL) dark rum or Grand Marnier

1 pound 11 ounces to 2¼ pounds (750 to 1000 g) *caramel blond* (see page 108)

20 to 30 Jordan almonds

1 Punch a hole in the bottom of each *chou*, using the tip of a ⅜-inch (1 cm) plain pastry tube (Ateco 4).

2 Flavor the *crème pâtissière* with the rum or Grand Marnier. Transfer the *crème pâtissière* to a pastry bag fitted with the ⅜-inch (1 cm) plain pastry tube (Ateco 4). Insert the tip of the tube in the bottom of each *chou* and pipe in the *crème pâtissière* until the *chou* is filled.

3 Place the *nougatine* base on a serving plate, hollow side down.

4 Warm the *caramel blond* over low heat, being careful not to let it color more. As soon as it is melted, remove it from the heat, but briefly return it to low heat later as needed to keep it liquid.

5 Dip the top of one of the *chou* in the *caramel* ①, sweep the top over the rim of the caramel pot to clean off the excess, and then turn the *chou* right side up and place it on a rack to cool. Repeat with the remaining *choux*.

6 Dip the side of one of the *choux* in the *caramel* and stick it on the perimeter of the *nougatine* base, with the glazed side facing out ②. Dip the side of a second *chou* in the *caramel*, wipe off the excess on the side of the first *chou*, and stick the second *chou* on the perimeter of the *nougatine* base, right next to the first *chou*. Continue until you have arranged a circle of *choux*, glazed sides facing out, on the *nougatine* base. Dip your paring knife in the *caramel* and wipe it off between the *choux* on the *nougatine* base to cement them together more securely ③. Repeat with a second circle of *choux*, arranging them on top of the first circle. Continue building a conical tower by arranging one circle of *choux* on top of the other, making each successive circle slightly smaller than the previous one. Use the larger *choux* in the lower rows and the smaller *choux* in the upper rows. To keep the tower symmetrical, look down on

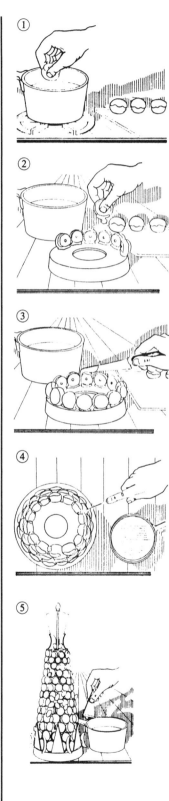

it from above and imagine the cone shape you are building ④. The top circle of *choux* should be about 4 inches (10 cm) in diameter.

7 Dip your paring knife in the *caramel* and wipe it off on the tops of the final circle of *choux* three or four times. Place the circle of *nougatine* on the last row of *choux* before the *caramel* sets. Dip the cut-off tip and the 6-inch (15 cm) side of each triangle of *nougatine* in the *caramel* and glue it on top of the circle of *nougatine*, tip down and radiating out from the center. Space the three triangles equally so they meet at 120° angles, with the 6-inch (15 cm) sides cemented together with caramel ⑤.

8 Finish decorating the *croquembouche* by sticking Jordan almonds in the cracks between some of the *choux*, using *caramel* to cement them in place.

NOTE: Another way to decorate the top of the *croquembouche* is to replace the triangles of *nougatine* with a pompon of *sucre filé*. To make an even more elaborate *croquembouche* cut more *nougatine* into triangles and crescents, or pipe and bake (no egg wash) some *pâte à choux* in crescent or scroll shapes; then glue the crescents, scrolls, and triangles around the *nougatine* base and on the *nougatine* platform on top. You can highlight the decoration of the *croquembouche* by piping *rosaces* of *meringue italienne* around the edge of the *nougatine* platform on top, between some of the *choux*, and on the edges of the crescents and scrolls.

Négus

Named for an Ethiopian king, *négus* is a rarity—it is the only *pâte à choux* dessert we know that is molded. Filled with *praliné*-flavored *crème au beurre au lait* and glazed with chocolate, it is also exceptionally rich.

For a small pastry serving 8 to 10 people or a large pastry serving 12 to 15

SMALL NÉGUS

Melted butter for brushing mold

1½ tablespoons (10 g) sliced almonds

1 cup (240 g) *pâte à choux speciale* (see page 78)

1 cup (180 g) *crème au beurre* (see page 85)

⅓ cup (90 g) *crème pâtissière* (see page 83)

¼ cup plus 1 tablespoon (90 g) *praliné* (see page 414)

Either 6 ounces (170 g) *pâte à glacé* (see page 110); *or* 4½ ounces (130 g) semisweet chocolate, 1½ ounces (43 g) barely melted butter, and 2 teaspoons (1 cL) water

1 Preheat the oven to 400° F (200° C).

2 Choose a 2-cup (½ L) *savarin* mold for the small *négus* or a 3-cup (¾ L) *savarin* mold for the large size. Brush the inside of the *savarin* mold heavily with melted butter. Sprinkle the sliced almonds over the inside of the mold.

3 Transfer the *pâte à choux* to a pastry bag fitted with a large plain pastry tube (Ateco 8 or 9). Pipe the batter into the *savarin* mold to fill it evenly to about half its height ①. If necessary smooth the top surface with a pastry cornet or rubber spatula.

4 Place the mold on a baking sheet and bake, using a wooden spoon to hold the oven door ajar, until the *pâte à choux* is well puffed and a uniform medium brown, about 45 minutes to 1 hour.

5 Remove the mold to a cooling rack and let the pastry cool in the mold.

6 Unmold the pastry. Punch eight to ten holes in the bottom (which was on top in the oven) with the tip of a sharpening steel or the handle of a slender wooden spoon.

7 Stir the *crème pâtissiére* into the *crème au beurre* with a wooden spoon to make a *crème au beurre au lait*. Then beat this *crème au beurre au lait* into the *praliné* with the wooden spoon, adding it gradually, to be sure there are no lumps of *praliné*.

8 Transfer the *crème au beurre au lait* to a pastry bag fitted with a ⅜-inch (1 cm) plain pastry tube (Ateco 4). Pipe the *crème au beurre au lait* into each hole in the bottom of the pastry until you feel resistance when you press on the pastry bag, indicating that this part of the pastry is filled.

LARGE NÉGUS

Melted butter for brushing mold

2½ tablespoons (15 g) sliced almonds

1½ cups (360 g) *pâte à choux spéciale* (see page 78)

1½ cups (270 g) *crème au beurre* (see page 85)

½ cup (135 g) *crème pâtissière* (see page 83)

½ cup (140 g) *praliné* (see page 414)

Either 8 ounces (225 g) *pâte à glacé* (see page 110); *or* 6 ounces (170 g) semisweet chocolate, 2 ounces (57 g) barely melted butter, and 1 tablespoon (1½ cL) water

9 If you have *pâte à glacé* on hand, temper it to get the right consistency for coating the *négus*. Otherwise, prepare a *pâte à glacé* as follows: Melt the chocolate and stir in the butter. When smooth, stir in the water. Dip the bottom of the pot of chocolate in cold water and stir until it begins to thicken. Return this *pâte à glacé* to the heat and gently warm it a second time, stirring until just melted.

10 Pour the *pâte à glacé* into the savarin mold in which the *négus* was baked. Turn the *négus* upside down and dip it in the *pâte à glacé,* rotating the pastry in the mold to be sure it is coated evenly ②. Remove the *négus* from the mold and place it, right side up, on a serving plate. Allow the *pâte à glacé* to set before serving.

①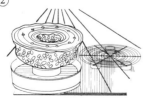

②

Chapter Twelve

BAVAROIS AND CHARLOTTES

*B*avarois and charlottes are molded desserts that get their lightness from whipped cream and their stability from gelatin. They are very different from the other desserts in this book because here the filling becomes the essential element, with the mold defining the shape and structure of the dessert.

Bavarois are the simplest molded desserts. In their most basic form, they are just Bavarian cream poured into a mold, refrigerated until set, and then unmolded onto a serving plate. Embedding layers of liquor-soaked fruit and cake in the Bavarian cream adds variety of texture and flavor.

The original *charlotte aux pommes*—an apple compote baked in a mold lined with toast slices—was created in the eighteenth century and named for the wife of King George III of England. The nineteenth-century French chef Marie Antoine Carème adopted the name and radically refined the concept in response to a kitchen disaster. At a banquet to celebrate the return to Paris of Louis XVIII in 1815, the supply of gelatin was insufficient for the Bavarian creams Carème was preparing. So the great chef buttressed the sides of his sagging desserts with ladyfingers. The result became known as *charlotte russe*. In an even fancier version, called *charlotte royale,* the ladyfingers are replaced by slices of a multilayered spongecake and jam sandwich.

While Bavarian creams are the traditional fillings for charlottes, we prefer our light, intensely flavored fruit mousses. You can make these from just about any fruit, but those with strong, distinctive flavors are best. We give recipes for eight—strawberry, raspberry, blueberry, cranberry, pear, sour cherry, lemon, and mango—and recommend a particular form—*charlotte russe* or *charlotte royale*—for each.

TOURS DE MAIN

Bavarois can be molded in just about any shape, and some very elaborate molds have been created for them. We like our Bavarians creamy, with just enough gelatin to hold their shape. This makes them somewhat delicate, and you will find them easier to handle if you choose molds that aren't too deep. We have chosen the quantities in our recipes for a 6-cup (1½ L) ring mold. If you have a more elaborate mold, increase or decrease the quantities in the recipe to fill it.

Classically, charlottes are molded upside down, in deep molds with sloping sides for *charlottes russes* or in deep, dome-shaped bowls for *charlottes royales*. Our unconventional—and easier—method is to mold both types of charlotte right side up in *vacherin* rings or springform pans. So the delicate operation of inverting and unmolding the fragile charlottes is replaced by the trivial step of lifting off the *vacherin* ring or opening the springform.

Charlottes Russes

We recommend a *vacherin* ring or springform pan 8 to 9½ inches (20 to 24 cm) in diameter. (Remove the bottom of the springform pan, since you need only the ring.) Place the ring on a round serving plate.

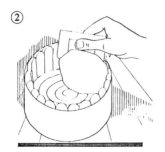

You will need about twenty-five ladyfingers to line the sides of the ring. The ladyfingers should each be about 3 inches (7½ cm) long by 1 inch (2½ cm) wide. They will be much easier to handle if they have been piped adjacent to each other so they hold together in a strip ①. Given the size of home ovens and baking sheets, two strips of ladyfingers will be required to get the necessary total length.

You will also need two 8-inch (20 cm) circles of *biscuit à la cuillère,* one for the bottom of the charlotte and the other for a layer in the center. If you have on hand some *génoise,* you can substitute it for the *biscuit à la cuillère* circles. To do that, cut a 1½-inch (4 cm) thick round of *génoise* horizontally into four ⅜-inch (1 cm) thick slices—enough for two *charlottes russes*. As a third alternative, you can substitute trimmings from the ladyfingers and one of the *biscuit à la cuillère* circles for the circle that is used in the middle of the charlotte.

Trim off one side of each strip of ladyfingers with a bread knife to make the ladyfingers the same height as the ring (about 2½ inches, or 6 cm) and give the strip a straight bottom edge. Brush the back side of the ladyfingers with a syrup flavored according to the charlotte you are making. Line the inside of the ring with the strips of ladyfingers, trimming the ends of the strips so they don't overlap.

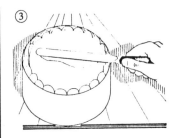

Trim the circles of *biscuit à la cuillère* to fit inside the ladyfinger-lined ring. Place one circle inside the ring on the serving plate and brush it with the flavored syrup.

You are now ready to fill the ring with fruit mousse ②-③.

There is a variation of the above method that omits the layer of *biscuit à la cuillère* in the middle of the charlotte and replaces it with a decorative circle of *biscuit à la cuillère* on top. We like this method for pale-colored fruits in general, and pears in particular. In this case, you must trim both top and bottom of the strips of ladyfingers in straight lines so the ladyfingers are precisely the height of the ring ④. And the decorative circle must be piped in a size that will just cover the top of the charlotte.

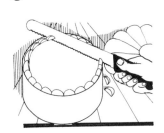

Charlottes Royales

We like the *royale* presentation for lemon and sour cherry charlottes, because the sweetness of the jam in the lining balances the tartness of the fruit in the filling. The spongecake we use for the lining is *joconde* (see page 70), which, since it contains ground almonds, adds another dimension of flavor and textural contrast.

The multi-layered *joconde*-jam sandwich that will be used to line the sides of the ring freezes well, so it makes sense to prepare enough for two or three charlottes at once. A 12×16-inch (30×40 cm) or 13×20-inch (33×50 cm) sheet of *joconde* will be sufficient, respectively, for two or three 8- to 8½-inch (20 to 22 cm) charlottes. We use raspberry jam for both lemon and sour cherry charlottes, and you will need about ½ cup (170 g) or ¾ cup (250 g) of it to spread on the *joconde,* depending on the size of the sheet.

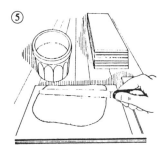

To make the *joconde*-jam sandwich, first trim the edges of the sheet of *joconde* with a bread knife. If the *joconde* is dry, moisten and soften it by brushing with a little *sirop à trente* (see page 398). Cut the sheet of *joconde* into four equal rectangles, each 11½ to 12½ inches (29 to 32 cm) long. Spread raspberry jam on three of the rectangles ⑤, neatly pile them one on top of the other, and place the rectangle without jam on top. Slice this four-layer sandwich in half lengthwise. Spread raspberry jam on one half and neatly place the second half on top. You should now have a sandwich 11½ to 12½ inches (29 to 32 cm) long and 2 to 2¼ inches (5 to 5½ cm) thick, with eight layers of *joconde* and seven layers of jam. It will be about 1¾ inches (4½ cm) or 2¼ inches (5½ cm) wide, depending on whether you used a 12×16-inch (30×40 cm) or 13×20-inch (33×50 cm) sheet of *joconde*.

Wrap the *joconde*-jam sandwich in waxed paper, enclose it in a plastic bag, and freeze it so it will slice cleanly and evenly. It can be kept frozen for up to 2 months.

When you are ready to make your charlotte, remove the *joconde*-jam sandwich from the freezer and cut it lengthwise with your chef's knife into slices ⅜ inch (1 cm) thick. Two slices 11½ to 12½ inches (29 to 32 cm) long should be sufficient for one charlotte 8 to 8½ inches (20 to 22 cm) in diameter. Return the remainder of *joconde*-jam sandwich to the freezer.

You will also need two 8-inch (20 cm) circles of *biscuit à la cuillère,* one for the bottom of the charlotte and the other for a layer in the center of the *charlotte.* If you have on hand some *génoise,* you can substitute it for the *biscuit à la cuillère* circles: Cut a 1½-inch (4 cm) thick round of *génoise* horizontally into four slices ⅜ inch (1 cm) thick—enough for two *charlottes royales.*

Choose a *vacherin* ring or springform 8 to 8½ inches (20 to 22 cm) in diameter. (Remove the bottom from the springform, since you need only the ring.) Place the ring on a serving plate. You can line the inside of the ring with slices of the *joconde*-jam sandwich in two ways.

HORIZONTAL STRIPES: The easiest is to line the ring with the two ⅜-inch (1 cm) thick slices standing horizontally along the inside of the ring and the ends of the slices meeting at opposite sides ⑥. Trim the ends so they don't overlap. The width of the slices should be ¼ to ½ inch (6 to 12 mm) shorter than the height of the ring, so a thin band of fruit

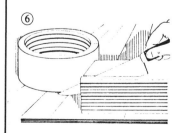

mousse will show at the top of the finished charlotte.

VERTICAL STRIPES: Cut each slice of the *joconde*-jam sandwich into rectangles 2¼ inches (5½ cm) long. Arrange the rectangles adjacent to each other around the inside of the ring, with the jam stripes vertical ⑦ . As for horizontal stripes, the rectangles should be a little shorter than the height of the ring. Trim the last rectangle so the slices don't overlap.

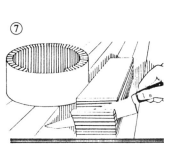

Whether you have used horizontal or vertical stripes, trim the *biscuit à la cuillère* circles so they fit neatly inside the lined ring. Place one circle inside the ring of the serving plate. Brush both the circle and the inside of the *joconde*-jam lining with a syrup flavored according to the charlotte you are making.

You are now ready to fill the ring with fruit mousse.

Charlottes Royales à l'Ancienne

This is an alternate form of the *charlotte royale,* in which slices of a jelly roll are used to line the outside of the charlotte. These are molded upside down in a layer-cake pan. Since the mold is very shallow, unmolding the charlotte poses no problem. We especially like this form for mango charlotte, in which we use *joconde* (see page 70) rolled with orange marmalade to contrast with the unctuous texture and sweet-spicy flavor of the mango.

As for the other *charlottes royales,* the *joconde* jelly roll can be frozen, and it is advantageous to prepare enough of the jelly roll for two or three charlottes at once. One 13×20-inch (33×50 cm) sheet or two 12×16-inch (30×40 cm) sheets of *joconde* will be enough for two or three 9- to 10-inch (23- to 25-cm) diameter layer-cake pans, respectively.

Trim the edge of each sheet of *joconde* with a bread knife and place it, top side up, on a sheet of waxed paper. If the *joconde* is dry, brush it with a little *sirop à trente* (see page 398) to moisten and soften it.

You will need about ¾ cup (250 g) or 1 cup (340 g) of fine-cut orange marmalade for one 13×20-inch (33×50 cm) sheet or two 12×16-inch (30×40 cm) sheets of *joconde,* respectively. Warm the marmalade over low heat, stirring occasionally, until melted. Brush the marmalade over the sheet of *joconde.* Then use the end of the sheet of waxed paper to lift the long edge of the sheet of *joconde* and begin rolling the *joconde.* Once the roll is started, let go of the waxed paper and finish rolling the *joconde* into a cylinder approximately 19 inches (48 cm) or 14½ inches (36 cm) long, depending on which size sheet of *joconde* you started with. Cut a 19-inch (48 cm) cylinder in half to make two cylinders, each 9½ inches (24 cm) long. Cut each 14½-inch (36 cm) cylinder into two pieces, one 9½ inches (24 cm) long and the other 4¾ inches (12 cm) long.

Wrap the rolled *joconde* in the waxed paper, enclose it in a plastic bag, and freeze it so it will slice cleanly and evenly. It can be stored in the freezer for up to 2 months.

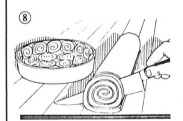

When you are ready to make your *charlotte royale,* remove one 9½-inch (24 cm) or two 4¾-inch (12 cm) cylinders of rolled *joconde* from the freezer. Using a chef's knife, cut each 9½-inch (24 cm) cylinder or pair of 4½-inch (12 cm) cylinders into about 24 slices, each ⅜ inch (1 cm) thick ⑧.

Brush melted butter over the inside of a layer cake pan 10 inches (25 cm) in diameter and 1½ inches (4 cm) deep or 9 inches (23 cm) in diameter and 2 inches (5 cm) deep. Spoon 2 tablespoons (25 g) of sugar into the mold, and tilt and shake the mold to coat the buttered surface evenly. Invert the layer-cake pan and tap it to dislodge the excess sugar.

Line the sides of the prepared layer-cake pan with the slices of rolled *joconde,* placing the slices adjacent to each other and pressing them down slightly if they project above the top of the mold. Arrange the remaining slices over the bottom of the layer-cake pan. Brush the slices with a syrup flavored according to the charlotte you are making.

You are now ready to fill the mold with fruit mousse.

STORAGE

Bavarois can be kept in the refrigerator, covered airtight with plastic wrap, for up to 2 or 3 days before unmolding. After unmolding they should be kept refrigerated, and they should be served within an hour or two after filling with *crème chantilly*.

Charlottes can be stored in the refrigerator, uncovered, for 2 or 3 days before unmolding and decorating or glazing. They can also be frozen for up to 15 days in the mold. Cover the frozen charlotte airtight in a plastic bag, being careful not to damage the top surface. The day before serving, remove the frozen charlotte from the plastic bag, glaze the top if required, and defrost overnight in the refrigerator before unmolding and decorating.

Bavarois à l'Orange, Bavarois aux Pêches, and Bavarois aux Fraises

Our recipes call for a liqueur-flavored *crème bavaroise*, and we recommend serving them with a plain *crème anglaise*. If you prefer you can omit the flavoring in the *crème bavaroise* and put it in the sauce instead.

For 6 to 8 people

BAVAROIS À L'ORANGE

2 large navel oranges

3 tablespoons (4½ cL) dark rum or Grand Marnier

Half of a 9-inch (23 cm) round of *génoise* (page 59)

1½ tablespoons (2 cL) *sirop à trente* (page 398)

3½ to 4 cups (8½ to 10 dL) *crème bavaroise* (page 95) flavored with 3 tablespoons (4½ cL) dark rum or Grand Marnier

BAVAROIS AUX PÊCHES

2 or 3 ripe fresh medium freestone peaches

3 tablespoons (4½ cL) kirsch

Half of a 9-inch (23 cm) round of *génoise* (page 59)

1½ tablespoons (2 cL) *sirop à trente* (page 398)

3½ to 4 cups (8½ to 10 dL) *crème bavaroise* (page 95) flavored with 3 tablespoons(4½cL)kirsch

BAVAROIS AUX FRAISES

½ pint (225 g) fresh strawberries

3 tablespoons (4½ cL) Curaçao or Grand Marnier

Half of a 9-inch (23 cm) round of *génoise* (page 59)

1½ tablespoons (2 cL) *sirop à trente* (page 398)

3½ to 4 cups (8½ to 10 dL) *crème bavaroise* (page 95) flavored with 3 tablespoons (4½ cL) Curaçao or Grand Marnier

INGREDIENTS

About 3 cups (7 dL)
crème chantilly
(page 82)

Candied fruits for
decoration

Optional: 1 cup (2.4
dL) *crème anglaise*
(page 126)

1 Prepare the fruit.

Oranges: Grate the aromatic zest from the outside of one of the oranges and reserve the zest. With a paring knife, carefully peel the orange, removing all of the bitter white pith and the outer membrane surrounding the flesh of the orange. Remove each segment of orange flesh by carefully cutting down to the core along the membranes that separate the segments.

Peaches: Peel and stone the peaches. Cut them into wedges ¼ inch (6 mm) thick, and dip the wedges in acidulated water to prevent them from discoloring.

Strawberries: Leave small strawberries whole. Cut large berries in halves, quarters, or slices, depending on their size.

2 Marinate the strawberries in the orange liqueur, the peach slices in the kirsch, or the orange segments in the rum or Grand Marnier for 2 to 3 hours. Then drain well, reserving the liquid.

3 Trim the crust from the *génoise*. Cut the *génoise* into strips about 2 to 2½ inches (5 to 6 cm) long and 1 inch (2½ cm) square. Mix 1½ tablespoons (2 cL) of the liquor reserved from soaking the fruit with the *sirop à trente*. Brush the *génoise* strips with this syrup.

4 For *bavarois à l'orange,* stir the grated orange zest into the *crème bavaroise*. Or, better yet, add the zest to the milk at the beginning of the preparation of the *crème bavaroise*.

5 Rinse a 5- or 6-cup (1¼ to 1½ L) ring mold with cold water and shake it out. Pour about one third of the *crème bavaroise* into the mold ①. Arrange the peach slices, strawberries, or orange segments over the *crème bavaroise* ②. Pour in half of the remaining *crème bavaroise* to cover the fruit. Arrange the *génoise* strips in a continuous circle in the mold and press them down gently into the *crème bavaroise*. Pour in the remaining *crème bavaroise* to cover the *génoise* strips and fill the mold. Smooth the surface with your palette knife ③.

6 Refrigerate until the *crème bavaroise* is set, at least 3 to 4 hours.

7 Remove the *bavarois* from the refrigerator and run the tip of a small knife or spatula around the rim of the mold to loosen the top edge of the *bavarois*. Briefly dip the mold in hot water. Wipe the mold dry. Place a round serving plate upside down on top of the mold and invert the plate and mold together to unmold the *bavarois*. If the *bavarois* does not slide out easily, repeat this procedure. After unmolding, if the surface of the *bavarois* has softened too much and is runny, return the *bavarois* to the refrigerator until the surface has set again.

④

8 Place the *crème chantilly* in a pastry bag fitted with a medium star tube (Ateco 6). Pipe the *crème chantilly* into the center of the *bavarois*, mounding the *crème chantilly* slightly. Pipe rosettes of *crème chantilly* to cover the mound ④.

9 Decorate the *bavarois* with candied fruits, arranging them around the top of the ring. Cut candied cherries in half. Cut larger candied fruits (such as pineapple, apricots, peaches, or pears) into triangle- or diamond-shaped slices.

10 Serve the *bavarois* accompanied, if you wish, by the *crème anglaise*, or, for *bavarois aux fraises* substitute *coulis de fraise*.

Charlotte Fraise, Charlotte Framboise, Charlotte Myrtille, and Charlotte Airelle

These, respectively, are strawberry, raspberry, blueberry, and cranberry charlottes. Because of their deep, beautiful colors, these charlottes look especially good in the *charlotte russe* form with ladyfingers around the sides and the fruit mousse showing on top.

For 8 to 10 people

INGREDIENTS

About 25 *biscuits à la cuillère* (ladyfingers), piped and baked adjacent to each other (see page 68)

Two 8½-inch (22 cm) diameter circles of *biscuit à la cuillère* (see page 68)

2 tablespoons (3 cL) *sirop à trente* (see page 398)

CHARLOTTE FRAISE

2 tablespoons (3 cL) *coulis de fraise* (see page 127)

1 tablespoon (1½ cL) kirsch

6 cups (1½ L) *mousse aux fraises* (see pages 96–97)

Optional: about 1 cup (200 to 250 g) fresh strawberries

Crème chantilly (see page 82) for decoration

A few fresh strawberries for decoration

Optional: 1½ cups (3½ dL) *crème anglaise* (see page 126) flavored with 1½ tablespoons (2 cL) kirsch, *or coulis de fraise* (see page 127)

CHARLOTTE FRAMBOISE

2 tablespoons (3 cL) *coulis de framboise* (see page 127)

1 tablespoon (1½ cL) kirsch or *eau de vie de framboise*

6 cups (1½ L) *mousse aux framboises* (see pages 96–97)

Optional: about 1 cup (200 to 250 g) fresh raspberries

Crème chantilly (see page 82) for decoration

A few fresh raspberries for decoration

Optional: 1½ cups (3½ dL) *crème anglaise* (see page 126) flavored with 1½ tablespoons (2 cL) kirsch or *eau de vie de framboise, or coulis de framboise* (see page 127)

CHARLOTTE MYRTILLE

2 tablespoons (3 cL) blueberry purée (see page 98)

1 tablespoon (1½ cL) kirsch

6 cups (1½ L) *mousse aux myrtilles* (see pages 96, 98)

Optional: about 1 cup (200 to 250 g) fresh blueberries

Crème chantilly (see page 82) for decoration

A few fresh blueberries for decoration

Optional: 1½ cups (3½ dL) *crème anglaise* (see page 126) flavored with 1½ tablespoons (2 cL) kirsch

CHARLOTTE AIRELLE

2 tablespoons (3 cL) cranberry purée (see page 98)

1 tablespoon (1½ cL) bourbon

6 cups (1½ L) *mousse aux airelles* (see pages 96, 98)

Crème chantilly (see page 82) for decoration

A few fresh cranberries, poached for 3 to 5 minutes in *sirop à trente*, for decoration

Optional: 1½ cups (3½ dL) *crème anglaise* (see page 126) flavored with 1½ tablespoons (2 cL) bourbon

1 Place a *vacherin* ring or the ring of a springform pan 8½ to 9 inches (22 to 24 cm) in diameter on a serving plate.

2 Trim one side of each strip of ladyfingers to make them the height of the ring and give them a straight bottom edge. Mix the *sirop à trente,* fruit *coulis* or purée, and kirsch, *eau de vie de framboise,* or bourbon. Brush the backs of the strips of ladyfingers with some of this fruit syrup. Line the inside of the ring with the ladyfingers. Trim the circles of *biscuit à la cuillère* to fit neatly inside the ladyfinger-lined ring. Place one of the circles inside the ring on the serving plate and brush it with fruit syrup.

3 If you are including the optional fresh berries, gently fold them into the fruit mousse. If you are using large fresh strawberries, cut them in halves or quarters first.

4 Fill the lined ring about halfway with fruit mousse ①. Smooth the surface and place the second circle of *biscuit à la cuillère* on top of this first layer of *mousse.* Brush the *biscuit à la cuillère* with fruit syrup. Then add more *mousse* to fill the ring to the top of the ladyfingers. Smooth the top of the *mousse* with your palette knife for a flat top surface ②.

5 Refrigerate until set, at least 3 or 4 hours.

6 When ready to serve, lift off the *vacherin* ring or open and remove the springform. Transfer some *crème chantilly* to a pastry bag fitted with a small star tube (Ateco 0), and pipe rosettes of *crème chantilly* in a decorative pattern on top of the charlotte ③. You can also pipe rosettes of *crème chantilly* between the ladyfingers around the base of the charlotte. Finish decorating the top of the charlotte with some fresh strawberries (whole, halved, quartered, or even sliced, depending on their size), raspberries, blueberries, or *sirop à trente*–poached cranberries. Raspberries, blueberries, cranberries, and very small fresh strawberries look nice on top of rosettes of *crème chantilly*. Larger strawberries should be placed directly on the surface of the charlotte—for example, slices of large strawberries could be arranged in a circle in the center of the charlotte, with the slices overlapping like the blades of a fan.

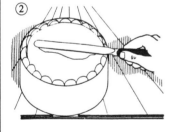

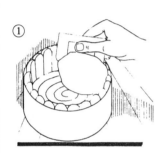

335

7 Serve the charlotte accompanied, if you wish, by a *crème anglaise, coulis de fraise,* or *coulis de framboise*.

Charlotte Poire

To enhance the delicate pear flavor, serve this charlotte with a *sauce au chocolat*.

For 8 to 10 people

INGREDIENTS

About 25 *biscuits à la cuillère* (lady-fingers), piped and baked adjacent to each other (see page 68)

One 8-inch (20 cm) circle of *biscuit à la cuillère* (see page 68)

One 8-inch (20 cm) decorative circle of *biscuit à la cuillère* (see page 68)

2 tablespoons (3 cL) *sirop à trente* (see page 398)

1 large or 2 small poached fresh pears (see page 422)

2 tablespoons (3 cL) syrup reserved from poaching the pears

1 tablespoon (1½ cL) *eau de vie de poire*

1 Place a *vacherin* ring or the ring of a springform pan 8 to 8½ inches (20 to 22 cm) in diameter on a serving plate.

2 Trim both sides of each strip of ladyfingers to make them precisely the height of the ring. Mix the *sirop à trente,* poaching syrup, and *eau de vie de poire,* and brush the backs of the strips of ladyfingers with this pear syrup. Line the inside of the ring with the ladyfingers. Trim the first circle (but not the decorative circle) of *biscuit à la cuillère* to fit neatly inside the ladyfinger-lined ring. Place it inside the ring on the serving plate and brush it with some of the pear syrup.

3 Fill the lined ring about halfway with the *mousse aux poires* and smooth the surface. Cut the poached pear into slices ¼ inch (6 mm) thick and arrange the slices over the *mousse* in the ring. Then add more *mousse* to fill the ring to the top of the ladyfingers. Smooth the top of the *mousse* with your palette knife.

4 Brush the back of the decorative circle of *biscuit à la cuillère* with pear syrup, and place it on top of the charlotte.

5 Refrigerate until the *mousse* is set, at least 3 or 4 hours.

6 When ready to serve, lift off the *vacherin* ring or open and remove the springform.

6 cups (1½ L)
mousse aux poires
(see pages 96–97)
1½ cup (3½ dL)
sauce au chocolat
(see page 128)

7 Serve the charlotte accompanied by the *sauce au chocolat*.

Charlotte Montmorency and Charlotte Citron

Sour cherry and lemon charlottes, respectively, these are greatly enhanced by serving with a sauce—kirsch-flavored *crème anglaise* for sour cherry and *coulis de framboise* or *coulis de fraise* for lemon.

For 8 to 10 people

INGREDIENTS

Two slices of a *joconde*-raspberry jam sandwich (see page 327) 11½ to 12½ inches (29 to 32 cm) long, 2 to 2¼ inches (5 to 5½ cm) high, and ⅜ inch (1 cm) thick

Two 8-inch (20 cm) circles of *biscuit à la cuillère* (see page 68)

1 Place a *vacherin* ring or the ring of a springform pan 8 to 8½ inches (20 to 22 cm) in diameter on a serving plate.

2 Line the inside of the ring with the slices of the *joconde*-jam sandwich. Trim the circles of *biscuit à la cuillère* so they fit neatly inside the lined ring. Place one of the circles inside the ring on the serving plate. Mix the *coulis de cerise, sirop à trente*, and kirsch or the lemon syrup and *sirop à trente*, and brush the bottom circle of *biscuit à la cuillère* and the *joconde*-jam lining with this syrup.

3 Fill the lined ring about halfway with *fruit mousse*. Smooth the surface and place the second circle of *biscuit à la cuillère* on top of this first layer of *mousse*. Brush the *biscuit à la cuillère* with fruit syrup. Then fill the ring to the rim with mousse. Smooth the top of the *mousse* with your palette knife to give the charlotte a flat surface.

CHARLOTTE MONTMORENCY

2 tablespoons (3 cL) *coulis de cerise* (see page 127)

2 tablespoons (3 cL) *sirop à trente* (see page 398)

1 tablespoon (1½ cL) kirsch

6 cups (1½ L) *mousse aux cerises* (see pages 96–97)

3 tablespoons (60 g) cherry jelly

CHARLOTTE CITRON

2 tablespoons (3 cL) lemon syrup (see page 424) mixed with 2 tablespoons (3 cL) water

1 tablespoon (1½ cL) *sirop à trente* (see page 398)

6 cups (1½ L) *mousse au citron* (see page 99)

3 to 4 candied lemon slices (see page 424)

4 Refrigerate until the *mousse* is set, at least 3 to 4 hours.

5 *For charlotte montmorency:* Place the charlotte in the freezer for several hours so you can decorate the top without damaging the surface. Strain the cherry jelly through a fine sieve. Brush the cherry jelly on top of the frozen charlotte until evenly coated and glistening.

For charlotte citron: Cut the candied lemon slices in half and arrange them like a pinwheel on the center of the charlotte.

6 Dip a kitchen towel in hot water, then wring it out. Wrap the hot towel around the outside of the ring briefly to warm the ring so the charlotte won't stick to it. Then wipe the ring dry. Lift off the *vacherin* ring or open and remove the springform. For *charlotte montmorency,* defrost overnight in the refrigerator before serving.

7 Serve the charlotte accompanied, if you wish, by a *crème anglaise* (page 126) flavored with kirsch for a *charlotte montmorency* or a *coulis de framboise* or *coulis de fraise* (page 127) for a *charlotte citron.*

Charlotte Mangue

MANGO CHARLOTTE

A sauce of *crème anglaise* flavored with white rum is the perfect accompaniment to this luxurious charlotte.

For 8 to 10 people

INGREDIENTS

One 9½-inch (24 cm) cylinder, or two 4¾-inch (12 cm) cylinders, of *joconde* rolled with orange marmalade (see page 329)

Melted butter for brushing mold

2 tablespoons (25 g) sugar for dusting mold

2 teaspoons (1 cL) *sirop à trente* (see page 398)

2 teaspoons (1 cL) white rum

6 cups (1½ L) *mousse aux mangues* (see pages 96, 97)

6 to 8 tablespoons (120 to 160 g) strained apricot jam

1 Cut the *joconde*-marmalade cylinder (or cylinders) into twenty-four slices, each about ⅜ inch (1 cm) thick.

2 Brush melted butter over the inside of a layer cake pan 10 inches (25 cm) in diameter and 1½ inches (4 cm) deep or 9 inches (23 cm) in diameter and 2 inches (5 cm) deep. Dust the inside of the mold with sugar. Line the sides of the mold with slices of the *joconde*-marmalade roll, placing the slices adjacent to each other. Arrange the remaining slices over the bottom of the mold.

3 Mix the *sirop à trente* with the white rum and brush the slices lining the mold with this syrup.

4 Fill the lined mold to the rim with *mousse* and smooth the surface with your palette knife.

5 Refrigerate until the *mousse* has set, at least 3 or 4 hours.

6 Cut a cardboard cake-decorating circle (see page 383 for details and sources) to the size of the base of the charlotte. Place the cake-decorating circle upside down over the mold and invert the circle and mold together to unmold the charlotte onto the cake decorating circle. Place the *charlotte* on a wire rack.

7 Warm the apricot jam over low heat, stirring occasionally, until melted. Brush the entire outside surface of the charlotte with jam until lightly coated and glistening ①. Transfer the charlotte to a serving plate.

8 Serve the charlotte accompanied, if you wish, by a *crème anglaise* (page 126) flavored with white rum.

Chapter Thirteen

EQUIPMENT

This is more than just another book of pastry recipes. Our goal is to teach you how to make elegant French pastries with skill and efficiency in an American home kitchen. Having the right equipment and knowing how to use it is the first step in achieving that objective, and will make the time you spend in the kitchen that much more enjoyable.

We are well aware that few American home kitchens (and even fewer French ones) are equipped with the classic tools of the pastry chef's art. Consequently, we have kept to a minimum the number of special-purpose tools needed to follow our recipes. The French tools we do use are explained in this chapter, and we list sources for the ones that may be particularly hard to find.

There is also a wealth of American baking equipment that can be utilized in the preparation of French pastry. Since you are much more likely to have American equipment at hand, we have sought out the very best American products available and will explain how to use them to make French pastries. To our delight, some of the American alternatives we have discovered are equal or superior to their French counterparts.

Some of the most important sections of this chapter concern electrical appliances. While this book had its origin in a professional pastry kitchen, with great banks of deck ovens and huge mixing, kneading, whipping, and rolling machines, we have redesigned our recipes and methods from scratch using domestic appliances. Every recipe was tested on a GE electric range in Bruce's kitchen, and we can say without hesitation that the pastries you bake at home can be every bit as good as they would be if made in the finest pastry kitchen in Paris. We have experimented with a variety of convection ovens, electric mixers, food processors, blenders, and even a unique ventilator hood with infrared heat lamps in search of ways to make home pastry making easier. We will tell you about the appliances we found most valuable and explain how to use them.

Ovens

The most central and absolutely indispensable piece of equipment for pastry making is the oven. Indeed, it is such an obvious necessity that we often take it

343

for granted. But understanding how different types of ovens work makes it possible to use the one you have to best advantage.

Deck Ovens

The ovens used at Pâtisserie Clichy and most of the other great French pastry shops are deck ovens. These are ideal for baking in a professional kitchen, but they have no place in the home kitchen because they are big, expensive, and slow to heat and cool. We include them only to enlarge your perspective of what ovens are all about.

There are no racks in the traditional deck oven. The baking sheets sit directly on the oven floor, which may be steel or fire brick. This gives strong, direct, and immediate bottom heat to pastries baked in it.

Roasting Ovens

The range or wall oven in your home kitchen is a roasting oven. It is heated from the bottom, by either an electric element inside the oven cavity or a gas element beneath the oven floor. Heat is circulated within the oven cavity by radiation (the invisible infrared light waves emitted from the heating element and the hot oven floor and walls) and natural convection (air circulation produced by pressure differences between air masses at different temperatures). The predominant direction of heat flow is up, with the hottest air at the top of the oven.

Electric and gas ovens heat somewhat differently. An electric heating element gets much hotter than a gas flame. As a result, there is relatively more heat conduction by radiation and less by convection in an electric oven than in a gas oven, and the electric oven preheats more quickly.

When cooking in a roasting oven, the food is placed on wire racks, which can be positioned at several heights. The height of the rack in the oven and the position of the food on the rack both affect how the food will cook. For proper air circulation, there must always be at least 1 to 1½ inches (2½ to 4 cm) of air space between the walls of the oven and anything you put in it. Placing food closer to the oven walls would force air currents to travel past the edge of the food more quickly, which has the same effect as a higher temperature and cooks the edge of the food more rapidly.

It is usually desirable to bake on one of the middle rack positions, where the oven heat is most even. But, for browning the tops of pastries quickly, it is better to use one of the top rack positions, where the air in the oven is hottest. If your oven bakes unevenly, it helps to rotate the pastries half way through the baking period.

While most home ovens are equipped with two racks, it is rarely a good idea to bake on both simultaneously. Heat circulation in the horizontal direction is very poor in a roasting oven. So, if you position pastries one above the other, the top of the pastry on the upper rack and the bottom of the pastry on the lower rack will cook quickly, but there won't be enough heat circulation between them; so the bottom of the upper pastry and the top of the lower pastry will cook slowly. On the occasions when the limits of your oven capacity make it necessary to bake on two racks at once, you can partially compensate for the unevenness by switching the pastries between the upper and lower racks several times during the baking period.

Self-cleaning ovens have two advantages for pastry making. These ovens are called "pyrolytic" because they use a very high heat cycle to vaporize foods (including sugar syrups) baked on the oven walls. The intense heat requires much better insulation than is used in conventional ovens, and as a fringe benefit this makes self-cleaning ovens bake more evenly and preheat faster.

In contrast to self-cleaning ovens, continuous-cleaning ovens have no particular advantage for pastry making. Continuous-cleaning ovens have porous walls with a catalytic treatment designed to burn off fats at ordinary baking temperatures. However, this does nothing to remove baked-in sugar syrups, and continuous-cleaning ovens don't have the extra insulation that makes self-cleaning ovens bake better.

One big difference between home wall ovens and range ovens is their size. The oven cavity on our GE range will accommodate a 13 × 20-inch (33 × 50 cm) baking sheet or a "half-size," 13 × 18-inch (33 × 45 cm), jelly-roll pan. A typical self-cleaning wall oven will accommodate a 12 × 16-inch (30 × 40 cm) baking sheet but not the larger size pans. For pastries such as sheet cakes, where the size of the baking sheet is a determining factor, we give recipes appropriate to both range ovens and wall ovens.

Restaurant Ranges

Occasionally restaurant ranges are used in home kitchens. The ovens in restaurant ranges are also roasting ovens, and their only advantage over domestic ovens for baking pastries is their larger size—they are designed to accommodate a "full-size" 18 × 26-inch (45 × 66 cm) jelly-roll pan. However, no commercial manufacturer makes a self-cleaning (pyrolytic) oven, and the oven doors on restaurant ranges aren't sealed nearly so well as those on domestic self-cleaning models. In our experience, a good self-cleaning electric oven such as our GE bakes more evenly than the roasting ovens on restaurant ranges.

Convection Ovens

A convection oven is altogether different from both deck and roasting ovens. Its distinctive feature is a fan that circulates the air in the oven cavity. This forced convection evens out the heat and makes it possible to bake on several oven racks at a time. Thus the advantage of a convection oven is that it gives a larger baking capacity for a given amount of space.

A convection oven also bakes differently from other ovens. The circulating air operates like a wind chill factor in reverse, depositing heat on the food more quickly than does the radiant heat and natural convection in a roasting oven. We found that, when baking pastries in a convection oven, the temperature should be lowered by 25° to 50° F (15° to 30° C) compared with what you would use in a roasting oven. Precisely how much the temperature should be lowered depends both on the particular convection oven (especially the power of the fan) and what you are baking. Sometimes the baking time may also be reduced.

Another difference is that a convection oven heats the top and bottom of the food uniformly and does not naturally provide bottom heat. For pastries such as brioches and feuilletés, a strong initial bottom heat is important. The way to get it in a convection oven is to preheat the oven 50° F (30° C) above the baking temperature with a heavy baking sheet in the oven; then reduce the oven temperature when you place the pastry on the baking sheet.

When baking in a convection oven, always use the smallest possible baking sheets in order to minimize obstruction of the air circulation.

COUNTERTOP MODELS: About half a dozen manufacturers make countertop convection ovens for home use, and these can provide a very convenient way to expand your baking capacity without taking up too much space. All are smaller than a home wall oven but can bake on two racks simultaneously. We have used two models that should give you an idea of the results you can expect.

The Rival Model 4021 convection oven has one of the largest oven cavities of any countertop model. It will accommodate a 12 × 16-inch (30 × 40 cm) baking sheet in a pinch, but if you want to use both racks simultaneously you should stick to a 10 × 14-inch (25 × 35 cm) baking sheet or molded pastries without baking sheets. We found that the oven bakes evenly across each rack. The heating element and fan are at the top of the oven, so, not surprisingly, pastries baked on the upper rack tend to cook a little more quickly than those on the lower rack. The thermostat dial is continuously adjustable from ''off'' up to 475° F (245° C). By choosing a very low setting (below ''warm''), you can use the Rival as a proofing oven for leavened pastry doughs and for defrosting frozen components quickly.

The Moulin-Air Model CTC-400 convection oven has a smaller oven cavity but includes a conventional broiling element, which is useful for glazing pastries with sugar. The fan and heating element are located on the left-hand side, and, while pastries baked on two racks cook identically, there is a tendency for pastries on the left side of the oven to cook faster than those on the right. To compensate, the baking sheet holding the pastries should be rotated halfway through the baking period. The thermostat has settings from a low "defrost" up to 400° F (200° C), and this oven can also be used for proofing yeast doughs.

In using countertop convection ovens for proofing leavened pastry doughs, note that this should be done only with unmolded dough in a bowl covered with a damp kitchen towel. Do not proof molded pastries in a convection oven because the air flow will dehydrate the surface of the pastry.

PROFESSIONAL CONVECTION OVENS: There are many commercial convection ovens on the market, but even a standard "half-size" convection oven is a bit large for most home kitchens. We did find one, the Market Forge Model 2200 Compact Convection Oven, which is ideal for home pastry baking. It is comparable in size to a small home wall oven, yet the oven cavity holds three racks, each large enough to accommodate a 13 x 20-inch (33 x 50 cm) baking sheet. The oven has five heating elements and a heavy duty squirrel-cage fan, providing uniform heat and making it possible to bake on three racks simultaneously with nearly identical results. That gives it three to four times the capacity of a home wall oven, triple the capacity of a home range oven, and 50 percent more capacity than a restaurant range oven. And if you are baking pastries for a moderate-size party or to stock your freezer with components, that much capacity is easy to use.

About Oven Temperature, Preheating, and Baking Times

Since oven temperature is important in baking pastries, you should check your oven themostat every couple of months with an oven thermometer. If it is inaccurate, either have it corrected or adjust the oven setting when you bake to get the temperature called for in the recipe.

Whatever type of oven you use, it should always be preheated for baking pastries. When you open the oven door to place the pastries inside, the temperature will drop, and even a well-insulated oven will take a minute or so to come back up to the thermostat setting. For pastries such as brioches and *feuilletés*, which depend on quick initial heat, you should compensate by preheating the oven to 25° F (15° C) above the baking temperature, then lowering the thermostat when you load the oven. We have included this step in the recipes where it is most important, but even for other pastries it is a good procedure to follow.

Oven type and temperature are just two of many factors that affect the way pastries bake. Some others are the material and surface of your bakeware (bright and shiny aluminum or dull black steel), humidity, altitude, the thickness of your pastry (did you roll that dough ⅛ inch thick, or was it 3/32 or 5/32?), and the position in the oven cavity. The baking temperatures we give in our recipes have worked for us under a wide range of conditions in Boulder, New Haven, and Paris. However, the baking time for any given pastry can vary, depending on the factors we have just mentioned. Consequently, we have given precise visual and manual tests to determine when pastries are finished baking, and a range of baking times during which you should be testing the pastry.

Cooktops

Most professionals prefer gas burners to electric because gas responds instantly, whereas electric burners heat and cool more slowly. Thus, when cooking on an electric burner, you must anticipate more and adjust the heat before you actually need the change; or you can reduce the heat reaching the saucepan by lifting it and holding it above the surface of the burner. This is especially important when you are cooking sugar or a delicate custard such as a *crème anglaise*.

One nice feature available on restaurant ranges is an option called a "hot-top section." This is a thick sheet of steel with a heating element underneath that replaces a pair of open burners. Hot-top sections respond slowly to temperature changes, but they provide a very even heat, which can be a big advantage if your saucepan is less than ideal. And the single large cooking surface will accommodate oversize pots or several small pots—great when you need to gently heat small amounts of several components and ingredients in putting together an elaborate pastry. The open gas burners on some restaurant ranges also provide a more even heat distribution than those on most domestic cooktops, but, on the negative side, they are larger than the bottoms of many saucepans and don't have pilotless ignition, so they can waste heat.

We found only one cooktop, a four-burner model with broiler and griddle from Chambers, that combines the advantages of domestic and commercial cooktops. Like the best commercial cooktops, the Chambers has cast-iron gas burners with more holes and a more even heat distribution than conventional aluminum ring burners. We found that the thick aluminum griddle on the Chambers cooktop can be used in exactly the same way as a hot-top section. In contrast to the commercial models, it has electronic pilotless ignition and the right size burners for most domestic pots and pans. So it heats the kitchen less, which, as you will see later, is important for pastry making.

Broilers and Salamanders

Pastries can be glazed with sugar, using either the broiler on your roasting oven or a salamander.

A salamander is a small iron disk attached to a long handle. It is the best tool for glazing because it allows you to glaze the top of the pastry without burning the crust. The iron disc of the salamander is heated on your cooktop or with a more intense heat source. If possible it should be heated until red hot. You won't be able to get it that hot on a domestic cooktop, but your fireplace or outdoor barbecue could do the trick. When the salamander is as hot as you can get it, sprinkle the top of the pastry with granulated sugar and "iron" or pat the sugar with the salamander to caramelize the sugar. Reheat the salamander as often as necessary and scrape it on your burner grate to remove charred sugar.
Sources: Lamalle, Bridge, and La Cuisine.

Caramelizing sugar generates smoke. A red-hot salamander will ignite the smoke, making the sugar burn cleanly. But if the iron isn't red hot, you must have good ventilation to eliminate the smoke quickly.

If you don't have a salamander and are using your broiler, the pastry should be dusted with confectioners sugar rather than granulated sugar. The glazing should be done as quickly as possible, to avoid burning the crust of the pastry.

The Kitchen Environment

By controlling and utilizing the temperatures within your kitchen environment, you can make pastry making much easier.

First there is the overall kitchen temperature. While most home cooks feel quite comfortable at 70° to 75° F (21° to 24° C), that is above the melting point of butterfat and is far from ideal for working with pastry doughs. In the traditional French pastry kitchen, the *tours* station, where pastry doughs are prepared, rolled out, and molded, is in the basement and is kept at about 57° F (14° C). At that temperature, butter never melts and is always near the ideal temperature at which it just begins to soften. You probably aren't ready for that extreme, but the point is the cooler the kitchen the better.

A natural consequence of cooking is heat, and the first step in controlling the overall kitchen temperature is to get the heat out of the kitchen quickly. The way to do that is with a kitchen ventilator hood. If you live in an apartment, you may have to put up with a ventilator that merely filters and recirculates the air. But, given the choice, you should have over your cooktop a ventilator hood with an exterior exhaust. The hot air generated by cooking is contained under the canopy and drawn out through a filter, which traps steam and grease.

Be sure that the fan of your ventilator is powerful enough to do the job. A small fan drawing 300 cubic feet per minute (cfm) might be fine if you are baking a single cake layer in midwinter but totally inadequate if you are using four burners and your oven all afternoon on a summer day or creating smoke by glazing the sugar on a tarte with a salamander. The Thermidor ventilator we use is one of the most powerful domestic units on the market, drawing nearly 1,000 cfm and removing heat and smoke before they can accumulate. To keep kitchen noise to a minimum, have the ventilator unit mounted on the roof or exterior wall of the house.

Once you are in a position to remove the heat your cooking produces, you can adjust your thermostat to a temperature you feel comfortable with. If you want to bake in hot summer weather, you might also consider utilizing an air conditioner. No one, not even a skilled professional, has an easy time making pastries when the kitchen temperature gets above 80° F (27° C).

So far we have concentrated on the overall kitchen temperature, but within your kitchen environment there are many microclimates that you can use to advantage.

A professional pastry chef will melt chocolate by putting it near the oven door, where the heat is gentle, free, and always available. When you are cooking at home, a naturally warm place is above the range or cooktop. That space, just below the ventilator hood, is usually wasted. But the Thermidor "Keep Hot" hood we use takes advantage of it. This hood has infrared heat lamps mounted in the hood canopy and a pair of wire racks that fold down from a backsplash mounted on the wall below the canopy itself. It is intended for keeping foods (such as your breakfast croissants and brioches) hot before serving. We have found that, with the heat lamps off, the wire racks make a convenient spot for proofing leavened pastry doughs while other cooking is going on. And turning the heat lamps on provides a gentle, even heat that is perfect for melting chocolate, fondant, butter, and jam.

Here are some other places where you might look for temperature variations in your kitchen. The top of your refrigerator should be slightly warm and could be just right for proofing yeast doughs. If you have a gas oven with a pilot light, you could put chocolate in it overnight to melt. In winter, a countertop near an exterior door or window could become a good spot for preparing pastry doughs. Every kitchen is different, so get out a thermometer and explore.

Work Surfaces

Marble is an ideal work surface for pastry making. It is hard, durable, smooth, and nonporous. Most important, it is cool, which is really a shorthand way of saying that it has a high thermal mass and thus isn't easily warmed by the heat transferred from objects touching it. So when you roll out a pastry dough on marble, the marble absorbs the heat generated by the rolling process and both the marble and the dough stay cool. Also, when you pour hot sugar syrup onto marble to make fondant, the syrup cools very quickly.

Unfortunately, few of us have the luxury of marble countertops in our home kitchens. Plastic laminates are the customary alternative since they are also smooth and nonporous, though they lack marble's coolness.

For the occasions when the coolness of marble plays an especially important role, you can get a portable marble slab. The slab should be ¾ to 1 inch (2 to 2½ cm) thick and as large as you can conveniently handle. We find an 18 × 24-inch (45 × 60 cm) slab about right. Much smaller than that and it is too small for most tasks; and a much larger slab would require bringing in helpers whenever you want to move it. **Source:** Ranier Devido.

If you have a portable marble slab, you might chill it in the refrigerator before making fondant to speed the cooling process. For rolling pastry doughs, lightly chilling the marble can also be good. But the marble should not be more than 15° to 20° F (8° to 12° C) below room temperature or it can produce condensation, making your dough stick to the marble.

Marble and plastic laminates are good for everything but cutting boards. Don't use them for chopping, slicing, and other types of cutting because the blades of your knives will dull quickly. For those tasks, use a butcher-block cutting board. Conversely, you shouldn't roll out pastry doughs, *pâte d'amandes,* or *nougatine* or work with chocolate or fondant on the porous surface of your butcher block.

Rolling Pins

A good rolling pin should be straight and smooth, to roll pastry doughs into sheets of uniform thickness, and heavy, so its weight does some of the work of flattening the dough for you. The cylinder of the rolling pin can be made of hardwood, marble, or steel, and it may or may not have handles attached to each end. Which material and style you choose depends both on personal preference and the task for which it is used. A long cylinder is preferable to a short one for rolling out large sheets of dough.

A hardwood rolling pin should be made of a tight-grained wood that won't absorb moisture or fats. It should never be washed, since that can distort the grain of the wood. Just wipe the cylinder clean with a dry paper towel. However, after rolling out *feuilletage* on sugar, it will be necessary to wash the rolling pin, so for that purpose a marble or steel rolling pin, or an old wood one that you no longer value, is the tool to use.

The Rouleau

The classic French-style rolling pin is a cylinder of hardwood about 20 inches (50 cm) long and 2 inches (5 cm) in diameter, with smoothly rounded ends. It has no handles. Boxwood is considered best because it is both very tight-grained and heavy. Beechwood is a good second choice. This type of rolling pin is versatile and easy to maneuver. It gives you a better feeling for the dough you are rolling than does a larger and heavier rolling pin, but it requires you to supply most of the muscle. **Sources:** Lamalle, Dean & DeLuca, BIA Cordon Bleu, and La Cuisine.

The Thorpe

The Thorpe Rolling Pin Company makes what is generally conceded to be the finest professional version of the standard American rolling pin. A Thorpe rolling pin has a large, heavy, and very smooth hardwood cylinder that spins smoothly on ball bearings around a steel shaft down the center. Long hardwood handles are attached to both ends of the shaft. The smooth ball-bearing action and perfect balance of these rolling pins enable you easily to flatten your dough into an even thickness without tearing. Thorpe makes them in many sizes. For general purposes, we recommend a rolling pin with a cylinder 3 inches (7½ cm) in diameter and 15 inches (38 cm) long, or one 18 inches (45 cm) long if you have plenty of counter space. For rolling *pâtes feuilletées*, the weight of an even heavier cylinder, 3½ inches (9 cm) in diameter is an advantage, and again we suggest the longest cylinder you can use on your counter—either the 15-inch (38 cm) Bakers' Special or the 18-inch (45 cm) Master Baker.

The Devido

Marble is often touted as an ideal material for rolling pins because it is heavy and has a high thermal mass, which makes it stay cool. Unfortunately, most marble rolling pins seem to be designed more as ornaments than serious kitchen tools. We turned up only one exception. The Devido is to other marble rolling pins as the Thorpe is to a supermarket-variety wood model. The one we use has a marble cylinder 12 inches (30 cm) long and 3 inches (7½ cm) in diameter, and it weighs 8½ pounds (3.8 kg). It is constructed in much the same way as the Thorpe, with ball bearings, a stainless-steel shaft and long solid-walnut handles. In our experience, the Devido is the best rolling pin for making sheets of *pâte d'amandes* and *chocolat plastique*. Its weight and polished surface make it ideal for both the turns and the final rolling of *pâtes feuilletées*, and it is without equal for rolling *feuilletage* on sugar. The Devido is also outstanding for rolling all other types of pastry doughs. **Source:** Ranier Devido.

The Tutové

The Tutové is designed for doing the turns on *pâtes feuilletées*. It is constructed like the Thorpe, but its 16-inch (40 cm) hardwood cylinder is covered with a thick skin of longitudinally ribbed plastic. The ribbing reminds us of the old Armstrong Tire commercials—it ''grips'' the dough. The Tutové is also fairly heavy, and the weight and ribbing make it the best choice for its admittedly limited purpose. Do not use it for the final rolling of the *pâte feuilletée* or for other rolling tasks, since it would produce an unwanted bumpy surface. **Source:** Kitchen Glamor.

Steel Rolling Pins

While a steel rolling pin is intended primarily for rolling out *nougatine*, it is also excellent for pastry doughs, *pâte d'amandes,* and anything else. It is just a length of steel pipe, which you can have cut at your local hardware store or steel yard. We use a piece of stainless-steel pipe 20 inches (50 cm) long and 2 inches (5 cm) in diameter, but it could just as well be ordinary steel if you season it with oil to prevent rust. The heavier the pipe, the better.

Knives

Traditionally, professional chefs have preferred carbon steel knives, which are easy to keep sharp but pit and rust easily. Stainless-steel knives avoid those problems but are more difficult to sharpen. A modern alloy called ''high carbon stainless'' combines the virtues of both, and we think knives made from this metal are the best for home use. In our opinion, the finest high carbon stainless knives are made in West Germany by Wüsthof-Trident and F. Dick.

Here is the basic set of knives we recommend for pastry making:

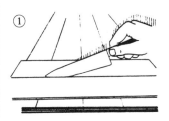

Chef's Knife

You will use this for chopping (almonds and chocolate, for example) and for cutting sheets of pastry doughs, as well as for an assortment of slicing and trimming jobs ①. We suggest a 10-inch (25 cm) blade to give long, straight cuts; and the blade should be wide and heavy enough that its weight does the work of chopping for you.

Bread Knife

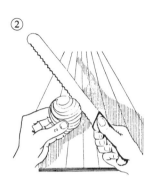

This should have a wavy or scalloped edge with sharp, pronounced teeth to give you a good purchase on delicate cake layers and leavened pastries and for sawing through fragile flaky pastry layers without shattering them ②. Since you want to be able to slice through at least a 9-inch (23 cm) round of *génoise* in one cut, we recommend a blade 10 to 12 inches (25 to 30 cm) long. The shape of the tip of the blade doesn't matter, so you can equally well use a true bread knife or a scalloped-edge slicing knife with pointed or rounded tip.

Paring Knife

This is used as a decorating tool and for cutting fruits. The point of the blade is used to pierce and score pastries before baking and for cutting circles of pastry dough. A short blade—3 to 3½ inches (7½ to 9 cm)—gives you the most control ③.

Slicing Knife

A slender slicing knife is used when the width of the chef's knife blade would produce too much drag and a bread knife won't give a clean cut—for example, in slicing lemons. An 8-inch (20 cm) long blade is good for most purposes.

Sharpening Steel

You need something to keep those edges razor sharp. We prefer a 12- to 14-inch (30 to 35 cm) sharpening steel, but we have found that many of our students don't feel comfortable with it. A good alternative is a small ceramic sharpener such as Forschner's 3-inch (8 cm) ceramic sharpening steel, which you stroke across the blade rather than vice versa. Whichever sharpener you choose, use it regularly.

Tarte Knife

Both Wüsthof-Trident and F. Dick make knives specifically designed for cutting tartes and *gâteaux*. The symmetrical, wedge-shaped blades have two cutting edges, one honed and the other serrated. These go beyond the basics, but we include them because they are the best implements we know for serving French pastries.

Measuring Tools

French pastry demands more precision than any other area of cooking. The tools you use to measure quantities and temperatures should be accurate and appropriate to what you are measuring.

Scales and Balances

A kitchen scale or balance is the best device for measuring out dry ingredients and most pastry components.

Two mechanisms are employed in kitchen balances—the spring and the balance beam. Spring balances are inherently less reliable than beam balances. If the spring is distorted by a sudden jolt, it can't be recalibrated. Most of the inexpensive kitchen scales are of this type, but there are also some well-constructed spring balances. Some of the best are made by Terraillon.

A beam balance is a much more sensible weighing device, since it depends only on the incorruptible principle of the lever. Professional bakers use an equal arm balance with a flat plate on each side, one to hold ingredients and the other for the balance weights. The weights are graduated in 1-pound (454 g) intervals, and a brass beam is used to divide each pound (454 g) into ¼-ounce (7 g) increments. While most of these scales are rather large and heavy for home use, Penn Scale makes a small, 6-pound (2.7 kg) capacity counter scale of the same design that is fine for home pastry making. **Source:** Penn Scale Mfg. Co.

Perhaps the best kitchen scale is the Terraillon double beam balance. It has a 7 × 12-inch (17 × 31 cm) tray across the top of the scale to hold ingredients and a more complicated system of levers than the single beam balance. The second beam takes the place of the balance weights. The Terraillon is especially good for small quantities since it measures in units of 1 gram, and it can also measure weights up to 22 pounds (10 kg). **Source:** Kitchen Bazaar.

While there are less expensive kitchen scales on the market, many are unreliable. So when purchasing a kitchen scale, try it first to be sure it has the sensitivity to measure at least to the nearest ¼ ounce (7 g) and that it does so consistently.

Measuring Cups and Spoons

Liquids are customarily measured by volume. Measuring cups for liquids should be clear glass or plastic so you can see the level of the liquid through the cup.

Dry ingredients such as sugar can be measured in dry measure cups. These are normally employed only for the American system, not the metric system. They are usually made of metal and are filled above the top, then levelled off at the rim to get the volume of the cup.

A set of measuring spoons is indispensable for measuring small amounts of both liquids and dry ingredients. Much as we like the accuracy of weighing dry ingredients, there is no particular advantage to measuring say 1 teaspoon (4 g) of salt by weight when a measuring spoon is available.

Thermometers

Temperature plays an important role in many areas of pastry making, and here again accuracy is important. For example, if melted chocolate is a couple of degrees too warm when used for glazing, it will lose its sheen and become streaked with gray. Even professionals who are adept at judging temperatures by visual or manual tests frequently resort to thermometers when precision is crucial.

Mercury thermometers are the most accurate. The inexpensive glass thermometers filled with a black or red liquid aren't nearly so reliable.

Dial thermometers measure temperature by the relative expansion of two metals. While not quite so accurate as mercury, they are sometimes more convenient. Small instant-reading ones allow you to check temperatures quickly without leaving the thermometer in the food while it cooks.

Top-quality thermometers in sizes and temperature ranges suitable for every kitchen task are made by Taylor; they are widely available and can be obtained by mail order from Maid of Scandinavia.

OVEN THERMOMETERS: Since oven thermostats are not necessarily accurate, the only way to be certain of your baking temperature is to use an oven thermometer. A mercury thermometer on a stainless steel stand that can sit or hang on an oven rack is both convenient and reliable.

CANDY THERMOMETERS: Unless you are really expert at judging the temperature of sugar syrups by feel, a candy thermometer is a must. Forget the dime-store variety with big clumsy dials. The best is a mercury thermometer on a stainless steel backing. Taylor's twelve-inch-long confectionery/deep-fry thermometer is calibrated in $2°$ F ($1°$ C) divisions and will give an accurate reading for even a small quantity of syrup. Choose the size of your pot according to the quantity of syrup so the level of syrup is sufficient to cover the bulb of the thermometer.

CHOCOLATE THERMOMETERS: When tempering chocolate, you must have the correct temperature at each stage of the process. Just right for this purpose is Taylor's instant-reading Bi-Therm thermometer with a stem 5 inches (13 cm) long and a 1-inch (2½ cm) dial that measures from 25° to 125° F (−4° to 52° C) in 2° F (1° C) divisions.

DOUGH THERMOMETERS: The temperature of butter determines its consistency, which in turn is important in preparing pastry doughs; and leavened pastry doughs rise best within a narrow temperature range. For measuring the temperatures of butter and pastry doughs, the same instant-reading thermometer we recommended for chocolate is excellent. For even more accuracy Taylor makes what it calls its Pocket Dough Test Thermometer, with a mercury-filled glass tube, 6 inches (15 cm) long, calibrated in 1° F (0.5° C) divisions from 60° to 100° F (16° to 38° C).

Rulers and Straightedges

A ruler is valuable both for measuring sizes and for cutting straight edges on sheets of pastry dough and cake layers. We suggest an aluminum or stainless-steel ruler 18 inches (45 cm) in length as the most convenient and durable.

Sifters, Tamis, and Dredges

These are all tools for sifting and dusting dry ingredients, though the tamis can also be used as a strainer.

Sifters

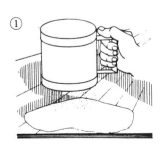

The flour sifter is a hollow metal cylinder with a handle, a wire screen across the bottom, and some sort of agitator ①. The models with more than one screen sift slowly and are difficult to clean. The best and most durable type of agitator is a wire rotor that is turned by a crank. The screen is contoured to the rotor, so it is effective in sifting flour quickly.

When making pastry doughs, you will often be sifting large quantities of flour. A professional baker's flour sifter will hold up to 3 pounds (1,350 g) of flour and minimize the number of times you must refill the sifter. **Source:** Maid of Scandinavia.

Never wash your flour sifter, since water makes the flour congeal on the wire screen in glutenous lumps. Just shake out the sifter and wipe it clean with a dry paper towel.

Always sift flour and other powdered ingredients onto a large sheet of kitchen paper so you can use the paper as a funnel for pouring (see Papers, page 382).

Tamis

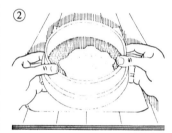

The alternative to the flour sifter is the tamis. This is a drum-shaped sieve with the mesh stretched across a wood or metal frame ②. Various types of mesh are available. For sifting flour you want a coarse metal screen. To sift with the tamis, place your hands on opposite sides of the frame with your fingertips underneath. The frame should rest loosely on your fingertips. Bounce the tamis back and forth between your palms to agitate the flour and sift it through. A coarse-screened tamis is also valuable for sifting ground almonds.

Tamis with fine brass and nylon meshes are used for other purposes—brass for dusting confectioners sugar and nylon for straining fruits and vegetables. These meshes are usually too fine for sifting flour effectively.

In choosing a tamis, the best size to get is about 12 inches (30 cm) in diameter. The French wood-framed ones are lightweight and inexpensive. **Sources:** Lamalle and Bridge.

After sifting with a tamis, it should be cleaned in the same way as a flour sifter—by shaking it out and wiping the frame with a dry paper towel. If you use it for sifting ground almonds, you will have to scrub it occasionally with a nylon brush and hot water to keep the mesh around the frame clean.

Dredges

A dredge is a metal shaker with a perforated lid ③. We use it for dusting confectioners sugar and cocoa powder. To dust with a dredge, shake it horizontally

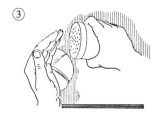

③ and at the same time tilt it. Do not invert the dredge or too much will come out.

Mixing Bowls

A collection of mixing bowls in various sizes is essential for pastry making. For most purposes, stainless steel is the best material. It is durable and lightweight, it doesn't interact with foods, and it transmits changes in temperature quickly. The latter property is important when, for example, you want to warm or chill a filling or topping to get the right consistency for spreading.

In addition to a set of stainless-steel mixing bowls you may want to invest in a copper bowl for whipping egg whites. It should have a rounded bottom and gently sloping sides for most effective whipping with a wire whisk. Never use this bowl for any other purpose. To keep the unlined copper clean, before each time you use it, toss in some coarse kosher salt and vinegar and wipe it around with a sponge or paper towel to remove oxidation on the copper. Then rinse out the bowl and dry it thoroughly. After whipping your egg whites, wash the bowl in hot sudsy water, rinse well, and dry thoroughly. Do not use harsh abrasive or caustic cleaners, which could stain or pit the copper.

Mixing Tools

For mixing ingredients you need a small battery of hand tools—wooden spoons, wire whisks, rubber spatulas, pastry cornes, and dough scrapers. Each implement is best suited to a particular group of tasks, and, even if you have an electric mixer, you will have occasion to use all of them.

Wooden Spoons

The wooden spoon is ideal for a wide variety of mixing functions, from the heavy-duty tasks of mixing thick batters and creaming butter to more delicate ones, such as stirring *crème anglaise* or apricot jam over the heat without incorporating air bubbles. Wooden spoons have numerous advantages. They are strong, lightweight, and won't damage the tin linings of your copper pots.

Like your rolling pin, they should be made of a tight-grained hardwood—boxwood or beechwood—and should never be soaked in water. The shape we find most useful is really not a spoon at all but a flat wooden paddle or spatula. For heavy mixing, a wooden spoon 14 to 16 inches (35 to 40 cm) long and 2 inches (5 cm) wide at the broadest part of the paddle is a good size, and it must be strong enough to transmit the full force of your right arm without breaking. The same shape is also useful in smaller lengths, down to about 8 inches (20 cm). **Sources:** Lamalle, La Cuisine, and BIA Cordon Bleu.

Wire Whisks

While a wooden spoon is great for mixing and beating ingredients to make them smooth, it is not effective for whipping cream or eggs to incorporate air. For that you need a wire whisk, preferably in two or three sizes for whipping both small and large quantities. The whisk should have many thin, flexible wires arching up from the handle to enclose a space shaped like an incandescent light bulb. Whisks 12 to 16 inches (30 to 40 cm) in length are about right for the quantities of cream and eggs you are likely to whip in a home kitchen, and the wire loops should be 3 to 4 inches (8 to 10 cm) across at the widest point. If you have a heavy-duty electric mixer, then you can get along fine with just the smallest of these sizes.

For some heavy stirring and beating you can also use a whisk, but the thin wires of the whipping whisk are too delicate. Here you want one with a smaller number of stronger, less flexible wires; a 10- to 12-inch (25 to 30 cm) size is about right. Use this whisk instead of a wooden spoon when rapid mixing is essential to keep the mixture smooth (as in making *crème pâtissière*) or to lighten the mixture by beating in a little air (in creaming butter for example).

Resist the temptation to use batter whisks for mixing small quantities of very heavy batters or you will end up with all of the batter inside the whisk. And never use a whisk when it is important that you don't work the batter too much, as in making *pâte à choux*. A wooden spoon is the better implement for these purposes.

Rubber Spatulas

Because a wooden spoon is rigid, it isn't effective for scraping mixtures from the sides of bowls. So for folding together delicate ingredients and for emptying a bowl of batter, a rubber spatula is a better tool. The blade of the rubber spatula should be flexible, so it will conform to the contours of a round-bottomed bowl. The spatulas made by Rubbermaid Professional are by far the best ones we know.

Folding is a method of combining two mixtures, one of which is fragile. The fragile element is most frequently whipped cream or eggs. If the other mixture is a heavy batter, you should first stir about one third of the fragile mixture into the batter, mixing thoroughly to lighten it. Then scoop the rest of the fragile mixture on top and begin the folding operation: Insert the edge of the spatula blade in the center of the bowl and cut down vertically to the bottom. Turn the blade horizontally and move it toward you across the bottom of the bowl. Finally bring the blade up to lift the batter from underneath onto the top. The motion is roughly circular. Rotate the bowl and repeat this motion. Continue, working gently so you don't deflate the fragile component, until the two mixtures are thoroughly blended and homogeneous.

To fold a dry ingredient into the fragile component, the motion is the same, but the dry ingredient should be dusted or sprinkled over the fragile one either as you are doing the folding or by alternately dusting and folding. If you add a large amount of the dry ingredient at once it tends to lump, and you end up deflating the mixture before you get it smooth.

Pastry Cornes

A corne is a rubber spatula without the handle. The name derives from the fact that in the old days they were made from the horns of animals, but the modern ones are plastic or nylon.

While you won't use it for folding, the corne is really superior to the rubber spatula for scooping up ingredients or batters in measured quantity, for scraping out bowls, and for smoothing fillings and toppings.

A pastry corne should have sharp edges and measure about 4½ to 5¾ inches (12 to 14½ cm) wide by 3¾ inches (9½ cm) high. One long edge should be curved for scooping and scraping, the other flat for smoothing. Large inexpensive plastic ones are sold in restaurant supply shops. Smaller and stiffer nylon ones are usually imported and more expensive, but they are better for scraping out small to medium-size bowls. Some suppliers may refer to pastry cornes as bowl or dough scrapers. **Sources:** Maid of Scandinavia, Dean & DeLuca, La Cuisine, and Nussex.

Dough Scrapers

The baker's dough scraper is a dull, flat, rectangular steel blade with a handle across one long side. You may not think of it as a mixing tool, but that is one of its most important functions. You will use it to lift, scrape, push, and stir as you mix pastry doughs, smooth and cream butter, and work fondant, to name just a few. Of course you will also use it as a cutting tool for dividing pastry doughs and blocks of butter into smaller pieces, and for scraping your countertop clean.

Choose a dough scraper with a 6 × 3-inch (15 × 7½ cm) stainless-steel blade. The handle can be wood, plastic, or a rolled steel extension of the blade itself.

Kitchen Machines

Electric mixers, food processors, and blenders have the potential to perform some of the most laborious kitchen work and eliminate drudgery.

Electric Mixers

With rare exceptions there are only two basic mechanisms used for electric mixers, the eggbeater and planetary action.

The eggbeater has two beaters that rotate on fixed axes in opposite directions. When used to beat a liquid, this mechanism sets up two whirlpools, which constantly circulate the liquid in the bowl and draw it through the space between the beaters. Unfortunately, if the liquid becomes very viscous—as it does in whipping cream or egg whites—the flow breaks down and you overbeat the mixture surrounding the beaters while not reaching the rest of the contents of the bowl. Some attempts, such as making the bowl itself rotate, have been made to circumvent this inherent weakness, but we have never found them completely successful. In our experience, you can get much better results by doing your whipping with a wire whisk and kneading yeast doughs by hand than you can with an eggbeater-style electric mixer. If you already own one and want to use it, keep in mind that you may have to compensate for its shortcomings by doing part of the mixing or kneading by hand.

The planetary-action mixer employs a single beater rotating on a vertical axis at the same time the axis itself (which is mounted on the circumference of a wheel) revolves around the bowl. Thus the beater constantly reaches the mixture in all parts of the bowl, regardless of its consistency. These machines are usually equipped with three beaters: a wire whisk for whipping, a flat leaf beater for mixing heavier batters and creaming butter, and a dough hook for mixing and kneading pastry doughs.

Of all the kitchen machines you can buy, a planetary action electric mixer is the most versatile for pastry making. There are five models made by three manufacturers on the market. They are all fairly large, with mixing bowls ranging in size from 4 to 7 quarts (4 to 7 L); but the bowls have steep vertical sides, so the machines are as effective in mixing small quantities as large. Since the motor heads on these machines cover much of the top of the mixing bowl, when adding dry ingredients during mixing you should always weigh or sift them first onto a sheet of paper and use the paper as a funnel to pour the ingredients into the bowl without stopping the machine.

KitchenAid makes two mixers, the K45 with a 4½-quart (4½ L) bowl and the K5 with a 5-quart (5 L) bowl. On the K45 the bowl locks into the base and the motor head tilts up to lift the beaters when you are attaching or removing the bowl. The K5 is unique among domestic mixers in having a fixed motor head. The bowl is held by two arms, which can be cranked up to position the bowl for mixing or down to lower the bowl for removal. The bowls of both machines are stainless steel. Copper insert bowls are available for whipping egg whites. In addition to being the larger and more powerful of the two, the K5 has the advantage for pastry making that an ice/hot water jacket is available. This is extremely convenient for making *génoise,* and we have also devised a method for using the K5 with ice jacket to prepare fondant. In using the K5 to knead large quantities of leavened pastry doughs, we have found that, because the machine has a high center of gravity, it sometimes "walks" around the counter, especially if operated above medium speed. If this happens on your machine, either turn down the kneading speed or hold the machine in place so it doesn't walk off the counter.

Kenwood also makes two machines, the 5-quart (5 L) Chef and the 7-quart (7 L) Major. Both have stainless-steel bowls that lock into the base and motor heads that tilt up and back for easy positioning and removal of the mixing bowl. The motors on these machines are mounted lower than those on the KitchenAid K5, and in kneading even very large amounts of leavened pastry doughs we have never seen them walk around the counter. The advantage of the Major is its 7-quart (7 L) capacity—the largest of any home mixer. It can handle enough *génoise* batter for three 9-inch (23 cm) rounds and enough *détrempe* for three *patons* of *feuilletage* or *pâte à croissant*—as compared with two rounds of *génoise* or two *patons* of *feuilletage* for the 5-quart (5 L) mixers. To go with that large capacity are the most magnificent whip, leaf beater, and dough hook we have ever seen outside of a professional kitchen. The whip has twice as many stainless-steel wires as the one on the K5, and as a result the Major can turn out enormous volumes of whipped cream and egg whites very quickly. Yet it is as adept at handling 3 egg whites as a dozen.

Unlike the other machines, Magic Mill's Bosch II mixer (formerly the West Bend Food Preparation System) includes a blender, vegetable slicer, and meat grinder as part of the basic package and it has no optional attachments. The mixer has a 4-quart (4 L) plastic mixing bowl and a planetary-action mechanism that is slightly different from the conventional planetary action of the Kitchen-Aid and Kenwood machines. The single beater spins on its axis at the same time as the axis pivots around the point at which it is inserted in the motor head. The Bosch II has a wire batter stirrer instead of a leaf beater. This batter stirrer performs well in nearly all of the same roles as the leaf beaters of the other machines; the exceptions are in mixing the *détrempe* for a *pâte feuilletée* and in making a large batch of *pâte à choux*—in both cases it works the dough or batter more than a leaf beater. The Bosch II is relatively slow at kneading *pâtes levées* but extremely quick and effective for whipping and mixing.

Food Processors

The food processor is a close second to the planetary-action electric mixer in its versatility for pastry making. It is excellent for preparing pastry doughs and fruit purées and the best machine for grinding nuts to powders and pastes in the home kitchen.

This machine is a recent innovation, created in France by Robot Coupe in the mid-1960s. It was originally designed for grinding, slicing, shredding, and the like in professional kitchens. The first home model made by Robot Coupe was introduced in the United States by Cuisinart in the early 1970s.

There are now many home food processors on the market, and for many tasks any of them are adequate. However, because a food processor operates at high speed it should have a strong direct-drive motor to handle pastry doughs (especially yeast doughs) and to grind nut pastes such as *pâte d'amandes* and *praliné*. Not all food processors have the power and capacity for these purposes.

Since there is an extreme variation in the capabilities of home food processors, we have chosen as a standard the original Robot Coupe home food processor, which, with minor variations, has been marketed as the Cuisinart CFP4, CFP5, and CFP9 series and the Robot Coupe RC2000 and RC2100 in the United States, and as the Magi-Mix in France. The quantities in our recipes have been chosen so they work in these machines, which all have a 7-cup (1¾ L) workbowl and a moderately powerful motor. In a less powerful machine, you may have to reduce the quantities in some of our recipes.

For preparing pastry doughs the workbowl of the basic food processor is rather small, accommodating only enough *pâte à foncer* (short or sweet pastry dough) for two 9½-inch (24 cm) diameter *tarte* shells—half the quantity we recommend preparing by hand or in an electric mixer. Robot Coupe makes an inexpensive Dough Dome Kit, which fits all of the basic machines listed above and expands their capacity for pastry doughs by almost 50 percent. If you want to make *pâtes feuilletées* in the standard food processor, the Dough Dome is a must, since without it the workbowl isn't large enough to handle the *détrempe* for even a single *paton* of *feuilletage*.

If you adopt our strategy of making pastry components in large quantities, then you should consider getting a larger and more powerful food processor than the standard machine. One of the largest home food processors is the Robot Coupe RC3600, which has an enormous 12-cup (3 L) workbowl and an extremely powerful motor. This machine will handle the same amounts of pastry doughs as we recommend making by hand or in a heavy duty electric mixer, and double the amounts you could make in the standard food processor. It will also handle twice as much *praliné, pâte d'amandes,* and ground almonds as will the standard machine. And for processing smaller quantities, it sometimes does a better job than the smaller machine. For example, it kneads the *pâtes levées* faster and thus heats them less; and, in making the *détrempe* for *feuilletage,* its wider workbowl makes it possible to keep fluffing up the flour as you add the liquid without packing the dough together and activating the gluten in the flour.

The Robot Coupe R2 is the original professional machine that inspired the home food processor, but it is very different from the domestic models. For slicing and shredding, it is operated in a continuous feed mode so the processed ingredients don't accumulate in the workbowl. Its wide 10-cup (2½ L) workbowl gives it a greater capacity than the basic home model for grinding nuts and for preparing the *détrempe* for *pâtes feuilletées.* However the R2 was never intended for making large batches of pastry doughs such as *pâtes levées.* Its fan-cooled motor is designed for long continuous use but isn't exceptionally powerful. So stick to the quantities of pastry doughs in our recipes and you can make pastry doughs (or anything else) all day without overheating it.

Electric Blenders

The blender's fortes are making liquid purées, emulsifying sauces, and grinding small quantities of ingredients. For pastry making, that includes puréeing fruits for charlottes and *coulis des fruits* (fruit sauces), and smoothing and reconstituting a slightly overcooked *crème anglaise.*

In grinding nuts into powder for *TPT* or pastes for *praliné* and *pâte d'amandes,* a blender can't handle the large quantities that a food processor can, but it will produce a finer texture.

In recent years the food processor has overwhelmed the electric blender to such an extent that a well-constructed home blender has become almost a thing of the past. To get one with a sturdy base and a powerful and durable motor, you must look to commercial blenders. Most of these are simply designed with only one or two speeds. The blades should be mounted very low and the bottom of the container should be narrow, otherwise you can't process small quantities, and, when you grind solids, you end up with too much packed down below the blades. A glass container is preferable to stainless steel, since it allows you to keep an eye on the processing without stopping the machine. The blender we found that best meets these criteria is a Waring two-speed commercial model, no. 7011HG. It has an exceptionally powerful motor and a 40-ounce (1¼ L) container with a clover-leaf shape that forces foods down into the blades. Waring's single-speed commercial blender shares the same container and blade design. An effective ice crusher is available as an optional attachment and is very convenient when you want crushed ice to rapidly chill a bowl of *crème anglaise* or make fondant in a KitchenAid K5 with the ice jacket.

Pastry Bags and Tubes

If you haven't done much pastry making before, you are probably intimidated by pastry bags and tubes. You shouldn't be! The pastry bag is one of the real time- and effort-saving tools in the kitchen. To be sure, there are a few simple techniques to learn, but nothing particularly difficult. And the same techniques are used over and over, whether you are piping *pâte à choux* or *meringue* or decorating the top of a *gâteau* with butter cream.

Pastry Bags

The pastry bag should be either canvas with a plastic-coated interior or nylon. Canvas is stiff when new but softens quickly with use and won't slip in your hands. Nylon is supple from the start and dries faster after washing, but it can be slippery and more difficult to hold.

For piping batters, you need a large pastry bag. Refilling the bag is a minor nuisance, so it is best to have one large enough to hold all of the batter at once. On the other hand, if the pastry bag is too large it becomes unwieldy. For home use, the most convenient sizes are 16 to 20 inches (40 to 50 cm) long. If possible, get two in this range so you have a choice of sizes and, when a recipe calls for piping batter with two different pastry tubes, you can switch without stopping to clean out one bag, change the tube, and refill.

To accommodate the largest pastry tubes, cut off the tip of the pastry bag in a straight line with a scissors to enlarge the opening to ¾ inch (2 cm) wide. Don't make the hole any larger than that or the smaller pastry tubes can fall through.

For decorating, you must have a smaller pastry bag. Not only would the large pastry bags be ridiculous and clumsy for small amounts of decorative piping, but a small decorating tube would fall through the hole in the tip of the large pastry bag. An 8- to 10-inch (20 to 25 cm) pastry bag is about right for decorating, and for smaller work you use a parchment cornet.

Pastry and Decorating Tubes

There are two types of tubes. Pastry tubes are used with large pastry bags for piping batters, fillings, and toppings; and decorating tubes are used with small pastry bags for decorative piping of toppings.

In the United States, the principal manufacturer of pastry and decorating tubes for both home and professional use is Ateco, and to our knowledge they are the only manufacturer that provides a complete range of tubes for all purposes. Since in any case this is the brand you are likely to find, we use the Ateco system of numbering the tubes so you won't have to measure them each time you reach for one. We also describe the size and shape called for in each recipe.

Pastry tubes are usually about 2 inches (5 cm) long. The opening can be any shape, but the only ones of interest to us are the plain and fluted (or star) round tubes.

Plain tubes are numbered from 0 to 9 and have openings ranging in diameter from $\frac{5}{32}$ to $\frac{11}{16}$ inch (4 to 18 mm).

Star tubes have fluted or toothed openings. There are two sets, depending on the number and size of the teeth. American style star tubes (numbered from 0 to 9 in increasing size) have wide deep teeth and are used for batters or fillings that aren't fine enough to hold a very delicate shape or to make deep distinctive fluting in the piped batter. French style star tubes (numbered from 0B to 9B) have short narrow teeth and are used with batters and fillings that will hold a very precise shape or when you want fine, shallow fluting on the piped batter.

In each recipe we suggest the pastry tube we consider ideal, but using a pastry tube of the next size up or down makes little difference. Also, you can use an American style star tube in place of a French style one or vice versa.

Decorating tubes are much smaller than pastry tubes. They are usually about 1⅛ inch (3 cm) long, and the shapes of the openings are even more varied than those of pastry tubes. However, for the type of decorating we do in this book you need only one decorating tube. An open star tube with a $\frac{3}{32}$ inch (2 mm) diameter opening and six teeth (Ateco 17 decorating tube) is about right.

TOURS DE MAIN

Fitting the Tube into the Bag

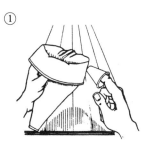

Drop the tube into the pastry bag, tip down ①, and slide it tightly into the opening at the end of the bag. Twist the bag just above the butt end of the tube and press the twisted fabric down inside the tube ②. This tightens the grip of the bag on the tube and at the same time obstructs the tube so that, when you fill it, the batter or filling doesn't drip out through the tube.

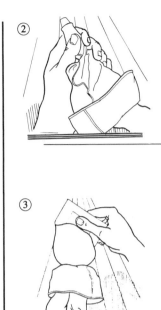

Filling the Pastry Bag

Hold the pastry bag, tip down, with one hand encircling it and fold the top third of the bag inside out over the top of your hand. This will hold the pastry bag open like a funnel for filling.

Filling the bag is especially easy with a pastry corne, but a rubber spatula will also do. Scoop some batter from the bowl and invert it into the funneled bag ③. Scrape the corne or spatula off on the inside edge of the rim of the bag to remove any batter sticking to it ④. Repeat until the bag is filled to the rim.

When you become more adept at handling the pastry bag, you can start with more of the bag draped over your hand to make filling the bottom of the bag easier, then gradually drop the bottom of the bag down relative to your hand until only one quarter to one third of the length of the bag overlaps your hand and the bag is filled to the rim of the funnel.

Closing the Pastry Bag

Unroll the fabric folded over your hand and twist it to close the bag ⑤. This will be easy if you haven't overfilled the bag.

Wrap the thumb and index finger of one hand around the twisted top of the bag to hold it tightly ⑥. You will be able to apply pressure on the batter in the bag with the palm and the other fingers of your hand, and, as the batter is piped out, you will gradually twist the fabric tighter to push the batter down toward the tube.

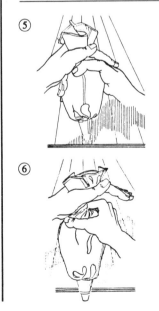

At this point the bottom of the bag should still be sealed with the fabric twisted into the tube.

Opening the Tube

Hold the tube with the fingertips of your free hand. This hand will guide the tube as you are piping. If the batter is very liquid, you can use your index finger as a tap to open and close the tube, and at the start you should cover the tube with your index finger so none of the batter drips out ⑦.

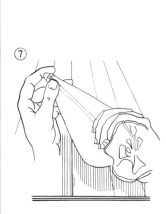

Pull down the tube and untwist the fabric pushed inside it. Gently press on the pastry bag from the top until the batter fills the bottom of the bag and comes to the tip of the tube.

Whenever you want to stop the flow of batter you release the pressure on the bag and cover the tip of the tube with your index finger, if necessary. If you need a free hand, turn the tip of the pastry bag up so it won't drip and support the weight of the bag with the hand wrapped around the top.

Piping

You are now ready to pipe the batter, filling, or topping ⑧. Piping is based on squeezing and releasing the bag with one hand while guiding the tip of the tube with the other to obtain different shapes. The methods of piping can be analyzed into four very general types of motions for manipulating the tube—filling, spreading, dropping, and dragging. One batter can be piped by different motions to get different shapes, and sometimes you must use a combination of motions to make a single shape. But isolating these four motions makes them easier to understand.

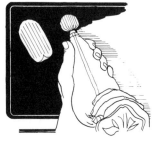

FILLING: This is just a squeeze and release motion for filling molds or baked *choux* ⑨. You judge when you have piped enough by sight or by the pressure in the filled pastry.

SPREADING: This is the method for making dome shapes, for example. Place the tip of the tube on the baking sheet or pastry and hold the pastry bag at an angle of 60° with respect to the surface you are piping on. Start pressing on the bag, and when the batter begins to spread around the tip of the tube, slowly

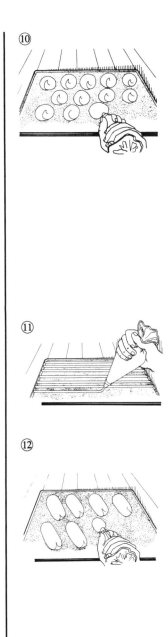

lift the tip of the tube in a smooth continuous motion ⑩. The tip of the tube should always be inserted in the batter, with the batter spreading around it in a mound of increasing width and height. It is like inflating the mound of batter from inside. The mound can be shaped or elongated by driving the batter with the tip of the tube, for example moving the tip in a small circle to make large fluted domes for *choux*.

DROPPING: This method is used to pipe rings and circular discs (or rounds) of batter. Start with the tip of the tube ¾ to 1½ inches (2 to 4 cm) above the baking sheet or pastry, and hold the bag at an angle of 60° with respect to the surface you are piping on. Press on the bag and, when the batter starts to come out of the tube, let it drop onto the baking sheet. As you continue pressing evenly on the bag, move the tip of the tube to trace out the shape you want to pipe. Adjust the pressure on the bag and the speed at which you move the tube so that a uniform rope of batter drops onto the sheet ⑪.

DRAGGING: You can make ribbons or fingers of various shapes by the dragging method ⑫. Place the tip of the tube on or just above the baking sheet or pastry and drag the batter across the surface as you press on the pastry bag. Depending on the pressure you exert on the bag and the angle the tube makes with the sheet, you can get ribbons of batter of various widths and thicknesses. Holding the bag nearly vertical would make a thin, wide ribbon, while holding it closer to the horizontal would make a more cylindrical, rope-shaped ribbon. You can get more complicated shapes such as pears and teardrops by changing the pressure on the bag as you pipe.

Terminating

You can terminate the piping motion in several ways, depending on the result you want to achieve. Always release the pressure on the bag before you reach the size or shape you want, since the batter will continue flowing for a moment. If you continue the motion of the tube after releasing the pressure, you will draw out a thin elongated tail of batter, and you can adjust the shape by the speed and direction of the

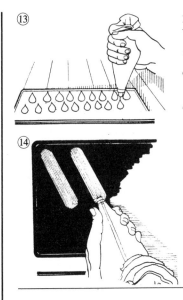

motion. That is how you finish a ring or disk of batter or a mushroom stem ⑬, but for other shapes, such as domes and fingers, a tail is undesirable.

To terminate the batter with no tail, you must ''cut'' it by a quick lateral movement of the tip of the tube. To keep the fluid rhythm of the piping motion as you move from piping one pastry to the next, this is done with a semicircular flick of the tip of the pastry tube; or if the batter was piped by the dragging method, you stop the piping motion and flick the tip of the pastry tube in the reverse direction ⑭. In either case the tip of the tube should move across the surface of the batter so the edge of the tube severs the connection between the batter in the tube and the batter already piped.

Refilling the Pastry Bag

If you must refill your pastry bag, first empty the batter remaining in it into your bowl. Twist the bag just above the tube and press it down inside the tube. Scrape down the inside of the bag with your pastry corne or a rubber spatula, then proceed to fill it in the usual way.

Palette Knives

What we call a ''palette knife'' is a metal spatula with a straight, thin blade. It is one of the most versatile tools in the French pastry chef's arsenal. Palette knives are used for spreading and smoothing batters, fillings, and toppings; for moving cake layers and pastries; for lifting *gâteaux* in the process of assembling; and for a variety of decorating tasks.

To be used for fine decorative work, the design and construction of the palette knife are crucial. The blade should be flexible, but its base should have enough rigidity to allow you to lift a *gâteau*. It should have a rounded end and straight parallel edges on both sides for most of its length, then taper in sharply to meet the handle. The handle should be slim and smoothly rounded for fingertip control. For most purposes, the blade should be 8 to 12 inches (20 to 30 cm) long and the balance point should be in the tapering section of the blade.

The American palette knives we have tried are fine as lifting and spreading tools but too clumsy and heavy for elegant decorative work. For palette knives of the type we have been describing you must look to European manufacturers, and only a few are widely available. The Swiss-made Victorinox palette knives from R. H. Forschner are excellent and come in 8-, 10-, and 12-inch (20, 25, and 30 cm) lengths. They are well proportioned and balanced and very comfortable to use. French palette knives of similar weight and balance are also available. **Sources:** La Cuisine and Nussex.

Wüsthof-Trident and F. Dick make luxurious forged spatulas that are very different from the classic Victorinox and French ones. Both have blades 10 inches (25 cm) long and 1⅜ inch (3½ cm) wide. While not as efficient for spreading large amounts of batter as the wider 12-inch (30 cm) Victorinox and French spatulas, these palette knives are outstanding for assembling and decorating *gâteaux*. They have slim bolsters and full tangs, which make them heavier but lower their balance points to the base of the blade so the blades feel almost weightless. The superb balance of these palette knives gives you extraordinary control. The blades have exceptionally long, straight edges (long enough to sweep the top of a 9-inch or 23-cm *gâteau*) for their size, and extremely flexible tips, but their bolsters give them plenty of rigidity at the base of the blade for lifting.

For very small decorative work and for spreading fillings in small pastries, choose a palette knife with a very flexible blade 4 to 4½ inches (10 to 12 cm) long, and ¾ inch (2 cm) wide. **Source:** BIA Cordon Bleu.

Pastry Brushes

You will use pastry brushes for painting pastry doughs with egg wash, for glazing the surfaces of many desserts with jams, jellies, and *glace à l'eau*, and for coating molds and baking sheets evenly with melted butter.

The best brushes have natural hog bristles, called "Chinese bristles," clamped to a wooden handle with a leather or stainless steel ferrule. Nylon bristles can melt if exposed to heat.

Pastry brushes are made in two shapes, flat and round. The flat, paint-brush type is the one used by professional French pastry chefs for all purposes. For home baking, you can get along quite well with three sizes, a 1-inch (2½ cm) width for brushing small molds and pastries, a 1½-inch (4 cm) width for larger molds and pastries, and a 2-inch (5 cm) width for baking sheets. A round brush ½ to ¾ inch (1½ to 2 cm) in diameter is less versatile than the paint-brush style, but is fine for brushing the insides of small molds.

After using a pastry brush, wash it out thoroughly with detergent and hot water (but not in the dishwasher). Then press it dry with an absorbent towel and hang it, bristles down, to finish drying. Don't hang it bristles up or moisture will stay inside the ferrule and eventually rot the base of the bristles.

Bakeware

There are several factors to consider in deciding which bakeware to choose. First is quality, and, while good heavy-gauge bakeware isn't cheap, it will repay your investment in both better results and durability.

Material

Nearly all of the bakeware we use is made from black steel, tinned steel, or aluminum, and each material has its distinctive characteristics and advantages.

TINNED STEEL: This is relatively inexpensive. If heavily plated it is quite durable, though we wouldn't recommend it for baking sheets, which must be able to take some abuse. Most of the French molds are tinned steel, and Chicago Metallic makes an extensive line of American tinned-steel molds that easily match the finest French ones in quality. Since tin has a low melting point (450° F, or 232° C), tinned-steel molds should never be exposed to direct heat or placed empty in a hot oven.

BLACK STEEL: This is heavy and can rust if it isn't kept totally dry. Otherwise it is almost indestructible, and like tinned steel it is not expensive. Black steel absorbs radiant heat more quickly than bright, shiny materials, which reflect heat. The proponents of black steel bakeware are always telling us how wonderful that is, but in fact it can be an advantage or disadvantage, depending on the situation. Professional French pastry chefs always use black steel baking sheets but rarely black steel molds. However, good imported (BIA Cordon Bleu) and domestic (Stone Hearth and Brick Oven) black steel molds are available and are sometimes the best choice.

When you get a new black steel mold or baking sheet, wipe off the oil used to protect its surface during shipping. Using a paper towel, coat the surface of the baking sheet or mold with a film of neutral vegetable oil. Then season it in a 350° F (175° C) oven until it begins to smoke. Let it cool, then wipe off the excess oil with a paper towel. Black steel should never be washed, and there should always be a thin film of grease coating its surface to protect it and give it better baking properties. After each use, black steel baking sheets should be scraped clean with a dough scraper. Wipe both molds and baking sheets with a paper towel to remove excess grease. If food sticks to the inside of a mold, use some coarse kosher salt as an abrasive and rub it with a paper towel dipped in vegetable oil, then wipe out the salt.

ALUMINUM: This is superb for bakeware because it is lightweight and an excellent heat conductor. It is also more expensive than either black steel or tinned steel, and consequently it is rarely used for French bakeware. However, there is an enormous selection of American aluminum bakeware ranging from the lightweight and flimsy foil variety to the heavy-gauge bakeware made by Chicago Metallic and Wear-Ever Professional (Lincoln Manufacturing).

A natural finish is used on most of the moderate-weight aluminum bakeware (such as Wear-Ever's Preferred Bakeware) and some of the heavy-gauge lines (Chicago Metallic and Wear-Ever Professional).

Anodized aluminum bakeware is made by Chicago Metallic under the trade name Bakalon. This is a heavy gauge aluminum with a dark gray surface produced by a process called ''hard-coat'' anodizing. It combines the advantages of aluminum with the heat-absorption properties of black steel.

Most aluminum bakeware does not have to be seasoned because it doesn't rust and the molds are always brushed with butter before baking. However, we recommend that natural-finish and anodized aluminum baking sheets and cookie sheets be seasoned in the same way as black steel. The film of oil produced by seasoning prevents *choux* and other pastries from sticking to the baking sheet. After each use the seasoned baking sheets should be wiped with a dry paper towel to remove excess grease. They should not be washed, or they will have to be re-seasoned. If food sticks to the surface of the baking sheets, clean them by rubbing with a paper towel dipped in vegetable oil and use coarse kosher salt as an abrasive. Do not scrape them with a steel dough scraper.

Surface—Dark versus Shiny

The surface of your bakeware can be as important in determining its baking characteristics as the material from which it is made. A dark, dull surface such as black steel or Bakalon absorbs radiant heat faster than a bright, shiny one like polished aluminum or tinned steel. However, the surface makes little difference for absorption of convection heat. So the surface finish of the metal is most important in an electric roasting oven, less important in a gas oven, and least important in a convection oven.

Faster heat absorption results in more rapid browning and shorter cooking times. That can be good for most *tarte* shells, but not so good if the *tarte* is made with a very juicy fruit that requires long baking to dry it out. While good browning is desirable for *babas,* for most cakes like *génoise* you want to minimize browning. If you find that you are getting excessive browning with a dark-surfaced bakeware, reduce the oven temperature next time around.

Baking Sheets

The baking sheet is the single most important piece of bakeware in your kitchen. Many pastries—including *tartes, choux, feuilletés,* sheet cakes, meringues, and some forms of brioche—are baked directly on the baking sheet. Even when you are baking a pastry in a mold, the mold is often placed on a baking sheet.

FRENCH BLACK STEEL BAKING SHEETS: The professional French baking sheet is stamped from a sheet of heavy-gauge black steel $\frac{1}{16}$ inch ($1\frac{1}{2}$ mm) thick. All four sides and corners are enclosed by a $\frac{1}{4}$-inch (6 mm) high rim sloping up from the bottom of the sheet at a shallow 30° angle.

These baking sheets are incredibly versatile. The low, sloping rim makes it easy to remove *tartes* and *feuilletés* baked on them. Yet the rim is just high enough to enable the baking sheets to be used for thin sheet cakes, and the rim serves as a guide in sweeping the cake batter smooth with your palette knife. Furthermore, the heavy black steel holds and distributes the heat. When you preheat the oven with one of these inside and then place a molded pastry on the hot baking sheet, the pastry gets tremendous bottom heat.

French black steel baking sheets are made in three sizes—12 x 16 inches (30 x 40 cm), 13 x 20 inches (33 x 50 cm), and 16 x 24 inches (40 x 60 cm). Only the first two will fit in home ovens. **Sources:** Dean & Deluca, La Cuisine, BIA Cordon Bleu.

THE GRIDDLE AS BAKING SHEET: No American manufacturer makes a baking sheet in the style and quality of the French black steel ones. However, there are a few aluminum griddles that are very similar and that make excellent baking sheets. Wear-Ever's Premium Cookware rectangular griddle is heavy-gauge aluminum lined with Dupont's nonstick SilverStone surface. It measures 12 x 19 inches (30 x 49 cm) and has a rim $\frac{5}{8}$ inch ($1\frac{1}{2}$ cm) high. It can be used in any recipe that calls for a 13 x 20-inch (33 x 50 cm) baking sheet. Nordic Ware's 10 x 17 inch (26 x 42 cm) rectangular griddle has a rim $\frac{1}{2}$ inch (12 mm) high and is available in polished aluminum or with SilverStone lining. It is a good substitute for the 12 x 16-inch (30 x 40 cm) French baking sheet.

The SilverStone linings on these griddles should be conditioned by wiping with vegetable oil the first time they are used, but they do not have to be seasoned in the oven.

COOKIE SHEETS: We distinguish between a baking sheet, which is enclosed on all four sides and corners, and a cookie sheet, which is not. The typical American cookie sheet has a turned-up rim on the two short ends and is open on the long sides. This makes sliding *tartes* and other pastries off the cookie sheet even easier than from a baking sheet, but you can't bake a sheet cake on a cookie sheet.

There are only a few heavy-gauge aluminum cookie sheets on the market. Leyse makes two sizes—12 x 15 inches (30 x 38 cm) and 14 x 17 inches (35 x 43 cm)—in their professional-weight polished aluminum called Toroware. Chicago Metallic makes 10 x 14-inch (25 x 35 cm) rectangular and 14-inch (35 cm) square cookie sheets in both natural-finish aluminum and the dark gray Bakalon.

ROUND BAKING SHEETS: Round baking sheets are called *tourtières* in French and are constructed of black steel with turned-up rim just like the rectangular baking sheets. You would use them for baking a single round pastry such as a *tarte* or *pithiviers,* or for holding a round mold such as a layer-cake pan.

They are available in several sizes, including 11-inch (28 cm), 12¾-inch (32 cm) and 14½-inch (37 cm) diameters. **Sources:** La Cuisine, Dean & Deluca, and BIA Cordon Bleu.

Leyse has gone one better by making a griddle of the same shape in their dark-gray Leysón anodized aluminum and adding a metal loop handle for easier maneuvering. The griddle is 12 inches (30 cm) in diameter and is also available in a buffed natural-finish aluminum or with a SilverStone lining.

JELLY-ROLL PANS: Jelly-roll pans, or "bun pans," are similar to baking sheets but much deeper—usually about 1 inch or (2½ cm) deep.

They aren't quite so convenient for baking thin sheet cakes as baking sheets, and you could mutilate a fragile *tarte* in the process of removing it from a jelly-roll pan. But for other purposes they are acceptable alternatives to baking sheets. Because the jelly-roll pan has those high, steep sides, it can be used to catch the drippings when you drain a rum-soaked *baba.*

Jelly-roll pans are sold in two standard sizes: 18 x 26 inches (45 x 66 cm), or "full size"; and 13 x 18 inches (33 x 45 cm), or "half size." Only the half-size pan is suitable for home ovens. While jelly-roll pans are never made in the very thick aluminum used for baking sheets and cookie sheets, good, moderately heavy-gauge examples are produced by Wear-Ever Professional, Leyse, and Chicago Metallic.

Molds

Molds for French pastry come in so many sizes and shapes that not even the largest pastry shop has them all. We have tried to limit the number of specialized molds used in this book, and for most pastries a small number of general-purpose molds (layer-cake pans, loaf pans, flan rings, and ring molds) is all you need. Some pastries, including most *choux* and *feuilletés,* require no molds at all. For others, like brioches and *savarins,* special shapes are what distinguish one pastry from another.

Pastries that are low in sugar and high in butter (such as brioches) tend to cook evenly without burning even in a thin, inexpensive mold; but those high in sugar or low in butter need the protection of a heavy-gauge mold. Pastries that will be subjected to high heat or must be browned very well need the uniform heat provided by a heavy-gauge mold to prevent burning in spots. Placing a light-weight mold on a heavy baking sheet helps even out the heat and partially compensates for the flaws of the mold.

We advise you to get the best general-purpose molds you can afford and select a few moderately priced tinned-steel specialty molds.

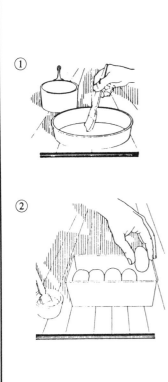

LAYER-CAKE PANS: French layer-cake pans, called *moules à manquer*, have sloping sides and are typically 1½ to 1¾ inches (4 to 4½ cm) deep. Tinned steel ones are available in diameters ranging from 6 to 12 inches (16 to 30 cm) ①. **Sources:** BIA Cordon Bleu, Bridge, and La Cuisine.

Most American household-style layer-cake pans (Wear-Ever, Mirro, Leyse) are very similar to the French, with sloping sides and a depth of 1½ inches (4 cm). Professional style ones (Chicago Metallic, Wear-Ever Professional) have vertical sides, with a depth of 1½ or 2 inches (4 or 5 cm). In both domestic and professional layer-cake pans, the most common diameters are 8, 9, and 10 inches (20, 23, and 25½ cm).

LOAF PANS: The classic French loaf pan has sloping sides and is relatively narrow ②. **Sources:** BIA Cordon Bleu, Lamalle, Kitchen Bazaar, and La Cuisine.

American loaf pans are usually wider and deeper than the French ones. While most (such as Wear-Ever Professional) have nearly vertical sides, a few (Chicago Metallic) have sloping sides like the French.

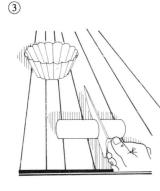

TARTE MOLDS: Sold as deep quiche molds in the United States, these are called *moules à tarte* in France, They are round and about 1¾ inches (4½ cm) deep, with steep fluted sides. Their original use was for neither *tartes* nor quiches, but as cake pans. **Sources:** BIA Cordon Bleu, Lamalle, and La Cuisine.

The only American *tarte* mold we have seen is an aluminum Quiche-Flan Set from Wear-Ever. In addition to the standard removable flat bottom, this set has a decorative *rosace,* or rose window, bottom that is very nice for baking *biscuit de savoie.*

BRIOCHE MOLDS: While brioche can be molded in many forms, there is one shape designed explicitly for *brioche parisienne* and *petites brioches.* These round molds have deeply fluted, sloping sides ③-④.

Sources: Nussex, La Cuisine, BIA Cordon Bleu, Lamalle, and Bridge.

You can also mold *petites brioches* in cupcake pans. The sides of the cupcake pans aren't fluted and don't slope as much as those of the brioche molds, but the proportions are close enough to work quite well. These pans are usually made in a frame holding 12 or 24 cups. The frame makes molding the brioches more clumsy, but moving a dozen framed molds in and out of the oven and unmolding the brioches become much easier. Chicago Metallic's "teacups" are just right for breakfast size *petites brioches*. For slightly larger brioches you could use the standard cupcake pans made by Chicago Metallic and Wear-Ever Professional.

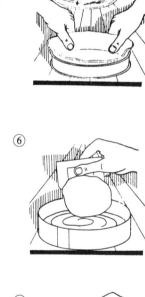

FLAN RINGS: This is just a ring of steel, with no bottom, used to mold *tartes* on baking sheets ⑤. Most flan rings are tinned steel with rolled top and bottom edges. They are quite shallow, either ¾ or 1 inch (2 or 2½ cm) deep. For most *tartes* either will do, but a few pastries require the 1-inch (2½ cm) deep flan ring. The most commonly available diameters in the United States are 4, 8, 9½, and 11 inches (10, 20, 24, and 28 cm). **Sources:** La Cuisine, BIA Cordon Bleu, Lamalle, and Bridge.

ENTREMET RINGS: These rings are deeper (1⅜ inches or 3½ cm) than flan rings and are usually stainless steel ⑥. They are used as forms for assembling *gâteaux*, where they greatly simplify the decorating process. Also, very deep *tartes* are occasionally baked in *entremet* rings. **Sources:** La Cuisine, Nussex, and Dean & DeLuca.

VACHERIN RINGS AND SPRINGFORM PANS: We normally mold large charlottes in a stainless steel ring 2⅜ inches (6 cm) deep ⑦, called a *vacherin* ring. **Sources:** Lamalle, Nussex, and La Cuisine.

A good alternative to the *vacherin* ring is a springform pan. You need only the outside ring, not the bottom of the springform. The ring should have rolled rims on top and bottom and an embossed rib to hold the bottom of the pan. If the bottom rim of the ring is turned in to hold the bottom of the pan, as many are, unmolding the charlotte will be difficult.

The only springforms we think suitable are the German tinned steel ones from Dr. Oetker and Kaiser. **Sources:** BIA Cordon Bleu and Maid of Scandinavia.

CHARLOTTE MOLDS: These are deep, round molds with steeply sloping sides. They are the classical molds for *charlottes russes,* but we use them only for making *diplomate*. **Sources:** La Cuisine, BIA Cordon Bleu, and Bridge.

SAVARIN RINGS AND RING MOLDS: Large *savarins* are molded in plain, shallow ring molds, typically 7 to 9½ inches (18 to 24 cm) in diameter and 1½ to 2 inches (4 to 5 cm) deep ⑧. **Sources:** BIA Cordon Bleu, La Cuisine, Lamalle, and Bridge.

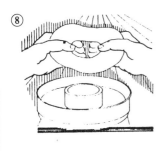

Another mold sometimes used for *savarins* is a ring mold with two indentations running around the inside and outside near the bottom. These are frequently called ''rice rings'' in French cooking, and aluminum ring molds of this shape are made by some American manufacturers (Leyse, Mirro).

INDIVIDUAL SAVARINS AND MARY ANN MOLDS: The molds for *individual savarins* are round, with a depression in the center of the bottom. They are similar to miniature ring molds, but the center is closed and the depression comes to just above half the height of the mold. Molds with open centers, or with closed centers coming up to the top of the mold, can't be filled properly. **Sources:** Lamalle, Dean & DeLuca, and Nussex.

An excellent American alternative is individual Mary Ann molds. These are usually deeper than the *savarin* molds, but, since you fill them only enough to barely cover the central depression, what matters is the height of the depression. It should extend about ½ inch (12 mm) up from the bottom of the mold. Chicago Metallic's tinned steel pan with twelve Mary Ann molds held in a frame fits the bill perfectly.

KUGELHOPF MOLDS: Kugelhopf is baked in a deep tube pan. The traditional earthenware molds are hard to find and very fragile ⑨. For home use, we recommend tinned steel.

The shape of the kugelhopf mold depends on the country it comes from. French ones have a diagonally fluted design with deep, wide fluting. German ones (also sold as Bundt pans) have shallower fluting and a more elaborate design, with short vertical fluting around the rim of the mold. **Sources:** BIA Cordon Bleu, Lamalle, and La Cuisine.

The Turk's head tube molds made by some American manufacturers of professional bakeware are very similar. American bundt pans have a different design and aren't quite so deep but work well. Or you could get one of the good German tinned-steel springform pans. (Dr. Oetker or Kaiser) with a tube bottom to use for both kugelhopf and charlottes.

TARTELETTES, BARQUETTES, AND MILLASSONS: These are three small molds used for a variety of pastries. The *tartelette* mold is round and shaped like a tiny pie pan, with shallow sloping sides. The *millasson* is a *tartelette* mold with steeper sides—like a miniature layer-cake pan. And the *barquette* is a boat-shaped *tartelette* mold with pointed bow and stern . These shapes are made with plain or fluted sides, the plain sides being more versatile and often easier to use. **Sources:** Lamalle, Bridge, and BIA Cordon Bleu.

TIMBALE MOLDS: Small thimble-shaped molds are used for the champagne cork–shaped *babas* called *bouchons* 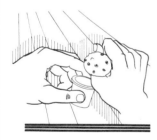. **Sources:** Lamalle and Dean & DeLuca.

BÛCHE DE NOËL MOLDS: There are special trough-shaped molds for *bûches de Nöel* (Yule logs). They can also be used for molding ice cream. **Sources:** Lamalle, Bridge, and La Cuisine.

VOL-AU-VENT-DISCS: These aren't really molds but guides for such procedures as cutting circles of pastry and marking circles on baking sheets. They are tinned steel with a slightly domed shape and a hole in the center so they can be lifted and positioned easily . *Vol-au-vent* discs are sold in sets of twelve sizes graduated from 4¼ inches (11 cm) to 9¾ inches (25 cm). **Sources:** Dean & DeLuca, Nussex, and La Cuisine.

Cooling Racks

When you remove most pastries from the oven, they should be transferred from the mold or baking sheet to a wire cooling rack. This makes them cool more quickly and prevents condensation, which could make their surface soggy. Some pastries (*choux* and meringues) are too fragile to move while hot, so these are left on the baking sheet while the baking sheet is placed on a rack to speed cooling.

We suggest that you have two or three wire cooling racks at least as large as your baking sheets. They should be made of tinned or chrome-plated steel wires spaced about ½ inch (12 mm) apart, with enough cross spokes to support the weight of the pastries or baking sheet without bending. The frame should have feet to hold the rack at least ½ inch (12 mm) above the counter.

Small round or rectangular wire racks are used to hold *gâteaux* when you are finishing them and are especially useful when you are glazing with fondant or *pâte à glacé*. They are also useful for holding and lifting *babas* when you soak them in rum syrup, and, since the *babas* are fragile, it is best to have closely spaced spokes for this purpose.

Saucepans and Caramel Pots

Stovetop cooking is a limited but important part of pastry making. You must be able to prepare custards and sugar syrups, poach fruits, and melt butter, jam, etc. Occasionally a sauté pan is useful for cooking apples in butter, but you could easily make do with only one pot, the *casserole russe* or saucepan, in a range of sizes and materials for different purposes.

The only materials of interest are copper and aluminum. Among the metals used for cooking implements, these two are by far the best heat conductors. Copper is a better conductor than aluminum, but, more important, it has a lower thermal mass, enabling it to react more quickly to changes in temperature. This feature is especially significant in cooking delicate sauces and sugar syrups, when you don't want heat stored in the pot to overcook the ingredients after you remove it from the burner. However, copper is heavy and expensive. Aluminum makes up for its higher thermal mass by being light in weight and considerably less expensive.

Whether a saucepan is made of copper or aluminum, the metal should be a heavy gauge to provide even heat distribution. The best thickness for both metals is about ⅛ inch (3 mm). Much thinner pots don't heat evenly and can warp, and thicker ones would be too heavy and have too much thermal mass.

Both copper and aluminum can interact chemically with certain foods. Some copper compounds are potentially harmful, and for this reason copper cooking utensils are always lined with another metal unless they will be reserved for a special purpose, such as cooking sugar or whipping egg whites. The very best French copper saucepans are hammered for extra strength and lined with tin. These are perfect for cooking custards and some sugar syrups. **Sources:** BIA Cordon Bleu, La Cuisine, Lamalle, and Bridge.

Tin lined copper pots should not be used for cooking sugar to the caramel stage because if you accidentally overcook the caramel, you can damage the tin lining (tin has a relatively low melting point). Copper pots lined with nickel (Coventry Copper) or stainless steel don't have this drawback. However, since stainless steel is a poor heat conductor, there is no advantage to a saucepan that is mostly stainless steel with only a thin layer of copper on the outside.

Unlined copper caramel pots are used for cooking sugar and melting chocolate. Most are made in the same shape as an ordinary saucepan, but there are also round-bottomed ones that are even better for making *nougatine* and *praliné*. All caramel pots have spouts to make pouring easier. The inside of a copper caramel pot should be cleaned with coarse kosher salt and vinegar, then rinsed out with water and dried before each use. After cooking sugar syrup, fill it with water and boil to dissolve sugar sticking to the inside of the pot. **Sources:** Lamalle (both round and flat bottomed), BIA Cordon Bleu, Kitchen Glamor, Bridge.

Aluminum can discolor eggs and foods containing acids. While these interactions aren't harmful, for aesthetic reasons it is undesirable to cook custards or fruits in a bare aluminum saucepan. To prevent interaction with foods, aluminum saucepans can be lined or the surface of the aluminum can be anodized. For lining, the best material is stainless steel because of its durability. Anodizing is an electrolytic process that chemically alters the surface of the aluminum. The best cookware of these types comes from American manufacturers (for example, the stainless steel–lined Master Chef and LTD pots from All-Clad Metalcrafters and the anodized Leysón pots from Leyse and Magnalite Professional pots from General Housewares).

Papers

Kitchen Parchment

This is a strong and stiff greaseproof paper used for making parchment cornets (decorating cones) and occasionally for lining baking sheets. We also use parchment to cover the tops of some pastries toward the end of the cooking period to prevent them from browning too much.

Waxed Paper

Waxed paper is also greaseproof and is less expensive than kitchen parchment. It is convenient for holding dry ingredients when you weigh them and to catch powdered ingredients as you sift them. You can then lift the sheet of paper holding the ingredients by two opposite sides and use it as a funnel for pouring.

Newsprint

We almost always use newsprint rather than parchment for lining baking sheets. It is inexpensive, and like waxed paper, it is convenient to use for weighing or sifting dry ingredients; and by lifting two opposite sides of the paper you can use it as a funnel for pouring the ingredients. Paper supply houses sell it by the ream in several sizes. Get the size that is a little larger than your baking sheets, or as large as two baking sheets. Artists newsprint is sold in smaller quantities but is more expensive.

Freezer Paper

In addition to wrapping foods for freezer storage, this heavy, glazed paper can be used like waxed paper or newsprint to weigh or sift dry ingredients. It comes in wider rolls than does waxed paper, so for holding large quantities of dry ingredients it is the better choice.

Tissue Paper

The white tissue paper you use for wrapping gifts is the best paper for lining *tarte* shells when you prebake them. Since it isn't stiff, it is less likely to damage a fragile pastry dough than, say, aluminum foil.

Cardboard Cake-Decorating Circles and Rectangles

The corrugated-cardboard cake-decorating circles sold in the United States are totally inappropriate for use in French pastry making.

For supporting *gâteaux* and other pastries, what you want are the lids for aluminum-foil take-out containers. These are made of a single layer of white cardboard with foil on one side. They are thin, they have just enough rigidity, and the foil is moistureproof. You should be able to get these lids at a local restaurant supply store. They are inexpensive, but unfortunately, they are sometimes sold in packages of 500 or, worse yet, in sets with the foil containers. If you can't find them locally, Hackensack Supply will take mail orders for packages of 100 lids. The largest sizes available from them are 9-inch (23 cm) circles for round *gâteaux* and pastries and 7 × 9½-inch (18 × 24 cm) rectangles for rectangular *gâteaux*. Some restaurant supply stores also carry 9½ × 11-inch (24 × 28 cm) rectangles.

Paper Doilies

It is customary in France to serve *gâteaux* and many other pastries on paper doilies. They can add a nice decorative touch, but use them only under dry pastries, which won't make the doily soggy. Choose a doily that will give you a 1- to 1½-inch (2½ to 4 cm) border on all sides of the pastry.

Chapter Fourteen

INGREDIENTS

*T*he number of ingredients used in French pastry is relatively small, yet the variety of desserts that can be produced from them is infinite.

Butter, Cream, and Milk

Butter, and to a lesser extent cream and milk, is what makes French pastry special. There are, of course, substitutes for these dairy products, but if you are going to invest the time and effort in making elegant pastries, it would be a shame to spoil the results with the inferior taste and texture of artificial dairy products. We recommend using only the real thing, and the best quality you can get your hands on.

Milk

USES: Milk is a primary ingredient in *pâtes à choux, crème pâtissière, crème bavaroise,* and *crème anglaise.* Small amounts of milk are also used in some pastry doughs and cake batters.

FACTS ABOUT MILK: Cows' milk is the only one of interest for pastry making. It is predominantly water (about 87 percent), with the remainder about 3.5 percent each of butterfat and protein (mostly casein) and 5 percent carbohydrate (lactose).

To kill harmful bacteria, milk is pasteurized by heating to either 145° F (63° C) for at least 30 minutes or 161° F (72° C) for at least 15 seconds, after which it is rapidly cooled.

Most milk is also homogenized. Before homogenization, the butterfat, which is lighter than water, rises to the surface to form a layer of cream on top. Homogenization breaks up the milk fat into tiny globules, which are then kept separated and dispersed throughout the milk by Brownian motion.

WHAT TO LOOK FOR IN BUYING MILK: Freshness! Milk sours by a process of slow fermentation in which bacteria convert the lactose into lactic acid, making it lose its fresh, sweet taste.

The variability among different brands of homogenized milks is rather small. In contrast, cream-top (nonhomogenized) milk varies tremendously, depending on the breed of cows, what they eat, and the time of year. Look for rich, sweet flavor; high butterfat content (in cream-top milk it can vary from 3 to 6 percent), indicated by a thick layer of cream on top; and a herd of Jersey or Guernsey cows at the farm.

Certified raw milk is unpasteurized milk from government-inspected cows. It has a more natural flavor than pasteurized milk, but it spoils more quickly.

Whether you choose homogenized, cream-top, or certified raw milk, always use whole milk (never skim milk) in our recipes.

STORAGE: Fresh pasteurized milk can be kept refrigerated for over a week before going sour. But during that time its flavor deteriorates gradually.

CAVEATS ON COOKING WITH MILK: Choose a heavy saucepan and rinse it out with cold water before pouring in the milk. This helps prevent the milk from sticking. To avoid scorching or forming a film on top, cook the milk over low to medium heat, stirring occasionally. Do not boil, since that would alter its taste and make it overflow the saucepan. It should be heated only to the point at which it begins to simmer—about 180° F (80° C).

Cream

USES: As a primary ingredient in *crème chantilly, ganache, crème bavaroise,* and fruit mousses.

FACTS ABOUT CREAM: The cream that floats to the top of cream-top milk is relatively high in butterfat. At the dairy, a centrifugal separator is used to produce even richer creams. They are classified from light to heavy in direct proportion to their butterfat content, and hence in inverse proportion to their weight. The higher the butterfat content, the thicker the cream, and it is the higher viscosity that makes "heavy" cream seem heavier. Higher butterfat content also makes cream whip better. The only creams of interest for French pastry are heavy cream and whipping cream, which by law must contain at least 36 percent and 30 percent butterfat, respectively.

Almost all cream is either pasteurized, like milk, or ultrapasteurized. Ultrapasteurization is a high temperature sterilization that prolongs the shelf life of cream but destroys its fresh sweet taste and superlative whipping properties in the process.

WHAT TO LOOK FOR IN BUYING CREAM: Freshness, high butterfat content, and rich sweet taste. Always choose pasteurized over ultrapasteurized cream.

STORAGE: If fresh from the dairy, up to 1 week in the refrigerator. But, as for milk, the sooner you use it the sweeter it will be.

CAVEATS ON WHIPPING CREAM: Whipping incorporates tiny air bubbles, which increase the volume and viscosity of the cream. Cream whips best if it is at least 1 day old and at a temperature of 40° F (5° C). So always chill the cream, the bowl, and the whisk before whipping.

Whip the cream at medium speed, then slow down when it forms soft peaks to avoid overbeating. Continue whipping until the cream is light and thick. It should expand to double its original volume.

If the whipped cream is to be folded into some other ingredients, stop whipping when it holds medium-firm peaks. If it is too stiff, you will have to mix it too vigorously, which will deflate it. The other ingredients should also be cold, in order not to soften and thin the whipped cream.

If the whipped cream is to be piped from a pastry bag for decoration, it must be whipped a little longer until just stiff, so that it will hold a precise shape. Do not overbeat or the cream will become grainy, then curdle, and eventually turn to butter.

ABOUT CRÈME FRAÎCHE: American-style sweet cream is called *crème fleurette* in France. *Crème fraîche* (literally "fresh cream") is actually a matured heavy cream that has a full, nutty, and slightly sour taste. The name came about in the days before refrigeration and rapid transportation when naturally occurring bacteria soured the cream before it got from the farm in the country to the market in Paris. Parisians developed a taste for *crème fraîche*, and today the cream is matured under controlled conditions to give it the desired flavor. *Crème fleurette* has only recently become popular in France.

In the United States the commercial availability of *crème fraîche* is rather limited, but it is easy enough to make *crème fraîche* from heavy cream at home. The Crayon Yard Corporation (see Sources for Specialty Ingredients, page 434) makes a simple and foolproof culturing device called the Solait and provides real *crème fraîche* starter cultures.

Crème fraîche can be used whenever heavy cream is called for, except that it requires more care in whipping (see the recipe for *crème chantilly* on page 82 for more details).

Butter

Butter is the soul of French pastry. *Always* use unsalted butter in pastry making.

USES: In all pastry doughs and *pâtes à choux* and some cake batters and fillings—especially *crème au beurre*. Also, for brushing molds and baking sheets to prevent sticking.

FACTS ABOUT BUTTER: Butter is made by churning heavy cream until the butterfat solidifies. The mass of butterfat is the butter, and the remaining liquid is buttermilk. The butter is then washed to eliminate most of the milk protein and lactose, which spoil more quickly than does butterfat, and kneaded to eliminate excess water. By law all butter sold in this country must be at least 80 percent butterfat, with the remainder mainly water (about 18 percent) and residual milk solids.

In large part, the quality of the finished butter is determined by the cream from which it is made. Butter is graded by the USDA on several characteristics, including taste, aroma, body, texture, and uniformity of color. Grades AA (93 score, the highest) and A (92 score) must be made from fresh sweet cream and have a delicate sweet taste. Grade B (90 score) butter is made from soured cream and has a slightly acid flavor.

For comparison, French butters are made from matured cream. They have a rich nutty aroma and a fuller flavor than butters made from sweet cream, but of course they aren't as sweet. On the average, French butters also have a slightly higher butterfat content—typically 82 to 86 percent—than American butters, and thus contain less water.

Salt is often added to butter as a preservative. However, salt can mask the off-flavor of rancid butter, and, furthermore, by using salted butter you lose control of the amount of salt that goes into a recipe. Do not use salted butter for making French pastries.

For sautéing and some other purposes, butter can be clarified to remove the residual milk solids, which burn at a lower temperature than does the butterfat. However, much of the flavor of butter is in those milk solids. Clarified butter should not be used in pastry making, except possibly for brushing molds and baking sheets.

WHAT TO LOOK FOR IN BUYING BUTTER: Choose only sweet butter! Not salted, not whipped, and not—heaven forbid!—margarine. Unsalted butter is usually packaged in ¼-pound (114 g) sticks or 1-pound (454 g) blocks. In some areas of the country, fresh-from-the-dairy tub butter, cut from 68-pound (31 kg) cubes, is also available. The finest American butter we have been able to find has been tub butter from the Axelrod dairies in New York State. Land O'Lakes butter is also excellent and is more widely distributed.

To assess the quality of butter yourself, first let it soften at room temperature until it reaches about 50° F (10° C). It should taste sweet, with no off-taste or pronounced sourness, and its texture should be smooth and creamy. When you cut it with a knife it should look creamy, not crumbly. To judge the water content of the butter, cream it by hand on your countertop (see below). If there is excess water in the butter, it will show up as droplets on the surfaces of the counter and the butter. Get the driest butter you can find.

STORAGE: If fresh from the dairy, butter can be kept in the refrigerator for 2 to 3 weeks. Or you can freeze it for up to 2 or 3 months. After that, it loses flavor and eventually goes rancid. In either case, always keep the butter covered airtight to avoid picking up off-odors. If frozen, defrost the butter overnight in the refrigerator before using.

CAVEATS ON USING BUTTER: Butter begins to soften at about 59° F (15° C), and butterfat melts at about 68° F (20° C). In pastry making the consistency of the butter is frequently important. Above 59° F (15° C) it gets too soft and oily for many purposes; so pay close attention to how long the butter is left at room temperature, and chill softened butter briefly in the refrigerator if it becomes too warm. When the butter melts, the emulsion that holds the butterfat, water, and milk solids together breaks down, and the butter will never be its smooth, creamy self again. Butter that has been once melted should be used only where melted butter is called for. When you do melt butter, warm it gently over low heat and don't let it burn.

As mentioned above, there is some variability in the water content of butter. However, the difference between the water contents of really good American butter and watery butter (with the legal minimum of 80 percent butterfat) is only a couple of percent, amounting to perhaps 1 tablespoon (1½ cL) of water in a pound of butter. In most recipes, that small percentage of excess water is insignificant. You might notice a very slight difference in pastry doughs, but for most of them you can easily adjust the amount of liquid or flour in the recipe to compensate for variations in the moisture content of the butter, as well as the flour. Only the *pâtes feuilletées* are a little tricky; the method for handling excess water in the butter for those doughs is discussed on page 13.

ABOUT CREAMING BUTTER: In order to mix solid butter with other ingredients, it is frequently necessary to knead or beat the butter to give it a smooth, creamy consistency. This is called ''creaming,'' and it can be done by hand, in an electric mixer equipped with the leaf beater, or in a food processor. Butter is usually creamed with sugar (and sometimes ground nuts) to facilitate the mixing process. Creaming can also incorporate some air in the butter, and this effect can make a small contribution to the lightness of cakes containing a large amount of butter.

Creaming butter is fastest if you remove it from the refrigerator in advance, letting it soften slightly and warm to about 59° F (15° C). If you are creaming a large amount of butter, you can hasten the softening by cutting the butter into smaller pieces.

However, if your kitchen is very warm, you must be careful not to let the butter soften too much. In that case, we advise you to take the butter straight from the refrigerator, cut it into pieces of about 2 tablespoons (50 g), and cream the butter without letting it soften first.

By hand: To cream butter for use in sweet pastry doughs and cookies, place it on your countertop and add the sugar (and ground nuts, if called for). Smear the butter across the counter a little at a time with the heel of your hand. Then gather the butter together with your dough scraper and repeat until the butter is soft, smooth, and creamy. If before you finish the butter becomes greasy, it has warmed too much. In that case, wrap it in waxed paper and chill it briefly in the refrigerator.

To cream butter for use in cake batters or fillings, place the softened butter in a stainless-steel mixing bowl. (Or if it is cold from the refrigerator, start creaming it on your countertop by the previous method, and when it has softened transfer it to a bowl.) Add the sugar (and ground nuts, if called for), and beat the butter and sugar vigorously with a wooden spoon or a stiff wire whisk, warming it gently over low heat. When it just begins to melt around the side of the bowl, remove it from the heat and continue beating vigorously until it becomes light and fluffy. This is called *beurre pommade* in French.

In an electric mixer equipped with leaf beater or in a food processor fitted with the steel blade: Cut the butter into pieces about 2 to 4 tablespoons (25 to 50 g) in size, and place it in your electric mixer or food processor. Add the sugar (and ground nuts, if called for). Turn on the machine and process, at medium speed if you are using an electric mixer, until the butter is soft, smooth, and creamy. If you are making a sweet pastry dough or a cookie dough, stop when the butter reaches this consistency. If you are making a cake batter or filling, continue processing until the butter becomes light and fluffy, but not so long that it melts.

ABOUT BUTTERING MOLDS: Butter is used to coat molds and baking sheets. There are two ways to do this. As a rule, the easiest is to melt the butter and brush it onto the surface of the mold or baking sheet with a pastry brush. The butter should be liquid but not hot to coat the metal well. This method gives you complete control over the thickness and uniformity of the butter coating.

The second method is to take a piece of softened butter on your fingers and rub it over the surface to be coated. If you are coating a single small surface—one flan ring for example—this is more convenient than brushing on melted butter.

By either method, try to coat the mold or baking sheet evenly. How heavily the mold or baking sheet needs to be buttered depends on what kind of dough or batter is to be baked in it (the more butter in the dough or batter, the less you need to brush) and on the shape of the mold (a deep or complicated shape, or one with sharp corners, requires more butter than a shallow, smooth one).

TO MEASURE BUTTER: Butter can be measured by weight or volume, whichever you find most convenient. ½ cup (1.2 dL) of butter weighs about 4 ounces (114 g).

Eggs

Eggs are the most versatile ingredient in French pastry, and indeed in all of French cooking. While eggs from a variety of birds are used for culinary purposes, only hen's eggs are widely available and standardized. Throughout this book, when a recipe calls for eggs it means large hen's eggs.

USES: Throughout French pastry, as liquid and for leavening, thickening, emulsifying, and brushing.

FACTS ABOUT EGGS: The egg is composed of three parts—yolk, white, and shell.

The yolk contains primarily water, protein, and fat. The mixture of fat and water, which are not soluble in each other, is called an "emulsion." Microscopic globules of fat are suspended in the water, and this suspension is stabilized by the action of an emulsifying agent. The emulsifying agent here is lecithin, and it operates by surrounding each fat globule with lecithin molecules, which, in turn, bond loosely to water molecules and thus keep the fat globules separated. One of the reasons eggs are so important in cooking is that the yolk contains more lecithin than it needs to keep itself emulsified. Thus egg yolks can aid in the formation of other fat in water emulsions (including many sauces, such as hollandaise). In addition, the yolk contains a second emulsifying agent, cholesterol, which facilitates formation of water in fat emulsions. While the emulsifying ability of egg yolks plays a minor role in many areas of French pastry (from pastry doughs such as *pâte sucrée* to fillings like *crème pâtissière*), it is crucial in the preparation of *crème au beurre*.

The egg white is composed almost entirely of water and a water soluble protein called "albumin." Two thin, twisted, opaque white filaments of albumin, called "chalazas," connect the yolk with the inner membrane of the egg shell and keep the yolk anchored near the center of the egg.

The egg shell consists of two parts. The outer shell is the hard, porous, calcified part which the word "shell" calls to mind. Its exterior surface is protected by a film of albumin. The inner shell is really a pair of membranes separated by a thin layer of air. At the top, wide end of the egg, the cushion of air is thicker and is called the "air cell." As the egg gets older, moisture slowly evaporates through the shell and the air cell gets larger. For this reason, while a freshly laid egg will sink in cold water, a 4-day-old egg will rise to the surface and a 2-week-old egg will float, lying on its side.

At the simplest level, raw eggs are a liquid (70 to 75 percent water) that, used in place of, say, water, enriches the taste of a wide range of components. This is especially noticeable in pastry doughs.

When a mixture containing eggs is heated, the proteins in the whites and yolks coagulate, turning from liquid to solid. Egg whites coagulate at about 145° F (60 to 65° C). If not diluted with liquid, yolks coagulate at about 155° F (70° C); on the other hand, if diluted with liquid, it is sometimes possible to raise the temperature of egg yolks as high as 175 to 185° F (80 to 85° C) before coagulation. For both whites and yolks, as the protein coagulates it absorbs liquid in the mixture. This thickens pastry creams and sauces such as *crème pâtissière* and *crème anglaise*.

391

Diluting eggs with liquid is not the only step that will alter their rate of coagulation. Sugar slows coagulation (for example in *crème pâtissière* and *crème anglaise*), whereas acids (such as lemon juice) promote coagulation.

If eggs are heated above the temperatures at which they coagulate, the protein molecules can shrink and lose some of their capacity to hold liquid. This is what happens when, for example, a *crème anglaise* curdles. Egg whites, which contain no fat, lose their softness when overheated and eventually become rubbery. For that reason, meringues are always cooked at low temperature.

Yet another important property of eggs is their ability to form foams when whipped. The foams are formed by trapping air bubbles in the liquid. Most frequently we think of this property in terms of whites, but whole eggs and egg yolks can also be whipped to frothy lightness. If the foam is cooked, then the egg protein coagulates, and it is this combined foaming and coagulation that is behind the preparation of nearly all French cake batters.

HOW EGGS ARE GRADED: Eggs are graded according to both size and quality, with the latter grading voluntary. Large eggs, for example, must have a minimum weight of 24 ounces (685 g) per dozen.

The quality judgment of eggs is made by a process called "candling." The egg shell is not totally opaque, and by holding a light (e.g., a candle) behind the egg and rotating the egg, it is possible to assess the size of the air cell, the condition of the shell and the white, and the size, color, consistency, and mobility of the yolk. Based on this visual test, the eggs are graded AA, A, B, or C, in descending order of quality. The higher the grade the smaller the air cell, the thicker and more viscous the white, and the firmer and plumper the yolk.

WHAT TO LOOK FOR IN BUYING EGGS: As for other dairy products, freshness comes first. Fresher eggs have thicker whites, firmer yolks, and more flavor. Eggs deteriorate much more quickly at room temperature than in the refrigerator, so buy eggs that have been kept refrigerated.

All of our recipes call for large eggs. Either grade AA or A are fine, and you aren't likely to find the lower grades in supermarkets in many areas.

STORAGE: If fresh, eggs can be kept for over a month in the refrigerator. The coldest part of the refrigerator is best, and the eggs will last longer if stored upright, that is, large end on top. For the best flavor, use the eggs within a week to 10 days.

After separating, cover unbroken egg yolks with cold water, seal airtight, and keep in the refrigerator for at most 1 or 2 days. Obviously, they should be drained before using.

Store egg whites in an airtight container in the refrigerator for up to 4 or 5 days. Whites can also be frozen, either in bulk, covered airtight, or in ice-cube trays, one white per compartment. Unmold the frozen cubes and store in plastic bags for as long as several months. Defrost frozen egg whites in the refrigerator before using.

CAVEATS ON COOKING WITH EGGS: Generally, eggs should be brought to room temperature before using. This is especially important for whipping and in preparing *pâtes levées,* where cold eggs would slow the action of the yeast. Remove the eggs from the refrigerator at least 45 minutes before you intend to use them. If you forget to take them out of the refrigerator in advance, you can warm the eggs quickly (before cracking) by immersing them in warm water for 5 to 10 minutes.

Do not cook or beat eggs in bare aluminum, because direct contact with aluminum discolors eggs. However, pastry doughs and cake and pastry batters can be baked on bare aluminum because the butter brushed on the mold or baking sheet or the butter in the pastry dough provides a barrier between the metal and eggs.

When using eggs to thicken a pastry cream or sauce, it is essential to raise the heat of the liquid evenly. Use a heavy saucepan and stir constantly. We recommend that you cook pastry creams and custard sauces over direct heat. You can always lower the heat quickly by lifting the saucepan if the mixture is cooking too quickly. When the egg-thickened mixture has reached the required consistency, remove it from the heat and pour it into a bowl. Do not leave it in the saucepan because heat stored in the metal of the pan can continue to cook the mixture after you have removed it from the heat. If, after the pastry cream or sauce is in the bowl, you decide that it has not cooked enough, you can always return it to the saucepan and cook it more.

Always be careful when you mix eggs with flour or cornstarch. If there isn't enough liquid in the mixture, these carbohydrates can dehydrate and "burn" the eggs, making them grainy. There are two places in pastry making where this is a potential problem: in mixing *pâtes levées* the dough must not be allowed to become too dry; and in preparing pastry creams, you should not mix the starches with the eggs too long before adding the hot milk.

TO SEPARATE EGGS: Cold eggs are easiest to separate, because in cold eggs the whites and yolks have greater viscosity and surface tension. Very fresh eggs are easier to separate than older ones because the membranes around their yolks are stronger.

Crack the side of the egg shell with a sharp tap on your countertop. Do not crack the shell on the edge of a bowl, since that increases the possibility of puncturing the yolk with a jagged edge of the cracked shell. Hold the egg vertically over a bowl, insert the tips of your thumbs in the crack, and pry the shell open. Let the white drop into the bowl, then pour the yolk back and forth between one half of the shell and the other until all of the white has been separated from the yolk. Remove the chalazas (the thin white filaments) from the yolk by running your finger over the edge of the shell, and let these filaments drop into the bowl with the rest of the white.

If a speck of yolk gets in the white, remove it with the edge of the shell; or blot it up with the corner of a paper towel. After you separate each egg, pour the white into another bowl so that if by chance you puncture a yolk and too much of it drops into the bowl with the white, you will lose only one egg rather than all of the whites you have separated up to that point.

ABOUT BEATEN EGGS: When a recipe calls for lightly beaten eggs, the eggs are to be stirred vigorously with a fork until yolk and white are mixed. The object is to have a fairly homogeneous liquid, but not to incorporate air in the eggs.

Some recipes call for beating egg yolks and/or whole eggs with sugar (and in some cases flour and cornstarch). This is usually done before adding a hot liquid (most often milk) to the eggs, and the purpose is to mix the eggs and sugar well so that when the liquid is added the result will be a smooth mixture with no lumps (remember that sugar retards coagulation). The eggs and sugar should be beaten with a wire whisk, but only until smooth, thick, and pale yellow.

TO WHIP EGGS: Whole eggs, yolks, and whites can be whipped to produce thick, light foams. Whip eggs with a wire whisk in a nonporous, round-bottomed bowl. Stainless steel is excellent, and glass is also all right; for whipping whites, copper is best. Both the bowl and the whisk should be clean, dry, and at room temperature.

To incorporate the most air and get the maximum volume, eggs should be at room temperature before whipping and at least 3 days old (fresher eggs have too much viscosity).

For whole eggs and yolks, sugar is added at the beginning of the whipping process. For whites, sugar is added at the end.

Always start whipping at low speed to incorporate many small air bubbles in the eggs. If you are whipping by hand, tilt the bowl and sweep the whisk around the bottom in a rythmical circular motion. Each revolution should lift the entire mass of egg and incorporate air in the process.

As the eggs get foamy, gradually increase the speed at which you whip them. In an electric mixer, gradually increase the speed to medium-high.

Yolks are whipped until cream colored, thick, and light. When the whisk or beater is lifted from the whipped yolks, slowly dissolving ribbons should form on the surface. Whole eggs are whipped to a similar consistency and color. They can be whipped to an even larger volume by carrying out the early stage of the whipping in a warm bowl (see the recipe for *génoise*, page 59).

Eggs whites require more care than whole eggs or yolks. It is essential that there be no specks of yolk in the white and no grease or oil on the bowl or whisk. Copper bowls are best for whipping whites because the copper produces a slight acidity that firms the protein in the egg whites, making it possible to incorporate more air and stabilizing the whipped whites. If you don't have a copper bowl, add a little cream of tartar (⅛ teaspoon, or a pinch, for 3 egg whites) or lemon juice (¼ teaspoon, or 1 mL, for 3 egg whites) to the whites when they begin to froth.

At the outset, the egg whites will be transparent, with a slight yellowish tint. As you whip in air bubbles and the whites become foamy, the color will change to white and they will become opaque. Gradually the egg whites will increase in volume and become thick enough to hold soft, bending peaks as you lift the whisk from the bowl. At this stage, the whites still slide down the sides of the bowl.

Then, as you continue beating, the whites will become stiff but still moist, and the mass of egg white won't slip when the bowl is tipped. Lifting the beater will produce firm, sharp peaks. This is the stage when you would stop beating if you were making a soufflé.

For meringues, briefly continue whipping until the egg whites just begin to slip and form streaks around the side of the bowl; but do not beat them so long that they become grainy. This will give the meringue a consistency firm enough for piping from a pastry bag and a volume that will rise, dry out, and stabilize when baked (rather than rising in the oven, then falling as it cools).

At this point, "meringue" the egg whites by adding the sugar or sugar syrup and continuing to whip until smooth and shiny, about 10 to 20 seconds longer. Then stop beating or your meringue will be too elastic and become chewy after baking.

When whipping very fresh egg whites (which can be overwhipped and become grainy more easily) or making an exceptionally delicate nut meringue with very little sugar, alter this procedure slightly. As the whites form soft peaks, gradually add a little sugar while you continue whipping. This will make the meringue smooth and shiny, and it will become very stiff without forming jagged peaks or streaking and slipping on the sides of the bowl as you whip it. Stop whipping as soon as the meringue is very stiff and still moist and shiny. It must not become at all grainy. Then gently fold in the remaining sugar.

ABOUT EGG WASH: Pastries are brushed with lightly beaten egg for a variety of reasons: to prevent the surface of a *pâte levée* from drying while rising, and to moisten it before baking so that it will rise evenly in the oven; to seal the surface of a *tarte* shell and prevent the filling from making it soggy; and to give the tops of pastries a beautiful golden color. The egg wash is applied with a flat pastry brush. Use it sparingly; only a thin coating is needed, and if you use too much you will get a thick, undesirable crust.

For the small quantity of egg wash you will need in the home kitchen, simply beat a whole egg with a fork until homogeneous. For an especially large batch of pastries, you can extend the egg wash by beating in a little cold water, but this will give the pastries less color. If you have some extra egg yolks on hand, you can thin them with a little water and use instead of whole eggs to get an even richer color.

TO MEASURE EGGS: Our recipes call for specific numbers of large eggs. In terms of volume, there are 5 whole eggs, or 8 whites, or 14 yolks in 1 cup (¼ L).

To substitute eggs of other sizes or use stored egg whites in our recipes, first convert the number of eggs in the recipe to volume, using these equivalents, then measure the required volume of eggs.

Sugar

USES: Every recipe in this book contains sugar in one form or another.

FACTS ABOUT SUGAR: All sugars are sweet and share a common chemical composition ($C_6H_{12}O_6$ for simple sugars). However, their molecules are structured in different ways, and thus they have different properties.

Sucrose: Ordinary sugar, or sucrose, is one of the more complicated. It is a disaccharide, or double sugar, composed of the two monosaccharides (simple sugars) fructose and dextrose. Sucrose is found in sugar cane, sugar beets, and maple syrup.

Pure sucrose is a brilliant white, hard, odorless crystalline solid. It is heavier than water (the density of solid sucrose is 1.6 g/cc as compared with 1 g/cc for water) and is very soluble in water. On the other hand, sucrose is insoluble in alcohol and poorly soluble in alcohol solutions, so it should always be dissolved in water before adding alcohol.

As mentioned earlier under Eggs, sugar raises the temperature at which eggs coagulate. Also, it is hydrophilic, meaning it absorbs water from its environment. This combination of properties gives cake batters more time to rise before setting and makes it possible to obtain a moist, soft cake without sogginess.

In whipped eggs, sucrose becomes part of the cell walls of the foam. By absorbing moisture it firms the eggs, giving the foam strength and rigidity. This effect is especially apparent in meringues where, added at the end of the whipping, sugar prevents graininess and produces a smooth and stable meringue.

Finally, sucrose enhances other flavors, retards discoloration in fruits, depresses the freezing point of water, and promotes fermentation of yeast in *pâtes levées*. It gives a rich color to many pastry doughs and to the tops of pastries that are sprinkled with it before baking.

Dextrose: Dextrose is also known as glucose (and sometimes as "corn sugar," since it occurs naturally in sweet corn), but since the term "glucose" also refers to a commercial syrup, we never refer to the pure sugar dextrose as glucose. Dextrose is less than half as sweet as sucrose. Like sucrose, it is very soluble in water, and it melts at 293° F (145° C), or 27° F (15° C) below the melting point of sucrose.

Dextrose does not crystallize itself and inhibits crystallization of sucrose. For this reason, a small amount of glucose or corn syrup is often added to sucrose in preparations where crystallization is a potential problem.

Fructose (or levulose): This is a simple sugar found in ripe fruits and honey. It is about 50% sweeter than sucrose.

Invert sugar: When sucrose is dissolved in acidulated water and boiled, some of it transforms into "invert sugar," a mixture of equal parts of dextrose and fructose. Like dextrose, invert sugar doesn't crystallize, and this process plays a role in keeping jams and jellies smooth and preventing crystallization in *caramel blond* and *nougatine*. Also, invert sugar is even better than sucrose in its ability to absorb water.

Lactose and maltose: Like sucrose, lactose and maltose are double sugars. Except for the small amount of lactose in milk, this sugar has no role in French pastry. Maltose is crystalline, less sweet than sucrose, and very soluble in water. Its importance in pastry making is in leavened pastry doughs, not as an ingredient but as an intermediate stage in the breakdown of starch and the fermentation process.

COMMERCIAL FORMS OF SUGAR: Sugar is sold in many forms. Most refined sugars are sucrose, derived from either sugar beets or sugar cane, and from the culinary point of view they are indistinguishable.

Granulated sugar: Pure white crystalline sucrose, ground to fine granules. Unless otherwise specified, this is what we mean when we call for sugar in a recipe.

Superfine sugar: A very finely ground granulated sugar that dissolves more quickly than ordinary granulated sugar. It is often used in cake batters because when it is beaten into the batter the smaller crystals drag in more air with them.

Confectioners sugar: Granulated sugar that has been crushed to a fine powder. A little cornstarch is included to prevent caking. Confectioners sugar dissolves more quickly than even superfine sugar.

Crystallized sugar: Very coarse granulated sugar which, used as decoration, gives a jewellike appearance. A good substitute is rock candy. Coarsely pulverize the rock candy using a meat pounder or hammer. Then sift out the fine powder to separate the larger crystals of sugar. Ideally, you want crystals about ⅛ inch (3 mm) in diameter.

Molasses: A by-product of refining sugar cane, molasses is a thick, viscous syrup that is about 50 percent sucrose. It can vary in color from amber to dark brown. Molasses contains minerals and nitrogenous substances that contribute to the development of yeast, and used in small quantities it adds flavor, color, and softness to some leavened pastries. Choose light unsulphured molasses, and definitely not the strong, bitter blackstrap molasses.

Honey: Before refined cane sugar became widely available in Europe in the seventeenth century, honey was the predominant sweetener and was used throughout French pastry. Today it has been almost completely replaced by refined sugars. Honey contains both dextrose and fructose.

Glucose: This viscous syrup is primarily dextrose, with some maltose, water, and a gummy substance called "dextrin." It is produced by an incomplete hydrolysis of starch, usually potato starch in France and cornstarch in the United States. Glucose is sold in candy-making and cake-decorating shops and by mail order from Maid of Scandinavia. You can sometimes substitute light corn syrup (see below) for it. When pouring glucose, cut the flow of syrup by sweeping your index finger down over the mouth of the container. Dip your finger in cold water first to prevent the glucose from sticking to it; and, if you are measuring by volume, first rinse out the measuring cup with cold water.

Light corn syrup: This is a glucose-type syrup manufactured from cornstarch and diluted with water to give it a more fluid consistency. Some manufacturers flavor their corn syrup, so, if you are buying it as a substitute for glucose, read the label carefully (a little citric acid or vanilla is fine, but avoid salt). In recipes that contain glucose, sugar, and water, the correspondence we use is:

¼ cup (75 g) glucose + 1 tablespoon (1.5 cL) water + 1 tablespoon (12 g) sugar = ⅓ cup (100 g) corn syrup

Malt extract: Malt extract is a syrup made from germinated barley in which the starch content has been converted to the sugar maltose. Malt extract is rich in enzymes, including amylase. When added to leavened pastry doughs, it facilitates fermentation, making the baked pastry lighter, and like molasses it gives the pastry a richer color and flavor. Malt extract must never be mixed directly with salt, which destroys some of its enzymes. Get light malt extract without hops, and don't use the nondyastatic variety, which lacks the important enzymes (diastases).

SUGAR SYRUPS: Sugar syrups play important roles in pastry making. The principal syrups used in this book are: *sirop léger,* a light syrup used for poaching fresh fruits (see the section on Fruits, page 422); *sirop à baba* (see page 221), another light syrup that is flavored with rum and used to soak *babas;* and a heavy syrup called *sirop à trente.*

Sirop à Trente

HEAVY SYRUP

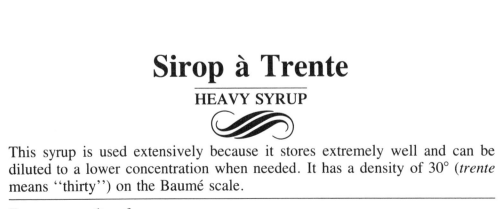

This syrup is used extensively because it stores extremely well and can be diluted to a lower concentration when needed. It has a density of 30° (*trente* means "thirty") on the Baumé scale.

For any quantity of syrup

INGREDIENTS

Sugar and cold water
in the ratio of 2
cups sugar per 1
cup water (1,750 g
sugar per liter of
water)

1 Combine the sugar and water in a saucepan and bring to a boil, stirring occasionally to dissolve all the sugar.

2 Allow the syrup to cool.

3 Pour the cooled syrup into a dry container, cover airtight, and keep at room temperature for up to several months. If sugar crystallizes from the syrup, add a little water (about 2 tablespoons, or 3 cL, for each 1 cup, or ¼ L, of syrup) and bring to a boil to dissolve the crystals, then cool again before using.

STORAGE OF SUGAR: Stored dry, sugar doesn't ferment. Because it absorbs odors and moisture, it should be kept in an airtight container.

In high concentrations, sugar solutions can provide an environment hostile to bacteria growth—a principle that is vital in canning and making jams and jellies. *Sirop à trente* has the ideal concentration for storage. Syrups with lower concentrations can begin to ferment in a few days, and those with higher concentrations have a tendency to crystallize.

ABOUT COOKING SUGAR: Sugar can be cooked either dry or after dissolving in water.

We begin with the method for cooking sugar dry, which is used in preparing *nougatine* and *praliné*. The pot in which the sugar is cooked must be large enough to accommodate the nuts, which are added after it has melted and begun to color. There is no reason to use a candy thermometer since you can easily recognize the stages of cooking by color alone.

Place the sugar in the saucepan and cook it over medium to high heat without stirring. As soon as it begins to melt around the edge of the pot, start stirring with a wooden spoon. When the sugar becomes fluid, with small white lumps of unmelted sugar floating in the syrup, reduce the heat to low and continue cooking, stirring constantly and crushing the solid lumps with the wooden spoon, until completely melted.

Sugar melts at 320° F (160° C). If it were cooked very evenly, then it would be clear and nearly colorless. However, in practice the sugar cooks unevenly, and it will turn a pale to medium amber. Also, stirring incorporates air bubbles, which sometimes make the syrup translucent or even opaque.

As you continue cooking, stirring constantly, the sugar will gradually turn a deeper amber. At 355° F (180° C) it will lose one-sixth of its weight by evaporation of water contained in the sugar molecules themselves, and it will begin to boil.

When the temperature of the sugar is raised still higher, the sugar darkens and gives off a faint burnt odor; then it begins to smoke and turns almost black. At

400° F (200° C), the sugar decomposes and only carbon remains. Burned sugar has a bitter taste, so cook it to a dark caramel only if it is to be used as a food coloring.

Bear in mind that, above the melting point, sugar cooks very quickly and can rapidly pass from a desirable pale caramel to an unusable bitter state. Even when you remove the pot from the burner, heat stored in the pot can continue cooking the sugar. So have a large bowl of cold water handy, and, if you think the caramel is becoming too hot, briefly dip the bottom of the pot in the water to cool it and then quickly remove from the cold water so you don't cool the caramel.

For all purposes other than *nougatine* and *praliné,* sugar is dissolved in a little water, then boiled to gradually increase the density of the syrup and raise its temperature. The syrup goes through a succession of well-defined stages by which you can recognize its density and temperature. The stages that are of primary interest in this book are the soft ball, firm ball, and hard crack, and the degrees of caramelization discussed earlier.

For some purposes (notably fondant and *sucre filé*), the sugar should be cooked to an especially precise temperature, and even experts use a candy thermometer. For other uses, you can judge the temperature with sufficient accuracy by touch or color, and we feel that this is much more convenient, especially for small quantities of syrup.

The first important point in cooking a sugar syrup is to choose the right pot. Ideally, it should have a spout for pouring the syrup in a thin stream; and it should be about half to two thirds full.

Measure the sugar into the pot and add the water. Use at least ¼ cup (6 cL) of water for each 1 cup (200 g) of sugar. Stir to thoroughly moisten the sugar. Then stop stirring, place the saucepan over moderate heat, and bring to a boil. It is not necessary to stir the sugar while you are bringing it to a boil. In fact, stirring splashes syrup on the walls of the pot, and the syrup on the walls dries to form unwanted sugar crystals.

At the moment when the syrup comes to a boil, the impurities in the sugar will rise to the surface and appear as a white foam or scum. Most sugar sold for domestic use in the United States is quite low in impurities. However the impurities can cause the sugar to crystallize, so it is a good idea to skim the foam or scum off the surface of the syrup with a spoon at this point. This is especially important if you are cooking sugar above the hard ball stage (see page 402).

Never stir the syrup after it has come to a boil since stirring can lead to crystallization of the sugar.

Right after the syrup has come to a boil it will have a tendency to foam up and can boil over if the heat is too high or the pot is too small. Adjust the heat so the syrup cooks quickly without foaming up.

At this point, you have two choices. The simplest is to cover the pot loosely while you continue cooking the syrup. The water vapor that condenses inside the lid will dissolve sugar crystals forming on the walls of the pot. The pot should be kept covered (except for occasional observation) until enough water has evaporated that the syrup no longer splatters onto the sides of the pot.

If you choose not to cover the pot, then sugar crystals will form on the walls of the pot, and you must wash down the walls with a moistened pastry brush to dissolve the crystals. Use as little water as you can so you don't slow the cooking. This is done only at the early stage of cooking, right after the syrup comes to a boil. After that, there should be no more crystals forming on the walls of the pot.

If you use too large a pot, then in washing down the walls of the pot you will add too much water to the syrup. Also, if the level of syrup is too low, cooking is irregular and it is difficult to use a candy thermometer.

As you continue cooking the syrup, the water in it evaporates and its temperature increases. Below 293° F (145° C), that's all that is happening, so if you heat the syrup above the required temperature, you can always lower the temperature (and correspondingly the concentration of the syrup) by adding a little hot water.

Checking the Stages of Sugar

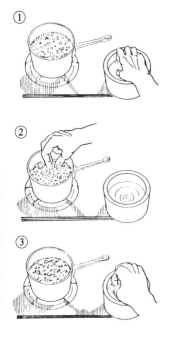

If you are not using a candy thermometer, then after the syrup stops foaming up and splattering on the walls of the pot, you must start testing it to check the stage of cooking. Have a large bowl of cold water next to the saucepan. Dip your hand in the cold water ①, quickly dip the tips of your thumb and index finger in the syrup to pluck out a little syrup ②, then immediately immerse them in the cold water again ③. (Don't worry, you won't get burned. The cold water will protect your fingers, so they will feel barely warm. However, if this procedure makes you too nervous, you can spoon a few drops of the syrup into the cold water instead.) Feel the syrup between your thumb and index finger. At first it will be watery and will dissolve immediately in the cold water. Repeat this test every minute or so. Gradually the syrup will become viscous and won't dissolve so quickly. Soon you will be able to roll it between your fingertips into a small, very soft ball that flattens when you lift it. This is the soft ball stage, which corresponds to a temperature of 234° to 239° F (113° to 115° C). For fondant, the sugar is cooked to the upper end of the soft ball stage.

When the syrup reaches about 243° F (117° C), the ball you form between your fingertips will be about the size of a pea, and, while still soft, it will hold its shape ④. This is the beginning of the firm ball stage, called *petit boulé* in French. It is used for *crème au beurre*.

Within the firm ball stage, French chefs differentiate a second stage called *boulé*. At this point, when you test the syrup in cold water, you can roll the cooled syrup into a slightly larger ball. The temperature of the syrup is about 248° F (120° C), and this is the best stage to use for *meringue italienne* and for a very firm *crème au beurre*.

If you did not wash down the walls of the pot carefully at the outset then, when you test the syrup for the soft ball or firm ball stage, it will feel grainy because it contains undissolved sugar crystals. Do not use a grainy syrup because it will produce a grainy fondant, *crème au beurre,* or *meringue italienne*. If the crystals are transparent, add more water to the syrup to lower the temperature and dissolve the crystals. Then continue cooking, bringing the syrup back up to the soft ball or firm ball stage. However, if the crystals are white and opaque, you cannot dissolve them, and the only way to use the syrup is to cook it further and make a caramel, *praliné,* or *nougatine*.

Above 250° F (121° C), the syrup becomes progressively more viscous. From 250° to 268° F (121° to 130° C) it is in the hard ball *(grand boulé)* stage and will form a very firm, but still malleable ball when tested in cold water. From 270° to 290° F (135° to 140° C) it is in the soft crack stage (*petit cassé*, in French) and can no longer be rolled into a ball; instead it forms hard threads or sheets that bend before breaking. If you bite a piece of the cooled sugar, it will stick to your teeth ⑤.

In making *sucre filé* and *caramel blond,* a few drops of acid (such as lemon juice) are frequently added to the syrup during the hard ball or soft crack stage to help prevent crystallization.

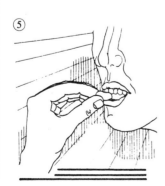

At 293° F (145° C), the syrup has lost all of its water by evaporation. However, as long as there are no crystals on the walls of the pot, it will remain liquid, even though this is below the melting point of sucrose.

From this point on, be especially careful not to cook the sugar beyond the required temperature, because, as you raise the temperature still higher, the structure of the sugar will change and you can't reverse the process by adding water and cooling it. When the sugar reaches the desired stage, immediately plunge the bottom of the pot into a large bowl of cold water to stop the cooking. Then quickly remove it from the cold water so you don't lower the temperature of the syrup, and wait briefly until any bubbles in the syrup rise to the surface and disappear.

Next is the hard crack *(grand cassé)* stage. It corresponds to a temperature of 300° to 320° F (150° to 160° C). When you test the syrup in cold water, it forms hard sheets and threads that shatter easily. If you bite a piece of the cooled sugar, it no longer sticks to your teeth.

At 320° F (160° C), the true melting point of sucrose, the sugar yellows very slightly. In contrast to the dry cooking method, it should be transparent (because this method of cooking sugar is slower and more even). If the syrup were cooled to room temperature, it would form a glassy mass and would no longer crystallize.

As you continue cooking the sugar, it will gradually turn golden at about 330° F (165° C) and then amber, and will go through the same stages of caramelization as sugar cooked dry.

In practice, the sugar will probably be slightly darker than the color appropriate to its temperature because syrup around the edge of the pot cooks more quickly than syrup in the center of the pot, especially if the flames on a gas burner lick the sides of the pot.

When you have cooked sugar a few times, you will be able to anticipate the stages of cooking as they come along and remove the pot from the heat before the syrup reaches the desired temperature. Be careful not to let the heat stored in the pot raise the temperature of the syrup above what you are aiming for. This is especially important for cooking caramels, since there the structure of the sugar is changing irreversibly.

To clean a pot in which sugar has been cooked, fill it about half to two-thirds full of water and boil to dissolve the sugar clinging to the inside of the pot.

When cooking sugar at high altitudes—above, say, 3,000 feet (900 m)—you must take into account the change in the boiling point of water due to reduced atmospheric pressure. This affects the temperature of each stage between the boiling point and the point at which all of the water in the syrup has evaporated—that is, between 212° and 293° F (100° and 145° C) at sea level. Within this range, reduce the temperatures we have given for each stage by 1.8° F (1° C) for each 1,000 feet (300 m) above sea level. Altitude has no effect on the hard crack and higher stages (above 293° F or 145° C), and for cooking sugar dry.

TO MEASURE SUGAR: Granulated and superfine sugars can be measured equally well by weight or volume. Most syrups are measured by volume, but for very viscous syrups (such as glucose) it is more convenient to measure by weight if a scale is available.

Solid sugar is heavier than water, but granulated and superfine contain air between the granules and thus have a lower density. One cup of granulated or superfine sugar weighs about 7 ounces (200 g).

While not very accurate, confectioners sugar can also be measured by volume. Scoop the (unsifted) confectioners sugar into a dry measure cup (or measuring spoon) without packing it down and sweep a palette knife or pastry corne over the top of the cup to level the surface. Measured this way, 1 cup of confectioners sugar weighs about 4⅔ ounce (130 g).

Flour

Use unbleached all-purpose flour for all recipes in this book that call for flour.

USES: Gives body and structure to all pastry doughs and most cake and pastry batters. Gives elasticity to *pâtes levées*. Thickens some fillings, including *crème pâtissière* and *crème d'amandes*.

FACTS ABOUT FLOUR: Flours are milled from a variety of grains. By far the most important is wheat, and whenever the word flour is used alone it refers to wheat flour.

The wheat kernel is composed of three parts. The bran is the outer envelope and is rich in vitamins and minerals; but it is tough and papery. The germ is the embryo and contains proteins and fats. And the endosperm is the farinaceous (starchy) body of the kernel.

Only the endosperm is used in white flour. The process of milling breaks the kernel and separates the endosperm from the other components by bolting—a process of sifting through successively finer sieves.

The endosperm contains primarily starch, water, and a combination of albuminous proteins called gluten. The proportions of starch and gluten in the flour depend on the type of wheat (typically, winter wheats have a lower gluten content than spring wheats) and how the flour was milled (the proportion of gluten is greater in the peripheral part of the kernel than in the center). Wheats high in gluten are called ''hard'', those low in gluten, ''soft.''

After milling, flour has a yellowish color and poor baking qualities. Aging lightens the color, improves the flour's ability to absorb fats, and develops the elasticity of the gluten. Similar results can also be achieved by chemical means, and flours so treated are called ''bleached.'' Those aged naturally are called ''unbleached.''

Starch is the predominant part (typically 73 to 78 percent) of most flours. The salient feature of starches in cooking is their ability to absorb water. Flour thickens liquids because the starch is a solid and because the starch granules absorb water. Heating the liquid swells the granules and increases their water retention, thus increasing their thickening power. When the liquid cools, water remains trapped in the starch granules, and the viscosity of the liquid increases still further. On the other hand, excessive heating overstretches the granules, reducing the amount of water they can hold. Also, the presence of sugar or acids reduces the thickening power of starches.

Gluten typically makes up 6 to 12 percent of the composition of wheat flour. The characteristic that distinguishes gluten is its elasticity. When a mixture containing gluten is moistened, the gluten fibers link together in a meshlike network. Manipulating the dough increases the elasticity of the individual gluten fibers. This combination of effects makes leavened pastry doughs possible.

The mechanism by which yeast leavens breads is this: Enzymes produced by the yeast ferment sugar in the dough, releasing carbon dioxide. This gas inflates the fibers of gluten like tiny balloons. Baking expands the ''balloons'' and coagulates the gluten protein, giving the bread its characteristic spongelike structure. The minimum percentage of gluten for breadmaking is considered to be 7 percent, and a higher percentage is usually desirable.

In addition to its role in leavened pastry doughs, gluten plays an essential part in other pastry doughs. The strength of the gluten-fiber network prevents pastry doughs from tearing too easily and makes it possible to roll them into thin layers. And the flakiness characteristic of many pastry doughs depends upon the structure they get from gluten. To a lesser extent, gluten contributes to the stability of cell walls in cakes. However, while in breads gluten's elasticity and strength is paramount, tenderness is an essential characteristic of other pastry doughs and of cakes, and too much (or too strong) gluten must be avoided because it would make them tough.

The elasticity of gluten can be modulated by other factors. For example, the development of gluten's strength by manipulation is retarded by lowering the temperature. Fats coat the gluten fibers and inhibit linking (this is why *pâtes à foncer* are so much more tender than *pâtes feuilletées*, where the butter is kept separated from the flour). The presence of sugar (notably in *pâte sablée* and *pâte sucrée*) or acids also reduces the linkage of gluten fibers, but, on the other hand, salt or milk will strengthen the gluten and raise its coagulation temperature.

Just as important as the percentage of gluten in the flour is its quality, assessed in terms of its retentiveness (ability to absorb water), extensibility, and suppleness. For bread to be soft and not too dry, the gluten must have good retentiveness. The more elastic (or extensible) the gluten, the more the dough will rise and the lighter the bread will be. The suppleness of the gluten depends on the wheat from which it came (flour from durum wheat is never used in pastry or bread making because its gluten is not supple), the milling and aging of the flour, and the way the dough is handled. Proper kneading enhances the suppleness of the gluten.

Yet another essential property of gluten for pastry making is its ability to absorb fats. Without gluten, pastry doughs would not retain their high butter content during baking.

The primacy of wheat flour in pastry making derives from the fact that gluten is found only in wheat. While proteins similar to gluten exist in other cereals (rye, for example), these proteins don't have gluten's elasticity. Thus, other flours are of interest only for their starch content.

ABOUT OTHER STARCHES: The other starches significant in French cooking are cornstarch, potato starch, and arrowroot. Their advantage as thickeners is that they produce a smoother, more refined texture and have greater thickening power than does flour. A given weight of cornstarch or potato starch will thicken twice as much liquid as the same weight of flour, and arrowroot has two and one-half times the thickening capacity of flour. Also, whereas flour produces opaque sauces, cornstarch and potato starch can be used to thicken a translucent sauce, and arrowroot a transparent sauce.

On the other hand, flour is a more stable thickener than these starches, and it can withstand more prolonged contact with heat.

Cornstarch and potato starch can be used interchangeably, and the only reason for choosing one over the other is availability. In this book we use cornstarch, whereas in France, we would use potato starch. Arrowroot is much more expensive than cornstarch, and, since the clarity it give to sauces is of no advantage in pastry making, we never use it.

TYPES OF WHEAT FLOUR: Several types of white wheat flour are widely available in the United States. Some brands (Gold Medal and Pillsbury are the biggest producers) are marketed nationally and standardized, while others are available regionally, or even locally. Packaged flours are labeled with their carbohydrate and protein contents (as well as fat and sodium, which are present in small amounts) in grams per 4-ounce (113.5 grams) portion. From this information, you can easily compute the percentages of protein (about 85 percent of which is gluten) and carbohydrate (starch) in the flour. The remainder is primarily water and a small amount of ash (natural minerals from the wheat). Most white flours are enriched to replenish vitamins and minerals removed in the milling process.

Unbleached all-purpose flour: A blend of soft and hard wheats intended for everything, including cakes, pastry doughs, breads, and thickening. It is aged, rather than chemically bleached, and is a soft cream color. For the two major national brands, the breakdowns of components (based on the information on their labels) are:

	Gold Medal (%)	Pillsbury's Best (%)
Carbohydrate	76.6	75.8
Protein	9.7	10.6
(gluten)	(8.2)	(9)
Water (not labeled)	12.3	12.3
Fat	0.9	0.9
Ash (not labeled)	0.5	0.5

All-purpose flour, bleached: Also a blend of soft and hard wheats, and intended to be suitable for everything. Bleached chemically, it is a bright, strident white. For both Gold Medal and Pillsbury's Best, the breakdown of components on the label is the same as for Gold Medal's unbleached all-purpose flour.

Bread flour: A very high protein (12 to 13 percent) flour made from hard wheats, usually chemically bleached and treated with potassium bromate to further improve the gluten's elasticity. Suitable only for making breads.

Cake Flour: A highly refined, very soft flour. It is bleached with chlorine which, unlike the chemicals used to bleach all-purpose flour, does not develop the gluten's strength and in fact inhibits the linkage of gluten fibers by raising the acidity of the flour. Cake flour's low protein content (about 7 percent) and low gluten strength make it suitable only for cakes.

Regional flours: Unbleached flours marketed regionally in the northeastern United States often have slightly higher gluten contents than the national brands of all-purpose flour. Southern all-purpose flours have lower gluten content. Some all-purpose flours marketed in the Northeast and the West have a higher water content and a correspondingly lower carbohydrate content than do the nationally marketed all-purpose flours.

Whole-wheat, bran, and related flours: These are flours that contain, in addition to the endosperm, all or part of the bran and/or germ of the wheat. They contain more of the natural vitamins, minerals, and proteins of the wheat kernel than do white flours, but their textures are totally unsuitable for making French pastries.

CHOOSING THE RIGHT FLOUR: In developing the recipes for this book we used Gold Medal unbleached all-purpose flour. We chose the Gold Medal because, of the two major nationally available brands, it has the lower protein content (by about 1 percent) and is closer to the flour we would use for pastry doughs in France. With this flour, we found that we were able to get perfect results for all types of pastries.

The bleached all-purpose flours of both Gold Medal and Pillsbury have the same proportions of protein, carbohydrate, and water as does the Gold Medal unbleached, so these three could be used interchangeably. If you prefer to use another brand, choose a flour with the proportions of components as close as possible to those of the Gold Medal unbleached all-purpose flour (87 g carbohydrates, 11 g protein, and 1 g fat per 4-ounce portion). Otherwise you may have to alter our recipes to compensate for the differences in the properties of the flour.

STORAGE: Covered airtight to prevent loss or absorption of moisture, white flour can be kept at room temperature for up to 2 or 3 months before it begins to deteriorate in quality.

CAVEATS ON COOKING WITH FLOUR: When thickening with flour, it is essential to keep the starch granules separated in order to produce a smooth result. If you mix flour directly into a hot liquid, it will form lumps—dry inside and surrounded by a layer of moistened starch granules that prevent water from penetrating to the interior of the lump. The classic methods of thickening are designed to avoid this, and, if you follow the instructions in our recipes, you will never have a problem with it. Also, raw flour has an unpleasant starchy taste. Thus, any starch-thickened filling must be thoroughly cooked—either during its preparation or when baked in a pastry.

When making pastry doughs, pay strict attention to how much the gluten should be activated. For *pâtes levées,* do not shortchange the kneading or you will not activate the gluten enough and the pastry will not rise properly. For other pastry doughs, don't work the dough too much or it will become elastic (and difficult to use) and the finished pastry will be tough rather than tender. Keep in mind that the gluten will gradually relax and lose its elasticity when you stop manipulating the dough. A rest of 20 minutes is sufficient from the practical point of view, and after 1 hour the gluten will be totally relaxed. Also, keeping the dough cold reduces the activation of the gluten. However, when frozen the gluten maintains its elasticity and does not relax.

The water content of flour is variable, depending on the brand of flour, the season (flour loses more moisture by evaporation in winter when the air is drier), and how long the flour has been stored. The flour on your supermarket shelf contains typically 1 to 1½ percent less moisture than it did when it was packaged. When a recipe (especially for pastry dough) calls for a high percentage of flour and the amount of liquid is crucial to the final texture, it may be necessary to compensate for variations in the moisture content of the flour by adjusting either the amount of liquid or the amount of flour in the recipe.

DUSTING WITH FLOUR: It is frequently necessary to dust molds, baking sheets, or your countertop with flour.

Molds and baking sheets are always brushed with melted butter before dusting with flour. For molds, the flour fixes the butter (so it won't run down the side during baking) and forms a light crust when baked. On baking sheets, the flour prevents batter from sliding around when it is spread.

Spoon the flour into the mold or onto the baking sheet, adding more than will be needed to coat it. Then tilt, shake, and tap to distribute the flour and coat the butter evenly. Once a thin layer of flour is on the butter, no more flour will adhere. Invert the mold or baking sheet and tap it to remove the excess flour.

When rolling out pastry dough, you must dust your countertop and the top surface of the dough with flour to prevent the dough from sticking to counter or rolling pin. In order to avoid altering the proportion of flour in the dough, use as little flour as possible.

Most home cooks use a sifter or strainer to dust with flour, but this method tends to put too much flour on the counter. The method used by professionals is this: Take a little flour in your hand, holding it between the tips of your thumb and fingers. Slowly and smoothly draw back your hand (without snapping your wrist—you don't want the flour on the floor behind you); then, without releasing your fingertips, throw your hand in a horizontal motion—like skimming a rock across the surface of a pond—over the front half of the countertop. Do not open your hand to release the flour. There will be enough loose flour around your fingertips to make a light film across the counter. To dust evenly, move your hand nearly parallel to the counter and 4 to 6 inches (10 to 15 cm) above it. Repeat several times until there is just enough flour on the counter to roll the dough without sticking. (A soft, sticky dough such as *pâte à brioche* will require more flour than a firm, dry dough like *feuilletage*.) Place the dough on the flour-dusted counter and lightly dust the dough with flour by the same method. After you start rolling the dough, occasionally lift it from the counter and dust a little more flour under and on top of the dough so you can continue rolling it without sticking. This method of dusting flour on the counter takes a little practice, but it works extremely well.

HOW TO MEASURE FLOUR AND CORNSTARCH: The only accurate way to measure flour and cornstarch is by weight. The volume of 1 pound (450 g) of flour can vary from 3 to 4½ cups, depending on how much moisture it contains and whether it is sifted before measuring or packed down in the cup.

If you don't have a kitchen scale and must measure flour and cornstarch by volume, then *measure it before sifting*. Scoop the flour or cornstarch directly into a dry-measure cup (or measuring spoon) without packing it down. Then level the top by sweeping the edge of your palette knife or pastry corne across the rim of the cup. Measured in this way, 1 cup of flour or cornstarch weighs approximately 4¾ ounces, (135 g), or equivalently 1 pound (454 g) equals 3⅓ cups.

Nuts

USES: Finely ground, to give texture and flavor to *pâte sucrée* and *crème d'amandes;* in *praliné,* to flavor various fillings; as a topping in *pâtes d'amandes;* and as decoration in a variety of forms.

FACTS ABOUT NUTS: Botanically speaking, a nut is the dry fruit or seed of a tree or plant. It develops inside a fibrous hull, which opens to release the "fruit" when ripe. The nut itself consists of a dry inner shell encasing the nutmeat or kernel. The kernel is the edible portion and is usually covered with a brown, paperlike skin.

Nuts are typically high in proteins and fats, as well as vitamins and minerals. The fat content may be polyunsaturated (in almonds, walnuts, and pecans, for example) or saturated (in cashews and macadamias).

ABOUT BUYING NUTS: Most nuts are available either in the shell or shelled. While they stay fresh longer in the shell, we recommend buying shelled nuts. Many of our recipes require large quantities of nuts and it would be very tedious to shell them yourself. Shelled nuts are available in bulk and vacuum packed in plastic bags and cans.

Freshness is very important in nuts. Choose nuts with plump, firm kernels. If they look dry or shriveled, they are stale. Do not use salted, smoked, or flavored nuts in pastry making.

If in the shell, the shells should be shiny and not cracked, dusty, or gray. A good general rule is that 1 pound (450 g) of nuts in the shell will yield 6½ to 7½ ounces (185 to 215 g) of nutmeats.

STORAGE: Shelled nuts should be kept sealed in their original container if vacuum packed, or covered airtight in a plastic bag. At room temperature or (preferably) in the refrigerator, they will keep for weeks—and longer if vacuum packed. They can also be frozen for several months. If frozen, defrost at room temperature before using.

Hazelnuts and pistachios are especially perishable and should be kept refrigerated. If the oil in the nuts does go rancid, you will be able to recognize it by their smell and taste.

Unshelled nuts can be kept for months in a cool place, and they can also be frozen.

ROASTING NUTS: Nuts are frequently roasted to enhance their flavor and reduce their mosture content. Spread them out loosely on a baking sheet or jelly-roll pan. Place in a preheated 350° F (175° C) oven and stir occasionally so they roast evenly. Chopped or sliced almonds should be roasted until lightly browned, about 10 minutes. Whole almonds and hazelnuts are roasted until light brown in the center. After about 15 minutes check one by cutting it in half with a sharp knife. Usually it takes about 20 minutes to roast whole almonds or hazelnuts, but check every 2 or 3 minutes to avoid burning them. Remove the roasted nuts from the oven and either use hot (for example in *praliné* or *nougatine*) or let cool on the baking sheet.

You can give sliced almonds a sweeter taste by tossing with a little *sirop à trente* (see page 398) before roasting. We usually do this when the almonds will be used for decorating *gâteaux*, but it is optional. Use 1 tablespoon (1½ cL) of syrup for each 3½ ounces (100 g) of sliced almonds.

TO CHOP NUTS: You can chop nuts in a food processor or electric blender, on a cutting board with a chef's knife, or in a wood chopping bowl. They should be chopped into bits about 1/16 to 3/32 inch (1½ to 2 mm) in size, but you won't get bits of uniform size. After chopping, sift out the very fine, powdery bits with a coarse sieve.

ALMONDS (AMANDES): Almonds are the most widely used and versatile nut in French pastry. Sweet almonds are the edible ones. Bitter almonds can also be eaten, but they are toxic if ingested in large quantity and are not sold in the United States. The oil derived from bitter almonds is not toxic and is used as a flavoring in the form of almond extract. We dislike the taste of almond extract and never use it.

From now on we will concentrate on sweet almonds. They contain albuminous protein (about 15 percent), sugar, oil (typically about 50 percent), and gum. The kernel has a brown skin, which is frequently removed by blanching.

Almonds are sold both raw (unblanched) and blanched, but if necessary you can blanch them yourself. To do that, pour boiling water over the raw almond kernels and let stand about 3 to 5 minutes. They are ready when squeezing the almonds between your thumb and index finger makes the skins slide off easily. Drain the almonds and slip off their skins while still warm by pinching each almond between your thumb and index finger. After blanching, dry the almonds in a warm (250° F, or 120° C) oven for a few minutes.

Almonds are available in several forms, including:

Raw almonds: Whole, unblanched, shelled almonds. Also called "whole natural almonds."

Blanched whole almonds: These can be used as is for decoration, or chopped or ground.

Blanched slivered almonds: Can be chopped or ground.

Sliced almonds: Sliced blanched almonds are preferable for garnishing, but difficult to find. You will probably have to settle for sliced raw almonds.

HAZELNUTS (NOISETTES): These are also called "filberts," though to be precise the term "filbert" should be reserved for the large, oval, cultivated variety. Hazelnuts have a sweet, distinctive flavor. They are always sold raw (whole and unblanched) or in the shell.

Blanching hazelnuts is tedious, and we advise it only if they are to be used as a garnish. Roast the hazelnuts in a preheated 350° F (175° C) oven until the skins begin to pucker. Then, while they are still hot, remove most of the skins by rolling them between two rough kitchen towels or on a coarse tamis. Don't expect to remove all of the skins completely.

PISTACHIOS (PISTACHES): Pistachios are, like almonds, the seed of a stone fruit. Their oval kernels are a pale yellowish green and are split into two halves. In French pastry, they are most often used as a garnish. They play a larger role in candy making as well as in flavoring ice creams.

Pistachios are almost always sold in the shell. The shells are naturally an off-white, but are sometimes dyed a hideous red.

Pistachios are sometimes blanched before using. The method is the same as for almonds.

WALNUTS (NOIX): There are several varieties, most common of which are English and black walnuts. Of the two, black walnuts have the more pronounced flavor.

Shelled walnuts are usually sold in halves or in pieces because the halves separate easily in the shelling process. In French pastry, walnut halves are used primarily for decoration.

CHESTNUTS (MARRONS): Unique because of their high starch and low fat contents, chestnuts play a special—if limited—role in pastry making. Peeling and candying chestnuts are so tedious that we recommend using canned *marrons glacées* and *purée de marrons,* which are imported from France and are quite good.

Marrons glacées are whole candied chestnuts. They are expensive, and used primarily for decoration. *Pâte de marrons glacées* is a thick, hard chestnut paste made from chestnuts broken in the candying process. This is the proper chestnut purée for pastry making, but you aren't likely to find it in the United States. We have devised a method for preparing an excellent substitute from *purée de marrons,* a purée made from cooked chestnuts, water, and glucose. See the recipe for *crème de marrons* on page 92. **Sources:** Balducci's and Dean & DeLuca.

OTHER NUTS: Pecans, brazil nuts, macadamias, and cashews are rarely used in French pastry, but if you enjoy experimenting with different tastes, you might try substituting them in our recipes. For example, pecans could be substituted for walnuts or hazelnuts, Brazil nuts for almonds, and macadamias for blanched hazelnuts in decorating. The only nut we do not recommend using in French pastry is the peanut. On that we agree with the botanists—the peanut is a legume, not a nut.

TO MEASURE NUTS: The best way to measure nuts is by weight. Measuring by volume is not very accurate, especially in small quantities. Nonetheless, here are the weight-volume equivalences for some of the most often used nuts.

Almonds:	1 cup whole = 6 ounces (170 g)
	1 cup slivered = 4½ ounces (130 g)
	1 cup sliced = 3½ ounces (100 g)
	1 cup chopped = 5 ounces (145 g)
Hazelnuts:	1 cup whole = 5½ ounces (150 g)
	1 cup chopped = 4½ ounces (130 g)
Walnuts and pecans:	1 cup halves = 3½ ounces (100 g)
	1 cup chopped = 4½ ounces (130 g)

Since nuts are sold by weight, you can also measure out the amount you need by comparing with the weight of the package.

ABOUT GRINDING NUTS: Three forms of ground nuts—*tant pour tant, praliné,* and *pâte d'amandes*—are used repeatedly throughout this book. A food processor will supply the muscle required by these jobs and produce professional-quality results. An electric blender will also do an excellent job, but can't handle nearly as large a quantity.

Tant pour tant and *praliné* are used as ingredients in pastry doughs, cake batters, and fillings, and we give the recipes for them here. *Pâte d'amandes* is a topping, so it is included in Chapter 4.

Tant Pour Tant

If you try to grind nuts to a fine powder in a blender or food processor, you extract oil from the nuts and end up with a paste. The trick is to mix sugar with the nuts before grinding. The sugar absorbs the oil and allows a much finer texture. The nuts and sugar are combined in equal proportions by weight, hence the name *tant pour tant* (*as much* sugar *as* nuts), which we abbreviate as *TPT*.

Almonds are the nut most often used for *tant pour tant*. The result is *TPT blanc* or *TPT brut*, depending on whether they are blanched or raw. A more strongly flavored *TPT brut* can be made with hazelnuts or a mixture of almonds and hazelnuts. You can also substitute walnuts or pecans for all or part of the almonds in *TPT brut*.

For 1 pound 1½ ounces (500 g), or about 3⅓ cups

TPT BLANC

9 ounces (250 g)
 blanched almonds

1¼ cups (250 g) sugar

If you have a tamis (drum sieve) with a coarse mesh, combine the nuts with half of the sugar in your food processor; or if you don't have a tamis, combine all of the sugar with the nuts. Process until the nuts are finely ground, and stop as soon as the mix-

TPT BRUT

9 ounces (250 g) raw almonds or hazelnuts, or a mixture of both

1¼ cups (250 g) sugar

①

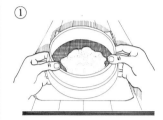

ture starts caking around the sides of the food processor bowl. (Note: if you use a blender instead of a food processor, process only about one fourth of the nuts and sugar at a time to avoid caking.)

2 If you have a tamis, sift the nut-sugar mixture through it ①. Combine the nuts that don't go through the tamis with the remaining sugar and return them to the food processor. Process again until the mixture starts caking around the sides of the food processor bowl, then stop.

3 Pour the ground nut and sugar mixture into a bowl (adding it to the sifted nuts and sugar if you used a tamis in step 2) and stir with a rubber spatula to fluff the mixture and eliminate any caking.

Storage: Covered airtight for up to 1 month at room temperature or, preferably, in the refrigerator.

Praliné

This *praliné* paste is used to favor fillings—*crème au beurre* and *crème au beurre au lait*—and ice creams. It was first made by the chef to the Duc de Praslin.

For about 1 pound 11 ounces (775 g), or 2⅔ cups

INGREDIENTS

7 ounces (200 g) raw almonds

7 ounces (200 g) hazelnuts

1 cup (200 g) sugar

1½ cups (200 g) confectioners sugar

1 Preheat the oven to 350° F (175° C).

2 Place the nuts on one or two large baking sheets and roast them, stirring occasionally, until brown in the center, about 20 minutes. Wipe another baking sheet with a light coating of vegetable oil.

3 While the nuts are roasting, put the granulated sugar in a 1½- to 2-quart (1½ to 2 L) caramel pot or saucepan and cook it over medium to high heat, without stirring. As soon as the sugar begins to melt around the sides of the pot, begin stirring with a wooden spoon. When the sugar becomes fluid, with small white lumps floating in the syrup, reduce the heat to low and continue cooking, stirring constantly and crushing the solid lumps with the wooden spoon, until the sugar is completely melted and turns a medium amber.

4 Stir the hot, roasted nuts into the caramel syrup. Continue heating, stirring constantly with a wooden spoon, until nuts and caramel are well mixed, with the caramel syrupy.

5 Pour the caramel-nut mixture onto the oiled baking sheet and let cool to room temperature.

6 Break the nut brittle into pieces. Combine with the confectioners sugar in the workbowl of your food processor and process until smooth. (If you use an electric blender instead of a food processor, process only about one quarter of the *praliné* at a time, and if necessary stop the blender occasionally and scrape down the mixture around the blades.) The puréeing will take a while and the praliné will become hot in the process. When finished, it will be smooth and viscous, with a slight grittiness.

7 Transfer the *praliné* to a bowl and let cool to room temperature.

Storage: Covered airtight, for up to 3 months at room temperature or in the refrigerator. If some of the oil from the nuts separates on top of the *praliné*, stir it back into the *praliné* before using.

Beans—Coffee, Vanilla, and Chocolate

Chocolate, vanilla, and coffee are among the most important and pervasively employed flavors in French pastry. While none of them come from leguminous plants, they are commonly referred to as beans.

Coffee

USES: For flavoring fillings, toppings, and syrups.

FACTS ABOUT COFFEE: The coffee bean is the seed of a shrub. It is said to have originated in Ethiopia and from there spread through the Middle East to Europe.

As a beverage, coffee is a subject of enormous complexity and interest. Its quality and character depend on the climate and soil in which it is grown, the details of its roasting, and the care taken in its blending. However, the subtleties that distinguish different types and qualities of coffee are lost in pastry making, where it must be intensely concentrated to use for flavoring and is also heavily sweetened.

To get the very concentrated coffee needed for flavoring fillings, toppings, and syrups we recommend the best available instant coffee. Put some in a small bowl and stir in just enough boiling water to dissolve it. This concentrate is what we mean when we call for ''very strong black coffee'' in our recipes.

There are, of course, other methods for getting a coffee concentrate. The Toddy Coffee Maker produces an excellent concentrate by cold water extraction. You could also reduce your favorite coffee, boiling it down until almost syrupy.

Vanilla

USES: For flavoring fillings, toppings, and occasionally cake batters; and to enhance other flavors, especially chocolate.

FACTS ABOUT VANILLA: The vanilla bean is the fruit of a climbing vine of the orchid family. It originated in Mexico and is now grown in tropical regions around the world.

The pod of the vanilla plant is about 6 to 8 inches (15 to 20 cm) long and contains many small black seeds in an aromatic pulp. The pods open when ripe, releasing their contents, so they must be harvested before they reach maturity.

After harvesting, the vanilla beans are cured. The first step is to warm them. In Mexico, this is done in ovens; in the Bourbon Islands (including Madagascar), the beans are either steamed or plunged into hot water. This initiates a 3 to 6 month fermentation process, during which the beans develop their aroma and eventually become dry.

Mexican vanilla beans are considered the best for pastry making, followed by those from the east coast of Madagascar.

Vanilla beans have a sweet and penetrating perfume that gives a special character to many fillings and toppings, *crème pâtissière* and *crème anglaise* being the most important examples. However, it must be used sparingly because in excess it can be cloying.

HOW TO USE VANILLA: To flavor a milk-based custard, cut the bean in halves or quarters crosswise and use one quarter to one half of the bean for each quart (liter) of custard. Slit the bean lengthwise and scrape out the seeds. Add both seeds and pod to the milk before cooking. After the custard has been prepared, the pod should be rinsed and dried, then covered with sugar in an airtight container.

The sugar in which used vanilla beans are stored takes on the vanilla aroma and is called ''vanilla sugar.'' It can be used in place of plain sugar in recipes that call for vanilla or vanilla extract.

When you have accumulated several used vanilla beans (and dried them thoroughly), you can grind them to a powder using a food processor, a blender, or a mortar. If you have at least 10 to 12 vanilla beans, you can powder them by themselves, sift through fine mesh, and use as a substitute for vanilla extract. If you have fewer beans, powder them with six times their weight in sugar (about 2 tablespoons, or 25 g, of sugar for 6 to 8 beans) and sift to get an even more aromatic vanilla sugar. In either case, the powdered vanilla should be covered airtight to preserve its aroma.

VANILLA EXTRACT: Vanilla extract is made by steeping vanilla beans in alcohol. You can make your own by immersing whole vanilla beans in vodka, using 1 cup (¼ L) of vodka for each 2 ounces (50 g) of beans. Cover airtight and let the beans infuse in the alcohol for at least 1 month. It will keep indefinitely.

Vanillin is a white crystalline compound found in the pulp of vanilla beans. It has an aroma reminiscent of natural vanilla, but thirty to forty times stronger and not as subtle or complex. It also evaporates more quickly than natural vanilla extract. Vanillin is manufactured commercially and used in artificial vanilla extracts. In our opinion, these are not acceptable substitutes for vanilla beans or natural vanilla extract.

Chocolate

USES: For flavoring fillings and toppings, and for decoration.

FACTS ABOUT CHOCOLATE: The tropical cocoa tree is native to Central and South America and was first cultivated by the Mayas, who used it to make a beverage. Fernando Cortez introduced chocolate to Europe in the sixteenth century, but it was not until three centuries later that someone had the idea of eating sweetened solid chocolate. Thus, the use of chocolate in pastry making is a surprisingly modern phenomenon.

The fruit of the cocoa tree is a pod about 6 to 8 inches (15 to 20 cm) long that contains 20 to 50 beans. The pods are harvested when ripe, and the contents are removed and fermented to separate the beans from the pulp and develop the cocoa aroma. The beans are sun dried and roasted at low temperature to further develop their aroma. After roasting, they are cooled, crushed, and sifted to separate the shell from the kernel. The crushed kernels are milled to produce a dark brown paste, which is the chocolate liquor. During milling, some of the fat content of the beans—called "cocoa butter"—is released. The chocolate liquor is processed in various ways to produce the different forms of chocolate.

UNSWEETENED CHOCOLATE: This is the pure chocolate liquor, with no sugar added. It contains about 50 percent cocoa butter and has a strong, bitter flavor. Sometimes called "baking chocolate," it is always melted and mixed with other ingredients.

COCOA BUTTER: Cocoa butter is a shiny yellowish white and has a mild flavor and aroma of chocolate. At room temperature it is quite hard, almost brittle. It is composed almost entirely of fat, or rather several fats, each with a different melting point. This is one of the reasons chocolate can be tricky to use.

Cocoa butter is used pharmaceutically as well as in pastry and candy making. It is expensive, and in poor-quality chocolate it is replaced by other, less expensive fats.

COCOA POWDER: Chocolate liquor can be passed through a hydraulic press to extract more of the cocoa butter. The mass which remains is pressed into cakes, dried, pulverized, and sifted to make cocoa powder. It still contains 10 to 25 percent cocoa butter.

Dutch-process cocoa is cocoa powder that has been treated with alkaline carbonates or ammonia to make it less bitter, give it a deeper reddish-brown color, and make it dissolve more easily in water.

Some cocoa powder is sold sweetened for use as a drink. However, only unsweetened cocoa is of interest for pastry making.

When combining cocoa powder with a liquid, first either sift the cocoa and mix it with the other dry ingredients in the recipe or gradually stir some of the liquid into the cocoa to form a smooth paste before adding the remaining liquid. If you don't take one of these precautions, the cocoa may form lumps.

SEMISWEET CHOCOLATE: To make chocolate for eating and decorating, sugar and extra cocoa butter are added to the chocolate liquor, and the mixture is kneaded mechanically—called "conching"—to give it a smooth texture. The quality of the finished chocolate is determined by the cocoa beans from which it is made, the proportions of chocolate liquor, sugar, and cocoa butter in the mix, and the length of time it is conched.

Semisweet, or bittersweet, chocolate contains about one third cocoa butter and 40% sugar. Increasing the cocoa butter content gives the chocolate more bite. Usually small amounts of vanillin (or sometimes real vanilla) and lecithin (an emulsifier) are included in these chocolates to enhance the chocolate flavor and keep the cocoa butter evenly distributed.

COUVERTURE: *Couverture,* or coating chocolate, is a semisweet chocolate with an especially high cocoa butter content that is used for decorative work and for coating chocolate bonbons. It has a glossy surface and a firm snap. When melted, it is more fluid than ordinary semisweet chocolate.

MILK CHOCOLATE AND SWEET CHOCOLATE: These are made by adding powdered milk or extra sugar to the chocolate during conching. They have less flavor than semisweet chocolate and are not used in French pastry.

ABOUT BUYING CHOCOLATE: The first criterion is that it be real chocolate and not artificially flavored or mixed with fats other than cocoa butter.

Unsweetened and semisweet chocolates from Baker's and Hershey's are widely available. Guittard and Kron make excellent unsweetened chocolates. The more luxurious semisweet chocolates from Lindt and Tobler in Switzerland and Guittard in San Francisco have finer textures and more sheen than the Baker's and Hershey's and are therefore much better for glazing *gâteaux* and for decorative work. Lindt's Excellence, Tobler's Bittersweet and Tradition, and Guittard's French Vanilla have moderate cocoa butter and sugar content and are suitable for most purposes. Tobler's Extra, Lindt's Courante Special, and Guittard's Bittersweet have less sugar and are correspondingly more bitter and intense. On the other hand, Lindt's Surfin and Guittard's Solitaire are couvertures, with a higher cocoa butter content. Two other good couvertures are the Belgian Callebaut and Peter's from Nestle.

Cocoa butter is difficult to find in food shops, but Hershey's and Lorann market 1-ounce (28 g) bars as a skin moisturizer. These are pure cocoa butter, so ignore the ''for external use only'' precaution on the label, which was designed to deter chocoholics from eating too much skin moisturizer and suffering the consequences of cocoa butter's mild laxative nature.

For cocoa powder, get the unsweetened variety and preferably a Dutch process cocoa. Three excellent brands are Droste, Poulain, and Kron.

Chocolate sprinkles are usually artificially flavored. However, Guittard makes them of pure semisweet chocolate with a sugar glaze.

Sources: Balducci's, Dean & DeLuca, La Cuisine, Maid of Scandinavia, and Kron.

STORAGE: At 60° to 75° F (15° to 24° C), chocolate can be stored for over a year. If it gets too warm, cocoa butter comes to the surface and forms a grayish-white film called ''bloom.'' This doesn't affect the usefulness of the chocolate.

Cocoa powder is best stored at the same temperature as chocolate and must be kept dry.

Cocoa butter must be covered airtight and kept away from foods with strong odors, which it would absorb. As long as it is kept cool or refrigerated, it can be stored indefinitely without becoming rancid.

ABOUT MELTING AND TEMPERING CHOCOLATE: Chocolate scorches easily and should not be melted over direct heat. Two suitable methods are to melt it either in a double boiler or bain-marie over hot (but not boiling) water, or in a warm oven. In either case, first chop the chocolate with your chef's knife, then warm it gently, stirring occasionally to make it melt more quickly and evenly. The temperature of the chocolate should never be allowed to exceed 120° F (49° C).

It is essential that no water get in the chocolate while melting because the addition of a tiny amount of liquid can make it "seize," becoming thick and granular. Unsweetened chocolate, which contains no emulsifier, is especially susceptible to seizing. If this happens, you can make the chocolate smooth again by stirring in more liquid, but it will no longer be usable for any purpose in which its consistency is important.

For coating a *gâteau* and for decorative work, semisweet chocolate must be tempered. The cocoa in chocolate is suspended in the cocoa butter, and the two can separate easily, with cocoa butter rising to the top and producing a dull, gray-streaked surface. Tempering avoids this by placing the chocolate just above the melting point so it will set quickly and not have time to separate. It also gives the chocolate an ideal working consistency—fluid enough to spread easily and coat thinly, but viscous enough that it won't flow off the surface you are trying to coat.

To temper chocolate, first melt it. Ideally, the temperature of the melted chocolate should be 113° to 118° F (45° to 48° C). Remove from the heat and dip the bottom of the pot of chocolate in cold water. Stir constantly until the chocolate starts to thicken. At this point, some of the cocoa butter is solidifying and the temperature is between 80° and 84° F (27° and 29° C). The chocolate must not be allowed to set, so remove it from the cold water immediately and warm it gently a second time, stirring constantly. When the chocolate has just melted again, remove it from the heat and use it right away. The temperature of the chocolate will now be 86° to 90° F (30° to 32° C). If it gets above 90° F (32° C) it will become too thin and take too long to set, so you will have to temper it again—cooling until it starts to thicken, then warming until it just melts.

While tempering chocolate requires careful attention, it is not difficult. We have given the temperatures at each stage of the process, but you don't really need a thermometer. The procedure is designed so that each stage corresponds to a distinct and easily recognizable change in the consistency of the chocolate.

TO MEASURE CHOCOLATE: Chocolate and cocoa butter are normally measured by weight, and since they are most often sold in premeasured and marked bars, this poses no problem, even if you have no kitchen scale. When melted, 1 cup (2.4 dL) of chocolate or cocoa butter weighs about 9 ounces (250 g).

Like other powdered ingredients, cocoa powder is best measured by weight. To measure by volume, scoop the unsifted cocoa powder into a dry-measure cup or spoon without packing and level the top with a palette knife or pastry corne. 1 cup of cocoa powder weighs about 6 ounces (170 g).

Fruits

USES: Fresh, in *tartes, charlottes, bavarois,* and some *babas* and *feuilletés;* jams and jellies, as glazes and fillings; candied fruits for decoration, and both candied fruits and raisins for flavor and textural contrast.

FRESH FRUITS: We will confine ourselves to a few comments on the most frequently used fruits, and give instructions on how to poach fresh fruits that aren't quite ripe enough.

Apples: Choose tart, full-flavored apples that won't discolor or disintegrate during cooking. The selection available varies regionally. Greenings, Winesaps, Jonathans, and Newtown Pippins are all good for cooking, as are the Granny Smiths that come from Australia in spring. Avoid Red and Golden Delicious and McIntosh.

Peaches: Since peaches are usually sliced for use in pastries, choose freestones. If they are to be incorporated in a dessert without cooking, they should be ripe and tender, but not too juicy. If not cooked, sliced peaches should be dipped in a solution of lemon juice and water to prevent discoloration.

Pears: We prefer Bartlett, Comice, and Anjou pears, in that order. Like peaches, pears for baking should be ripe but not too juicy, and they discolor quickly after peeling if they are not washed with lemon juice.

Plums: Small prune plums have the most flavor, and blood plums are also good. Most of the larger plums are too bland and juicy.

Cherries: Sour cherries such as Montmorency have the most flavor.

Oranges and tangerines: If they are to be peeled and sliced, they should be large and have as few seeds as possible. Choose navel oranges, Temple oranges (a cross between the orange and the tangerine) or Mineola tangerines.

Citrus zests: The outer surface of the skin of a citrus fruit is called the zest. Depending on the fruit and on whether it has been dyed or not, it may be orange, yellow, or green. The zest contains aromatic oils that add a distinctive and seductive flavor to some desserts. The white inner part of the skin is the pith and should not be used because it is bitter. When the zest of a citrus fruit is required in a recipe, it is usually grated. Grate the zest directly from the whole fruit with a very fine, flat grater.

More generally: Fruits that will not be cooked should be ripe but not mushy or excessively juicy. Flavor is important, so for each fruit choose the more intensely flavored varieties.

SALADE DES FRUITS: This is a mixture of diced fresh fruits that can be used in desserts or served on its own. There is no special recipe, and it is neither filling nor topping. We will give you some general ideas and let you make it according to your own taste and the fruits available.

Choose at least four or five fresh fruits, such as apples, pears, oranges, bananas, pineapples, peaches, strawberries, raspberries, blueberries, cherries, seedless grapes, and kiwi fruits. If you don't have a large enough variety, you might add canned pineapple or peaches in heavy syrup. Cut the larger fruits into ½- to 1-inch (1½ to 2½ cm) dice, oranges into peeled segments, bananas into slices, and large strawberries into halves or quarters. Pit cherries and leave grapes and small berries whole. Add a little superfine sugar and some liqueur (Grand Marnier, rum, or kirsch, for example) to sweeten and flavor the fruits, and toss with the juice of half a lemon or an orange for each pound (500 g) of fruit. If you like, you could also add some whole blanched almonds.

ABOUT POACHING FRESH FRUITS: Certain fruits that aren't quite ripe can be poached in a light syrup to soften and sweeten them. This works best for peaches, pears, apricots, and pineapple, and occasionally plums, sour cherries, and bananas.

Sirop Léger (Light Poaching Syrup)

The sugar content of this syrup can be varied according to the ripeness and sweetness of the fruits you are poaching. You can flavor it with a couple of tablespoons (a few cL) of liqueur (such as rum, Grand Marnier, or kirsch) or by substituting wine for half of the water in the recipe. Dry white wine is especially good for enhancing the flavors of pears and peaches, and pears can also be poached in dry red wine to give them a beautiful, rich color.

To poach about 2 pounds (1 kg) of fruit in *sirop léger*

INGREDIENTS

1 quart (1 L) cold water

3 to 4 cups (600 to 800 g) sugar, depending on the sweetness of the fruit to be poached

Juice of 1 lemon, strained

Half a vanilla bean, split lengthwise

About 2 pounds (1 kg) of fresh peaches, pears,

1 Combine the water, sugar, lemon juice, and vanilla bean in a large (at least 4-quart, or 4 L) saucepan and bring to a boil. This is the *sirop léger*.

2 Prepare the fruit: Peaches, apricots, plums, and sour cherries are poached whole. Pears are peeled and may either be left whole or cored and cut in half. Pineapples are peeled, cored and sliced. Bananas are peeled and thickly sliced.

3 Add the fruit to the boiling syrup and place a round wire rack or the lid of a smaller saucepan on top to keep them submerged. Bring the *sirop léger* back to a simmer, reduce the heat, and continue simmering very gently until the fruits are no longer hard and can be pierced easily with the tip of a skewer.

apricots, pineapple, plums, sour cherries, bananas, or other fruit

They must still be a little firm, or they will become mushy by the time they have cooled. The cooking time can be anything from 5 to 20 minutes, depending on the ripeness and size of the fruit.

4 Remove from the heat and let the fruit cool in the syrup.

Storage of poached fruits: The poached fruit can be kept in the refrigerator, submerged in the syrup and covered airtight, for up to 3 or 4 days.

CANNED AND FROZEN FRUITS: While we prefer fresh fruits in season, poaching them when necessary, canned or frozen fruits can sometimes be acceptable substitutes. The best canned fruits are those that can stand up to poaching without too much alteration of flavor or texture. For most desserts, you should use canned fruits in heavy syrup. Canned fruits in light syrup should be used for fruit *tartes* baked in the shell.

Very fragile fruits, including most berries, should never be poached, and the canned ones are not successful. While they aren't suitable for *tartes* or decoration, frozen berries can be good in charlottes and *coulis des fruits* (fruit sauces), where they are puréed.

JAMS AND JELLIES: Apricot jam and red currant jelly are used extensively for glazing pastries. Occasionally peach jam and cherry jelly are also used for that purpose. Raspberry jam, apricot jam, and orange marmalade are used as fillings.

When buying jams or jellies for pastry making, there is no reason to choose the very best. The qualities of flavor and texture that make them special would be obscured in most pastries. Save fine jams and jellies for eating with your brioches and croissants at breakfast. On the other hand, the poorest quality jams and jellies taste more of citric acid and sugar than they do of fruit. In between are name brand preserves in your supermarket, and these will do the job nicely.

DRIED FRUITS: The ones of primary interest are raisins, both for scattering over the fillings between the layers of *gâteaux* and for baking in some cakes. Prunes can be used in *tartes*.

Dark seedless raisins are made from sun-dried Thompson seedless grapes. Golden raisins are the same grapes, treated with sulphur dioxide to retain their original color and dried artificially.

Muscats are dark raisins made from Muscat grapes. They are large and sweet and have a nicer flavor than the Thompson seedless variety. Choose seeded ones, since the crunch of grape seeds adds nothing to French pastry.

All raisins can be stored for months at room temperature, and in the refrigerator they will keep for over a year.

To steam raisins: For many recipes, raisins are steamed to soften them. After steaming, we always soak them in alcohol (usually dark rum) to give them more flavor.

Fill a saucepan to a depth of 1 to 2 inches (2½ to 5 cm) with water and bring to a simmer. Put the raisins in a strainer and place the strainer over the saucepan. Cover and let the raisins steam over the simmering water until they just begin to soften, about 5 minutes. Transfer them to a small bowl and add dark rum to almost cover. Press the raisins down in the rum, cover airtight, and let steep for at least 2 hours and preferably overnight. Immersed in the rum, the raisins can be kept for up to 6 months in the refrigerator.

CANDIED FRUITS: We use candied (or *glacé*) fruits as decoration and also in the same ways as raisins. The best ones are made from soft fruits—apricots, pears, peaches, pineapple, and cherries. Citron, lemon, and orange peel are hard and so less good. For decorative purposes candied strawberries and orange slices are very nice. We sometimes use candied lemon slices on lemon *tartes* and charlottes, and you can make them easily yourself (see below).

Supermarket variety candied fruits are usually disappointing in taste. Vastly superior *glacé* fruits are imported from Australia and France. **Sources:** Balducci's and Dean & DeLuca.

Covered airtight, candied fruits can be kept in the refrigerator for 2 or 3 months, or they can be frozen for up to 6 months. If stored longer, they may dry and harden or some of their sugar content may come to the surface and crystallize. Soaking in alcohol will dissolve the sugar crystals and help to soften them.

To soak candied fruits in alcohol: For use inside desserts (but not for decoration), we usually soak candied fruits in alcohol (most often rum, kirsch, or Grand Marnier) to give them more flavor. Cut them into ¼- to ⅜-inch (6 to 10 mm) dice first, then place in a small container and add enough alcohol to almost cover. Press the dice down in the alcohol, cover airtight, and let steep for at least 2 or 3 hours, and preferably overnight. Immersed in the alcohol, the candied fruits can be stored in the refrigerator for up to 6 months.

Candied Lemon Slices and Lemon Syrup

Lemon slices can be poached in *sirop à trente* to make an attractive garnish. The poaching syrup becomes a strongly flavored lemon syrup, which can be used for brushing cake layers.

For 6 to 8 candied lemon slices and about 1 cup (¼ L) of lemon syrup

INGREDIENTS

1 medium fresh
lemon

1 to 1½ cups (2½ to
3½ dL) *sirop à
trente* (see page
398)

1 Cut the lemon into 6 to 8 thin slices with your slicing knife.

2 Place the lemon slices and the *sirop à trente* in a small saucepan and bring to a simmer. Reduce the heat and simmer gently until the lemon rind changes from an opaque white to translucent, 20 to 30 minutes.

3 Remove from the heat and allow the lemon slices to cool in the syrup.

Storage: Leave the lemon slices submerged in the syrup, cover airtight, and keep in the refrigerator for up to 1 week.

Alcohols

USES: To flavor fillings and toppings, and for brushing cake layers and soaking raisins and candied fruits.

RUM: Rum originated in the Caribbean islands, and most of the world production still comes from there. It is distilled from molasses and from sugarcane juice, as a by-product of refining sugarcane.

Rums range in style from light-bodied, dry Puerto Rican rums to the heavy, rich, and pungent ones produced in Jamaica. Whenever we call for rum—whether dark or white—in our recipes, we mean Jamaican rum or one of the full-flavored rums from Haiti, Martinique, or Guadaloupe.

EAUX DE VIE BLANCHES: *Eau de vie*—literally "water of life"—is the French term for brandy. It is most often used in connection with the *alcools blancs,* the clear, colorless brandies distilled from fresh fruits, including cherries, raspberries, and pears (but not grapes or apples). They are high in alcohol—typically 80 to 90 proof—and the best are produced in France, Switzerland, and Germany. We prefer the French ones, which tend to be more fruity. The *eaux de vie* we use most frequently are:

Kirsch (*Kirschwasser,* in German): Kirsch is distilled from cherries. Excellent as a flavor in its own right, it also enhances the flavors of other fruits such as berries and peaches.

Framboise (*Himbeergeist,* in German): Framboise is distilled from raspberries (about nine pounds or 4 kg per bottle). It is used in desserts containing fresh raspberries.

Poire (*Williams Birne* or *Birngeist* in German): Poire is distilled from fresh pears, of which the Williams pear is best. Sometimes a whole pear is included inside the bottle—a nifty trick arranged by placing the bottle over the blossom on the pear tree, and letting the pear develop inside.

CALVADOS: This French apple brandy, made in Normandy, is distilled from cider and aged in oak casks. It is dry, typically 80 to 100 proof, and strongly scented. Calvados is used in apple desserts. American applejack, which has much less apple character, is a possible substitute.

COGNAC AND ARMAGNAC: These are the finest French grape brandies, both distilled by strictly controlled methods and aged in oak casks. We use Cognac to flavor the *crème pâtissière* filling in grape *tartes,* and it is also excellent for enhancing the flavor of chocolate. Armagnac, which is stronger in flavor and more scented than Cognac, is very good with prunes. Since Cognac and Armagnac are both expensive, you may want to substitute another good grape brandy for them.

ORANGE LIQUEURS: There are several, all sweet and medium proof. The orange flavor is extracted from orange peels by steeping them in alcohol. The result is distilled and sweetened with sugar syrup.

Curaçao: This was originally produced by the Dutch from the skins of the green oranges grown on the island of Curaçao off the coast of Venezuela. Curaçao is now made in many countries, from a variety of oranges. It has a strong orange flavor, with a slight edge of bitterness.

Grand Marnier: Grand Marnier is a proprietary Curaçao-type liqueur made by the Cognac house Marnier-Lapostolle in France. It has a Cognac base and is one of the least sweet, and most elegant, of the orange liqueurs.

Cointreau: This is another proprietary orange liqueur. It is colorless and higher in alcohol than Curaçao. Originally it was called Triple Sec White Curaçao, but when it became widely imitated it switched to Cointreau, the name of the French family that makes it. Other liqueurs of this type are called Triple Sec.

OTHER SWEET LIQUEURS: Mandarine, a tangerine flavored liqueur, can be used in place of orange liqueurs and is especially good in tangerine *tartes*.

Amaretto: This liqueur is made in Italy from apricot pits. It is reminiscent of almonds, and we like to use it instead of almond extract.

Maraschino: This is distilled from fermented Marasca sour cherries. It originated in Yugoslavia, and it is now also produced in Italy.

BOURBON: We like Kentucky bourbon for enhancing the flavors of chestnuts and chocolate. Bourbons are very fruity, with a taste of charcoal and caramel from the charred white oak barrels in which they are aged.

Leavening

Loosely speaking, leavening is a process—whether mechanical, chemical, or biological—by which bubbles of gas are introduced into a dough or batter and make it rise when baked. The agent through which this is achieved can be whipped eggs, baking powder, or yeast. In the stricter sense, leavening is limited to the action of yeast.

USES: Yeast is the ingredient that gives *pâtes levées* (and croissants) their light, airy texture.

FACTS ABOUT YEAST: Yeast is a fungus. In the presence of air, sugar, liquid, and sufficient warmth, this microorganism multiplies rapidly and produces the enzyme zymase, which transforms sugars into alcohol and carbon dioxide. This is the process of fermentation.

A pastry dough is a very favorable environment for the development of yeast. Flour contains a small amount of sugar, plus the enzyme amylase, which naturally converts starch into the sugar maltose. Other sugars may also be mixed in the dough and promote fermentation.

The carbon dioxide produced by fermentation is trapped by the elasticity of the gluten in the flour. As the strands of gluten inflate, the dough rises.

When the dough is baked, the carbon dioxide trapped in the elastic gluten network expands, making the dough rise further; then the gluten coagulates and the starch hardens to form a stable structure that won't collapse when it is removed from the oven. The heat also kills the yeast and evaporates the alcohol produced during fermentation. The result is the familiar spongelike texture of leavened breads.

CAVEATS ON COOKING WITH YEAST: Yeast requires special attention to keep its environment hospitable. It needs sugar, but too much sugar can kill it. Salt and fats inhibit the growth of yeast; and a high concentration of salt will kill the yeast, so it should not be dissolved in salty water.

Yeast needs a temperature of at least 50° F (10° C) to activate its growth, and the ideal temperature is between 75° and 85° F (25° to 30° C). Above 140° F (60° C), the yeast dies. So while it is advantageous to dissolve yeast in warm water to get its growth started quickly, it must never be dissolved in hot water.

Yeast doughs must have sufficient time to rise in order to produce a light airy texture. The stretching of the dough by the expansion of the trapped carbon dioxide contributes to the activation of the elasticity of the gluten fiber network. If the dough is allowed to rise too rapidly, the interior of the bread will be weak and the yeast will produce a disagreeable odor and taste.

When the temperature in your kitchen is below 75° F (25° C), you can use your oven to provide the optimal 75° to 85° F (25° to 30° C) rising environment. A gas oven with pilot light may supply sufficient warmth. If not, or if you have a pilotless gas oven or an electric oven, then fill an earthenware or pyrex casserole with boiling water, cover, and place in the oven. The casserole will release the heat slowly and give the oven a fairly steady temperature. You can control the temperature by your choice of the size of the casserole or, if the oven becomes too warm, by leaving the oven door ajar.

ABOUT BUYING AND STORING YEAST: Yeast for baking is available in two forms, fresh yeast and active dry yeast.

We always use fresh yeast. It is sold in individually wrapped 0.6-ounce (17 g) cakes for home use. It should feel crumbly when pressed between your fingertips and be a uniform pale gray with no discoloration. Fresh yeast should be stored in the refrigerator and used before the expiration date on the wrapper. It can also be stored in the freezer, covered airtight, for several weeks. Fresh yeast will dissolve most readily if broken into small crumbs before adding warm (85° to 90° F, or 30° to 32° C) liquid.

Active dry yeast is sold in premeasured packets, each equivalent to an 0.6-ounce (17 g) cake of fresh yeast, and in jars. It can be stored in a cool dry place before opening. After opening it should be covered airtight and kept in the refrigerator. To substitute active dry yeast for fresh yeast in our recipes, use warmer (105° to 115° F, or 40° to 45° C) water to dissolve it. You may also have to increase the amount of liquid used to dissolve the yeast.

If you are not certain that your yeast is still active, prove the yeast by dissolving in the warm water called for in the recipe, adding a pinch of sugar, and letting it work for 5 to 10 minutes. If the yeast is good, it will begin to bubble within that time.

ABOUT BAKING POWDER: Baking powder is a dry acid and alkali mixture. When mixed with water and heated, carbon dioxide gas is produced. This chemical form of leavening is very rarely used in French pastry.

Gelatin

USES: As a stabilizing agent in *crème bavaroise, fruit mousses,* and *crème chiboust.*

FACTS ABOUT GELATIN: The protein gelatin is a transparent, colorless, odorless, and tasteless solid that is usually extracted from the bones, cartilage, and tendons of animals. Isinglass (obtained from the air bladders of fish) and agar-agar and carrageen moss (both from seaweed) are all forms of gelatin, but are not used in pastry making.

The key property of gelatin in cooking is its ability to increase the viscosity of liquids by absorbing water from its surroundings. The viscosity of a gelatin-thickened mixture depends on the ratio of gelatin to liquid, the temperature, and the other ingredients in the mixture. Lowering the temperature increases viscosity and, if sufficient gelatin is present, causes the mixture to set. This makes it possible for certain fillings to hold their shape after molding or piping. If the right proportion of gelatin is used, the filling can, at the same time, keep a soft, fragile consistency. But too much gelatin will make the filling rubbery.

Acids, sugar, and pineapple can affect the thickening ability of gelatin. Acids or sugar in excess will inhibit setting. Fresh pineapple contains bromelain, an enzyme that breaks down gelatin and destroys its setting capacity. Poaching fresh pineapple destroys the enzyme, as does the cooking involved in the commercial canning of pineapple.

CAVEATS ON COOKING WITH GELATIN: Before adding hot liquid or cooking, gelatin must always be softened in cold liquid. Otherwise, the granules of gelatin can lump, resulting in an undesirable consistency and reducing its thickening ability.

After softening, the gelatin must be heated—either directly in a liquid mixture or by adding a hot liquid—until completely dissolved and no longer grainy. If the gelatin has not dissolved (or rather absorbed enough liquid from the mixture), then the mixture won't set. However, excess heat damages the gelatin protein. Remove a mixture containing gelatin from the heat when steam begins to rise from the surface; and, if hot liquid is poured into softened gelatin, the temperature of the liquid should be below 180° F (80° C).

After the gelatin has dissolved, the mixture must be cooled to room temperature. At that point it will still be fluid. For all of the gelatin-stabilized fillings used in this book, the mixture is lightened by folding in either whipped cream or *meringue italienne*. The cream or meringue will deflate less if the gelatin mixture is first chilled until the gelatin just begins to thicken it: Place the bowl containing the gelatin mixture in another bowl containing ice water or crushed ice, and stir it constantly until it thickens slightly and flows more slowly off a wooden spoon. Remove from the ice immediately and quickly and thoroughly stir in about one third of the whipped cream or meringue. Then gently fold in the remaining whipped cream or meringue.

The step of chilling the gelatin mixture is a delicate one, since the gelatin can set very quickly. If, before adding the whipped cream or meringue, it becomes too thick, warm it briefly over low heat to return it to a fluid consistency and then cool again. However, after folding in the whipped cream or meringue, do not warm the filling because you will deflate it.

After the finished filling has been molded or piped, it must be refrigerated until completely set. Depending on the size of the dessert this will take from 2 to 6 hours.

TO MEASURE GELATIN: In developing our recipes, we used Knox unfla-vored gelatin, which is sold in envelopes containing ¼ ounce (8 g), or 2¼ teaspoons, of gelatin. We advise caution in using other types of gelatin in our recipes. Different gelatins differ in their thickening power, and you can not simply substitute the same weight or volume to get the same result. One enve-lope of Knox unflavored gelatin is designed to jell 2 cups (½ L) of liquid, so use this as a guide in determining equivalences.

Salt

USES: In pastry doughs and *pâtes à choux,* primarily as a flavor enhancer.

FACTS ABOUT SALT: Chemically, salts are a class of compounds formed by the neutralization of an acid with a base. The only salt of interest in the kitchen is sodium chloride.

Salt plays two vital roles in cooking, namely as preservative and as flavor enhancer. The first of these is irrelevant to desserts, and the second calls for only very small quantities. Too much salt conflicts with sweet flavors, but a small addition of salt to pastry doughs and *pâtes à choux* enhances the flavors of butter and eggs without producing any discernible saltiness. The balance is a fragile one, so you must keep strict and accurate control of the amount of salt that goes into a recipe. Measure carefully, and never use salted butter.

The other culinary functions of salt are less pervasive in their significance. In leavened pastry doughs, salt slows down the action of the yeast, allowing a more uniform development. And salt can affect the coagulation of proteins, a fact that has special importance in egg cookery but very limited significance in pastry making.

TO MEASURE SALT: Being granular, salt can be measured with reasonable accuracy by volume. Its density is about ¾ ounce (20 g) per tablespoon.

Food Colorings

Food colorings make it possible to enhance the natural colors of some ingredi-ents and to greatly enlarge the range of colors available for decorating desserts. They must be used sparingly—literally by the drop—to avoid strident or garish effects.

We use food dyes primarily to color fondant, *crème au beurre,* and *pâte d'amandes.* The color is chosen according to the flavor of the dessert (for example, pink or peach for Grand Marnier and green for kirsch) or for deco-rative representation (green for *pâte d'amandes* leaves).

You can make your own caramel food coloring to give a rich, natural tan color to fondants used in coffee- and *praliné*-flavored desserts. Cook about 1 cup (200 g) of sugar (or use leftover cooked sugar) to a dark caramel stage (see page 399). When it begins to smoke and is very dark brown, pour in a little water. Stand back, because it will splatter. Continue heating, stirring constantly, and gradually adding more water to thin the caramel. Altogether you should add about ½ cup (1.2 dL) of water. Remove from the heat and let cool to room temperature. Caramel food coloring can be kept in an airtight container at room temperature for months.

Flowers and Herbs

Crystallized violets are whole candied flowers—hard and sugary—that can serve, like candied fruits, as decoration atop desserts. They are especially elegant on individual *savarins chantilly*.

Orange flower water is a fragrant liquid distilled from neroli, an oil obtained from the flowers of orange trees. It gives a special flavor to certain pastries—for example *gâteau des rois* and *bostock*—but must be used very sparingly.

Candied angelica is made from the stalks of an aromatic herb. The stalks are large and can be sliced thin and cut into diamonds or triangles for use as decoration.

SOURCES FOR EQUIPMENT

*T*he first place to look for baking equipment is at your local gourmet cookware store, restaurant supply shop, department store, or hardware store. Many retailers are willing to place special orders for items they don't stock. Refer them to the wholesale sources listed below for French bakeware or to the American manufacturer or distributor of the equipment you need.

If you can't find what you want locally, you can purchase baking equipment by mail.

Mail-Order Sources for Baking Equipment

Bridge Kitchenware Corp., 214 E. 52nd St., New York, NY 10022. Telephone: (212) 688-4220. French and American cooking equipment, including wide range of molds, copper pots and pans, and black steel baking sheets.

Dean & DeLuca, 121 Prince St., New York, NY 10012. Telephone: (212) 431-1691. French and American bakeware and cooking equipment, including a large selection of molds and black steel baking sheets.

Kitchen Bazaar, 4455 Connecticut Ave. NW, Washington DC 20008. Telephone: (202) 363-4625. French and American baking equipment, including electric mixers and food processors, large assortment of bakeware, and gadgets. Catalog available upon request.

Kitchen Glamor, 26770 Grand River Ave., Redford Township, MI 48240. Telephone: (313) 537-1300. French and American baking equipment, including the Tutové rolling pin, copper pots and pans, and many molds.

La Cuisine, 323 Cameron St., Alexandria, VA 22314. Telephone: (703) 836-4435. French bakeware, utensils, and copper cookware. Catalog available at nominal charge.

Maid of Scandinavia, 3244 Raleigh Ave., Minneapolis, MN 55416. Telephone: (800) 328-6722 or (612) 927-7966. Primarily American baking equipment and supplies. Catalog available at nominal charge.

Nussex Bakery Eqpt. Co., 14752 Franklin Ave., Tustin, CA 92680. Telephone: (714) 832-9956. And 880 S. Five Point Rd., West Chester, PA 19380. Telephone: (215) 696-3324. MATFER French bakeware, pastry bags and tubes, rolling pins, and French palette knives.

Williams-Sonoma, P.O. Box 3792, San Francisco, CA 94119. Telephone: (415) 652-9007. Kitchen machines, gadgets, American and European bakeware. Catalog available upon request.

Specialty Equipment and Supplies

Hackensack Supply Co., 165 State St., Hackensack, NJ 07601. Telephone: (201) 487-9300. Take-out container lids for use as cake-decorating circles and rectangles.

Penn Scale Mfg. Co. Inc., 150 West Berks St., Philadelphia, PA 19122. Telephone: (215) 739-9644. Professional bakers scales.

Ranier Devido Stone & Marble Company, 2619 New Butler Rd., New Castle, PA 16101. Telephone: (412) 658-8518. Marble rolling pins and pastry slabs.

Wholesale Sources for French Bakeware and Cooking Equipment

Your local retailer can order just about any French baking equipment you could want from one or more of these importers.

BIA Cordon Bleu, 375 Quarry Rd., Belmont, CA 94002. Telephone: (415) 595-2400.

Charles F. Lamalle, 1123 Broadway, New York, NY 10010. Telephone: (212) 242-0750.

Nussex, see Mail-Order Sources for Baking Equipment, above.

European Sources for French Baking Equipment

David Mellor, 4 Sloane Sq., London SW1W8EE, England. Telephone: 01-730-4259. Extensive catalog available.

MORA et Cie., 13, rue Montmartre, 75001 Paris, France. Telephone: 508-1924, 508-1147. The premier supplier of professional French baking equipment. MORA's wholesale and manufacturing division is MATFER. MATFER equipment is available in the U.S. through several sources, including Nussex, La Cuisine, and Dean & Deluca.

SOURCES FOR SPECIALTY INGREDIENTS

*I*f you can't find the specialty ingredients you need locally, all of the ones called for in our recipes are available by mail order.

Balducci's, 424 Avenue of the Americas, New York, NY 10011. Telephone: (212) 673-2600. French glacé fruits, *marrons glacées,* fresh nuts, and Callebaut chocolates.

Crayon Yard Corporation, 75 Daggett St., New Haven, CT 06519. Telephone: (203) 624-7094. Solait Cultured Food Cooker and *crème fraîche* starter cultures.

Dean & DeLuca, 121 Prince St., New York, NY 10012. Telephone: (212) 431-1691. Extensive selection of specialty foods, including Australian glacé fruits and angelica, crystallized violets, Lindt chocolates, cocoa powder, fresh nuts, *marrons glacées* and *purée de marrons.*

Kron Chocolatier, 764 Madison Ave., New York, NY 10021. Telephone: (212) 472-1234. Baking chocolate and cocoa powder.

La Cuisine, 323 Cameron St., Alexandria, VA 22314. Telephone: (703) 836-4435. Cocoa butter, Lindt chocolates, cocoa powder, vanilla beans, nuts, crystallized violets, and candied angelica.

Maid of Scandinavia, 3244 Raleigh Ave., Minneapolis, MN 55416. Telephone: (800) 328-6722 or (612) 927-7966. Glucose, Peter's covering chocolate, and Mexican vanilla beans.

AMERICAN-METRIC-BRITISH CONVERSION TABLE

*I*n our recipes we give all measurements in both American and metric units. British units are the same as the American ones with the exception of volume measures, for which the conversions are included below.

Weight
1 kg = 1,000 g
       = 2.2 pounds
_____
1 pound = 16 ounces
          = 454 g
1 ounce = 28.4 g

Length
1 cm = 10 mm
       = ⅜ inch
_____
1 inch = 2.54 cm

Temperature
°F = °C × ⅗ + 32°
0° C = 32° F
100° C = 212° F
_____
 50° F = 10° C
100° F = 38° C
150° F = 66° C
200° F = 93° C
250° F = 121° C
300° F = 149° C
350° F = 177° C
400° F = 204° C
450° F = 232° C
500° F = 260° C

Volume
1 L = 10 dL
      = 1.06 quarts
1 dL = 10 cL
      = 6.8 tablespoons
1 cL = 2 teaspoons
_____
1 quart   = 4 cups
             = 0.95 L = 33 British
                  fluid ounces
1 cup   = 16 tablespoons
             = 2.4 dL = 8.3 British
                  fluid ounces
1 tablespoon = 3 teaspoons
             = 4.5 cL = 0.52 British
                  fluid ounce
1 teaspoon   = 0.5 cL = 0.17 British
                  fluid ounce

CROSS-INDEX OF COMPONENTS

Our recipes for many components and prepared ingredients produce larger quantities than you need for a single pastry recipe. We have determined the quantities according to how often each is used, how long it can be stored, and the economy of effort achieved by preparing a larger amount. As you prepare components for future use, keep an inventory indicating the quantity and date prepared for each. And periodically replenish your supply of the components you use most frequently.

In the cross-index that follows the components are grouped according to type, with pastry doughs, cake and pastry batters, fillings, toppings, and prepared ingredients listed separately. Each component is followed by the page numbers of the recipes in which it appears, with the recipe for the component itself listed first in **boldface** type.

When you are planning to make a dessert, choose components of different types (such as a pastry dough and a filling) from your inventory and compare the listings to see which pastries can be made by assembling these components. Then check the recipe for the pastry you select to see if any additional components are required. Plan ahead whenever possible so that you can defrost your components or remove them from the refrigerator in time to reach the required temperature or consistency.

TOPPINGS

PREPARED INGREDIENTS

GENERAL INDEX